T5-AVO-237

THE COLLEGIUM PHAENOMENOLOGICUM

PHAENOMENOLOGICA
COLLECTION FONDÉE PAR H.L. VAN BREDA ET PUBLIÉE
SOUS LE PATRONAGE DES CENTRES D'ARCHIVES-HUSSERL

105

THE COLLEGIUM PHAENOMENOLOGICUM
THE FIRST TEN YEARS

Comité de rédaction de la collection:
Président: S. IJsseling (Leuven)
Membres: L. Landgrebe (Köln), W. Marx (Freiburg i. Br.),
J.N. Mohanty (Philadelphia), P. Ricœur (Paris), E. Ströker (Köln),
J. Taminiaux (Louvain-la-Neuve), Secrétaire: J. Taminiaux

The Collegium Phaenomenologicum
The First Ten Years

edited by

JOHN C. SALLIS, GIUSEPPINA MONETA
and JACQUES TAMINIAUX

Kluwer Academic Publishers
DORDRECHT / BOSTON / LONDON

Library of Congress Cataloging in Publication Data

The Collegium Phaenomenologicum.

(Phaenomenologica ; 105)
1. Collegium Phaenomenologicum. 2. Phenomenology.
3. Philosophy, Modern--20th century. I. Sallis, John, 1938- . II. Moneta, Giuseppina Chiara. III. Taminiaux, Jacques, 1928- . IV. Series.
B829.5.C52 1988 142'.7 88-9276
B
829.5
.C52
1988
ISBN 90-247-3709-5

Published by Kluwer Academic Publishers,
P.O. Box 17, 3300 AA Dordrecht, The Netherlands

Kluwer Academic Publishers incorporates
the publishing programmes of
Martinus Nijhoff, Dr W. Junk, D. Reidel and MTP Press

Sold and distributed in the U.S.A. and Canada
by Kluwer Academic Publishers,
101 Philip Drive, Norwell, MA 02061, U.S.A.

In all other countries sold and distributed
by Kluwer Academic Publishers Group,
P.O. Box 322, 3300 AH Dordrecht, The Netherlands

All rights reserved
© 1988 by Kluwer Academic Publishers
No part of the material protected by this copyright notice may be reproduced or utilized in any form or by any means, electronic or mechanical, including photocopying, recording or by any information storage and retrieval system, without written permission from the copyright owner

Printed in the Netherlands

LIBRARY
McCORMICK THEOLOGICAL SEMINARY
1100 EAST 55th STREET
CHICAGO, ILLINOIS 60615

Contents

Appendices

Preface

It is our hope that this volume will serve to document both the history of the Collegium Phaenomenologicum during its first ten years as well as some of the philosophical work that has grown out of the annual gatherings in Perugia. The Introduction narrates the history and is supplemented by the Appendices, in which the programs and the participants for each of the ten years are listed. The essays, on the other hand, present in more finished form work that was developed in connection with courses, lectures, or seminars conducted during the first ten years of the Collegium.

Giuseppina Moneta
John Sallis
Jacques Taminiaux

Introduction

The Collegium Phaenomenologicum in Its First Ten Years

GIUSEPPINA C. MONETA

The idea of the Collegium Phaenomenologicum first took shape in a conversation that I had with Werner Marx at his home in Bollschweil in the Spring of 1975. Previously I had thought of the possibility of a gathering of phenomenologists somewhere in Italy during the summer months. And when I explained to Werner Marx that it would not be difficult to find accommodation for such a gathering in a Franciscan monastery in Umbria, he responded enthusiastically and assured me that such a project would have the support of the Husserl Archives in Leuven and in Freiburg.

During the following months I contacted Father Gianmaria Polidoro of the Franciscan monastery of Monteripido in Perugia and inquired about the possibility of accommodation for a small group of phenomenologists. In his generous response Father Polidoro explained that the ancient monastery had recently been renovated and the monks' cells provided with modern comforts. He assured me that the community would welcome a meeting of philosophers, provided, of course, that the guests were willing to conform to the daily rhythm of the monastery, as, for instance, in sharing meals with the monks in the common refectory.

In its early years the Collegium was to prove quite indebted to the enterprising spirit of Father Polidoro. He was himself a philosophy graduate and wanted the monastery to become progressively more open to cultural exchanges and international meetings. His hope was that it might regain something of the role it had had in the early Renaissance, when it served as a focal point for the growth of the Franciscan order and became the Studium Generalis for the entire region.

While still in Freiburg, I informed José Huertas-Jourda of my conversations with Werner Marx concerning the possibility of a meeting in Perugia. Professor Huertas-Jourda had established and was at that time in charge of the Centre for Advanced Research in Phenomenology, then located at the University of Waterloo in Canada. After my return to the United States, we continued to discuss the possible arrangement to convene a meeting at the

J.C. Sallis, G. Moneta and J. Taminiaux (eds.), The Collegium Phaenomenologicum, 3–9.
© Kluwer Academic Publishers.

monastery for the summer of 1976. Indeed the Centre was to continue to sponsor the Collegium for the next three or four years. Also to be mentioned is the encouraging support that the Collegium received from the Husserl-Archief of Leuven (Belgium), The Centre d'Etudes Phenomenologiques at Louvain-la-Neuve (Belgium), and the Husserl-Archives in Freiburg. In the Spring of 1976, letters were sent out by José Huertas-Jourda to a number of phenomenologists in the United States and in Europe informing them of the meeting at the monastery, which was to begin on July 14 and to run to the end of the month. No program was announced, and since the letters had not been dispatched in time for prospective participants to respond, we simply had to wait and see who would appear. In fact, right up to the last minute the monks were skeptical whether an international gathering of philosophers would choose the austere atmosphere of a medieval monastery for their meeting.

But come they did. Those who arrived at Monteripido that summer were: Jeffner Allen, Richard Grathoff, Mrs. Aron Gurwitsch, José Huertas-Jourda, Samuel IJsseling, Bernd Jäger, Emmanuel Levinas, Werner Marx, Giuseppina Moneta, J.H. Nota, Reiner Schürmann, Thomas Sheehan, Carlo Sini, Jacques Taminiaux, Michael Zimmerman.

We were cordially welcomed by the monks, and in the beautiful surroundings provided by the monastery we set to work. Our immediate aim was to make the necessary preparations for such gatherings to continue in future summers on a regular basis. Each morning we convened in a room that had just been restored to its original thirteenth-century style, and there we tried to put together guidelines that would serve for future years. Although no minutes of those intensive meetings were taken, they are documented in the report that José Huertas-Jourda prepared of that first session. Let me cite at length from that report.

> We worked long and hard, wrangling consensus from the clash of divergent ideals, temperaments, backgrounds, and disciplines. Each gave in where his or her position appeared too esoteric and extreme, but only when all efforts to convince the others had failed, or when the others' point of view eventually appeared the better. We found that by letting all air their views and by exploring each position fully, we could, as a matter of fact, reach one of what Aron Gurwitsch used to call 'the three unholy C's' (committee, compromise and consensus) without resorting to either of the other two. We achieved 'consensus' without 'compromise' and without the face-saving detour of the 'committee'. What we have achieved will doubtless need to be changed as we learn more and can attempt more. It is far short of some of the ideals towards which we turned ourselves in that initial meeting, in the Library of the Franciscan monastery at Monteripido. Intruders from another age, we so evidently disturbed its ancient elegance, its gilded fragility redolent with the pervasive smell of wax and book dust! Yet we were not unwelcome, and

the quietude of the place worked its enchantment upon us through its windows open on the luminous Umbrian night, as its high ceiling isolated our voices around the cartographer's table with a peculiar timelessness all its own. If walls can wait for centuries for men to bring to them the treasure of their hope, may not men learn from their patience, and, in order to improve it, to participate in, rather than reject out of hand, what they cannot totally commend?

The aim was to set up an international, multidisciplinary graduate and undergraduate seminar in phenomenology designed to introduce to the field selected students ranging from fourth-year undergraduate to post-doctoral professionals eager to fill a glaring professional lacuna. By the 'field' of phenomenology we meant not only the growing corpus of research claiming that methodological allegiance in the many disciplines in which it is now recognized but also the researchers themselves whose current activities illustrate and transform 'phenomenology'. True we were under no illusions that we might succeed in a summer, no matter how concentrated the work and illustrious the lecturers. And so we resolved not to attempt the impossible task of introducing the student to all phenomenology at once. Instead, we divided it into three 'concentrations' to each of which a summer would be devoted, a year apart and in succession: Husserlian, Heideggerian and 'further developments'. And we decided to devote some eighty hours of 'instruction' to each. Under each of these headings we resolved to show where the many ramifications take root which branch out as contributions to psychology, sociology, history, literary criticism, etc. The seminar would be named: *Collegium Phaenomenologicum* to make manifest its oecumenism ... Let us say that what we attempted here is intended to help in this collective effort by instituting a forum designed to bring together all those who, across continents and across disciplines, work through phenomenology to the realization of this hope: 'Philosophie als strenge Wissenschaft, der Traum ist *nicht* ausgeträumt'.

The opening of the Collegium took place in the sixteenth-century library of the monastery on the evening of July 14th with an informal talk by Werner Marx. In the days that followed, morning and afternoon meetings were devoted to the organization of the future Collegium; in the evenings papers were presented and followed by lively discussions among the various participants.

Participants at this first session of the Collegium began also to discover the cultural richness of the Umbrian Region, visiting several Umbrian towns such as Assisi, Spoleto, Gubbio and Fonti del Clitunno. But, above all these, as José Huertas-Jourda expressed it above

even Perugia itself with its incredible vistas and architectural marvels, the warm hospitality of the good fathers, the quiet of their routine, Monteripido itself with its inner gardens, outer terraces and vineyards, its incomparable distance from the frenetic rhythm within which we are normally caught, all conspired to instill us with the mood most propitious to work.

Even in later years, after the Collegium had left Monteripido, much of the spirit of what had been established there during that first summer remained: the quiet ambiance aloof from the frenetic world in which most of us otherwise lived; visits to other Umbrian towns and to favorite places in Perugia, to its old churches and art galleries, its museums and Etruscan tombs, even to the Communist bar and the swings in the luna-park, and, later, back to the monastery itself – all of these excursions experienced not as touristic events but rather as integral to participation in the Collegium.

The 1977 session, directed by José Huertas-Jourda, lasted for six weeks and was devoted to the study of Husserl's work. There were lectures and seminars, the latter conducted largely as workshops in which the ten students attending could actively participate. A formal lecture on the history of Perugia was delivered by a member of the Community, Father Ugolino Nicolini. On one memorable occasion we went off to a neighboring convent where Tom Clifton (piano) and Reg Lilly (guitar) provided us with musical entertainment. In this second session the number of faculty increased somewhat, even though – as was to remain the policy – faculty received no compensation whatsoever from the Collegium and were themselves responsible for their own expenses at the monastery. One result of this policy has been that the cost of tuition for students has been kept extremely low so as to allow as many qualified students as possible to attend. The policy has also helped to foster a spirit of community and collaboration among faculty and between faculty and students. Indeed, one of the most remarkable things about the Collegium has been the way in which personal associations formed there have in so many instances grown into enduring friendships and extended philosophical collaborations.

The 1978 session, directed by Thomas Sheehan, was devoted to the thought of Martin Heidegger. The number of faculty and students attending was nearly double that of the previous year, though communication about the Collegium continued to be largely by word of mouth rather than by the usual means of publicity. The five-week program was inaugurated by Werner Marx with a lecture 'Heidegger and the Task of Thought'. The series of morning courses and of evening lectures were supplemented by afternoon faculty seminars devoted to on-going discussion of *Being and Time.* One of the high points of the 1978 session was a spirited *Auseinandersetzung* between Werner Marx and Hans-Georg Gadamer. During this third session the Collegium was host to a special colloquium for which Carlo Sini, one of the Collegium's founders, invited to Monteripido the most prominent representatives of phenomenology in Italy.

The philosophy of Merleau-Ponty was the theme of the 1979 session, directed by Jacques Taminiaux, who was ably assisted by James Decker. This session lasted for four weeks, as have all sessions of the Collegium in subsequent years. The session included a special day devoted to lectures on the philosophy of Aron Gurwitsch; Mrs. Gurwitsch was in attendance.

Each year brought the Collegium some scholars who had not previously attended, and several of these became regular participants: Hans-Georg Gadamer, William Richardson, and David Krell in 1978; John Sallis in 1979. There were also students, Reginald Lilly, Robert Crease, Thomas Thorpe, Marylou Sena, and others, who continued to return year after year, providing that continuity of spirit that has remained throughout all the philosophical, pedagogical, and organizational reorientations, and even the abrupt change of location.

It came quite unexpectedly. Early in 1980, the Father Superior at Monteripido informed me that the monastery would no longer be able to offer accomodations for the Collegium. The City Administration was demanding that the monastery have a regular permit in order to function as a guesthouse. Because of the length of time needed for obtaining such a permit, the monastery was being forced to cease offering accommodations. For us to find another location suitable for the Collegium appeared, at first, quite impossible; all guesthouses in Perugia and in the vicinity were booked for the coming summer. We were on the verge of cancelling the 1980 session when I contacted the Casa del Sacro Cuore just outside Perugia. They were willing to host our group.

Hence the 1980 session took place at the Casa del Sacro Cuore. It was directed by Jeffner Allen. Its theme was 'Studies in Hermeneutics and Interpretation'. The uncertainty that, with the need for a new location, had accompanied much of the planning was to a degree balanced by the major contribution made to the session by Hans-Georg Gadamer, who spent more than two weeks at the Collegium conducting several seminars and engaging almost continually in informal discussion with students. The 1980 Collegium was one of the most cosmopolitan, with participants from eleven countries, including Poland and Japan. Again a group of Italian scholars convened for a special colloquium. Professor Gadamer gave the opening address to more than a hundred participants.

Though the new location was quite different in character from the monastery, there was much to be said for it; there were to be interminable discussions of the relative merits of the two locations. The Casa del Sacro Cuore, a classic Italian villa, is perched high above the Tiber valley; as one looks out, one can see Assisi in the distance, just across the valley. The grounds of the Casa are quite extensive and include gardens, a playing field, and woods. In the Casa excellent local Umbrian cuisine is prepared and served by a staff that includes several Italian girls whose charm and fine spirits have won the hearts of all participants. In 1983 a second building with more comfortable facilities was- completed; in the more recent sessions the courses and seminars have been held in this building. The additional rooms that it provides have also allowed the Collegium recently to accommodate more participants.

The 1981 session was directed by John Sallis. Its theme was 'Phenomenology and Aesthetics'. In view of the steadily growing number of students attending the Collegium, certain pedagogical changes were introduced: courses and seminars were to be more explicitly oriented to presentation and discussion of specific texts, which all were encouraged to study in advance. An effort was also made to give greater unity to the program by correlating more closely the morning courses and the afternoon seminars. During this session participants had the opportunity of attending the Festival of the Two Worlds in Spoleto as well as several concerts at the Perugia Town Hall as guests of the President of the Perugia Music Association, Mrs. Alba Buitoni. Joan Stambaugh treated the participants to a piano recital at the Casa. Again the Collegium was host to an Italian colloquium. The three-day meeting, organized around three specific themes ('Signs, Language, and History', 'Art, World, and Values in the Post-Metaphysical Age', 'Politics, Reason, and Necessity') received considerable attention in the Italian press. Several who first attended the Collegium in 1981 were to return regularly in the years to follow: Robert Bernasconi, Walter Brogan, Michel Haar, Charles Scott. Among the founding members, Jacques Taminiaux and Samuel IJsseling returned regularly; Thomas Sheehan also returned frequently.

John Sallis also directed the 1982 session, devoted to the theme 'Phenomenology and the Ends of Metaphysics'. In addition to the academic program, there was an organized visit to the Umbrian towns of Todi and Orvieto. A piano recital was presented at the Casa by Adriaan Peperzak, who was attending the Collegium for the first time; it was also the first time that Parvis Emad participated.

'Phenomenology and Language' was the theme of the 1983 session under the direction of Robert Bernasconi. At this time the Collegium received from the Assessorato alla Cultura of the Umbrian Regional Government a grant of two million lire, which was to be renewed in the following years. The grant made possible a number of fellowships for needy students. The Collegium was also awarded a travel grant by the Giunta Provinciale of Perugia, which financed an excursion to the Adriatic seashore as well as an all-day excursion to Siena with a memorable stopover at the Renaissance town of Pienza.

The 1984 session had as its theme 'Phenomenology and the Crisis of Reason'. It was directed by Parvis Emad. In addition to the regular program, regular elementary instruction in Italian language was introduced. The number of faculty and students interested in attending the Collegium had continued to increase rapidly.

The 1985 session, marking the tenth anniversary of the founding of the Collegium, was directed by Charles Scott. Its theme was 'Thinking after

Heidegger'. We celebrated the tenth anniversary with a four-day trip to Elea and Paestum in Southern Italy. On our way south from Perugia we stopped briefly at the park of the Royal Caserta Palace, then travelled on beyond Rome and Naples, arriving finally at the small town of Ascea Marina, where we were to stay. Our hotel was within sight of ancient Elea, the city of Xenophanes and Parmenides. The following day Kenneth Maly gave a lecture on Parmenides. Late in the afternoon we were given a tour of the archeological site. The immense wonder of the place stilled our voices, as we walked over the huge stones marking the area of the ancient school. Memorable also was the visit the next day to the Greek temples at Paestum, which were of special interest because of Heidegger's discussion in 'The Origin of the Work of Art'. Our visit to Paestum was followed by a lecture, 'The Place of the Work of Art', in which Edward Casey took up that discussion again. On the return trip to Perugia we stopped briefly in Naples for a visit, on invitation, at the Italian Institute for Philosophical Studies.

In its ten years the academic program of the Collegium has, of course, undergone many changes, not only changes in structure and in pedagogy but also changes that reflect contemporary developments in Continental philosophy at large. Whereas the earlier sessions were largely oriented to the classical phenomenological thinkers (Husserl, Heidegger, Merleau-Ponty), later sessions have focused attention also on the works of Nietzsche, Lacan, Derrida, and one of the most eminent founders of the Collegium, Emmanuel Levinas.

Throughout its ten-year history the Collegium has always, along with its academic program, also given some attention to the heritage of Umbria. There have been lectures on Umbrian history and on the civilization of the Etruscans. The interest in these pre-Roman inhabitants of the region has also been aroused by the fact that the Casa holds a small collection of gravestones from Etruscan times, all excavated in the immediate surroundings. Nor have we neglected to visit such examples of the contemporary cultural life of the region as the open-air 'Fuseum' of the Umbrian artist Brajio Fuso.

Especially in recent years the organizational structure of the Collegium has deliberately been kept quite minimal. An evening meeting of former directors and others long involved in the Collegium serves each year for choosing a new director and proposing a topic for the following year. Such tenuous organization has been successful only because of the dedication and hard work of those involved, especially the directors and their assistants. Though the Collegium has grown in size and complexity over the ten years, all have endeavored to maintain those delicate balances that have made the atmosphere of the Collegium so very exceptional.

Texts

The Crisis of Reason in the Nineteenth Century: Schelling's Treatise on Human Freedom (1809)

DAVID FARRELL KRELL
University of Essex

> Our age is the proper age of *critique*, to which everything must be subjected.
>
> Kant, KrV, A xi

> Thus the ground, in its freedom, achieves Allotment [*die Scheidung*] and Judgment (κρίσις), and precisely thereby the complete actualization of God.
>
> Schelling, S.W., *7*, 404

> I know my lot. One day the memory of something monstrous will attach itself to my name – the memory of a *crisis* the likes of which has never been seen on earth . . .
>
> Nietzsche, StA, *6*, 365

> – 'Well, Bannadonna', said the chief, 'how long ere you are ready to set the clock going, so that the hour shall be sounded'? . . .
> – 'To-morrow, Excellenza, if you listen for it, – or should you not, all the same – strange music will be heard. *The stroke of one* shall be the first from yonder bell,' pointing to the bell, adorned with girls and garlands, 'that stroke shall fall there, where the hand of Una clasps Dua's. *The stroke of one shall sever that loved clasp.'*
>
> Melville, 'The Bell-Tower'
> (*Emphases mine throughout*)

Introductory Note

The crisis of reason in *the* nineteenth century? As if there were but one 'crisis.' As if one could reasonably circumscribe what we call 'the nineteenth century.' As if, even granting that one might decide to remain within the confines of philosophy and intellectual history, one could reduce such events as Darwin, Marx, Nietzsche, and Freud to a single unified fable.

These were my first responses to the invitation to teach the first course of the 1984 Collegium, 'Phenomenology and the Crisis of Reason in the Nineteenth

J.C. Sallis, G. Moneta and J. Taminiaux (eds.), The Collegium Phaenomenologicum, 13–32.
© *Kluwer Academic Publishers.*

Century.' I realized that whatever I said about 'the crisis of reason' would be tangential, peripheral, even eccentric. Nevertheless, I played with the thought of *one* crisis, of a singular and central problem that might have begun with Kant, pervaded German Idealism, and come to implosion in Nietzsche. I played with the thought of the problematic role of *imagination* (as opposed to the transcendental unity of apperception) as the agent of synthesis for the manifold of intuition and the concepts or categories. Such play then led me from the *Critique of Pure Reason* to Kant's *Anthropology from a Pragmatic Point of View* (1798). In one of the sections on imagination I found the passage that I decided should open my course. It was a note to which Nietzsche had drawn my attention (see the *Studienausgabe, 7,* 149); and, because I wished to conclude the course with some reflections on Nietzsche, I prepared the following quotation and translation for the Collegium participants:

Man könnte die zwei ersten Arten der Zusammensetzung der Vorstellungen die *mathematische* (der Vergrößerung), die dritte aber die *dynamische* (der Erzeugung) nennen; wodurch ein ganz neues Ding (wie etwa das Mittelsalz in der Chemie) hervorkommt. Das Spiel der Kräfte in der Leblosen Natur sowohl als der lebenden, in der Seele ebensowohl as des Körpers beruht aus Zersetzungen und Vereinigungen (/) des Ungleichartigen. Wir gelangen zwar zur Erkenntnis derselben durch Erfahrung ihrer Wirkungen; die oberste Ursache aber und die einfachen Bestandteile, darin ihr Stoff aufgelöst werden kann, sind für uns unerreichbar. – Was mag wohl die Ursache davon sein, daß alle organische Wesen, die wir kennen, ihre Art nur durch die Vereinigung zweier Geschlechter (die man dann das männliche und weibliche nennt) fortpflanzen? Man kann doch nicht annehmen, daß der Schöpfer bloß der Sonderbarkeit halber, und nur um auf unserem Erd-Glob eine Einrichtung, die ihm so gefiele, zu machen, gleichsam nur gespielt habe; sondern es scheint, es müsse *unmöglich* sein, aus der Materie unsers Erdballs organische Geschöpfe durch Fortpflanzung anders entstehen zu lassen, ohne daß dazu zwei Geschlechter gestiftet wären. – In welchem Dunkel verliert sich die menschliche Vernunft, wenn sie hier den Abstamm zu ergründen, ja auch nur zu erraten es unternehmen will?*

One could call the first two kinds of combination of representations [i.e., *imaginatio plastica* and *imaginatio assozians*] the *mathematical* (having to do with enlargement); but one could call the third kind [i.e., *affinitas, Verwandtschaft*] the *dynamic* (having to do with generation), whereby an entirely new thing (somewhat like a salt in chemistry) is produced. The play of forces, in lifeless nature as well as in animate nature, in the soul as well as in the body, rests on dissolutions and unifications (/) of dissimilars. True, we attain knowledge of these whenever we experience their effects; yet their highest cause and the simple components into which their matter can be resolved are beyond our reach. – What might be the cause of the fact that all the known organic creatures reproduce their kind solely by means of the unification of two sexes (which one then calls the male and the female)? Surely we cannot assume that the Creator, merely on account of some eccentricity, and simply in order to devise an arrangement on our earthly globe that pleased him, was only playing, as it were; rather, it seems that it must be *impossible* to enable organic creatures to originate through reproduction from the matter of which our globe consists in any other way than by founding two sexes to that end. – In what obscurity does human reason lose itself when it undertakes, even by way of surmise, to ground here its lineage.

* I. Kant, *Anthropologie in pragmatischer Hinsicht,* 1798 (Akad.-Ausg., pp. 177–78n. Footnote to § 31, 'On the Sensuous Poietic Faculty of Affinity [*das sinnliche Dichtungsvermögen der Verwandtschaft*]'.

The very idea that the author of a *transcendental critique* of pure reason would envisage something like a *genealogy* of reason, a genealogy of 'Unifications' (a word I had associated with Hölderlin, but not Kant), a genealogy that would implicate reason itself in the 'dissimilars' of male and female, astonished me. For the Nietzschean texts that I had already chosen as points of culmination for my course – its outermost periphery, as it were – involved precisely this bifurcation and distinction of the sexes. Jacques Derrida's *Spurs* had reminded me of the disturbing presence of these texts in *The Gay Science.* Without knowning precisely how I would relate them to Kant's note on the imagination, indeed, without knowing whether or not I had anything at all to say about them, I prepared a second sheet with translations of sections 59 and 60 of *Die fröhliche Wissenschaft,* as follows:

59

We Artificers! – When we love a woman, we may well fly into a rage against nature, thinking of all the repulsive naturalnesses to which every woman is exposed; we gladly think right on by all these things, but if our souls should chance to graze against them it recoils impatiently and looks toward nature, as I have said, with contempt: – we are insulted, nature seems to be meddling with our possessions, and with the most profane hands. Here one stops his ears against all physiology and secretly decrees for himself: 'I want to hear nothing about human beings' consisting of anything more than *soul and form!*' The human being 'under the skin' is for all lovers a horror and an impossible thought, a blasphemy against God and against Love. – Now, in the same way that the lover is sensitive with regard to nature and naturalness, so in former times was each person who revered God and his 'holy omnipotence' sensitive: everything that astronomers, geologists, physiologists, and doctors said about nature he saw as an encroachment on his most precious possession, and consequently as a attack – to top it off, an attack by an utterly shameless attacker. The 'law of nature' itself sounded to him like a calumny against God; at bottom, he would have been all too happy to have seen all mechanics traced back to acts of moral will and unconstrained arbitration: – but because no one could render him this service he *concealed* nature and mechanics from himself as best he could and lived in a dream. Oh, these human beings of bygone days knew how to *dream*, and they didn't have to wait till they fell asleep! – and we human beings today, we too are still quite proficient at it, for all the good will we show to vigilance and daylight! It is enough for us to love, hate, desire, sense anything at all – immediately the spirit and force of the dream comes over us, and we climb the most hazardous winding ways, open-eyed, coolly confronting every danger, up to the rooftops and turrets of fantasy, without a hint of vertigo, as though we were born to clamber – we somnambulists of the day! We artificers! Concealers of naturalness! Moonsick, Godsick! Relentless wanderers, still as death, along heights we do not perceive as heights but as our level plains, our securities!

60

Women and Their Action at a Distance. – Do I still have ears? Am I now but an ear, nothing else besides? Here I stand in the midst of the surging surf, its white flames licking their way to my foot:

– from every side it threatens, howls, cries, and screams to me, while in the deepest depths the old earthshaker sings his aria, the muffled sounds of a bellowing bull: he beats out such an earthshaker's measure that the very hearts of these monstrous, weathered rocks tremble in their bodies. Then, suddenly, as though born of nothing, there appears beyond the doorway of this hellish labyrinth, only a few leagues removed, – a great sailing ship, gliding along, silent as a ghost. Oh, what ghostly beauty! With what enchantment it grips me! Could it be? Has all the tranquility and silence in the world embarked on this ship? Does my happiness itself have its seat there in that quiet place, my happier 'I', my second, dearly departed self? To be, not dead, yet no longer living? As a ghostlike, silent, gazing, gliding, hovering daimon? To be like the ship which with its white sails skims like a huge butterfly over the dark sea! Yes! To skim *over* existence! That's it! That would be it! – It seems the noise here has made me a visionary? All great noise causes us to posit our happiness in tranquility and remoteness. When a man stands in the midst of *his* noise, in his surf of plays and plans, he too will see tranquil, enchanting creatures gliding by him: he yearns for the happiness and seclusion of them – *it's the women*. He almost imagines that his better self dwells among the women: at these quiet places even the loudest surf would grow still as death and life itself become the dream about life. And yet! And yet! My noble enthusiast, even on the loveliest sailing ship there is so much hubbub, so much noise, and alas, such petty, miserable noise! The magic, the most powerful impact of women is, to speak the language of the philosophers, an action at a distance, *actio in distans*: to it pertains, in the first place and above all else – *distance!*

When I left England for Perugia I was certain of only one thing: the hiatuses in Kant's text ('. . . are beyond our reach. – What might be the cause . . .' and '. . . two sexes to that end. – In what obscurity does human reason lose itself . . .') opened up a *distance* similar to the one evoked in and by Nietzsche's discourse. And I believed that both sets of hiatuses would provide a new space, a radically decentered and incalculable space, in which to insert a reading or two of F.W.J. Schelling, *Philosophische Untersuchungen über das Wesen der menschlichen Freiheit und die damit zusammenhängenden Gegenstände* (1809).

A Peripheral Reading

A well-centered reading of Schelling's investigations *On Human Freedom* would pursue the problems of evil, existence, and origin. It would involve itself in Schelling's own quest for the origin of evil in existence, a quest plagued by a particular doubt. Schelling doubts whether any 'system of reason,' any *Vernunftsystem* past or present, whether monistic, dualistic, or even dialectical, can resolve the aporias that variously go under the rubrics of 'freedom and determinism', 'pantheism and fatalism', 'divine omniscience and beneficience', and so on. From Plotinus and Augustine through Leibniz and Spinoza, the question concerning the origin of evil in existence has been obfuscated rather than exposed. And Schelling wonders whether systems of reason 'merely displace the difficulty one point further down the line, but do not relieve it [*die Schwierigkeit nur um einen Punkt weiter hinausgerückt, aber nicht aufgehoben wäre*].'[1] A well-centered reading of Schelling's text would register each of Schelling's attempt to anneal traditional dualisms and complexify traditional monisms, attempts that become increasingly frantic as the scalpel of difference and scission, *Scheidung,* cuts deeper and deeper into the flesh of God. The hemorrhaging that occurs as a result of Schelling's strokes ceases only when the patient has become a bloodless shade. (Which Nietzsche will find hovering in a cave.)

Even an *indifferent* reading of Schelling's investigations (see Part II of this essay) would perceive that here it is a matter of crises: crisis of reason, crisis of divinity, crisis of ontotheology. My own *peripheral* reading, arbitrary and headstrong as it is, will be blind to the consequences of the crisis even as it tries to envisage κρίσις as such. According to the strictures of Schelling's own treatise, a peripheral reading strays from the center of divine Logos and Love, and also from the center of human freedom. Peripheral reading is thus evil.

On the final page of his treatise, Schelling writes of the 'unwritten revelation' that is nature. Nature contains proto-images, *Vorbilder*, which Schelling would have his readers contemplate. My peripheral reading will contemplate a series of proto-images of *Scheidung* and κρίσις in Schelling's text.[2] On the metaphoric perimeter of Schelling's treatise, I shall pay heed to two types of *Scheidung* and crisis, those of (1) self-mutilation and castration and (2) pregnancy and birth. For these are not entirely unrelated to the divine center – the Word – of Schelling's *Philosophical Investigations*.

Yet I cannot begin without invoking Schelling's own most striking simile for the very move from center to periphery I am here committing myself to – a move that is not only evil but also sick. Schelling writes:

> Illness here offers the aptest simile [*Gleichnis*]. As the disorder that comes into nature through the misuse of freedom, illness is the true replica of evil or sin. Universal illness never occurs without the emergence of the concealed forces of the ground. Illness originates when the irritable principle, which should reign in the tranquil depths as the innermost cincture [*Band*] of forces, actuates itself; or when Archaeus, suddenly disturbed, quits his tranquil dwelling in the center and moves to the circumference. In the same way, contrariwise, all original healing consists in the restoration of the relation of periphery to center; and the transition from illness to health can really happen only by virtue of the opposite, to wit, the reabsorption of separate and particular life into the inner beam of light in the essence [*Wiederaufnahme des getrennten und einzelnen Lebens in den innern Lichtblick des Wesens*], after which reabsorption the scission (crisis) again occurs.[3]

Turning now to the image of *Scheidung* as castration, I want to present three passages from various sections of Schelling's *Investigations*. First, a segment from what one might call the 'historical introduction' to the problem of evil in philosophy. Here Schelling pinpoints the principal flaw in modern philosophy since Descartes. Modern (idealistic) philosophy, because it contains no (real) philosophy of nature, has mutilated itself, emasculated itself. At the outset I shall leave in suspense the curious fact that precisely when the (masculine) modern philosopher ignores (feminine) nature he sacrifices his own (masculine) nature. As we shall see, the female in Schelling's text appears under two guises: first, as the plenitude of fecund nature, as the Mother; second, as absence and debility, affectation and hysteria, effeminacy and flaw. The second guise of the female thus brings us back to the (problematically masculine) modern philosopher: modern philosophy becomes effeminate insofar as it spurns the female. Yet how are we to divorce or divide these affirmative and negative guises? Schelling's image of the crises of modern philosophy will itself become the crisis of such imagery. All this in anticipation of the following (356–57):

> Modern European philosophy as a whole, from its beginning (in Descartes), has this common flaw: for it, nature does not exist, it lacks a living ground. Spinoza's realism is in this regard as abstract as Leibniz's idealism. Idealism is the soul of philosophy, realism its body; only the two together constitute a living whole. Never can the latter [i.e., realism, as the *Leib* of philosophy] provide the principle, but it must be the ground and the means [*Grund und Mittel*] in which the former actualizes itself, assumes flesh and blood. If a philosophy lacks this living fundament – which is usually a sign that the ideal principle too was originally only feebly at work in it – it loses itself in the kind of system whose attenuated concepts of aseity, modifications, etc. stand in sharpest contrast to the vital force and fullness of actuality. Yet wherever the ideal principle actually works its effects to a high degree, while unable to find the reconciling and mediating basis, it generates a turbid, wild enthusiasm that irrupts in self-mutilation or – as with the priests of the Phrygian goddess – self-emasculation [*da erzeugt es einen trüben und wilden Enthusiasmus, der in Selbstzerfleischung, oder, wie bei den Priestern der phrygischen Göttin* (i.e., Kybele), *in Selbstentmannung ausbricht*]. This transpires in philosophy when reason and science are surrendered.

When (idealist) philosophy neglects to assume flesh and blood in the womb of realism, its high spirits and presumed high-mindedness culminate in *Selbstzer*fleisch*ung* – as though there were already in idealism, in spite of itself, a *Fleisch* susceptible of mutilation – and *Selbstent*mann*ung*, a self-castration after the manner of the husbands of Kybele or, even though Schelling does not mention him, on the example of Origen.

Precisely how does such castration occur? When a philosopher abnegates the reconciling and mediating basis (*Grund*) of the ideal principle, he abjures reason and science – the philosophic potency. However, science establishes the distinction (*Unterscheidung*) 'between essence insofar as it exists, and essence insofar as it is merely the ground of existence' (357). The problem, as we shall see, is how to prevent this *Unter-scheidung* from itself developing into a scission that will unman science as definitively as idealism has done.

The second passage on *Scheidung* as castration comprises an extended quotation from Johann Georg Hamann (1730–1788), along with Schelling's commentary (401):

> 'If the passions are the members of dishonor, do they thereby cease to be weapons of manhood? Do you understand the letter of reason more discerningly than that allegorical chamberlain of the Alexandrian Church understood Scriptures when he made himself a eunuch for the sake of the kingdom of heaven?[4] – The prince of this aeon adopts as his favorites those who are perfect little demons toward themselves – his (the devil's) jesters are the harshest enemies of beauteous nature, which has Corybants and Galli as its renegade monks[5] but vigorous spirits as its true worshippers.' [Schelling cites Hamann's *Cloverleaf of Hellenistic Letters,* II, p. 196, and comments as follows:] It is only that those whose philosophy is made more for women's rooms [*Gynäceum*, from ἡγυναικεία, that part of a house in ancient Greece reserved for the women; cf. τὰ γυναικεῖα, defined by Liddell-Scott as the *partes muliebres*] than for the Academe or the palaestra of the Lyceum do not wish to bring those dialectical propositions [i.e., those that assert the identity of good and evil (400)] before a public which, misunderstanding both them and itself, sees in them a sublation of all distinction between justice and injustice, good and evil; before a public where they belong just as little as do the statements of the ancient dialecticians, Zeno and the other Eleatics, before the forum of effete spirits [*seichter Schöngeister*].

It is difficult to separate out the various levels of polemic here and their respective targets. Suffice for the moment to note once again the curious recoil of the castration imagery: the male member, dishonorable though it is, precisely because of its susceptibility to elements of the *Gynäceum*, is manhood's weapon *par excellence* (Schelling himself more often refers to the body in general as the 'tool' or 'implement' of spirit, *Werkzeug des Geistes*; Hegel too employs the phrase); only a womanly philosopher, a philosopher of the kitchen and the loom, not to mention the bedroom, would hesitate to assert the dialectical identity of good and evil merely because an effeminate public fears such identification. The effete and effeminate public in fact prefers a sterile dualism to a fructifying monism capable of sustaining profound *Scheidungen* and surviving severe *crises*. Such a monism girds its loins with the sheathe that swallows the sword, the flaming sword that announces in one stroke – not here, not yet, but in the sketches toward *The Ages of the World* (1810–1814), and even there only incipiently, never with full confidence – the invagination of God.[6]

One final passage on the *Scheidung* of castration – particularly revealing as regards the ambiguous plight of modern philosophy, which becomes womanly ('womanly', to be sure, only if one remains within the phallocratic equation of woman and castration) precisely in its recoil from womanly nature – appears in a footnote late in Schelling's text (409–10). Here Schelling is eager to join his voice to those that object to 'the unmanly pantheistic swindle' in contemporary German letters. Eager because it is he who is being accused of pantheism, and of swindle, by his 'brother-in-law,' once removed, Friedrich Schlegel. If modern philosophic idealsim from Descartes to Leibniz is unmanned, according to Schelling, then modern pantheism in Spinoza and his epigones is unmanly. Schelling thus finds himself caught between two eminently vulnerable positions. Too little devotion to a philosophy of nature and he joins the gelded ranks of the Kybeline priesthood; too much devotion and he capitulates to a simpering pantheism. *In either case the result is the same.* And yet. However much pantheism may imply both vertigo and fraud (*Schwindel* here suggesting both, as it does in Hegel's *Phenomenology*, where it is predicated of historical skepticism), Schelling is willing to dally with it. A year later he will conclude his *Stuttgarter Privatvorlesungen* (7, 484) by saying, 'Then God is actually all in all, and pantheism true.' Yet in the *Investigations* he will cut himself off from pantheism at the decisive moment, at the place where one clasps the hand of two, at the decisive moment of absolute indifference. He and his God, by grace of *Scheidung*, will cut themselves off by the stroke of One.

Let me now take up the images of *Scheidung* as fecundation, pregnancy, and birth. Of the many references to parturition in Schelling's text, I shall refer to three.

Quite early in his account (346–47), Schelling tries to express the relation of ground and existence in the (divine) essence without submitting to pantheistic excess. The passage begins cautiously enough, is delicate to the point of ambiguity:

> Consideration of the divine essence itself offers a much higher standpoint. The idea of that essence is of a consequence that would not wholly contradict generation, that is, the positing of something self-sufficient [*eine Folge, die nicht Zeugung, d.h. Setzen eines Selbständigen ist, völlig widersprechen würde*: the subjunctive mood and the periphrasis indicate Schelling's caution; the confusing contiguity of *nicht* and *Zeugung* is well-nigh equivocal in its effects, as though canceling the word 'generation' or 'procreation' before writing it]. God is not a God of the dead, but of the living. It is utterly incomprehensible how the most perfect essence of all [*das allervollkommenste Wesen*: one is tempted to translate *Wesen* here as 'creature', thus wreaking havoc with the traditional ontotheological distinction between the *ens creatum* and *ens increatum*, even though it is precisely such havoc that Schelling is about] could take his pleasure in even the most perfect machine

> [*auch an der möglich vollkommensten Maschine seine Lust fände*]. However one might think of the manner of procession of essences from God, it can never be a mechanical one, no mere effecting or putting in place, whereby what is effected is nothing for itself; just as little can it be emanation, whereby the efflux would remain the same as that from which it has flowed, and thus is nothing of its own, nothing self-sufficient [*Eignes, Selbstständiges*]. The procession of things from God is a self-revelation of God. However, God can only be revealed to himself [*kann nur sich offenbar werden*] in what is similar to him, in essences that act freely from out of themselves; for there is no ground for their Being, other than God; but they are in the way that God is. He speaks, and they are there.

If the procession of creatures from the primal essence cannot be mechanical – and we recall that for German Idealism and Romanticism as a whole the *machine* is sheer oppression and death[7] – then it must be a matter of *Zeugung*, procreation and generation. Since the Greeks there have been only two options: production (τέχνη) and reproduction (γένεσις) are the demiurgic modes, these and no others. Yet if τέχνη seems an utterly unworthy mode, paternity imposes its own attendant indignities. Schelling tries to displace these indignities onto *a second scene*, the scene of humanity; yet they cling to the primal scene of *Scheidung*, to (divine) Creation. And in the wake of these indignities – time, finitude, illness, and evil. Not long after the passage with which I began, on the self-emasculation of modern philosophy, Schelling writes the following concerning the scission between ground and existence in God (359–60):

> In order to be separated [*geschieden*] from God, they [i.e., *die Dinge*, the things of nature] must come to be in a ground that is different [*verschieden*] from him. Yet because nothing can be outside God [*außer Gott*], this contradiction can be resolved only thus: the things have their ground in whatever in God himself is not *He Himself*, that is, in that which is ground of his existence [*daß die Dinge ihren Grund in dem haben, was in Gott selbst nicht E r S e l b s t ist, d.h. in dem was Grund seiner Existenz ist*].

In a note to this passage, marked for insertion after the phrase, *was in Gott selbst nicht Er Selbst ist,* Schelling declares this 'the sole correct dualism', one that simultaneously 'admits of a unity' by virtue of the fact that it 'subordinates' the 'evil principle' to the good. How that *Unterordnung* is to occur is, of course, the question. At this point we are confronted with the conundrum that there is something *in God himself* that is *not He Himself*. The divine *selbst* is here writ twice, once small and without emphasis, a second time large and opened by spaced-type;[8] and, mediating these two invocations of the divine self, the negative (*nicht*) and the masculine pronoun, also capitalized and broadly spaced: *E r*. The passage continues:

> If we wish to make this essence more accessible in human terms [*menschlich*

> *näherbringen*], we can say that it is the longing [*Sehnsucht*] felt by the eternal One to give birth to itself [*sich selbst zu gebären*]. It [*Sie*: i.e., this longing] is not the One itself, yet is still co-eternal with it. It wants to give birth to God, that is, to the ungroundable unity [*Sie will Gott, d.h. die unergründliche Einheit gebären*]; but to that extent unity is not yet in it itself [*in ihr selbst*].

The translation obfuscates the curious pronomial play of Schelling's text. When the masculine *Er* is opened up there is suddenly room for feminine longing, gyneceal room, one might say; for *die Sehnsucht*, which in the subsequent lines commands the feminine pronoun *sie*. She, longing, is not the one itself (*das Eine, ne-uter,* 'neither the one nor the other'), although she is coeval with it (or him, inasmuch as the dative singular, *mit ihm*, is identical for masculine and neuter). She wants to become pregnant with God, to bear and parture him. *Gebären* derives from the Greek φέρω, to bear or carry, and the prefix *ge-*, expressing the *result* of the pregnancy, that is to say, looking forward to the Son – surely in the present case it can only be a matter of sons, not of daughters – that will eventually be *ge-boren*. Thus unity is not yet in her, in her self, *in ihr selbst.* Presuming that one can even speak of ground and longing as possessing selfhood. Juxtaposed to the phrase *Er Selbst* we now have an *in ihr selbst* – no, not merely juxtaposed, because she, the longing, is *in* God, himself. How did she get there? Did she not get there because *in* God himself there arose a longing, a longing (expressed in terms of the human scene) to give birth to himself? to make himself his own Mother? Are we certain that it will not be a matter of daughters?

Or may we discount all the above as a contingency of German grammar and its three genders of nouns and pronouns? And does not Schelling himself explicitly invoke that second scene in order to speak in parables, by way of analogy, merely in order to bring the essence nearer? Presumably the (divine) essence *itself* will suffer no such division? And yet. The essence *as such* is divided into ground and existence: such is the initial insight of Schelling's science of nature. And 'divided' here cannot here mean the empty, formal, abstract *Unterscheidung* of idealism. The division must be *real*.

It is no accident that precisely at this point – the point of longing, craving, the compulsion to conceive, hysteria – Schelling felt compelled to defend himself against the (mis)understandings of his contemporaries Eschenmayer and Georgii.[9] (Mis)understandings arise here, Schelling assures us, from the obduracy (*Eigendünkel*) that is the root of evil itself; and they ultimately betray themselves, not only as obduracy, but also as 'womanly wailing', *die weibischen Klagen* (360), the womanly wailing of philosophers who are afraid of the dark. It is not Schelling's God but Schelling's critics who show themselves to be womanly. (But why *womanly* when it is *longing herself* from which the philosopher-critics shrink?) Skipping now a page of Schelling's text – a page on the 'ruleless' and 'ungraspable basis of reality' which is 'ground', a page we really ought to read word-for-word – I return now to the passage in question:

> All birth is birth from darkness into light; the kernel of seed must be implanted in the earth, to die in gloom, in order that the more beautiful shape of light [*Lichtgestalt*] arise and unfold along the beams of the sun. The human being is formed in the mother's womb;[10] and from the darkness of what is without understanding (from feeling, longing, the magnificent mother (*aus ... der herrlichen Mutter:* literally, from the lordly mother] of knowledge) first burgeon luminous thoughts [*die lichten Gedanken*[11]]. Thus we must represent to ourselves the originary longing [*die ursprüngliche Sehnsucht*], which indeed orients itself toward the understanding that it does not yet know, just as we, in longing, yearn for some unknown, nameless good; and, vaguely apprehending, it bestirs itself, as does a swelling, seething sea, like Platonic matter, according to an obscure and uncertain law, unable to form for itself something lasting.

Longing longs for the intellect, of which it is only vaguely aware. It bestirs itself, orients itself in the direction of *Verstand.* Yet it heaves and subsides, *wogend wallend*, like the sea, presumably without direction. Thus Schelling reads Plato's *Timaeus*: the irresolvable enigma of the conjunction of *Logos* and *Ananke* in a world where 'female parts' subsist solely as supplements; where access to the mother and nurse of Becoming is granted solely by a kind of 'bastard reasoning'.[12] In order to rescue (divine) essence from this all-engulfing duplicity of *Logos-Ananke*, from what Melville calls 'the shroud of the sea', Schelling now endeavors to neutralize the metaphors of longing, procreation, fecundation, pregnancy, and birth:

> However, in accord with the longing which, as the still obscure ground, is the first stirring of divine existence [*Dasein*], there is generated in God himself [*erzeugt sich in Gott selbst*] an inner reflexive representation [*eine innere reflexive Vorstellung*], through which, because it can have no other object than God, God envisages himself in a likeness [*durch welche ... Gott sich selbst in einem Ebenbilde erblickt*].

The icon that God espies in his inner reflexive representation appears to transmogrify itself, Proteus-like, from scene to scene in Schelling's *Investigations.* At times that *Vorstellung* appears to be the Word itself, the full presence of the eye and voice of the Father; at other times it appears as the Son, as Christology; finally, it appears at the center of the circle of Man, who is made in the image and likeness of the Father. For the most part, Schelling successfully resists the shape of Proteus which both Goethe and Nietzsche perceived as the fruit of the original *Scheidung* in God's essence – the shape of Lucifer.

A peripheral reading cannot thematize or even summarize in any detail the *Scheidung der Kräfte,* the 'scission' or 'sundering' of forces, that now occupies Schelling's *Investigations*. It can merely observe that they conduct us to the point at which we began – the simile of illness, whereby Archaeus abandons the serene center and, in crisis, loses himself on the periphery. One final glimpse of this crisis, on the human scene, in the course of Schelling's description of the 'formal essence of freedom.' Schelling is discussing the 'eternal deed', *die ewige Tat*, by which humanity – in some time prior to all time, in some ineffable coeval eternity – performed (freely) the deed that determined its nature. He writes (387):

> This universal judgment of a proclivity to evil, which in terms of its origin is entirely unconscious and indeed irresistible, as an act of freedom points to a deed and thus to a life prior to this life; except that it may not be thought as preceding in terms of time, inasmuch as the intelligible is altogether outside of time.[13] Because there prevails in Creation supreme consonance, and because nothing occurs in separation and sequence, in the way we are constrained to represent it, but where the later is also at work in the earlier and everything happens simultaneously in One magic stroke [*alles in Einem magischen Schlage zugleich geschieht*], because of this, humanity, which appears here decisively and determinately, is captured in a determinate shape in the first Creation [*hat . . . in der ersten Schöpfung sich in bestimmter Gestalt ergriffen*]; and is born as what it was from all eternity, inasmuch as, by means of that deed, the very type and particular quality of its corporization is determined [*die Art und Beschaffenheit seiner Korporisation bestimmt ist*].

The passage has to do with determinations, *Bestimmungen.* These arise 'in One magic stroke', in a single *coup*, at Once, from all eternity. Not only is the human proclivity to evil, its obdurate inclination to things peripheral, explained by this deed, but also the peculiar nature of its embodiment, the very *Art und Beschaffenheit seiner Korporisation.* The word *Art,* in modern German, means (among other things) 'species', and it includes both sexes. Yet in Hegel's philosophy of nature (see the *Encyclopedia*, sections 367–70) the word for 'species' is *Gattung*, whereas the *Arten* are (or at least include) the male and female genders. However, the phrase *Beschaffenheit seiner Korporisation* is even more intriguing. It could refer to any specific (or intraspecific) property of embodiment. It may be excessive or eccentric to read it as *sexual difference* as such. Yet could a peripheral reading – preoccupied with the metaphorics of center and circumference, fecundity and sterility, wholeness and mutilation, the lordly mother *versus* womanly wailing – read it in any other way? However, why should there be any connection between sexual difference and the deed that ushered evil into the world? Is the magic blow of embodiment, the bifurcated embodiment of the human animal, the curse and plague of evil as such? Would such bifurcation go some way toward explaining the negative guise of the female in Schelling's text? Is bifurcated embodiment, on the stroke of One, in essence, female? Furthermore, if the human and divine centers coalesce, so that the 'likeness' of God – whether as Self, Christ, or Man – is radically undecidable, would not the eternal deed recoil on essence as such? If during the years 1810–1814 Schelling remains fascinated by the consequences of his insight that God's every path – the *finis viarum Dei* (*8*, 325) – culminates in embodiment, does not the opening of an ineluctable duality in *Wesen* itself both promise to advance science and threaten to annihilate it? If the ground of existence is that which in God himself is not He Himself, must not Schelling cross out *Selbst* and write (in dialect) *Anderst*; must not Schelling cross out *Er* and write *Sie*?

God Himother? God Herself?

And would that, in Schelling's view, amount to anything less than God's self-emasculation, the magic stroke of evil incarnate, so that the eunuchs of modern philosophy will have been right all along?

An Indifferent Reading

Even if we persist on the periphery of Schelling's treatise, advancing along the perimeter of his metaphorics of *Scheidung*, we will find our way to the point of absolute indifference. Schelling calls if (406) 'the supreme point of the entire investigation'. It is that point at which *Grund* achieves ultimate scission, the point at which Judgment (κρισις) expels all evil and proclaims the rule of Love. Even though our circling about the periphery has hardly prepared us to occupy this supreme point, let us try to follow Schelling's text quite closely here (406–08), if only, for the most part, by way of paraphrase.

Schelling returns to his starting-point, the insight of the philosophy or science of nature. What purpose does that first differentiation within essence – insofar as it is *ground* and insofar as it *exists* – mean to serve? If ground and existence share no midpoint, the inevitable result is dualism and the collapse of every system of reason. Science must therefore strive to find that *Mittelpunkt*. It cannot be found in the absolute identity of opposites (light and dark, good and evil), inasmuch as identity would mean stasis, the dull decrepitude of such systems. Science must therefore insist that there is *one* essence *prior to* every ground and *prior to* everything that exists – although, presumably, such priority can be thought in terms of neither time nor causality nor ontological eminence. How else can we call it, Schelling asks, than *primal ground* or, rather, *nonground*? In Schelling's text (*'wie können wir es anders nennen als den Urgrund oder vielmehr* U n g r u n d ?') the primal, primordial, incipient, or original ground and the nonground are brought as close together as possible: only a single letter distinguishes them, and not even an entire letter, inasmuch as it is here merely a matter of prolonging a single stroke of one, of one letter, extending the arc of the *r* in *Urgrund* to the *n* of *Ungrund*. That one stroke alters origins to nihilations. The (original) nonground (the nonorigin of all grounds) precedes both opposition and identity, binary sets and units, dualism and monism. It is insufficient to call it a *coincidentia oppositorum*, after the manner of certain traditional systems. In the face of every oppositional pair, *der Ungrund* can only be 'the absolute *indifference* [I n d i f f e r e n z] of both'.[14]

It is as though primal essence had already passed through *Scheidung* and so becomes *geschiedenes Wesen*, a thing apart, whose development lay always already far behind it. No predicates adhere to it, especially not those of 'good' and 'evil'. The essence that is nonground is, if we may say so, quite beyond good and evil. Yet Schelling shrinks from the consequences of such indifference. He quickly calls for a restoration of sorts. 'Nothing can stop us', he declares, *aber es hindert nichts,* from predicating both opposites *in disjunction*, not as opposites but as a bare *duality*. Nothing can hinder us – inasmuch as the original nonground is 'careless' of both: *gleichgültig*, indifferent in the sense of 'insouciant'. Nonground is a neither-nor from which all duality (and opposition?) can eventually proceed. '*Without* indifference, that is, *without* a nonground, there would be no twofold of principles.'

However, sensing that his 'dialectical discussion' of duality resembles the logical legerdemain he elsewhere derides, Schelling proceeds as follows (and here, at 407–08, I shall stop paraphrasing and quote at length):

> The essence of ground [*Wesen des Grundes*], like the essence of what exists, can only be what *precedes* every ground, hence the Absolute considered purely and simply, the nonground.

Whereas Schelling's text has heretofore concerned the ground of essence, a ground that is *in* essence but not *of* it, as a compelling and autochthonous longing, the danger of that *Scheidung* now prods the text to conjure an Absolute that is prior to ('prior to', in 'scare quotes', since it is impossible to say or to think this 'prior to') all scission. So far, the Absolute has only a negative name, a name Schelling prefers even to the invocation of origins: the proper name of the Absolute is not *Urgrund* but *Ungrund*. But to continue:

> Yet the nonground can be the Absolute (as demonstrated) in no other way than by diverging into two equally eternal commencements [*zwei gleich ewige Anfänge*]; not that he [*er: der Ungrund*] is both commencements *simultaneously* [z u g l e i c h], but that in each of them he is in the same way [g l e i c h e r w e i s e], is thus the whole in each, or is thus a proper essence [*in jedem das Ganze, oder ein eignes Wesen*].

Somehow the divergence into *two* commencements, *two* eternities (one thinks of the two eternities that 'affront one another' in the gateway *Augenblick* of *Thus Spoke Zarathustra*, Part II, 'On the Vision and the Riddle'), leaves the wholeness and ipseity of the Absolute untouched. By itself alone, ab-solute,

One becomes Two, clasps the hand of Two. Schelling must now explain (away) the bifurcation of nonground as both essential and transient. He must explain (away) the very possibility of a second, nonsimultaneous commencement, as one that leaves the wholeness and propriety of essence without a trace. The κρίσις of the Absolute, *Scheidung*, will conform to what Derrida in a different yet related context has elaborated as 'the logic of the supplement'.[15] But, again, to continue:

> Yet the nonground divides itself into the two equally eternal commencements solely in order that the two which are in him as nonground, and which could not be simultaneous or be One, become one through love. That is to say, he sunders himself only in order that there be life and love and personal existence. For love is neither in indifference nor there where opposites are joined, opposites that need joining in order to be; rather (to repeat a phrase already invoked), this is the mystery of love, that it joins such as could be each for itself alone, and yet is not, and cannot be without the other.

Love requires an initial divergence, an incipient sundering, as do life and personal existence. Schelling will later (7, 425) call this divergence a 'doubling', *Doublierung*, of essence, 'thus an enhancement of unity'. The mystery and enigma of love, *das Geheimnis der Liebe,* is that it (freely) fuses the duality it itself inaugurates; or, to put it the other way around, love initially severs that which it is destined to heal. Original violence, nihilation, is the secret life of love. Each fragment of the resultant duality *could be* for itself (*sein könnte*, subjunctive 'contrary to fact', *Irreales*), and yet each *is not* and *cannot be* (*nicht ist, und nicht sein kann*: indicative) without its other. Original violence is real.

> Therefore, just as duality comes to be in the nonground, so also does love come to be, a love that joins what exists (the ideal) with the ground of existence. However, the ground remains free and independent of the Word up to the final total scission [*bis zur endlichen gänzlichen Scheidung*[16]].

'Up to', 'until': *bis zur*. The nonground is thus in process, as we have been assured from the beginning. Something awaits it. What awaits it? The moment (of eternity, of two eternities) when nothing will remain independent of its Word. Yet that moment is now envisaged, not as a moment of conjunction, *Verbindung*, but as one of divorce, *Scheidung*. And not just any divorce. A scission that will be *endlich* and *gänzlich*. Presumably, *endlich* here means 'final', and not 'finite', inasmuch as the primal (non)ground could hardly be expected to suffer finite division – that would surely spell the *end* of its life, love, and personal existence. *Final*, then, in the sense of *ultimate*. Ultimate in the sense of a culminating, consummating, *apocalyptic* sundering. Apocalyptic and *gänzlich*. At long last, *endlich*!, a *total* sundering, a scission of the whole, *das Ganze*, the whole that each of the two eternal commencements sustains. Yet if the nonground initially diverges, *auseinandergeht*, solely in order to allow the doubling or fold of love, why and how should its process culminate in total divorce, *Scheidung*? Both predicates of scission thus prove troublesome. *Endlich*, we said, cannot refer to finitude; and yet Schelling's text now shifts to the scene of humanity. *Gänzlich*, we said, should refer to the restoration of wholeness by love and life, not by divorce and death; and yet Schelling's text now shifts to the scene of mortality. But to continue, now presenting the German text first, in order to allow the *er* to implicate *Grund, Ungrund, Gott* and *Mensch* in its tangled syntax of scission:

> Dann [d.h., in der endlichen gänzlichen Scheidung] löst er sich auf, wie im Menschen, wenn er zur Klarheit übergeht und als bleibendes Wesen sich gründet, die anfängliche Sehnsucht sich löst, indem alles Wahre und Gute in ihr ins lichte Bewußtsein erhoben wird, alles andre aber, das Falsche nämlich und Unreine, auf ewig in die Finsternis beschlossen, um als ewig dunkler Grund der Selbstheit, als *Caput mortuum* seines Lebensprozesses und als Potenz zurückzubleiben, die nie zum Aktus hervorgehen kann.

> Then [i.e., in the final total scission] it [i.e., the ground] is dissolved, as in man, when he [he, who? it? the ground? man?] goes over to clarity [a reference, presumably, to transfiguration, *Verklärung*, but of whom? God? Man? The Christ?] and grounds himself [itself?] as perdurant essence [creature?], the incipient longing dissipates when everything true and good in her [i.e., in longing, *die Sehnsucht*] is elevated to buoyant consciousness; but everything else, namely, the false and impure, is sealed off eternally in gloom, in order to remain back behind as the eternally dark ground of selfhood, as the dead-head of his life-process and as a potency that can never proceed to act.

The phrase *caput mortuum* refers to the lifeless, valueless residue of an alchemical or industrial process – the dross of a metal casting, for example, to be lopped off and cast away. Another name for the *caput mortuum* in alchemy is *Earth*. It ought to give us pause if the ultimate insight of the philosophy of nature is that Earth, the stuff of nature, is the waste product of divine elimination. Where would essence find the space to bury such excreta? For if its waste perdures back behind, *zurückbleibt*, will it not contaminate the perdurant essence, *das bleibende Wesen,* even and especially if it should appear to be lifeless? *Can* it *be* lifeless? A potency with no latency, without deferral, without life? Was it not a 'kernel of seed' that earlier was 'implanted in the gloom', not a dead-head but a living germ? The final, finite, whole and total reduction of living seed to dead waste, semen and egg to lifeless effluvia – would that not be a fatal stroke to divinity? But to continue, and to bring both this long quotation and the even longer indifferent reading as a whole to a close:

> Then all will be subordinate to spirit. In spirit whatever exists is one with the ground of existence; in spirit both are actually simultaneous; in other words,

spirit is the absolute identity of both. However, above spirit [*über dem Geist*] is the incipient nonground. It is no longer indifference (carelessness [*Gleichgültigkeit*]), yet is not the identity of both principles; rather, it is unity in general, which is equal with respect to all things yet captive of none, the beneficence that is free from all things while pervading them all – in One Word, Love, which is all in all.

An indifferent reading cannot resolve the most troubling questions Schelling's text raises – as to whether the 'will of Love' is at all distinguishable from incipient 'longing'; whether humanity (as the *Zentralwesen*) can be successfully differentiated from divinity, or whether the realm of evil which mankind endures will inevitably be coextensive with the kingdom of God; whether, when Schelling writes of evil that 'it is not an essence, but a nonessence', *ein Unwesen*, even if *Unwesen* should here have the sense of 'sinister doings', he merely displaces the problem of evil 'one point further down the line', without resolving it; whether the word 'resolution', *Aufhebung*, here makes any sense at all, when it can only be the stroke of One, *genitivus obiectivus*; whether the divine essence – become life, love, personality, and process – does not proceed unswervingly toward the abyss of its own death, so that the apocalypse of *endlicher gänzlicher Scheidung* is either the sudden self-mutilation or the progressive paralysis of God; whether the ultimate scission in essence is not a *crisis* of reason with which no *system* of reason can cope;[17] nor can an indifferent reading, adjunct to a peripheral reading, make clear the enormity of Schelling's undertaking in all these respects. Recalling William Faulkner's own estimation of his masterwork, *The Sound and the Fury*, I must be content to acclaim Schelling's *Philosophical Investigations* 'the most splendid failure' in the history of metaphysics. The most splendid failure *of* metaphysics.

And if at the end one were to try to correlate the peripheral/indifferent reading of Schelling with the texts of Kant and Nietzsche? Is Kant's reflection on the kinds of combination (*Arten der Zusammensetzung*), especially in the dynamic imagination of generation (*Erzeugung*), an early move in the direction of a philosophy of nature? The play of forces in nature (*Spiel der Kräfte*) points forward both to Schelling's cincture and scission of forces, perhaps even to Nietzsche's *Kraft des Traumes,* force as *actio in distans*. Kant's unification of dissimilars (*Vereinigungen des Ungleichartigen*) here seems to anticipate both Hölderlin and Schelling. However, when Kant invokes the word 'play' a second time, envisaging the demonic God who *gleichsam nur* gespielt *habe*, he conjures the laughing god, Aion, Dionysos. Finally, the darkness in which human reason loses itself – this crisis of reason – may well be the gloom in which Schelling would implant living seed, seed which a long tradition wants to kill, and does kill, but which Schelling would rescue.

Looking back to Schelling's text from the vantage-point of Nietzsche's *Gay*

Science, one final question concerning those 'repulsive naturalnesses' associated with *Weib* and *Natur*. Nietzsche explicitly relates such revulsion to those who revere God's omnipotence and who, spurning mechanics, trace everything back to unconstrained will – thus living in a dream. Is this the vertiginous dream of life itself: Schelling, up on the rooftops and turrets of fantasy, conjuring the sailing ship on swelling seething seas, in a sink or swim situation, yet dreaming the tranquil, remote dream of the *Mittelwesen*?

Beyond the polemical sallies in Schelling's text, beyond the bravado of its ontotheological maneuvers, beyond the dream of the Word, a 'source of sadness', *ein Quell der Traurigkeit*, flows free from Schelling's grand book into a troubled future.

> From it comes the pall of despondency [*der Schleier der Schwermut*] draped over the whole of nature – the profound and indestructible melancholy of all life [*die tiefe unzerstörliche Melancholie alles Lebens*] (399).

NOTES

1. F.W.J. Schelling, *Sämtliche Werke* (Stuttgart: Cotta, 1860 and seq.), 7, 355. I shall cite this edition throughout my text. The text I have actually used is the fine edition by Horst Fuhrmanns (Stuttgart: Reclam, 1964). The currently available English translation is unfortunately full of errors and inconsistencies – thus I do not refer to it.
2. See, e.g., 7, 366, 380, and 404. Cf. in the *Stuttgarter Privatvorlesungen* of 1810 (7, 483) a similar passage on *Krisis* and *Scheidung* in nature. In both texts *Krisis* means a series of decisive cuts and separations, *Scheidungen. Scheidung,* the root of *Entscheidung*, 'decision', and *Unterschied*, 'distinction', means separation, divorce, discrimination, apportionment, allotment, expulsion, elimination, 'scission'. *Scheiden*, related to the English word 'to shed', derives from the Greek σχίζω, to split or sunder. *Die Scheide* may be a limit or boundary, a 'watershed', or a 'sheathe'. At the end of the seventeenth century it becomes a translation of the Latin word *vagina*.
3. 7, 366. I will not attempt to discuss the various 'sources' of Schelling's center/periphery imagery. One might well search the pages of Kant's *Religion within the Limits of Reason Alone* (1793) for instances of such movement from center to periphery and back again. Schelling himself cites Franz Baader, who through Jakob Böhme would take us back to Plato's *Timaeus,* the Pythagorean Brotherhood, the Cabala, and all the hermetic doctrines, so that we could neither find a particular center for such 'sources' nor circumscribe their periphery. Baader himself (cited at 366–67n.) invokes the 'center (*mysterium*)' of primal fire, the 'periphery' of primal moisture within fire, and their economy of peaceful coexistence and discord (*Zwietracht*). When the center (ego) shifts to the periphery (egoism) and seeks to occupy the entire circle, evil reigns.

   > Where there was once ⊙ we now have ○ – that is: at one particular place in the planetary system, that dark center of nature is closed, latent; precisely for that reason it serves luciferously [*als Lichtträger*] to grant entry to the higher system (a shaft of light – or revelation of the ideal). Precisely for that reason this place is the open point (sun – heart – eye) in the system – and if the dark center of nature would rise or open there, then *eo ipso* the point of light would close itself, light would become darkness in the system, or the sun be extinguished!

Baader's ⊙ and ○ grant us a first glimpse of the radical undecidability of the center/periphery movement: the dark center of nature is marked not, as one might think, by ⊙ but by ○. When the center disappears in the periphery there is closure; yet closure is itself the opening of the point, it is the solar center written large, as it were. The eye ⊙ is most radically open to light at its black center: ○. Here the heart of the essence throbs through all space, from every point on the periphery. Yet if the heart of darkness is also the bearer of light, it is not clear how any scission or decision or distinction could ever separate one from the other. The marks of sanity and illness, good and evil, would no longer be distinguishable. They would signify nothing, would not be signs at all. There would be no periodization, no period ⊙ Period ○. Etc.

4. Doubtless, Origen. Schelling will thus not have mentioned him at the outset, relying on Hamann to introduce him at the end.
5. Corybants, i.e., the priests of Kybele (once again!), known for their frenzied dance – they are often compared to Whirling Dervishes – and their initiation rite of self-castration. *Gallier*, from the Latin *Galli*, Greek Γάλλοι, means not the Celtic Gauls but (yet again!) the Phrygian priests of Kybele. The singular, *Gallus*, is sometimes written in the feminine form *Galla*, 'humorously', the dictionaries say, inasmuch as *gallus* in the cock. Cf. in anatomy the *crista galli*, cited by Hegel in his Jena lectures on the philosophy of nature, *Gesammelte Werke, 8*, 173.
6. Schelling intensifies his polemic against the philosophy of his time during the period of his sketches toward *Die Weltalter*. In an unpublished essay of 1812 (Fuhrmans, pp. 171–72, citing *8*, 16) he writes:

   > You have maligned nature for deploying the senses, for failing to create man on the model of your own abstractions. You have abused and maimed [*geschändet und verstümmelt*] his nature to suit yourselves; in insolent fury you have raged against her, like those who in earlier times castrated themselves for the sake of heavenly bliss [*verschnitten um der Seligkeit willen*].

   I believe that it would also be possible to show (but elsewhere, and in detail) that Schelling's *Weltalter* sketches lead him beyond the merely abstract assertion of God's embodiment (which is something altogether different from orthodox phallic Incarnation) to the question of the essential bisexuality of divinity.
7. See my presentation of 'The Oldest Program toward a System in German Idealism,' *The Owl of Minerva*, vol. 17, no. 1 (Fall 1985), 5–19.
8. In the *Stuttgarter Privatvorlesungen* (e.g., *7*, 434, 458, and 475) and in the 1810 dialogue on the nexus of nature and the spirit-world ('Clara', at *9*, 75) Schelling writes: E r S e l b e r.
9. See Fuhrman's note, p. 147; for the Schelling-Eschenmayer correspondence, see *8*, 137–89.
10. In the first edition, the one Schelling himself saw through the press, the phrase reads *wird in Mutterleibe gebildet,* 'the human being is formed *into* the mother's womb.' Schelling's son, seeing the dative ending of *Mutterleibe*, quite rightly altered the Father's word *in* to *im*, thus rescuing the sense, thus rescuing sense, thus sensing rescue. Etc.
11. 'Light' is of course the opposite of darkness, *Dunkel.* Yet the shape-of-light *rises* to unfold on sunbeams. *Die lichten Gedanken* are not only luminous but also buoyant, ascensional thoughts: the original partner of 'light' in Schelling's text (358) is not darkness but gravity, weight, *Schwerkraft.* Thus one senses here intimations of what Heidegger will later call *Lichtung des Seins*.
12. See Krell, 'Female Parts in *Timaeus*,' *Arion*, New Series 2/3 (1975), 400–21, esp. 413. In Schelling's text (390) 'bastard reasoning', λογισμῷ νόθῳ, becomes 'false imagination'. The Zweibrücken edition which he cites (*9*, 349) offers Ficino's translation *adulterina ratione*. Yet *falsche Imagination* has as its opposite *wahre Ein-Bildung*, 'true, in-forming imagination', in the womb of knowledge (362), in such a way that one cannot divorce one from the other. For my earlier suggestion that imagination is *the* crisis of reason in the nineteenth century, it would

be crucial to juxtapose Schelling's adulation of *Ein-Bildung* as the gestation of intellect and reason and his fear of 'false imagination' as the very faculty of evil. Which is more than one can do on the periphery.

13. Cf. Schelling's earlier remarks (358) on the 'circle' of time and eternity, a circle which precludes both priority in time and priority of essence.
14. The notion of 'absolute indifference' is crucial for Schelling's thinking from early on – for example, in the period of his struggles with the subjective idealism of Fichte, the period of his 1795 essay, '*Vom Ich als Prinzip*.' (I am grateful to Peter Dews for this reminder.) Cf. the crucial role of 'absolute indifference' in Hegel's *Logic*, as the 'Becoming of Essence', the culmination of the doctrine of Being, which I can only note here without commentary. (See *Wissenschaft der Logik*, Part I, 'Objective Logic', Division 3, 'Measure', Chapter 3, 'The Becoming of Essence'.) Perhaps it is also worth noting that in his account of human genitality (in the 1805–06 Jena lectures on *Realphilosophie*) Hegel designates the uterus as *das Indifferente*. See Krell, 'Pitch: Genitality/Excrementality: From Hegel to Crazy Jane', *boundary 2, 12,* 2 (Winter 1984), 113–41, esp. p. 120.
15. See *De la grammatologie* (Paris: Minuit, 1967), pp. 207–34 and 441–45.
16. Cf. the phrase *der notwendige Weg zur endlichen wirklichen Differenzierung*, from the *Stuttgarter Privatvorlesungen* (7, 426).
17. On this system which 'is no longer system', a system destroyed by the scission of ground and existence, a cut no *Seynsfüge* can anneal, see M. Heidegger, *Schellings Abhandlung über das Wesen der menschlichen Freiheit (1809)* (Tübingen: M. Niemeyer, 1971), esp. p. 194. See also Heidegger's remarkable account of longing (*die Sehnsucht*) as longing for the other (*ein Anderes*), p. 150.

Perception, Categorial Intuition and Truth in Husserl's Sixth 'Logical Investigation'

RUDOLF BERNET
University of Leuven

The sixth *Logical Investigation* has played a central role in the development of Husserl's own thought and of the phenomenological movement as well. This text works out a new phenomenological understanding of truth, which is indeed what any phenomenological 'theory of knowledge' necessarily aims at providing. This notion of truth brings the phenomenological investigation of the cognitive achievements of intentional consciousness to an end and it also, inevitably, confronts Husserl with the issue of a phenomenological ontology. It is, in particular, the notion of a 'categorial intuition' which shows clearly how the epistemological and ontological stakes are inseparably linked. On the one hand, the categorial intuition is the true answer given to logical psychologism by a phenomenological theory of knowledge: it is about the intuitive givenness of ideal objects. The analysis of this phenomenon also shows the encompassing unity of all elements belonging to a phenomenological theory of cognition: signitive and intuitive intentional acts, sensuous and categorial intuitions, acts of thought and acts of language. On the other hand, the categorial intuition reveals the ontological distinction between sensuous and ideal entities, it forces one to investigate the difference between entities and their being, and it also shows, as Husserl says with Kant, that 'being is no real predicate'.

My text has no other pretense than to report how these issues are treated in the sixth *Logical Investigation*. Rather than developing a personal line of interpretation, I simply wish to familiarize the reader with Husserl's understanding of truth and the way it takes advantage of a phenomenological analysis of intentionality. An account such as this one can not only prepare us for a critical evaluation of Husserl's thought, it also indicates elements of an interpretation that are present already in my report. For example, my insistence on the fact that the legitimate interest in the unity of cognitive life and the unity of ontological and epistemological issues ought not lead us to overlook the *diversity* of these phenomena might be a trace of such a personal interpretation.

J.C. Sallis, G. Moneta and J. Taminiaux (eds.), The Collegium Phaenomenologicum, 33–45.
© Kluwer Academic Publishers.

INTUITIVELY FULFILLED CATEGORIAL ACTS AS COGNITIVE ACTS IN THE STRICT SENSE

The key concept in Husserl's doctrine of truth is clearly the concept of *intuitive fulfillment*. In the sixth *Logical Investigation* in particular, this concept receives detailed consideration. It is only in relation to the phenomenological process of fulfillment that the status and function of the concepts of cognition, evidence, and truth can be determined with greater precision. A fulfillment is a cognitive process in which an empty intention or assertion is brought into synthetic connection with a corresponding intuitive act such that by way of this synthesis the intention is confirmed and corroborated or, respectively, disappointed.[1] This complex interconnection among different forms of intentional consciousness can be broken down schematically into the following three elements: a) the act to be fulfilled or the (partially) empty act; b) the fulfilling act; and c) the act conjoining both these acts synthetically. With all three elements it is a question of relatively independently demarcated immanent experiences or psychical activities in which consciousness is intentionally related to objects. The synthetic nexus (*c*), which conjoins the fulfilling act with the act to be fulfilled, has the form of a synthesis of identification (§ 8). The *identity* constituted in this synthesis concerns the two conjoined acts (*a* and *b*) in accordance with the moments responsible for their intentional function (their 'intentional essence'). The two acts coincide (at least partially) in respect to their intentional relation to the object. They refer to the same object. However, the synthesis of identity of the two acts becomes epistemologically relevant only when both acts possess a different cognitive value (cf. §§ 13, 16). This *difference* between the two acts concerns their 'cognitional essence' (§ 28), that is, it concerns the manner in which each of these acts *intuitively* presents its intentional object (the same intentional object), and brings this object to intuitive (or partially intuitive or non-intuitive) givenness. In the *Logical Investigations* Husserl understands this intuitive givenness of the object as an act which apprehends primitive, that is, preintentional contents of consciousness and intentionally refers them to the object. Through this mode of apperception these contents become intuitionally representative data or appearances of the object (§§ 14b, 22). Husserl also says that by dint of this apperception of primitive sensational data the intentional act 'represents [*repräsentiert*]' its object. The cognitional difference between the fulfilling act and the act to be fulfilled, hence, the difference between two intentional acts which intend the same object, thus derives from their mode of intuitive representation [*Repräsentation*] or from the range and richness of the sensational material apperceived in both acts at any given moment. Formally conceived, the process of fulfillment is thus a complex act which brings two acts into synthetic relation in respect to both the identity of their intentional object and the difference between their intuitive representations of this object.

Let us now consider somewhat more closely the case of the synthesis of fulfillment in which an empty assertion is epistemologically proven by means of the intuitional self-givenness of its object. The assertion, 'The black bird flies off', is thus fulfilled in synthetic connection with our perceiving the asserted state of affairs. But can one account for the bird's *being* black, its determination *as* bird and as *the* bird, by means of the spectacle which presents itself to our eyes? Furthermore, might not what we see be expressed lingually in other ways than the one we have hit upon? Both questions lead us to the insight, firstly, that a sensuous perception can fulfill a (predicative) assertion only in limited measure, and, secondly, that an assertion owes its meaning only partially and indirectly to the lingually expressed perception. In Husserl's terminology, this means that in a perceptual judgment the lingual signs in the authentic sense express not the perception itself but the judgmental meaning. This meaning is consummated in a categorial meaning-intention and it is through this meaning that the assertion acquires its reference to the perceptual object (§ 4). The consequence of this is, in turn, that the aforesaid semantical intention is fulfilled not by a purely sensuous intuition but by a categorial intuition. Yet before we investigate more closely this synthetic nexus of categorial meaning-intention and categorial intuition, we must bring to mind, at least in broad outline, what it is that makes up the essence of a *categorial act* as such.

According to Husserl, categorial acts are mainly acts of conjoining, relating, distinguishing, and so on. These are complex acts which relate diverse, pregiven, intentional objects to one another and bring them into synthetic unity under a categorial point of view, for example, that of the part-whole relationship. As a complex or synthetic act, the categorial intention presupposes both the acts brought into synthetic unity and the intentional objects of these acts. The performance of the synthetic act is 'founded' in the performance of the synthesized acts (§§ 46, 48). As a thus founded, intentional act, the categorial act refers to a higher-order intentional objectivity first made present by the categorial act itself (§ 43). However, it is extremely important that one not understand the performance of the categorial act as an action which modifies real objects by means of physical manipulation (§ 61). Rather, the achievement of the categorial act consists in the merely intellectual formation and articulation of a pregiven stuff or in the merely logical transformation of a stuff already formed categorially. Yet if the categorial act is not a sensuous, physical activity, neither is its intentional object a sensuous, physical object. It is not an object, in other words, which one can see with one's eyes or upon which one can sit. Contrasting them with real, empirical objects, or sensuous objects, Husserl calls categorial objects 'higher-order' objects or 'ideal' objects (§ 46).

One must not, however, permit oneself to be misled by this terminology into regarding all categorial objects as essences. A state of affairs which I assert, that a dove is now sitting on my windowsill, for example, is no less an ideal, categorial object than is the concept of a particular number or the formal-logical concept 'object-as-such'. If, with Husserl, one calls all categorial objects 'ideal', then one must distinguish between empirical-ideal (or 'sensuous-mixed') and *a priori*-ideal (or 'pure') categorial objects (cf. § 60).

According as the intentional object of a categorial act is intuitively given or merely represented by a sign, one distinguishes between intuitive and signitive or empty categorial acts. Signitive categorial acts are the meaning-intentions conjoined with empty assertive acts of speech; but they are also the calculative operations carried out in accordance with an arithmetical calculus. Empty assertive acts of speech are distinguished from technical calculation, however, in not being a surrogate for operations of thought that are incapable of intuitive performance. Rather, such acts of speech gain cognitional relevance only when they are fulfilled by a corresponding categorial intuition. In this categorial intuition, the categorial referent of the speech-act is no longer merely intended, emptily asserted; rather, it is itself given in intuition. In the sixth *Logical Investigation*, Husserl conceives this intuitional self-givenness of a *categorial* object largely in analogy to the self-givenness of a *sensuous* object, and he postulates a categorial form of intuitive representation. However, in the 'Foreword' to the second edition of 1920, Husserl remarks expressly that he 'no longer approves of the doctrine of categorial representation' (V). It was the fatal error of this doctrine to define categorial representation as the *categorial* apprehension of a *sensuous* apprehensional content. Yet apart from this logical difficulty, it is not even clear in phenomenological terms, at least with respect to the pure categorial objects or formal categories, what could serve the latter as an intuitional representative (in the sense of immanent sensuous self-givenness). Husserl's most convincing answer to the question of the intuitional givenness of categorial objects must be sought in his later doctrine of eidetic variation. This is so even though this doctrine does not satisfactorily take into account either the distinction between 'sensuous-mixed' and 'pure' essences or the distinction between a generalizing and a formalizing grasp of essences.[2] Nevertheless, and this is already true of the *Logical Investigations,* Husserl resists the temptation to conceive categorial intuition in strict analogy to sensuous intuition. Indeed, as an essentially synthetic act, categorial intuition is distinguished in principle from the immediacy of sensuous seeing. Simply by being a *categorial* act, categorial intuition is a founded act. In addition, categorial intuition is also a founded act insofar as, being a cognitive act, it is a dependent moment in the synthesis of fulfillment. Nor is a categorial intuition, as a cognitive act, anything like an '*intuitus originarius*'. Rather, it is a possible moment in the complex process of a 'continuous enhancement of fulfillment', a process which is founded in sensuous experience.

Yet what does one really mean in saying that categorial intuition is to be designated as a cognitive act only insofar as it is a moment in the synthesis of fulfillment, that is, only insofar as it stands in synthetic connection with an act in need of fulfillment? It means in the first place that merely having the object intuitively given does not yet constitute a cognitive act. The intuitional givenness of the object is epistemologically relevant only once it has justified a cognitive pretension or satisfied a cognitive interest. Only in synthetic agreement with a corresponding empty representation, a 'lack' (§ 21), does an intuitive act become a cognitive act. For Husserl, as for Kant, mere intuition is epistemologically irrelevant, or 'blind', if it has not been subsumed under a corresponding empty intention and thereby been 'classified'. Correlatively, the empty intention is a merely 'empty' presumption if it lacks intuitional confirmation, differentiation, and 'approximation' to the intended object 'it self'. The fact that this empty intention, which is to be fulfilled in intuition, is by and large only partially empty (or already partially fulfilled) changes nothing in regard to the general characterization of the synthetic cognitive nexus of emptiness and fullness. By contrast, it is of decisive importance that it is the synthesis of fulfillment typical of *categorial* acts which is first able phenomenologically to found the strict concept of cognition, that is, the cognition of something *as* something.

If, with Husserl, one defines the empty categorial intention as a signitive intention, and this, in turn, principally as a categorial meaning-intention, then the intuitionally fulfilled speech-act, that is, the assertion which has been justified by the intentional givenness of its object, proves to be the authentic paradigm for the act of cognition in the strict sense. The synthetic nexus of fulfillment, connecting a meaning-intention and a corresponding categorial intuition, can also be described as a synthesis of the intentional objects of these acts. Talk of the cognition of an object *as* something is particularly well suited to this objectively oriented description of the synthesis of fulfillment which, following Kant, may be called a 'recognition of the object in the concept' (cf. § 8). It is striking that this concept of cognition would not even be susceptible of phenomenological formulation, did Husserl not have at his disposal the structure of a merely emptily intended, that is, possibly nonexistent intentional object: the epistemological reality of the referent can be conceived and proven only against the background of the possible absence or unreality of this referent.

The Truth of Judgments and the Laws of Authentic Thinking

Cognition, and for Husserl this means essentially *scientific* cognition, is a complex act of satisfied cognitive interest or justified cognitive pretension. Yet what is it toward which this interest is directed, and what does the cognitive intention pretend or posit? If we continue to confine ourselves to the case of lingually mediated acts of cognition, then the pretension lies in insisting that matters really stand just as we assert that they do. Regarded with greater precision, however, this pretension can be understood in still different ways, namely, 1) as an assertion about the actual existence of the object of reference; 2) as an assertion that certain properties actually belong to the object asserted to be of such and such a complexion; 3) as an assertion that the object is not merely thus and so but rather is *exclusively* thus and so and is not additionally otherwise. Since Husserl understands reference in respect of the meaning-intention, and since, according to Husserl, every intentional act not only designates (denotes) its object but at the same time also determines (connotes) it, the first and second pretensions listed above cannot be separated from one another. A valid act of cognition is thus either an assertion which says nothing more of the object than what is at the same time given in intuition; or it is an intuitively fulfilled assertion which says everything that can be said positively about the corresponding object. As assertions fully fulfilled in intuition, both assertions are regarded by Husserl as *evident* acts of cognition. For the first assertion, however, evidence means intuitive 'confirmation through a corresponding and fully adapted perception', whereas the second assertion is evident in the sense of the 'most complete (or 'ultimate' [§ 39]) synthesis of fulfillment' (§ 38).

Evidence thus exhibits varying degrees of completeness; and even evidence in the sense of an intention fully satisfied in intuition is, generally speaking, the result of a complex, and that is to say gradually progressive process of fulfillment. In the *Logical Investigations*, Husserl defines the goal regulating this process of steadily enhanced fulfillment as ultimate or adequate evidence. The telos implied in our cognitive interest is thus the complete 'agreement between what is meant and what is given as such' (§ 39), 'adequation to the "thing itself"' (§ 37). This consummation of the 'ultimate synthesis of fulfillment' is a synthetic act of phenomenological consciousness which forms the legitimate origin of the concepts 'evidence in the strict sense', 'truth', and 'being'. In this connection, wholly oriented toward the process of fulfillment or the act of cognition, 'being' means nothing other than the object's 'truly-being' or actually 'subsisting' (§ 39). If one defines truth, in an initial sense, as the objective correlate of the ultimate synthesis of fulfillment, and defines the consummation of this synthesis as evidence, then evidence is the synthetic experience of the 'full agreement between what is meant and what is given as such', that is, it is the 'immanent experience of truth', the intuitive proof that an object of cognition 'truly is'. If, by contrast, one orients truth, in a second sense, not toward the gradually fulfilled agreement between what is meant and what is given, but toward the agreement between the act of intending and the act of intuiting, then truth is no longer synonymous with actually-being, but rather with the idea of evidence, that is, that which belongs essentially to the experience of the ultimate synthesis of fulfillment.

These comments from the sixth *Logical Investigation* are by no means unproblematical, nor are they Husserl's final word concerning the problems of evidence and truth. In particular, the orientation of the strong concept of evidence toward the concept of the *adequate* synthesis of fulfillment appears to be questionable. Since the demand for adequate self-givenness of the object cannot be satisfied in large areas of scientific cognition, including the area of logical, a priori cognition, one must ask whether the function of the principle of evidence as a possible methodological norm for phenomenological science is not thereby undermined. One can also ask in general whether the orientation of scientific cognition toward the telos of adequation does not rather destroy than found the idea of a rational progress in cognition. We cannot here enter further into these questions. Instead, we should like to meditate briefly upon those positive aspects of the Husserlian theory of truth which promise still to bear fruit.

It is a primary characteristic of Husserl's concept of cognition and truth that the intuitionistic demand for the self-givenness of the object is not understood sensualistically. Husserl understands the epistemologically relevant form of the intuitional self-givenness of the object as a result of subjective, synthetic activity, not, for example, as the mere possession of 'little things [*Dingelchen*]' which function in consciousness as causally conditioned representatives of the thing-in-itself. Intuitional representation of the thing is essentially apperception of a hyletic stuff and actually establishes truth only in the synthesis of fulfillment, namely, when a connection has been established between the intuition and a cognitive intention. Accordingly, 'adequation to the thing itself' (§ 37) does not mean agreement of representatives in consciousness with the represented and in itself fully determinate thing-in-itself. It means rather an agreement, within the phenomenologically determined consciousness, between the intention and the givenness of the ultimately differentiated object. We shall not dispute the fact that in the sixth *Logical Investigation* Husserl was not yet able fully to free himself from the old concept of adequation (*adequatio rei et intellectus*). Yet the true sense of his remarks points clearly in the direction of an agreement, in fulfillment, between various subjective acts. It thus points at once in the direction of a concept of truth oriented primarily toward the coherence of cognitive life. In any case, it is perfectly clear that the old problem of the 'bridge' between subjective, cognitive activity and objective thing no longer presents itself for Husserl, and that even 'verification' in the sense of the comparison of lingual assertions with the 'actual' constitution of the thing as it is 'in itself' can not count for him as a criterion of truth.

Truth rather concerns the agreement among various intentional acts or their intentional objects. The phenomenological analysis of truth is especially dedicated to formulating the ideal conditions for the possibility of this agreement.

If we try now to investigate in greater detail the general conditions for this agreement in the case of lingual judgmental truth, this may not be taken to mean that judging is for Husserl the most primordial site of truth. It is, of course, correct that categorial acts are cognitive acts in a distinguished sense; yet not all categorial acts are lingual judgmental acts. Furthermore, in the definition of truth as 'agreement between what is meant and what is given as such' (the first concept of truth mentioned in the sixth *LI*), 'being-true' is a predicate belonging not to a judgmental act but to a state of affairs.

Husserl defines the concept of judgmental truth by taking as his point of departure the immanent experience of agreement between the meaningful speech-act animated by a cognitive interest, on the one hand, and, on the other hand, a corresponding act of categorial intuition in which the object of reference is given. Phenomenological exploration of the ideal conditions for possible judgmental truth thus has the form of an exploration of the conditions for the possible intuitional fulfillment of speech-acts. This, in turn, means nothing other than exploration of the conditions for the performance of categorial intuitions (§§ 62f.). The latter conditions fall under two types according as one has in mind the compossibility of categorial forms or their applicability to determinate sensuous stuffs. One must therefore distinguish between analytical and synthetic conditions for categorial intuition or for 'actual and possible fulfillments of meaning.'

On the basis of the intuitional givenness of the sensuous stuff, the synthetic conditions determine whether, in view of the 'respective particularity' of this stuff, a categorial form may be used, or whether a given 'categorial formation' of this stuff is 'actually able to be consummated' (190). By contrast, the analytical conditions abstract from the particular material determination of the sensuous stuffs. That is, they treat these sensuous stuffs as 'determinate but arbitrary' (189) 'variables' (195), maintained 'in identity with themselves' (189) in categorial formation and transformation. The positive task of exploring these analytical conditions concerns the formulation of ideal laws which regulate the 'ideally closed circle of possible transformations of any given form into ever new forms' (190). Thus, for example, according to these analytical laws the transformation of the proposition '*g* is a part of *G*' into '*G* is the whole covering *g*' is valid, whereas its transformation into '*G* is a part of *g*' is not valid. The assertion, '*g* is a part of *G*, and *G* is the whole covering *g*', satisfies the synthetic laws of possible categorial intuition only if the sensuous objects designated by *g* and *G* can be brought actually, and that is to say empirically, into the relationship of part and whole. However, we shall still see that the actualization not only of these synthetic laws, but also of the universally valid analytical laws, necessarily presupposes perception, i.e., the possibility of the intuitional givenness of individually determined, sensuous objects.

Categorial acts which contradict the analytical and synthetic conditions for their possible intuitive performance, cannot be true. Yet such categorial acts, which can be performed only signitively, need not as a consequence be meaningless in the sense of nonsense. Signitive categorial acts such as lingual expressions are meaningful if they obey the grammatical laws; but the possibility of their being true arises only when *in addition* they obey the laws of possible categorial intuition. If we call the signitive categorial acts 'inauthentic acts of thought', and the intuitive categorial acts 'authentic acts of thought ' (193), then the authentic acts of thought are necessarily subject to the laws of possible inauthentic acts of thought, but the inauthentic acts of thought are not necessarily subject to the laws of possible authentic acts of thought. '... The domain of meanings is much more comprehensive than that of intuition' for there is an 'unlimited multiplicity of complex meanings ... which are, indeed, consolidated into uniform meanings, but meanings to which no possible, uniform correlate of fulfillment can correspond' (192). Thus the only true assertion is the assertion whose meaning-intention, or inauthentic act of thought (193), can be intuitively fulfilled by a corresponding categorial intuition, by a corresponding authentic act of thought. The truth of a lingual utterance, or of a speech-act, is derived from the possibility of performing a corresponding authentic act of thought. This comes about in such a way that, firstly, the meaning-intention (in the unity of fulfillment) corresponds unambiguously with the authentic act of thought; and that, secondly, the meaning-intention finds 'unambiguous expression' in the lingual sign, the 'word' (cf. 191). Centered in the authentic act of thought or categorial intuition, this graduated sequence of unambiguous correspondence or isomorphism of 'word', 'meaning', and 'intuition', implies additionally an unambiguous correspondence between authentic thinking and its objects.

> 'The ideal conditions for the possibility of categorial intuition as such, are correlatively the conditions for the possibility of objects of categorial intuition, and (they are at once the conditions) for the possibility of categorial objects pure and simple' (189).

With these remarks Husserl does not accommodate himself unreservedly to the canon of a realistic theory of meaning which, having received its classical expression in the *De Interpretatione* (cf. 16a) of Aristotle, is oriented toward the unambiguous representations of the 'thing' in certain 'states of the soul', and of these, in turn, in the lingual 'word'? Surely this question may be answered only with a qualified affirmation, for in Husserl's system it is not the thing but authentic thinking which constitutes the supporting pillar for the multilevel complex of representations. In Husserl, the accent shifts, therefore, from the internalization of the external thing to the lingual externalization of the inwardness of thinking. The truth-value of a speech-act is derived from a corresponding act of authentic thinking. In view of the equivalence between the conditions for possible categorial intuition and the conditions for possible categorial objects, the truth-value of categorial objects can be seen similarly to be derived from a corresponding act of authentic thinking. The adequation of the meaning to the object is but a correlative formulation of the connection of fulfillment between the signitive meaning-intention and the corresponding categorial intuition. Without entering further into a discussion of these questions we would like nonetheless to consider some of the consequences of this Husserlian system of isomorphic correspondence or representation of expression, meaning, intuition, and object of cognition.

One consequence of this representational nexus, centered as it is in the concept of categorial intuition or authentic thinking, concerns the relationship between *language and thinking*. To be sure, authentic acts of thought do, under the proper conditions, fulfill meaning-intentions; authentic acts of thought and fulfilled meaning-intentions are 'parallel', but they are 'not identical'; the latter follow 'faithfully after' the former (§ 63). The authentic acts of thought, upon which the truth-value of cognition essentially depends, are prelingual. Lingual acts of cognition can be valid insofar as they 'follow faithfully after' or give 'unambiguous expression' to these prelingual, intuitive acts of thought (ibid). This demand for a relationship in which acts of prelingual thinking are unambiguously represented by the 'system of . . . meanings . . . expressing them' (ibid.), is problematical insofar as such a demand applies at best to the ideal language functioning as the 'garb' of thinking. It certainly cannot account for the language in which meaning is first instituted, the ordinary language of our usual dealings with lingual signs. The introduction of a prelingual criterion for truth has the further consequence that this criterion becomes to a certain extent private. It does so insofar as the performance of an authentic act of thought or a synthesis of fulfillment is an intrasubjective event which can be made accessible to the intersubjective lingual community of scientific investigators only secondarily.

In the aftermath of Heidegger, attention has also been drawn to the fact that Husserl's derivation of the determination and the being of actual objects from the performance of authentic acts of thought implies a problematical, preliminary decision in respect of the *ontological question*. Much as in the case of lingual expressions, the forms of objects and their being are but mirrorings of the determinations of corresponding acts of cognition. This relationship of representation, too, is one-sided. The being of that which objectively is, is determined with a view to the purely theoretically determined subject of cognition. It is determined, therefore, as being-known just as in the case of the ideal language, one can here ask whether this limited, epistemological understanding of being, represents a merely preliminary restriction or whether it does not rather represent an anticipatory decision concerning the question of being.

Perception as the Foundation of True Judgment

Husserl defines judging, but also thinking, as a categorial act. Categorial acts are mainly synthetic acts in which pregiven stuffs are given logical form or in which the resultant logical forms are transformed. This formational activity, however, is not an absolutely independent and spontaneous activity of the understanding, for it presupposes the necessary pregivenness of ultimately sensuous stuffs.

> 'It lies in the nature of the case that everything categorial ultimately rests upon sensuous intuition, indeed, that . . . thought . . ., apart from a founding sensuousness, is an absurdity' (§ 60).

If we recall that intuitively fulfilled categorial acts were designated as cognitive acts in the strict sense, then the question arises concerning the extent to which the pregivenness of sensuous stuffs founds not only the essential determination of these acts *as* categorial acts, but also their truth-value.

Talk of the foundedness of all categorial acts, whether signitive or intuitive, has a double sense according as one understands the concept of founding logically or phenomenologically-genetically. Taken in its logical sense, the foundedness of categorial acts means that as synthetic acts these acts imply the performance of the acts unified by them. Hence, as synthesizing acts, categorial acts are founded in acts of simple relation to the members which are to be synthesized just as the uniform whole is founded in its manifold parts. It is to be observed, withal, that these synthesized members can already be, perchance, (nominalized) categorial objects; that, however, the process of categorial complications has an absolute beginning; and, thus, that all categorial objects are ultimately founded (logically) in sensuous stuffs. If, placing ourselves in a phenomenological attitude, we contemplate the performance of the synthetic act, then it strikes us that the members which are to be synthesized also enjoy a chronological priority over the performance of the synthesizing act. Taken in this second sense, talk of the foundedness of categorial acts thus means that categorial acts are able to be consummated only when the appurtenant partial acts have already been performed.

Let us now pass on to the consideration of that special class of categorial acts capable of bringing fulfillment to signitive acts such as meaning-intentions. In this case, talk of the founding of categorial acts in the pre-givenness of sensuous stuffs acquires a new and narrower sense. In addition to the logical compatibility of the categorial forms employed, there belongs to the performance of a categorial intuition, and especially to the performance of a *synthetic* categorial intuition the adaptation of these forms to the particularity of the stuffs to which they are applied. Only when these stuffs are *intuitionally* or perceptually given in the particularity of their material determination is it assured that one does not incorporate them into an unsuitable categorial nexus. The possible performance of a categorial intuition and the possible truth of a categorial speech-act are thus founded in the perceptual givenness of sensuous objects functioning as stuffs of a logical formation. Thus, for example, the truth of the perceptual judgment, 'The pencil is red', is *founded* in the perception of a red pencil. (Yet the perceptual judgment, or its meaning, is not *contained* in the perception, since no perceptual givenness corresponds with the categorial form of the predicative synthesis of identification.)

What is the status of this necessary foundedness in the sensuous perception of stuffs, however, when we move on from synthetically true judgments to analytically true judgments, such as, '*G* is the whole covering *g*, and *g* is a part of *G*'? Still, mere variables function here as stuffs; and variable stuffs, that is, stuffs regarded independently of their particular material determination, 'arbitrary' stuffs, do not at all events fall into the realm of sensuous seeing. On the other hand, stuffs which function as arbitrarily variable, though thoroughly self-identical stuffs of categorial formation, are not for that reason necessarily to be designated as essences, whether material or formal.

In the *Logical Investigations*, Husserl seems clearly to take the view that even the intuitional performance of an *analytical* categorial act is founded in the intuitional givenness of sensuous stuffs, and founded in such a way that in the actual performance of the categorial act there is presupposed, at the very least, a phantasial presentation of a sensuous object which suits the terms of the categorial form employed (§ 62). In the *Formal and Transcendental Logic*,[3] Husserl supplements these early investigations by showing that it is not only in their apprehension that analytically true assertions, especially formal-logical laws, refer to the intuitional givenness of sensuous objects. Rather, even in their application these laws refer ultimately and necessarily to materially determined individuals. If the pure-logical laws come to be understood as laws of possible truth, then their 'idealizing presuppositions' (*FTL*: §§ 73ff.), related to their possible application in actual experience, require critical clarification. Thus, the formal logic of truth implies assertions which refer not only to materially determined individual entities but also to the intuitive-sensuous experience of such entities. The critical justification of these (implicit) assertions about individual entities is a task which can be accomplished not by formal logic itself but only by a transcendental logic of our living experience of the world. In his effort to found formal logic in a genetic phenomenology, Husserl went as far as to postulate a 'pre-predicative' 'syntactical accomplishment' of this 'founding experience' (cf. *FTL*: § 86).

The most important yield from Husserl's early analyses of judgmental truth is surely their hint at the necessary founding of acts of lingual cognition in nonlingual cognitive performances. Acts of true judgment are in the main mere lingual realizations or expressions of categorial intuitions or acts of 'authentic thinking', and these acts of authentic thinking are cognitive acts in the strict sense. According to Husserl's conception of the matter, however, authentic thinking is necessarily founded in sensuous intuition, and Husserl, therefore, does not hesitate to designate even these sensuous acts as cognitive acts. It is correct, to be sure, that such prelingual acts can be explored only in the medium of language. Yet Husserl, in contrast with a broad current in present-day philosophical thinking, refuses to conclude from this that all cognitive performances, as a matter of necessity, presuppose language from the very beginning and must consequently be designated as lingual performances.

Notes

1. E. Husserl, sixth *Logical Investigation*, §§ 6, 8, 11. When not otherwise indicated all references are to this text; page-references are to the German text (*Logische Untersuchungen, Zweiter Band/II. Teil: Elemente einer phänomenologischen Aufklärung der Erkenntnis,* M. Niemeyer, 1968[4]); translations are mine.
2. Cf. E. Husserl, *Ideen zu einer reinen Phänomenologie und phänomenologischen Philosophie. Erstes Buch: Allgemeine Einführung in die reine Phänomenologie*, § 13.
3. E. Husserl, *Formale und transzendentale Logik. Versuch einer Kritik der logischen Vernunft,* § 82.

Immanence, Transcendence, and Being in Husserl's Idea of Phenomenology

JACQUES TAMINIAUX
University of Louvain-La-Neuve

The purpose of this paper is to clarify the concepts of immanence and transcendence which play a decisive part in Husserl's foundation of Phenomenology. We shall base our investigation upon the five lectures delivered at Göttingen in 1907 under the title *The Idea of Phenomenology*,[1] which were first edited by Walter Biemel in 1950. In addition to the text of the lectures, Biemel's book includes a summary of them written by Husserl for his own use. In this paper I shall employ both the text of the lectures and the text of the summary.

According to Husserl's summary, the train of thought pursued in the lectures proceeds through four steps. The first one is a sort of preliminary stage corresponding to the awareness that a challenging situation in the epistemological field requires a new form of philosophy. The next three steps correspond to successive stages within phenomenology itself. Husserl uses either 'immanence' or 'transcendence' or both in his presentation of each of the four steps. Our task is to elucidate the meaning of these words in each step of the development.

1. Let us first consider the preliminary stage, i.e., the description of the critical situation which motivates the new form of philosophical investigation called Phenomenology. This preliminary stage is dealt with in the first lecture. While reading the text of this lecture, one realizes very soon that the situation which motivated phenomenology consists in a basic discomfort and perplexity with respect to the very possibility of cognition. Even the superficial reader may realize immediately that phenomenology was designed by Husserl as a method for overcoming once and for all the discomfort and perplexity which were prevailing at that time in the field of theory of knowledge. This raises the question: Why such a perplexity? But if we want to pose the question seriously perhaps we have to put it in a stricter form. Let us then divide it into two halves: 1) Which were those theories of knowledge entailing perplexity con-

J.C. Sallis, G. Moneta and J. Taminiaux (eds.), The Collegium Phaenomenologicum, 47–75.
© *Kluwer Academic Publishers.*

cerning the very possibility of cognition? 2) Is there anything in their methodological principles that inevitably entails perplexity?

Concerning the first problem, Husserl gives only two examples of epistemologies entailing perplexity as to the very possibility of cognition. In both cases the theories of knowledge evoked by Husserl ground their investigation upon what he calls 'a science of the natural sort' (13; 17) i.e., a science originating from the 'natural attitude of mind'.

Husserl insists that the 'natural attitude of mind' *per se* does not experience any perplexity at all since it is 'as yet unconcerned with the critique of cognition. Whether in the act of intuiting or in the act of thinking, in the natural attitude of mind we are turned to the matters (*den Sachen*) which are given to us each time and as a matter of course, even though they are given in different ways and in different modes of being, according to the source and level of our cognition' (13; 17). Within natural attitude we have no doubt that our perceptions and judgments relate to the world. True, the natural attitude often faces difficulties. This happens that our cognitions 'clash and contradict one another' (14; 17). But this clash does not result in any real perplexity: it merely raises problems which can be solved either by restoring formal consistency if the clash turns out to be of a logical nature, or by refining our observation if the clash is a conflict between two empirical evidences. In other words, the natural attitude of mind is basically assured. So, also, are the sciences which originate from this attitude and which may therefore be called 'sciences of the natural sort' (*naturlichen Wissenschaften*). These sciences include those which deal with real actualities such as the sciences of nature (physics, chemistry, biology *and* psychology), the sciences of culture (*Geisteswissenschaften*) and the sciences dealing with ideal actualities, such as the mathematical sciences and the sciences which 'investigate in their *formal* generality the a priori connections of meanings and postulated meanings and the a priori principles which belong to objectivity as such' (15; 19), such as pure grammar and pure logic. All these sciences are also assured. They do not experience perplexity, but only provisional difficulties. 'In every step of natural cognition pertaining to the sciences of the natural sort, difficulties arise and are resolved, either by *pure logic* or by appeal to *facts*, on the basis of motives and reasons which lie in the things themselves and which, as it were, come from things in the form of *requirements* that they themselves make on our thinking' (14; 18). These sciences of the natural sort are assured and without perplexity insofar as they trust the relation of cognition to its object. More exactly, 'what is *taken for granted* in natural thinking is the possibility of cognition. Constantly busy producing results, advancing from discovery to discovery in newer and newer branches of science, natural thinking finds no occasion to raise the question of the possibility of cognition as such' (15; 19). This question is the question raised by the theory of knowledge. In contradistinction to the sciences of the natural sort which take for granted the possibility of cognition, and which are assured that they really know, the theory of knowledge no longer takes for granted that possibility, but reflects upon it. Thereby perplexity appears. 'With the awakening of reflection about the relation of cognition to its object, abysmal difficulties arise' (14; 18). As a matter of fact the theories of knowledge entailing these abysmal difficulties are based upon sciences of the natural sort; more precisely upon natural sciences in the usual sense of the word. Husserl mentions as a first example the theory of knowledge that bases its investigation upon psychology. Psychology is a science of the natural sort inasmuch as it conceives of cognition as a 'fact in nature' (15; 19) occurring in a cognizing being and which can be treated like any natural fact, according to empirical procedures of observation, analysis, comparison, induction, hypotheses about the influence of other facts, and so on. Husserl contends that by being based upon empirical psychology a theory of knowledge is driven to an abysmal perplexity. The main issue in a theory of knowledge is the correspondence between cognition and the object cognized. In other words the main issue is truth construed as the very correspondence between the former and the latter. But as soon as you maintain, in agreement with empirical psychology, that cognition is merely a mental fact or process occurring, like any natural event, in a sector of nature, in that natural locus which is the mind of the cognizing subject, then the very possibility that 'there exist not only my own mental processes ... but also that which they apprehend' becomes enigmatic. Logically, Husserl argues, the one who maintains that cognition is merely a psychic fact has to become a solipsist: 'he never does and never can break out of the circle of his own mental processes' (16; 20). Consequently, the psychological, or psychologistic, theory of knowledge is driven to deny the very possibility of science in its double connotation: universality and objectivity.

If we look at the second example we become entangled in the same perplexity. Here we have a theory of knowledge based on biology. Cognition is treated as a biological fact, that is a process occurring in the intellect of a biological species whose present characteristics are the result of natural selection and adjustment. Accordingly, the way human beings cognize, including the logical rules and structures governing their judgments and reasonings, only expresses the accidental peculiarities of a species. Hence, in each case it turns out that cognition, if understood as a natural fact, is not fit to reach things as they really are.

The above theories of knowledge had been thoroughly scrutinized by Husserl earlier in the *Prolegomena* to his *Logical Investigations*. The first one had then been called psychologism, and the second, biologism. Together with a third one called anthropologism, they had been charged with many faults such as unclarity, inconsistency, self-contradiction, relativism, scepticism – all of which were eventually reduced to absurdity. All those accusations are repeated here but the main reproach now addressed to psychologism and biologism concerns the *relation* between cognition, its meaning and its object. Introducing his own phenomenological theory of knowledge Husserl states that the negative and critical task of the new theory is to '*stigmatize* the almost inevitable mistakes which ordinary reflection makes about the relation of cognition, its meaning and its object' (17; 22). Here, still within the preliminary stage, we reach the second half of our problem. We now see that the theories of knowledge entailing perplexity are those which are based upon sciences of the natural sort. Our second question is: Is there anything in the methodological principles of the theories of knowledge based upon natural sciences which inevitably entails perplexity? This question as such is not explicitly posed by Husserl, but he does assert that ordinary reflection or natural reflection on the possibility of cognition's reaching its object inevitably leads to a denial of that very possibility. This is why Husserl insists both at the beginning and at the end of the first lecture that a sharp distinction should be made between science of the natural sort and philosophical science: 'In contradistinction to all natural cognition, philosophy lies within a *new dimension* and what corresponds to this new dimension is a *new* and *radically new method* which is set over against the 'natural' method. He who denies this has completely failed to understand the whole of that level at which the characteristic problem of the critique of cognition lies, and with this he has failed to understand what philosophy really wants to do or should do, and what gives it its own character and authority vis-à-vis the whole of natural cognition and science of the natural sort' (21; 25–26). In other words, Husserl's critique of the theories of knowledge of the natural sort already presupposes another theory of knowledge which is no longer in any way of the natural sort but of a radically new sort, i.e., of a truly philosophical one. Hence the preliminary stage already presupposes the further stages. True the awareness that perplexities pervade the natural theories of knowledge motivates phenomenology but it may also be said conversely that the very description of those perplexities is carried out in the light of the new dimension won by phenomenology. Husserl makes this clear when he states: 'Only with the epistemological reflection (i.e., with the phenomenological reflection) do we arrive at the distinction between the sciences of a natural sort and philosophy' (18; 22–23).

But one could perhaps object: Does all this have anything to do with immanence and transcendence? The answer is yes. When he depicts the 'natural' theories of knowledge whose reflection upon the possibility for cognition to attain an object entail perplexity, Husserl characterizes their position in this way: 'Cognition in all its manifestations is a psychic act; it is the cognition of a cognizing subject. The objects cognized stand over against the cognition. But how can we be certain of the correspondence between cognition and the object cognized? How can knowledge *transcend* itself and reach its object reliably? The unproblematic manner in which the object of cognition is given to natural thought to be cognized now becomes an enigma' (15, 20). And a little further on he asserts that the psychologistic position leads to Hume, about whom he says two things: 1) Hume reduces 'all transcendent objectivity' to fictions lending themselves to psychological explanation in terms of 'actual "impressions" and "ideas"' within 'the sphere of immanence'; 2) in contradiction with this, however, Hume does in fact 'transcend the sphere of immanence'. Indeed 'by working with such concepts as habit, human nature, sense-organ, stimulus and the like, he is working with transcendent existences' (16; 20). Here we have the beginning of an answer to our second question. By stating that Hume reduces all transcendent objectivity to the sphere of immanence conceived of as a sequence of actual occurrences, Husserl supplies an answer to our question about why psychologism entails perplexity. If you state as a principle that cognition is nothing other than an inward succession of actual occurrences, it necessarily follows from your principle that cognition does not know since knowledge means a correspondence between cognition and its object. If you hold as a rule that there is a demarcation line between cognition and its object, then there is no hope of ever crossing the line. However, there is no doubt that Hume did cross the line, at least to some extent. He was unable to confine his statements to the mere succession of actual impressions occurring within the mind. By introducing universal concepts such as habit, nature and so on, he again and again transcended the actual impressions, thereby acknowledging, though reluctantly, that immanence is much more than a stream of factual occurrences. But it is one thing to acknowledge this reluctantly and implicitly and another thing to demonstrate it. Such a demonstration is part of the very task of phenomenology. But how do we have to enter into phenomenology? Here we leave the preliminary stage to make what Husserl calls in the summary the 'first step in the phenomenological orientation'.

2. The result of the preliminary step seems to be clear: the theories of knowledge of the natural sort were forced to deny the possibility of knowledge because they decided that their field of investigation was immanence conceived of as a succession of actual occurrences within a sphere out of which it is impossible to escape. Consequently if we want to establish a theory of knowledge free from any form of perplexity, it seems clear that we should not establish it within the sphere of immanence. If phenomenology has to be set over against the natural attitude as a whole, and if the establishment within the sphere of immanence seems to be just a prejudice of natural attitude, then we had better find another ground. Still, the first step in the phenomenological orientation is a settlement on the ground of immanence. How do we have to understand this puzzling development?

Let us look at the way Husserl argues when he makes the first step in the phenomenological orientation. Since the theories of knowledge of the natural sort entail unclarity, enigma and doubt, let us try, says Husserl, instead of basing our investigation upon a cognition of the natural sort, as psychologism does when it bases itself upon psychology which is a natural science, to suspend all cognitions of the natural sort, either prescientific or scientific. 'At the outset of the critique of cognition (the phenomenological critique of cognition) the entire world of nature, physical and psychological, as well as one's own human self together with all the sciences which have to do with these objective matters are put in question. Their being, their validity, are suspended' (22; 29). In this general suspension nothing is presupposed as already given. Such an overall suspending is called *epoché*. Husserl says that like the cartesian doubt, it 'begins with the doubt of all cognition, its own included'. But like in Descartes, it is impossible to remain in such a doubt, for 'while I am judging that everything is doubtful, it is indubitable that I am so judging'. 'And likewise with every *cogitatio*' (23; 30).

The cogitatio is, according to Husserl, the 'primal cognition' with which the new theory of knowledge must begin. When we focus upon those 'cogitationes', Husserl says, we are 'working on an absolute foundation'; with the whole realm of the cogitationes 'a sphere of the absolutely given can be indicated at the outset' of the theory of knowledge (25; 32). But here we must be very careful. In order to understand Husserl correctly we must pose the question: What then is absolutely given in this primal cognition? Is it the fact that this or that particular cogitatio (perception, imagination, judgment, inference, memory, etc.) *is*, here and now, actually lived by my mind? That it is an existing *Erlebnis* of my mind? True, to some extent, the absolute givenness of the cogitatio includes the fact that the cogitatio *is* here and now. Husserl says: 'it is given as something that is, that is here and now, and whose being cannot be sensibly doubted' (24; 31). However, if we read the text carefully we soon realize that Husserl is less concerned with the existence of the cogitationes or of cognition in general than with the essence of cognition. When he insists that 'every intellectual *Erlebnis* and indeed every mental *Erlebnis* whatever, while being enacted, can be made the object of a pure "seeing" and understanding, and is something absolutely given in this "seeing"', the point is not that I can see that this mental process *is* actually enacted by me here and now. If the point was the existence of the cogitatio, Husserl would not say in the same context: 'I have here put on the same level the 'seeing act' of reflective perception and the seeing act of reflective imagination. If one followed the cartesian view, one would have to emphasize perception first: i.e., the perception corresponding in some measure to the so-called inner perception of traditional epistemology, though this is a pseudo-concept' (24; 31). This apparently mysterious passage is quite understandable if we link it with a previous sentence: 'Perception itself stands open to my inspection as actually or imaginatively given to me'. The sentence means that what is at stake after the epoché in that particular type of cogitatio named perception (in the sense of the perception of a thing) is not the possibility of my having an inner awareness of its actual occurrence here and now. Rather the point is this: there can be an absolute givenness of perception not only when a perception actually occurs but also when we imagine a perception which does not actually occur at all. This clearly indicates that Husserl does not argue in terms of existence but in terms of essence. The absolute givenness of perception as a cogitatio does not mean its actual occurrence here and now, since it can be absolutely given when merely imagined and not at all actually occurring. In other words, the absolute givenness of perception means the presentation of the essence of perception, or of what Husserl calls briefly 'perception itself'. Now perception is a cognitive phenomenon among others. For all those cognitive phenomena the point is not to see *that* they occur, but to see what sort of cognition is exemplified in them, and more generally to see what cognition is, or, as Husserl says, 'to make the essence of cognition directly self-given' (25; 32).

What about immanence and transcendence in this context? Precisely, when he recapitulates the movement of this first step Husserl insists that the absolute givenness of the cogitatio is due to its immanence, and that it is 'because of this immanence' that the point of departure of phenomenology is 'free of the puzzlement which is the source of all sceptical embarrassment' (26; 33). Here it is our turn to be puzzled. We believed that a bias for immanence was a flaw in theories of knowledge, prompting puzzlement. And now we hear that immanence annihilates puzzlement. Does Husserl contradict himself, or does he attribute to the same word two different meanings? As a matter of fact, Husserl seems to have been aware of the difficulties caused by his terminology, for he develops a long analysis of what he means when using either the word 'immanence' or the word 'transcendence'. Let us follow his analysis:

> One thing one can mean by transcendence is that the object of cognition is not actually (*reell*) contained in the cognitive act so that one would be meaning by 'being truly given' or 'immanently given' that the object of the cognitive act is actually contained in the act ... (27; 35).

Husserl says later:

> There is still another transcendence whose opposite is an altogether different immanence, namely, absolute and clear givenness ... which consists of a simply immediate 'seeing' and apprehending of the intended object itself as it is ... (28; 35).

Let us try to elucidate the distinction.

According to the first meaning, 'immanent' means: actually contained in the cogitatio as a mental process; and consequently 'transcendent', as the antonym of immanent, means: not actually contained in the mental process. According to the second meaning, 'immanent' means: absolutely and clearly given to an immediate seeing; and consequently 'transcendent' means: not evidently given to a seeing.

Now in order to overcome the contradiction we seem to be confronted with we have to understand in what sense immanence prompts puzzlement in the natural theories of knowledge, whereas immanence annihilates puzzlement in the phenomenological theory of knowledge. In order to understand this point we must inspect first the way the natural theories of knowledge pose the problem with which they are concerned. Their problem is a problem of *relation*, namely the relation between cognition and the cognized object. Husserl argues that the way the natural theories of knowledge pose the problem implies the impossibility of solving it, hence puzzlement. Indeed, when they pose the problem of the relation between cognition and the cognized object, the natural theories of knowledge base their investigation at the outset on 'the unspoken supposition that the only actually understandable, unquestionable, absolutely evident givenness is the givenness of the moment which is actually contained within the cognitive act and this is why anything in the way of a cognized objectivity that is not actually contained within that act is regarded as a puzzle and as problematic' (28; 35–36). Such an unspoken supposition, Husserl says, is a '*fatal mistake*'. But before trying to understand why it is a 'fatal mistake', we can already notice that the two meanings of both words, 'immanence' and 'transcendence', are implied in the unspoken supposition of the natural theory of knowledge.

The natural theory of knowledge implicitly states at the outset: What is absolutely evident (second meaning of immanence) is what is actually contained within the mental process (first meaning of immanence). Therefore and inversely, what is not actually contained within the mental process (first meaning of transcendence) is not absolutely evident (second meaning of transcendence). Now it is clear that the object as a physical thing is not contained in the actual mental process. Consequently, the object is problematic.

Husserl says that there is a 'fatal mistake' in this unspoken supposition which is the very ground of the natural theory of knowledge. What is the fatal mistake?

The fatal mistake consists of believing that '*cognition and its object are actually separate*' (30; 37) or, if we use the two meanings of transcendence and immanence, it consists of believing that cognition as an actual mental process (first meaning of immanence) is absolutely given or seen (second meaning) whereas the object is neither in the mental process nor seen. As soon as you maintain this, Husserl argues, it is impossible to understand how cognition can relate to an object. Neither is it possible to find as a part of cognition what is no part of it, nor in what is seen the invisible. In other words, if the very *relation* cognition-object is not at the outset given to a seeing, then every attempt to understand the possibility of a relation between cognition and object is, as Husserl says, 'patent folly' (30; 37).

Now we are in a position to understand what Husserl means when he insists that immanence, in the case of phenomenology, annihilates puzzlement, whereas it prompts puzzlement in the case of the natural theory of knowledge. The core of the debate with the natural theory of knowledge on this point is a matter of 'seeing'. The natural theory of knowledge says: I see cognition as an occurrence in the mind, I do not see the object, therefore I do not see the relation of cognition to the object. However, the natural theory of knowledge goes on to argue, it is still possible to deduce or to infer some explanation of the relation of cognition to the object from what natural sciences make us know about, i.e., nature as a whole. Husserl's objection is very simple: '*"Seeing" does not lend itself to demonstration or deduction*' (31; 38). Or: it is absurd to 'draw conclusions (concerning what is a matter of seeing) from existences of which one knows but which one cannot "see"' (31; 38). And Husserl gives this illustration: 'A man born deaf knows that there are sounds, and that sounds produce harmonies . . . but he cannot intuit such things and in intuiting grasp the "how" of such things' (30; 38). It is with reference to such a seeing of the how that we have to understand the attitude of phenomenology towards the natural theory of knowledge. When Husserl maintains that by focusing upon immanence or (and this is the other side of that very focusing) by excluding transcendence, phenomenology liberates itself from puzzlement, *he merely states that the theory of knowledge has to be based at the outset upon a 'seeing' and to remain constantly based on it.* The bracketing of transcendence is by no means the exclusion of objects out of the field of the theory of knowledge. It is the exclusion of the unseen, including all the absurd attempts to demonstrate, upon the basis of the unseen, something that is, in principle, open to a 'seeing' only.

As a matter of fact, we have here a third meaning of the word 'transcendence'. This meaning was probably the original meaning of the word, for the Latin word 'transcendentia' was coined to translate the Greek word 'metabasis' which designated a transfer or a displacement from one region to another. The alleged demonstration of the seen by inference from the unseen is a transcendence in the sense of such a confusing displacement from one region to another, it is *a metabasis eis allo genos*. Still the question remains about how the exclusion of transcendence in all these meanings of the word entails a liberation from puzzlement. In order to understand this we need to take a further step in the phenomenological orientation. Yet before proceeding to this second step, let us summarize the result of the first one as far as immanence and transcendence are concerned. If we try to describe in terms of immanence and/or transcendence the picture Husserl gives of the natural theories of knowledge, we have the following:

- the terms of their problem are cognition, object, and relation between cognition and object.
- the concepts they have of the terms are: cognition is immanent, which means that it is evidently seen by the theorist as a fact actually contained in the mind; the object instead is transcendent in the twofold meaning of not-actually-contained in the mental process and of not-seen-in-it; likewise the relation cognition-object is also transcendent in both meanings of the word.
- as a result, there is no solution to the problem of the possibility of knowledge.

  By contrast the first step within phenomenology already allows Husserl to give in a provisional way the following picture of his theory of knowledge:
- the terms of the problem are the same.
- as to the meaning of the terms, we already know that 'everything transcendent is bracketed', which means that everything that is either not-actually-contained in the cogitatio or not-evidently seen in the cogitatio is excluded. However, Husserl insists that the relation cognition-object can be absolutely seen.
- this implies, as a result, that there is a solution to the problem of the possibility of knowledge.

The above contrast between both positions obviously implies that Husserl's concept of immanence, more precisely, the phenomenological immanence, is much broader than the type of immanence which prevails in natural theories of knowledge.

The immanence dealt with by the natural theorist of knowledge is strictly limited to what is actually contained in the mental process. It is taken for granted that this actual content alone can be seen. In Husserl's immanence we no longer find such a limitation.

Husserl insists that after the epoché the immanence which is the field of the phenomenological theory of knowledge is *pure*. This implies that the immanence which is treated by the natural non-phenomenological theories of knowledge is not pure. Why this contrast? The contrast depends on the quality of reflection. When reflecting upon knowledge in general, the natural theory of knowledge treats its subject matter in an impure way, because its way of treating it has recourse to procedures, rules and concepts which are not required by the matters themselves as given to a pure seeing, but imported or borrowed from pre-given natural sciences. In other words, the natural theorist of knowledge claims to stick to what is contained and visible in the sphere of immanence, but he decides beforehand that only actual occurrences here and now are contained and seeable in the sphere of immanence. Such a decision is a prejudice because it is not based upon what is visible in the sphere of immanence but upon what he knows on the basis of pregiven natural sciences for which the real is limited to what is the case. In his reflection he thus mixes what he sees in the given matter with what he knows from elsewhere: that there are only facts explainable by other facts. This mixing procedure results in an impure reflection, i.e., a reflection which to a large extent is blind towards the reflected. His so-called immanence is thoroughly polluted by transcendence. Instead phenomenological reflection pretends to be pure because in it 'every intellective lived experience (*Erlebnis*) and indeed every lived experience, while being enacted, can be made the object of a pure seeing and apprehending and is an absolute givenness in this seeing' (24; 31). Here reflection is pure of any interference of pregiven knowledges with the given matter. But what is then to be seen in this purified immanence? Is it a variety of facts occurring in the mind? A set of factual cases? To be sure the *cogitationes* to be seen or reflected may be given here and now and in that sense they are facts. But what is to be considered in them is not at all their actual occurring here and now. It is rather their way of being given. It is not *that* they are given but *how* they are given. If the 'that' were the topic of phenomenology, phenomenology would deal with psychological facts and therefore would be a psychology. But the aim of phenomenology, says Husserl, 'is not to explain cognition as a psychological fact; it is not to inquire in the natural causes and laws of the development and occurrence of cognitions ... Rather the task of the critique of cognition is to clarify, to cast light upon, the essence of cognition and the legitimacy of its claim to validity that belongs to its essence' (25; 32). In other words, the purely immanent *cogitatio*, as offered to a pure seeing reflecting on it, is not a here and now fact or occurrence; it is an example, either factually enacted here and now or simply imagined, of a type of *cogitatio* or of an essence. Moreover, in addition to being given as an essence, the purely immanent *cogitatio* is given right away as having in its essence a claim to a specific validity, which means a specific intending of a specific intended, or a specific relatedness to an objective correlate. This relatedness is in no way to be explained; it is given in the *cogitatio*, not in addition to it, not as a supplement or complement of it, but as an essential feature of it.

Two further steps are thus anticipated in the first one: the eidetic reduction and the analysis of intentionality to which the former opens the way.

3. The epoché was the first step within phenomenology. The eidetic reduction here called 'epistemological reduction' is the second. Reduction is the topic of lecture III in *The Idea of Phenomenology*.

Right at the beginning of the lecture Husserl recalls the result of the *epoché*.

'We have indubitably secured the whole realm of *cogitationes*. The being of the *cogitatio*, more precisely the phenomenon of cognition itself, is beyond question; and it is free from the riddle of transcendence . . . It is also clear that the *cogitationes* present a sphere of *absolutely immanent data; it is in this sense that we understand immanence.* In the "seeing" pure phenomena the object is not outside cognition or outside "consciousness", while being given in the sense of the absolute self-givenness of something which is purely "seen"' (33; 43). Reduction, here called 'epistemological reduction', is designed to assure the conquest of this pure immanence as the whole realm of *cogitationes* taken as absolutely self-given and therefore purely seen. We have noticed so far that the equation 'seen = actually contained-in-the-mind-as a fact' was the very definition of immanence in the natural, non-phenomenological theories of knowledge, and the basic reason for the abysmal puzzlement prompted by them. Reduction aims at overcoming once and for all such a puzzlement by overcoming that equation which defines impure immanence. Reduction is needed precisely 'in order to prevent the evidence of the being of the *cogitatio* from being confused with the evidence that my cogitatio is, with the evidence of the *sum cogitans* and the like' (33; 43). The above sentence clearly indicates that in Husserl's view 'the Being (*Sein*) of the *cogitatio*' is not at all the fact that the *cogitatio is*. Being here means absolute self-givenness, not as the presencing of such and such a *cogitatio* but rather as the presentation of its essence. Being means essence. Over against this sense of being which claims to be purely phenomenological, the fact that the *cogitatio* exists does not interest phenomenology but psychology, i.e., a natural science and even a science of natural phenomena. More precisely, the fact that *my* cogitatio exists, that it belongs to me, its existential mineness, its individuation is not a property of the phenomenon in the phenomenological sense. Husserl states this very clearly: 'If I, as a human being employing natural modes of thought, look at the perception which I am undergoing at that moment, then I immediately and almost inevitably apperceive it (that is a fact) in relation to my ego. It stands there as a lived experience of this living person, as his state, his act; the sensory content stands there as what is given to him or sensed by him, as that of which he is conscious; and it integrates itself like him within objective time. Perception, and any other *cogitatio*, so apperceived, is a *psychological fact*. Thus it is apperceived as a datum in objective time, belonging to the mentally living ego, the ego which is in the world and lasts through its duration. This, then, is the phenomenon which is investigated by the natural science we call psychology' (34; 44). Hence it does not pertain to the pure immanent cogitatio that it exists, that it belongs to an existing ego, that this ego is in the world. All these features are transcendent, they must be excluded from the phenomenon in the phenomenological, purely immanent, sense of the word.

Likewise the existence or non-existence of the object to which the cogitatio is related in its very intention is also suspended. When I see or behold perception, for example, as a pure, immanent and reduced phenomenon, I may undoubtedly reach the pure vision of the pure 'phenomenon' perception on the basis of this actual perception, let us say, for example, this perception here and now of this chair. But what is at stake in my pure vision is not the question of whether my perception here and now really does reach the chair, or whether there really *is* a chair out there corresponding to my perception. What is at issue is not this perception here and now with its existential properties and claims, but the essence of perception, perception as such, of which my perception of a chair is just an example. In other words, the phenomenological seeing of perception as a specific cogitatio is a seeing apprehension of a universal on the basis of the here and now. Phenomenology is a seeing or 'theory of the essence of pure cognitive phenomena' (37; 47). What is gained by phenomenology is not the fact that while reflecting or beholding I can say that this or that reflected *cogitatio* is actually occurring in my mind, for this would mean that the field of pure phenomena is a 'Heraclitean flux' (37; 47). It is psychological reflection which is concerned with the actual occurrence in me of particular *cogitationes*. Phenomenological reflection instead is concerned with the self-presentation or givenness of the essence of each specific *cogitatio*. It is in this way that '*to each psychic lived experience (Erlebnis) there corresponds through the device of phenomenological reduction a pure phenomenon, which exhibits its intrinsic (immanent) essence (taken individually) as an absolute datum.* Every positing of a 'non immanent actuality' of anything which is not contained in the phenomenon, even if intended by the phenomenon, and also of anything which is not given in the second sense (i.e., absolutely given or seen) is bracketed, i.e., suspended' (35; 45). The pure phenomenon 'perception of a thing' is an essence which can be seen with its universal properties on the basis of a particular perception of a particular thing – a perception either actually occurring or merely imagined. But even if the basis for the pure phenomenological seeing is an actually occurring perception, the phenomenological inspection is not concerned with its actual occurrence but with its essence. This essence, universal by definition, can be reached and contemplated with the help of an 'eidetic abstraction' or ideation which is neither inductive nor deductive but thoroughly intuitive. On the other hand, phenomenological seeing is not concerned with the problem of the existence of what the particular perception of a particular thing claims to perceive, for example, a chair. However, the phenomenological inspection or seeing reveals that it belongs to the essence of perception to be open to a specific correlate. The actuality of a concrete correlate, the actual existence of a chair out there, is not at issue. What is at issue is the essential relatedness or openness of the cogitatio called 'perception' to a specific *intentum*, the 'perceived'. This essential relatedness can be seen in the pure phenomenon: it is an absolute givenness in it. Within the sphere of pure immanence, 'the existence of objectivities to which (the cogitatio) is related insofar as it is transcendent, is not given to me'. However, the 'relation to the transcendent' even if the existence of the transcendent is bracketed by the phenomenologist is still 'somehow graspable within the pure phenomenon. The relating-oneself-to-the-transcendent, the meaning-the-transcendent in this or that way is still an inner feature of the phenomenon' (36; 46). Because a 'relating-oneself-to-the-transcendent' belongs to the pure phenomenon which is the essence of a specific *cogitatio*, the pure immanence is at once an eidetic field and a transcendental field. Indeed in pure immanence there is absolutely given or seen not only the essence or sense of each self-relatedness but also the possible validity of it: 'Where else could I investigate both the *meaning* of this intending-something-beyond-oneself, and also along with its meaning, its possible *validity,* or the meaning of such validity?' (36; 46). In this context Husserl evokes Kant's synthetic unity of transcendental apperception. However, he says, 'the transcendental apperception, consciousness as such, will soon acquire for us a completely different meaning, one which is not at all mysterious' (38; 48). Indeed the synthetic unity of transcendental apperception in Kant is not given to a seeing, it cannot be intuited. In Kant only space and time, the a priori forms of sensibility, are pure intuitions, are purely given to an immediate seeing, whereas the a priori concepts or categories together with the a priori principles of understanding are not intuitively given, are not offered to a seeing. By taking up the very notion of 'transcendental apperception' for characterizing the phenomenological immanence, Husserl acknowledges, by the same token, that the phenomenological immanence is a field of a priori conditions of possibility and validity. But by saying that transcendental apperception in his sense is not at all mysterious he is obviously claiming that the whole realm of a priori conditions is given to a seeing.

Consequently the purely immanent a priori is to be taken in two senses. Phenomenology as the seeing of the immanent is an a priori cognition in the sense that it is 'a cognition which is directed to general essences and which entirely bases its absolute validity on essence' (41; 51). But it is also an a priori cognition in the transcendental sense of the word, in the sense of 'the critique of reason, not only the theoretical, but also the practical and any other kind' (42; 52): it aims at setting and evaluating principles, i.e., conditions of possibility.

At this stage we are in a position to refine again the definition of phenomenological immanence. As Husserl writes in the summary outlining the train of thoughts pursued in the lectures, the step taken in this second phase 'makes clear to us in the first place that '*reelle Immanenz*' (or transcendence) is but a special case of the broader concept of immanence as such' (6; 9). In Husserl's language the adjective 'reell' means: 'as an actual content'. The '*reelle Imma-*

nenz' is the mental flux or stream of lived experiences (*Erlebnisse*), the latter taken as actually contained within the former. To be sure, when as a phenomenologist I see, in the way of pure seeing (*Schauen*), after phenomenological reduction, a *cogitatio* – for example, the 'perception-of-a-thing' – my act of seeing is actually contained within the stream of my lived experiences. As such my act of seeing is 'something singular. At any given time, it is a moment in the stream of consciousness'. Likewise my act of seeing a category (substance, totality, identity and so on) is something singular, a '*reell*' moment in the stream of my consciousness. But what I see – the perception-of-a-thing or this category – is nothing singular but a universal. And it 'is absolutely given but is not "*reell*" immanent', which means that it is not actually contained within the flux of my lived experiences. Therefore "no longer is it a commonplace and taken-on face value that the *absolutely given* and the '*reell*' *immanent* are one and the same". Indeed 'the universal itself, which is given in evidence' in such a seeing of the universal 'is nothing singular but just a universal, and therefore it is transcendent in the "*reell*" sense of the word' (67; 9), though it is not at all transcendent in the phenomenological sense of the word (assumed as existing but not seen). 'Consequently, the idea of *phenomenological reduction* acquires a more immediate and more profound determination and a clearer meaning. It means not the exclusion of the "*reell*" transcendent' (for then it would mean the exclusion of the universal since the universal is not actually contained within the stream of my singular acts of seeing) 'but the exclusion of the transcendent in general as something which is to be accepted as existent, i.e., everything that is not evident givenness in its authentic sense, that is not absolutely given to a pure "seeing"' (7; 9).

4. The third step within phenomenology is the exploration of the eidetic and transcendental immanence. As Husserl insists at the beginning of lecture IV: 'The singular cognitive phenomenon, coming and going in the stream of consciousness, is not the object of phenomenological statements' (44; 55). The subject matter of phenomenological statements is a 'generic' cognitive phenomenon. The absolute self-givenness of a cogitatio is a 'generic' absolute datum. It is an eidetic datum, an essence. But it is also an intentional immanence. The *cogitatio* taken as a 'generic' or 'eidetic' datum is essentially intentional. 'Cognitive lived experiences (and this belongs to their essence) have an *intentio*, they refer to something, they are related in this or that way to an object. This activity of relating itself to an object belongs to them even if the object itself does not. And what is objective can appear, can have a certain kind of givenness in appearance, even though it is at the same time neither actually contained (*reell*) within the cognitive phenomenon, nor does it exist in any other way as a *cogitatio*. To clarify the essence of cognition and the essential connections which belong to it and to bring this to self-givenness, this involves examining both these sides of the matter; it involves investigating this relatedness which belongs to the essence of cognition; (43; 55). In other words, not only the *intentio* of the cognitive phenomenon but what is *intended* by it can be absolutely given: both the *intentio* and the *intentum* are purely immanent. But the *intentum* in the phenomenological sense is not the object taken in the usual sense as when I say that this chair is the object of my perception. Such an object has been reduced. But what remains of it after reduction is its generic way of presenting itself, its *Erscheinen*, its appearing. This is the *intentum*, which, being one side of the intentional relation, is, like the other side, given as a universal. This raises two questions. The first question is: How are those sides given as universalities? Answer: They are given on the basis of something singular. The *intentio* 'perception of' is given in its universal properties on the basis of a singular perception of something. We already know that the elevation from the singular to the universal is an eidetic abstraction. This abstraction which is also called ideation, is an intuition of the universal through the singular. The universal overcomes the singular but only on the basis of a singular can it be phenomenologically seen. This phenomenological relationship between singular and universal is called relation of *Fundierung*. The singular provides a basis for the phenomenological intuition or seeing of the universal. On the basis of the singular perception that I have now of this particular thing, I may see phenomenologically that perception – envisaged in its *intentio* – is of an intuitive nature. It belongs universally to perception as such to be a fulfillment intention. I see that perception is a fulfillment intention. Likewise, on the basis of this singular assertion that I may make about something without perceiving it, I may see that this type of assertion is an intention without fulfillment, an empty intention. The second question is: What is the extension of the sphere of the absolutely and universally given? As a matter of fact, the answer is already implicit in what has been said above. What is absolutely given includes all the constituents of each side of the intentional relation. Here a precision is required as far as the *intentum* is concerned. Not only can each type of *intentio* be absolutely given in its specific universality but its very *intentum* also – hence, not only all the *cogitationes* but their correlated *cogitata*. The examples Husserl gives suffice to suggest the variety of these universal *cogitata*. He first mentions sensory universals, like the species 'red', redness as such, which can be ideated on the basis of a singular red. He then mentions sensory relations, like the relation of similarity, which can be ideated as a generic givenness on the basis of a singular similarity between, say, two singular samples of red. But Husserl insists that the whole realm of cognitive phenomena, in other words, the 'many forms and types' of cognition taken as such but also in their 'essential relations' and 'teleological interconnections' can be given to a 'pure seeing and ideation' (45; 57). They can be given together with what they intend, together with their specific *cogitatum,* which means that 'phenomenology proceeds by seeing, clarifying and determining meaning (Sinn), and by distinguishing meanings' (46; 58). In this clarification all the basic categories and structures which determine any type of objectivity whatsoever may be seen in a pure way, including no only the categories which determine perceptual objectivity (like color, space, form, etc.) together with the categorial forms by which we articulate what we perceive, and 'which find expression in words like "is" and "not", "same" and "other", "one" and "many", "and" and "or"' (56; 71), but also the 'basic concepts and principles" (*Grundbegriffe und Grundsätze*) which are 'the ideal conditions of possibility of scientific objectivity' (46; 58).

Here again the reference to Kant's transcendental problematic is obvious. Phenomenology, in its foundation, renovates Kant's project with the help of the eidetic method. 'This method', says Husserl, 'belongs essentially to the meaning of the critique of cognition and so generally to every sort of critique of reason (hence also evaluative and practical reason)' (46; 58). In Kant the critique of theoretical reason aims at determining the conditions of possibility of knowledge and its objects. In Kant such a critique shows that only mathematical and physical cognition have objects. Mathematics is a knowledge to the extent that it restricts itself to construction of concepts within time and space as a priori intuitions. And empirical physics is a knowledge insofar as it deals with the empirical content of space and time as a content which is a priori articulated by the categories and principles of pure understanding. In Husserl we no longer have this limitation of knowledge to mathematics and physics. The a priori realm, as far as knowledge is concerned, is no longer limited to the a priori conditions of mathematical entities and of physical objects. The phenomenological reduction shows that it makes sense to say that perception, and imagination as well, also have their objects. Thus the phenomenological transcendental field is much broader than Kant's transcendental field. And because the transcendental field is broader than in Kant, it can ground as sciences disciplines which were not scientific in Kant's view, like psychology or history, for example, and even the *Geisteswissenschaften* in general.

Moreover, phenomenology is also in continuity with Kant as far as metaphysics is concerned. In Kant the critique of theoretical reason opens the way to a metaphysics of nature. Likewise the critique of practical reason opens the way to a metaphysics of morals. Though expanded, this metaphysical aim is also reappropriated by Husserl, who writes the following: 'Whatever, in addition to the critique of reason, is called philosophy in the strict sense, is intimately related to this critique: hence metaphysics of nature and metaphysics of spiritual life as a whole (*des gesamten Geistesleben*), and thus metaphysics in general in the widest sense' (46; 58–59).

Hence pure immanence, as the transcendental realm offered to a pure eidetic seeing, is the field for an investigation both critical and metaphysical.

The phenomenological investigation is critical when it determines, within a pure seeing, the specific validity of specific forms of cognition. It is metaphysical when it determines, on the basis of the critique but, again, in a pure seeing, the ontological categories and structures which characterize being as a whole. *The Idea of Phenomenology* seems to take for certain – which means to be purely self-given to a pure seeing – that being as a whole is divided into two ontological realms: nature and spiritual life. Hence 'metaphysics in the widest sense' is composed of metaphysics of nature and metaphysics of spiritual life.

We have thus obtained a full characterization of phenomenological immanence. It is the eidetic sphere of essences and essential structures which determine each type of intentionality on both its sides, the side of the *intentio* and the side of the *intentum*. Immanence is also a transcendental sphere in the critical sense of the word since in it the categorial and axiomatic conditions of validity of each type of intentionality are self-given in purity. Moreover, it is a transcendental sphere in the metaphysical sense of the word since in it the ontological categories and structures of being as a whole (nature and spiritual life) are also self-given.

Either as eidetic or as transcendental, pure immanence is a priori. In each of these three lines of investigation, phenomenology is a matter of seeing. Such a seeing presupposes a bracketing of any existence other than the existence of the *cogitatio* itself. But as soon as the *cogitationes* are secured as the specific topic of investigation, their very existence, i.e., their actual occurring here and now, is of no interest for the phenomenologist. The fact that this *cogitatio*, say this perception, actually occurs in my cogito is not phenomenologically relevant. What is phenomenologically relevant in this case is the essence of perception with its intentional and transcendental features. And such an essence may be seen upon the basis of a perception which does not actually occur but is merely imagined. 'Hence phenomenological reduction does not entail a limitation of the investigation to the sphere of actual immanence, to the sphere of that which is actually contained within the absolute this of the *cogitatio* . . . but to the sphere of that which is purely self-given . . . the sphere of pure evidence' (48–49; 60–61). Within this sphere of pure evidence it turns out that pure immanence, because of its eidetic and transcendental properties, is in a position of overcoming or of surplus with regard to the actual immanence with which the psychologist is concerned. Envisaged as an actually immanent occurrence the *cogitatio* is a closed, atomic entity, deprived of any openness or relatedness to an object and therefore of any internal capacity for truth. Envisaged as a purely immanent phenomenon the same *cogitatio* is intrinsically open; it bears in itself a relatedness to an object, which means a specific claim to validity, to verification. Likewise the actually immanent *cogitatio* 'perception' is deprived of any temporal consciousness since it is encapsulated within a mere now moment. Instead, the same reduced *cogitatio* gives itself to the pure phenomenological seeing as pervaded by an internal time-consciousness in the form of 'the *retention* which is necessarily bound up with every perception' (52; 67). Finally the actually immanent *cogitatio* is deprived of any internal capacity for ideation, or for generalizing, or for categorial insight. Instead, reduction enables us to see that even a simple *cogitatio* like the perception of a thing is pervaded by categorial intuition. This is why Husserl writes the following: 'In the perception of an external thing, just that thing, let us say a house standing before our eyes, is said to be perceived. The house is a transcendent thing and forfeits its existence after the phenomenological reduction. The house-appearing, this *cogitatio*, emerging and disappearing in the stream of consciousness, is given as actually evident. In this house-phenomenon we find a phenomenon of redness, of extension, etc. These are evident data. But is it not also evident that a house appears in the house-phenomenon, and that it is just on that account that we call it a perception of a house? And what appears is not only a house in general, but exactly this house, determined in such and such a way and appearing in that determination. Can I not make an evidently true judgment as follows: on the basis of the appearing or in the content of this perception, the house is thus and so, a brick building, with a slate roof, etc.?' (57; 72). This passage somehow condenses the whole issue we are dealing with here. What is bracketed as transcendent in this analysis under the name of an existing thing is obviously an entity inserted as a portion within the processes which define nature from the point of view of what Husserl called earlier 'the natural attitude'. As a result of such a bracketing of the so-called natural objectivity, the immanent field, in the pure sense of the word immanent, is given to a seeing. What is thus given in this case is this perception-of-this-house in its essential features. Such a perception is a *cogitatio*. The word *cogitatio* here encompasses an intention and an *intentum*. The *intentum* here given is the appearing of the house. This appearing, also called phenomenon, includes in itself universal components such as redness, extension, house in general, brick, roof and so on. These components can be made the object of an ideation or categorial intuition, for instance of the eidetic seeing of redness as such. I can see redness as such in an eidetic abstraction on the basis of the particular redness of the bricks. But conversely those universals which are in a position of excess or superfluity with regard to the particular features of this particular thing also pervade the very appearing of this particular thing to me. A transcendantal seeing pervades my empirical seeing in such a way that I have the right to say at once that I see what I say, and that I say what I see. By this it is meant that I see empirically what I say in universal words expressing possible correlates of a transcendental seeing, and that the verbal account I give of what I perceive refers to a seeing which combines an empirical layer and a transcendental one. The passage that we are commenting on clearly shows that phenomenology does not drop existence for the sake of essences dwelling in a Platonist heaven. Indeed the investigation into the immanent sphere, the pure sphere of essences, is carried out with a view towards discovering the validity, i.e., the specific truth of each type of intentionality. This validation implies a return from the transcendental to the empirical. As Husserl said earlier, in the same lectures, about the phenomenon of perception as purely seen after reduction: 'this perception is, and remains as long as it lasts, something absolute, something here and now, something that is in itself what it is, something by which I can measure as by an ultimate standard what being (*Sein*) and being given can mean and here must mean, at least, obviously, as far as the sort of being and being given is concerned which a "here and now" exemplifies'. (24; 31). In other words, the phenomenological seeing of the essence of *perceptio* (for example, as a fulfillment-intention) and the correlative essence of the *perceptum* (for example, as a bodily presence given through a variety of profiles and exhibiting universal properties like extension, color, etc.) is an a priori standard by which I can measure the claim raised by this or that particular empirical perception to be indeed a perception, and to reach in truth what it claims to perceive. Consequently the transcendental immanence is by and large the ground of all the empirical *cogitationes*, or of all the *Erlebnisse* which might actually occur. But for the same reason transcendental immanence compels us to discard the picture psychology gives of the cognitive phenomena, i.e., the picture according to which perception, for example, is a psychic event occurring within me, an event of which the relation to a thing 'outside' should be explained because such a relation is supposedly a supplement to the event itself.

The above comment is another way of saying that the sphere of pure immanence is the sphere of *constitution*. Constitution, which is the main topic of lecture V, is neither the creation of beings out of nothingness nor the shaping of entities out of a pre-given matter. It does not designate an activity by which consciousness would let its objects emerge in existence, nor an activity by which consciousness would give to itself its objects. It does not even designate any onesided, centrifugal giving by consciousness. Rather it designates a correlation between a giving by consciousness – a specific *intentio* – and a corresponding *self*-givenness of the intended. It is one and the same thing to say that consciousness constitutes its objects and to say that its objects constitute themselves with respect to consciousness. In this double giving the issue is essence and not existence. Constitution as a correlation is not a relatedness in which consciousness would give existence to its correlates or would let them be. It merely lets them appear or give themselves as what they are as intended by consciousness. What is at issue in this relatedness – more precisely in the teleological connections between several types of relatedness – is not a giving of existence but a giving of sense (*Sinngebung*). The one who lives in the natural attitude posits existences, his own existence and the existence of the world. The one who purely sees the pure immanent sphere does not posit existences; he discloses sense, the sense of every intention and the sense or way of appearing of its correlative *intentum.*

This is why Husserl concludes his foundational account with these words:

> Originally the problem concerned the relation between subjective psychological experience (*Erlebnis*) and the actuality (*Wirklichkeit*) grasped therein, as it is in itself-first of all real actuality and then the mathematical and other sorts of ideal actualities. But first we need the insight that the radical problem must rather concern the *relation between cognition and object,* but in the reduced sense, according to which we are dealing not with human cognition but with cognition as such (*überhaupt*) apart from any reference, including an existential position, to the empirical ego or to a real world. We need the insight that the truly significant problem is that of the ultimate sense-giving of cognition and also of objectivity as such, which only is what it is in correlation with possible cognition. (60; 75–76)

Apparently written in a sort of fever, the fever of discovery, for advanced students already convinced by the *Logical Investigations* that phenomenology was a revival of philosophy, the text of the five lectures, precisely because it is a foundational text, shows at once, in a very vivid way, the fertility of Husserl's phenomenological problematic and the dark spots within the new light shed by it.

No one was better able than Heidegger at once to take advantage of the master's discoveries and to reveal the dark spots in the Husserlian concept of phenomenology. The lecture courses offered by Heidegger in Marburg, before the publication of *Being and Time,* express in many ways both his tribute to those discoveries and his awareness of these points of obscurity. Among those lecture courses, the course on the *History of the Concept of Time,*[2] offered in the summer of 1925, which consists in an early version of *Being and Time,* provides a very clear survey of both the discoveries and the dark spots. To be sure, in this survey there is no mention whatsoever of Husserl's lectures on *The Idea of Phenomenology*. Heidegger grounds his account on Husserl's publications available at that time, i.e., the *Logical Investigations,* the article on *Philosophy as a rigorous Science,* and *Ideas I*. Nevertheless it is not artificial to read the Göttingen lectures, analyzed in this paper, in the light of Heidegger's account. Indeed, for one thing, the Göttingen lectures express the discoveries to which Heidegger pays a tribute in the 1925 lecture course, and for another, leave the reader with a feeling of uneasiness due to their blind spots.

While remaining always within the framework of our attempt to clarify immanence and transcendence, recalling the discoveries and by trying to discern the blind spots.

According to Heidegger, there are at least three decisive discoveries in Husserl's phenomenology: 1) intentionality, 2) categorial intuition, and 3) the original sense of the a priori.

1) Husserl discovered that 'intentionality is a structure of lived experiences and not just a supplementary relation' (37; 47–48). More precisely he discovered, thereby overcoming the uncertainties of Brentano who never brought 'into relief intentionality as such, as a structural totality', that 'the basic constitution of intentionality' is 'a reciprocal belonging-together of *intentio* and *intentum*' (46; 61–62). Our commentary above suffices to show that this discovery is at the core of *The Idea of Phenomenology*, and is already involved in the very description by Husserl of the perplexities entailed by the theories of knowledge based on the natural attitude. Over against these theories Husserl insists in the first lecture that 'cognition, according to its essence, is *cognition of objectivities*, and it is this through its immanent *sense*, by virtue of which it *relates* itself to objectivities' (15; 19).

2) The second discovery is categorial intuition, by which is meant 'the demonstration, first, that there is a simple apprehension of the categorial, such constituents in beings which in traditional fashion are designated as categories and were seen in crude form quite early in Greek philosophy, especially by Plato and Aristotle'. But Heidegger insists that such a discovery is 'above all, the demonstration that this apprehension is invested in the most everyday of perceptions and in every experience' (48; 64). In order to prepare his audience for a correct appreciation of the two constituents of categorial intuition, Heidegger recalls Husserl's teaching about '1) intentional intending and its intentional fulfillment and 2) intentional comportments as expressed – intuition and expression' (id.). What is at issue in the correlation of the intending and its fulfillment is what Husserl calls the act of *identification* (*Aufweisung*), also called *evidence*, by which is meant the act of obtaining an intuitive insight of the coincidence between intention and intended.

Evidence, Heidegger insists, is both regional and universal (50–51; 68). It is regional in the sense that each intentional act, perception for instance, aims at a specific fulfillment and therefore has its specific evidence or revealing function with regard to its intentional correlate. It is also universal in the sense that it concerns all intentional acts. All this is present in Husserl's five lectures. Husserl's analysis of the perception of the house is done in terms of an example of regional evidence. Likewise the universality of evidence is emphasized by Husserl when, after having listed a series of regional evidences or givennesses, 'the givenness of universals, of predicates, of states of affair, (. . .) of an absurdity, of a contradiction, of non-existence', he concludes the list with these words: 'Uberall ist die Gegebenheit' (59; 74). Likewise, we find in *The Idea of Phenomenology* a retrieval by Husserl of what he had already taught in the sixth *Logical Investigation* about the relation intuition-expression. Heidegger summarizes that teaching very clearly: '*Assertions are acts of meaning*, and assertions in the sense of a formulated proposition are only specific forms of expressness, where expressness has the sense of expressing lived experiences or comportments through meaning. It is essentially owing to phenomenological investigations that this authentic sense of the expressing and the expressedness of all comportments was made fundamental and placed in the foreground of the question of the structure of the logical. This is not surprising when we consider that our comportments are in actual fact pervaded through and through by assertions, that they are always performed in some form of expressness. It is also a matter of fact that our simplest perceptions and constitutive states are already *expressed*, even more, are *interpreted* in a certain way' (56; 75). In this intrinsic expressness of each apprehension, categorial intuition is involved. When I give expression to my perception by saying that 'this thing is red', I do not merely announce that I now have a perception. I communicate what I perceive. 'A perceptual assertion is a communication about the entity perceived in perception and not about the act of perception as such' (57; 76). In my communication about the entity there are components which cannot be given in a merely sensory way: sensory universals, structures (like S–P), categories (all, and, or, but, etc.). Those components are in a position of surplus with regard to the strictly sensory datum here and now. However, they can be given to a non-sensory intuition, the categorial intuition. This intuition of a category is an act which is always founded in a simple founding act. But the founded is not a formal repetition of the founding on an ideal level. On the contrary 'the founded acts disclose the simply given objects *anew*, such that these objects come to explicit apprehension precisely in what they are' (62; 84) Here again our commentary suffices to show that one of the major themes in Husserl's five lectures is this discovery of which Heidegger acknowledges the significance of having opened 'the path of the understanding of universal objects and of the being of the ideal' thereby arriving 'at the form of research sought by ancient ontology' (72; 99).

3) The third discovery is what Heidegger calls 'the elaboration of the sense of the a priori' (72; 99). When dealing with this discovery Heidegger does not quote any specific text of Husserl. Moreover, he says right away that 'this discovery can be characterized more briefly 1) because despite some essential insights into phenomenology itself the a priori is still not made very clear, 2) because it is still by and large intertwined with traditional lines of inquiry, and 3) above all because the clarification of its sense really presupposes what we are seeking' *time*' (72; 99). This is a way of suggesting that Husserl's discovery of the a priori was insufficient. However, Heidegger praises Husserl for having shown, over against Descartes and Kant, 'that the a priori is not limited to the subjectivity' since it has a universal scope: there are essences not only in the field of the ideal but also in the sphere of the real and the material. Conse-

quently, says Heidegger, it is not a title for our intentional comportments, 'but a title for being (*Sein*)', more precisely, 'a feature of the being of entities and not a feature of entities themselves' (74–75; 102–103). In that sense 'it is not only nothing immanent, belonging primarily to the sphere of the subject, it is also nothing transcendent, specifically bound up with reality' (74; 101). The reservations here included in the praise lead us back to our problem and to the discernment of the points of obscurity.

Those are already alluded to by Heidegger in his presentation of the first discovery about which he writes this: 'Intentionality is not an ultimate explanation of the psychic, but an initial approach toward overcoming the uncritical application of traditionally defined realities such as the psychic, consciousness, continuity of lived experience, reason. But if such a task is implicit in this basic concept of phenomenology, then 'intentionality' is the very last word to be used as a phenomenological slogan. Quite the contrary, it identifies that whose disclosure would allow phenomenology to find itself in its possibilities' (47; 63). In other words, we are invited to transpose to Husserl himself what Husserl says about Descartes in the five lectures: for him 'to discover and to abandon were the same' (7; 10).

Husserl again and again insists that discovery requires sticking with a pure seeing of the matters themselves and avoiding uncritical presuppositions. But in each step in the train of thought of the five lectures it is possible to detect the presence of uncritical presuppositions.

About the preliminary step it can be objected that the so-called 'natural attitude' is not natural at all. As Heidegger puts it: 'For man's way of experience vis-à-vis the other and himself, is it his natural mode of considering (*Betrachtungsart*) to experience himself as ζῷον, as a living being, in this broadest sense as an object of nature which occurs in the world? In the natural way of experience, does man experience himself, to put it curtly, zoologically?' (113; 155). Is this characterization of everyday experience seen in the matters themselves, or is it projected by the philosopher upon everyday experience on the basis of 'a well-defined theoretical position, in which every entity is taken a priori as a lawfully regulated flow of occurrences in the spatio-temporal exteriority of the world'? (id.) The very fact that the ordinary experience is called an attitude is significant in this respect. One must indeed 'so to speak "place oneself into" /*hineinstellen*/ this way of considering things . . . in order to be able to experience in this manner. Man's natural manner of experience, by contrast, cannot be called an attitude' (id.). As a matter of fact the so-called natural attitude accords much better with the peculiar way modern scientists consider nature than with the everyday manner of experience.

To be sure, Husserl's phenomenology starts by bracketing the so-called natural attitude. But again this very bracketing is questionable insofar as it is motivated by what it puts in brackets. What is bracketed is an attitude 'for which every entity is taken a priori as a lawfully regulated flow of occurrences in the spatio-temporal exteriority of the world' or of nature as a whole. This attitude is supposed to encompass firstly the everyday experience of man, secondly the theoretical stand of modern scientist exploring nature, thirdly the attitude of the one who, while sharing the theoretical stand of the modern scientist, makes an epistemological theory of such a theoretical stand. The bracketing is motivated by the perplexities entailed by the third attitude. It claims to introduce a thoroughly new dimension. However, the very bracketing preserves at least two elements of the bracketed. It preserves the idea that the new dimension should be dealt with in terms of an epistemology or theory of knowledge in general. In other words the very bracketing tacitly admits the uncritical presupposition that intentionality falls de jure under the scope of a theory of knowledge. Moreover, it also preserves from the bracketed sphere the conviction that nature should be considered as a lawfully regulated flow of occurrences in the spatio-temporal exteriority. Evenso, this concept of a flow of occurrences is preserved in the immanent sphere to which the epoché gives access. Where else would the notion of a 'flow of *Erlebnisse*' come from if not from a concept of nature belonging to the bracketed sphere?

To be sure, the flow of occurrences called *Erlebnisse* has to be reduced again and again since the phenomenological seeing does not bear upon these *Erlebnisse* as occurrences but as intentionalities, not as existing events but as essential correlations. Nevertheless how could the immanent sphere, however pure and reduced it pretends to be, have another ontological status than the transcendent sphere if the only being (*Sein*) or existence grounding the essential intentional correlations has the status of an occurrence? Ontologically speaking, how could the immanent sphere have another status than the transcendent one? Ontologically speaking, how could it be more than an inverted transcendence? Isn't it significant in that respect that the only definition of metaphysics given by *The Idea of Phenomenology* is made in terms of a distinction between nature and mind, i.e., between two ontical spheres, without even raising the ontological question of the being (*Sein*) of those spheres, thereby giving the impression either than it must be taken for granted that their being has the same sense or that the sense of being is not a metaphysical issue? Does not the distinction between nature and mind go back to Descartes's distinction between *res extensa* and *res cogitans*? Is it not taken for granted by modern philosophy ever since Descartes, by Kant, by Hegel, by Neo-kantianism? Does not the very distinction indicate that in Husserl 'the thematic field of phenomenology is not derived phenomenologically by going back to the matters themselves but by going back to a traditional idea of philosophy'? (107; 147)

It might seem that *The Idea of Phenomenology* discards those questions and objections by making a clear distinction between being (*Sein*) in the transcendent sense of occurring and being in the absolute sense of Selfgivenness. But here again it can be replied right away that this very distinction is based upon an uncritical presupposition. Indeed the distinction is a repetition of the traditional distinction between existence and essence. And this only increases the uneasiness we try to express as far as the black spots are concerned.

As a matter of fact we look in vain in Husserl's text for a determination of the being of intentionality. As Heidegger puts it there are four determinations of being given by Husserl to pure consciousness. But in none of them is the being of the intentional really an issue. When, for example, consciousness is determined as *immanent being*, what is at issue is just a 'real inclusion in one another' (103; 142) of the reflecting experience and the reflected. This inclusion is an ontic relation between entities (the reflecting and the reflected) and not an ontological determination of consciousness. Immanence is also called 'the absolutely given being' or 'absolute being'. This second determination is in no way more ontological than the preceding one: it merely characterizes the way the reflected is apprehended by the reflecting within a region (consciousness) whose being is not determined thereby (104; 143). The third determination is also ontic. When he says that pure immanence *nulla re indiget ad existendum*, thereby meaning '*res*' in the sense of a transcendent entity which is not consciousness, Husserl again characterizes an ontic relation between entities, the subject and the object, the latter depending upon the former (104–106; 143–145). 'The fourth determination of being, which regards consciousness as *pure* being, is even less than the other three a characterization of the being of the intentional, that is, of the entity which is defined by the structure of intentionality' (106; 145). Indeed this being is pure because it is detached from all concrete individuation of a concrete entity. It is pure because it is 'ideal' and 'not real' (id.). Hence what is at issue in this characterization of consciousness as pure being is not the being of the entity which is intentional, but a universal essence.

Those four determinations, says Heidegger, show that what guides Husserl in his delimitation of the thematic field of phenomenology, and in the very use he makes of the notion of being, is not an ontological concern but the 'idea of an absolute science' (107; 147), an idea which again is not derived from the matters themselves but from a traditional definition of philosophy since Descartes.

Our commentary of Husserl's lectures shows that Heidegger's critical remarks are already quite relevant with regard to *The Idea of Phenomenology*. Heidegger condenses his critique by pointing out two basic neglects in Husserl's concept of the thematic field of phenomenology: 1) the neglect of the being of the intentional, and 2) the neglect of the question of the sense of being.

The first neglect means that Husserl's 'conception of ideation as disregard of real individuation lives in the belief that the what of any entity (*Seiend*) is to be defined by disregarding its existence' (110; 152). Such a disregard is already conspicuous in *The Idea of Phenomenology* where Husserl, as we have seen, insists that 'the crucial problem must have to do . . . not with human cognition, but with cognition in general, apart from any existential assumptions either of the empirical ego or of the real world' (60; 75–76). To this Heidegger objects: 'But if there were an entity whose 'what' is precisely to be and nothing but to be, then this ideative regard of such an entity would be the most fundamental of misunderstandings' (110; 152). Such an entity is the human Dasein, i.e., the sole intentional entity in Heidegger's view, an essentially individuated entity whose being cannot at all be fixed as a real natural occurrence, like it is eventually fixed by Husserl.

The second neglect is connected with the first one. Husserl's disregard of existence implies that he doesn't raise the question of the sense of being for the simple reason that he takes for granted that the only sense of being is natural occurrence.

Nevertheless the paradox in Heidegger's relation to Husserl is that he discovered these two neglects, not at all by discarding Husserl or by looking for a better inspiration in other philosophies, but by radicalizing the three discoveries we discussed above. There is, first, the *radicalization of intentionality*, which eliminates the duality *res extensa – res cogitans* that weighs upon Husserl's concept of intentionality. Once radicalized intentionality is no longer a mixture of transcendence and immanence, of a flow of *Erlebnisse* and of a detached realm of eidetic structures, or of existing occurrences and of pure essences. It is, instead, our openness to the entities that we are not and to ourself as an individuated entity whose essence is to be. In that sense the radicalization calls for an ontologization. The being of the intentional is our openness to our own individual possibility of being. It no longer falls under the scope of a theory of knowledge but under the scope of a new ontology. *Radicalization of the categorial intuition*. Under the title 'categorial intuition' Husserl discovers what in intentionality goes beyond all real occurrences. Intentionality includes an articulated set of ideas, structures, categories which are in a position of surplus with regard to those occurrences. But this discovery of a surplus is again limited by the dualistic framework transcendence-immanence which weighs upon the concept of intentionality. Once intentionality is transformed, through its radicalization, into our ontological openness, categorial intuition is no longer a title for what in immanence is in a position of surplus with regard to transcendence. It is a title for what in our openness to entities and to ourself as an entity goes beyond the real predicates of those entities and of ourself as an entity. Such a beyond is being (*Sein*). Once ontologized in its turn, categorial intuition amounts to the understanding of both the being of the entities other than ourself and of our own being. Once ontologized categorial intuition amounts to the understanding of the ontological difference. To this again Husserl was opening the way when, in his investigation about categorial intuition, he reappropriated Kant's thesis about being: being is no real predicate.[3] We understand that beings are, says Husserl, in the light of an a priori intuition of *being* (*Sein*) as a category. But this discovery again is limited by the transcendence-immanence framework, which means by the traditional prejudices according to which there is no other sense of being than occurring in the whole of nature. In other words, Husserl's discovery doesn't open the way to an interrogation about the sense of being, let alone to an interrogation about the possibility of an articulated horizon for understanding the senses of being (presence-at-hand, permanence, life, existence). In this interrogation Heidegger was led to radicalize reduction together with categorial intuition in such a way that reduction no longer meant the return to the noetic-noematic structures of immanence but to the articulated horizon for an articulated understanding of the senses of being. Such a return involves a *radicalization of the a priori*. Ultimately the radicalized a priori is time. Time as the ultimate dimension of our finite existence is the horizon from which we understand the various senses of being. But here again, Heidegger's discovery of the authentic time as the ultimate a priori is a radicalization of Husserl's discovery that the investigation of time is as he says in *Ideas I*: 'The fundamental consideration of phenomenology'.[4] But again this discovery which is already clearly anticipated in the fifth lecture of *The Idea of Phenomenology* is limited in Husserl by the transcendence-immanence framework. By recognizing that a 'retention' is inherent to the simplest *cogitatio*, Husserl acknowledges by the same token that nothing could appear, nothing could be an *intentum* for intentionality if consciousness were not intrinsically temporal, not in the sense of the repeated present which characterizes nature, but in the sense of an intrinsic articulation, in intentionality itself, between the acts of retention, presentification and protension. However, this discovery of time as the basic dimension of intentionality does not entail the recognition in intentionality of any deeper temporality than the one which is required in order for objects to appear, i.e., in order to make possible the appearing of entities whose being is precisely not the being of intentionality.

The paradoxes we have tried to formulate are far from being the only ones. At least they explain why Heidegger, after having emphasized the prejudices which in Husserl limit the possibilities of phenomenology may conclude: 'It almost goes without saying that even today I still regard myself as a learner in relation to Husserl' (121; 168).

Notes

1. We quote according to both the English translation: Edmund Husserl, *The Idea of Phenomenology*, trans. W.P. Alston and G. Nakhnikian, (The Hague; Nijhoff, 1964) and the original German text: *Die Idee der Phanomenologie*, ed. Walter Biemel, Husserliana II, second edition (Nijhoff, 1958). The first figure or figures in brackets refers to the English translation; the second one(s) refers to the German text. We often had to modify the translation.
2. We quote according to both the English translation' Martin Heidegger, *History of the Concept of Time,* trans. Th. Kisiel (Bloomington: Indiana University Press, 1985) and the original German text: *Prolegomena zur Geschichte des Zeitbegriffs*, ed. Petra Jaeger, *Gesamtausgabe* 20 (Frankfurt am Main: Klostermann, 1979). Again the first figure refers to the English text, the second one to the original.
3. Cf. our essay: 'Heidegger and Husserl's Logical Investigations' in Jacques Taminiaux, *Dialectic and Difference* (Atlantic Highlands, NJ: Humanities Press, 1985), pp. 91–114.
4. The phrase is in the title of part two of *Ideas* I.

Heidegger's *Lehrjahre*

THOMAS SHEEHAN
Loyola University of Chicago

For Prof. Otto Pöggeler

1. Heidegger's *Habilitation*

By July of 1915 the young Dr. Martin Heidegger was ready to apply for a license to teach at Freiburg University.[1] Two years earlier, in the summer of 1913, he had obtained the doctorate in philosophy with his inaugural dissertation, *The Doctrine of Judgment in Psychologism.* He had then set to work on his qualifying dissertation (*Habilitationsschrift*), but events had conspired to interrupt him. On August 1, 1914 the First World War broke out, and between August and October Heidegger was in and out of active military service twice, both times with Infantry Reserve Battalion 113, once as a volunteer (ca. August 2–10, 1914) and once as a draftee (October 9–20, 1914). In both cases he was dismissed for reasons of health.[2]

By the spring of 1915 Heidegger, then twenty-five years of age, had managed to finish his qualifying dissertation, *Duns Scotus' Doctrine of Categories and Meaning,*[3] under the directorship of Professor Heinrich Rickert.[4] (Husserl was still at Göttingen and would begin teaching in Freiburg as Rickert's successor only in the spring of 1916). On Friday, July 2, 1915, Heidegger formally presented the work to the Philosophy Department for their approval, and in an accompanying letter he petitioned for a qualifying examination:

Freiburg in Breisgau
July 2, 1915

To the Esteemed Philosophy Department of the University of Freiburg.

Concerning the application of Dr. Phil. Martin Heidegger of Messkirch (Baden) for the licence to teach:

The undersigned respectfully submits his treatise, *Duns Scotus' Doctrine of Categories and Meaning,* to the esteemed Philosophy Department of the University of Freiburg in Breisgau.

J.C. Sallis, G. Moneta and J. Taminiaux (eds.), The Collegium Phaenomenologicum, 77–137.
© *Kluwer Academic Publishers.*

If this treatise should be found to be scientifically adequate, the undersigned then respectfully requests the esteemed Philosophy Department to grant him the *venia legendi* in philosophy.

If he should be admitted to the examination, the undersigned wishes to submit to the esteemed Philosophy Department the following three [topics] as [possible] themes of the requisite trial lecture:
first, the concept of time in history
second, the logical problem of the question
third, the concept of number.

With highest regards, he remains the esteemed Philosophy Faculty's most respectful

Martin Heidegger[5]

Philosophy Department regulations dating back to 1894 required that along with this letter and other documents, the candidate supply the department with 'a rather detailed curriculum vitae' (*ein ausführliches curriculum vitae*).[6] Heidegger complied by submitting an extraordinary, handwritten 749-word *Lebenslauf*. This curriculum vitae, which forms the centerpiece of the present essay, I shall call 'CV-1915.'

Two years earlier, on June 30, 1913, when he submitted his inaugural doctoral dissertation on the theory of judgment to the Philosophy Department, Heidegger had also turned in a much briefer (130-word) handwritten curriculum vitae, which I shall call 'CV-1913.' (The original text of CV-1913, heretofore unpublished, appears below in Part Two, Section III.) A slightly *amended* form of CV-1913 was published in 1914 at the end of the book-version of the doctoral dissertation, *Die Lehre vom Urteil im Psychologismus,* and has since appeared in an English translation. This slightly amended version of CV-1913 I shall call 'CV-1914.'[7]

However, the *Lebenslauf* that we are concerned with here – CV-1915, which Heidegger submitted with his qualifying dissertation on July 2, 1915 – goes far beyond the two earlier texts and provides important insights into how the young scholar developed from his high school days, through his university studies, to his post-graduate work. I present here an English version of CV-1915, made from the original handwritten text of five oversized pages that Heidegger submitted to the Philosophy Department. The paragraph breaks are Heidegger's own, and the numbers in brackets indicate the page breaks in his text.

Curriculum Vitae
1915

I, Martin Heidegger, born on September 26, 1889 in Messkirch (Baden), the son of the sexton and master cooper Friedrich Heidegger and of his wife Johanna née Kempf, attented elementary and middle school in Messkirch. Beginning in 1900 I received private instruction in Latin, so that in 1903 I was able to enter the third-year class [*Unterteria*] of the Gymnasium in Constance. I am grateful to Dr. Konrad Gröber, at that time the rector of the minor seminary and currently the pastor of Constance, for decisive intellectual influence. After completing the third year of high school [*Untersekunda*] I attended the Berthold Gymnasium in Freiburg in Breisgau until reception of the high-school baccalaureate (summer 1909).

During the fourth year [*Obersekunda*], when instruction in mathematics got away from merely solving problems and moved more onto theoretical tracks, my preference for this discipline became a really focussed interest [p. 2], which extended to physics as well. Incentives for this came from religion classes, which led me to do extensive reading in the theory of biological evolution.

In the last year of high school it was above all the Plato classes of Gymnasium Professor Widder, who died some years ago, that introduced me to philosophical problems more consciously, but not yet with theoretical rigor.

After completing the Gymnasium, I entered the University of Freiburg in Breisgau in the winter semester of 1909, and I remained there without interruption until 1913. At first I studied theology. The lecture courses in philosophy that were prescribed at the time did not satisfy me much, so I resorted to studying Scholastic textbooks on my own. They provided me with a certain formal-logical schooling, but as regards philosophy they did not give me what I was looking for and had [already] found in the areas of apologetics through the works of Herman Schell.

Besides the *Small Summa* of Thomas Aquinas and individual works of Bonaventura it was the *Logische Untersuchungen* of Edmund Husserl that [p. 3] were decisive for the process of my scientific development. At the same time the earlier work of the same author, *Die Philosophie der Arithmetik,* placed mathematics in a whole new light for me.

My intense engagement with philosophical problems, along with the tasks of my own professional studies [in theology] resulted, after three semesters, in severe exhaustion.

My heart-trouble, which had come about earlier from too much sports, broke out so severely that any later employment in the service of the Church was taken to be extremely questionable. Therefore in the winter semester of 1911–1912 I had myself enrolled in the Department of Natural Sciences and Mathematics.

My philosophical interest was not lessened by the study of mathematics; on the contrary, since I no longer had to follow the compulsory lecture courses in philosophy, I could attend a great quantity of lecture courses in philosophy and above all could take part in the seminar exercises with Herr Geheimrat Rickert. In this new school [p. 4] I learned first and foremost to understand philosophical problems as problems, and I acquired insight into the essence of logic, the philosophical discipline that still interests me most. At the same time I acquired a correct understanding of modern philosophy from Kant on, a matter that I found sparsely and inadequately treated in the Scholastic literature. My basic philosophical convictions remained those of Aristotelian-Scholastic philosophy. With time I recognized that the intellectual wealth stored up in it must permit of – indeed, demands – a broad, fruitful exploitation and utilization. Therefore in my dissertation on *Die Lehre vom Urteil im Psychologismus* I took my bearings both from modern logic and from basic Aristotelian-Scholastic views and tried to find a basis for further investigations regarding a central problem of logic and epistemology. On the basis of this work I was allowed by the Philosophy Department of Freiburg University to take the oral examination for the doctorate, which I passed on July 26, 1913.

The study of Fichte and Hegel, [p. 5] intense engagement with Rickert's *Die Grenzen der naturwissenschaftlichen Begriffsbildung,* the investigations of Dilthey, and not least of all lecture courses and seminar exercises with Herr Geheimrat Finke, resulted in the fact that my aversion to history, nurtured in me by my predilection for mathematics, was thoroughly destroyed. I recognized that philosophy should not be oriented onesidedly, either to mathematics and natural science or to history, but that the latter, precisely as the history of spirit [*Geistesgeschichte*], can fructify philosophy to a far greater degree.

My increasing interest in history facilitated in me an intense engagement with the philosophy of the Middle Ages, an engagement that I recognized as necessary for a fundamental development of Scholasticism. For me this engagement consists not primarily in a presentation of the historical relations between individual thinkers but rather in an interpretative understanding of the theoretical content of their philosophy. Thus my investigation into [p. 6] *Die Kategorien- und Bedeutungslehre des Duns Scotus* came about.

This investigation likewise generated in me the plan of a comprehensive presentation of medieval logic and psychology in the light of modern phenomenology, with equal consideration of the historical position of individual medieval thinkers. If I am permitted to take on the duties of scientific research and teaching, my life's work will be dedicated to the development of this plan.[8]

Thus far CV-1915, an extraordinary text for the information it provides on the earliest intellectual development of a man now recognized as one of the century's greatest thinkers. Of particular interest is the light it sheds on Heidegger's 'pre-phenomenological' *Lehrjahre,* that is, his training in philosophy before he met Edmund Husserl in the spring of 1916. However, in 1915 the document was probably read by the Philosophy Faculty (if it was read at all) simply as a pro-forma statement required of one more young scholar who was about to finish his studies. In any case Heidegger handed it in along with a copy of his book-length manuscript and his letter petitioning the examination.

Some two weeks later, on July 19, Professor Heinrich Rickert, who had directed the dissertation, wrote up a long and very positive evaluation (*Gutachten*) of the manuscript and recommended that Heidegger be admitted to the licensing examination.[9] Of the three topics that Heidegger, in his letter of July 2, had proposed he be tested on, the Philosophy Faculty chose the first; and therefore on Tuesday, July 27, 1915, Heidegger delivered his trial lecture on 'The Concept of Time in the Science of History.'[10] Later that day the dean of the Philosophy Department, professor of medieval history Heinrich Finke, forwarded a copy of Heidegger's curriculum vitae, along with Rickert's evaluation of the manuscript, to the University's Academic Senate. His accompanying memo said:

> I have the honor of informing the Academic Senate that the Philosophy Faculty has decided to confer the *venia legendi* in philosophy upon Martin Heidegger, who was born in Messkirch on September 26, 1889 and who was promoted to doctor in philosophy in Freiburg on July 26, 1913, and who has fulfilled the prescribed requirements for admission to teaching. I request that the Senate recommend the approval of the licencing on the part of the Grand Ducal Ministry of Education. I am appending [Rickert's] written evaluation of the inaugural dissertation, as well as Dr. Heidegger's curriculum vitae.
>
> Finke
> Dean[11]

The next day the Academic Senate made the recommendation that Finke requested, and on Saturday, July 31, the Grand Duchy of Baden's Ministry of Education in Karlsruhe concurred with the Philosophy Department's decision. On Thursday, August 5, Heidegger was informed by the university that he was now officially a *Privatdozent.*[12]

Two weeks later, on Wednesday, August 18, Heidegger was again drafted into the army for what was to be his third, but not last, stint in the military. By September 18 he was training in Müllheim (Berlin) as a rifleman with Reserve Battalion 142 of the Second Infantry Regiment, but he took sick again and spent some weeks recuperating in a hospital. On Saturday October 16 he was exempted from duty and sent back to Freiburg to work in a military capacity in the office of the Postal Censor (*Postüberwachungsstelle*). He began the job on Monday, the first of November.[13]

The academic semester had already officially begun, but Privatdozent Heidegger applied for a teaching assignment even while keeping his military job in the Post Office.[14] By Wednesday, October 27, he had submitted his application and his *Standesliste,* and during the second week of November 1915 he officially initiated his teaching career with the lecture course *Grundlinien der antiken und scholastischen Philosophie.*[15] He chose the topic of the course on the advice of his friend and colleague, Father Engelbert Krebs (1881–1950), a Privatdozent in theology, who at that time was also standing in as an adjunct professor of Christian Philosophy.[16] The course was supposed to meet for two hours per week, but given his duties in the Post Office Heidegger arranged matters so that the course met for four hours every other week.[17] Among the twenty-one students enrolled in the lecture was one Fräulein Elfriede Petri from Wiesbaden. A year later she and Heidegger would be engaged to be married.[18]

2. A Commentary on CV-1915

The text of CV-1915, composed in late June of 1915, is made up of eleven paragraphs that correspond to four stages of the young Heidegger's education prior to his personal encounter with Edmund Husserl. I propose to comment on CV-1915 under each of these four headings.

I. (¶¶ 1–3): *1895 to 1909, age 6-19:* Grammar school and high school, culminating in the baccalaureate.

II. (¶¶ 4–7): *1909 to 1911, age 20-21:* First phase of higher education: Theological studies at Freiburg University.

III. (¶¶ 8-9): *1911 to 1913, age 22-23:* Second phase of higher education: Study of mathematics, natural sciences, and philosophy at Freiburg University, culminating in the inaugural dissertation and the Ph.D. in philosophy.

IV. (¶¶ 9–11): *1913 to 1915, age 22–25:* Preparation of the qualifying dissertation for the *Habilitation* at Freiburg University.

I. 1895–1909, age 6–19: Grammar school and high school

Volksschule: 1895–1899, age 6–9. Heidegger was born on September 26, 1889, in Messkirch (the medieval Mösskirch), Grand Duchy of Baden, at what is now #16 Kolpingstrasse. All of his academic education, from the very beginning through university studies, would take place in state schools, where, in fact, religious instruction was provided.[19]

Since 1873 Messkirch had had a *Kleinkinderschule* or Kindergarten (today called the *Städtischer Kindergarten*), and Martin Heidegger may well have attended it. In the fall of 1895, when he was six years of age, he entered the first grade of the *Volksschule* or primary school in Messkirch. Today the building (now the *Hochschule*) still stands in Schlossstrasse, on the Kirchberg in the center of town, just west of St. Martin's Church and the District Court (*Amtsgericht*). Since 1904, however, the classes of the elementary school have met in the new school building in Conradin-Kreutzer-Strasse, a few blocks northeast of the Kirchberg. The old building now houses a Progymnasium.

Bürgerschule: 1899–1903, age 10–13. In CV-1913 (see Section III below) Heidegger mentions that in the fall of 1899 – therefore, at ten years of age – he entered the first year of the *Bürgerschule,* at that time housed in the same building as the *Volksschule* on Schlossstrasse.[20] This would correspond to the fifth grade in the United States system. A photograph of the ten-year-old student, looking just a bit shy, was published some years ago.[21]

It is probable that during the first year of the *Bürgerschule* Heidegger's parents, at the suggestion of the local Catholic clergyman Father Camillo Brandhuber (1860–1931), began planning an ecclesiastical career for young Martin as a priest of the Archdiocese of Freiburg.[22] From CV-1915 we learn that a year later, in the equivalent of the American sixth grade, Heidegger began private lessons in Latin (almost certainly under the instruction of Father Brandhuber) in order to prepare for eventual admission to the minor seminary and the liberal arts high school in Constance, some thirty miles south of Messkirch. In the summer of 1903, after the equivalent of the American eighth grade, he was graduated from the *Bürgerschule* with three years of Latin under his belt. In the archives of the Archdiocese of Freiburg, in the registration lists for the school year 1903–1904, there is a note that says: 'Martin Heidegger, 26. IX. 1889 Messkirch. Preparation: Has completed the 3rd class of the *Realschule* there and wants to enter freshman class.'[23]

High school in Constance: 1903–1906, age 14–16. In October of 1903, having just turned fourteen years of age, Martin Heidegger left home and began what would turn out to be eight years of preparation for the Roman Catholic priesthood. He entered the equivalent of the freshman year of high school at the State Gymnasium in Constance, and at the same time took up residence in Konradihaus, the archdiocesan *Gymnasialkonvikt* or *Knabenkonvikt* (high school seminary or minor seminary) that had been named after the city's patron saint. There he would live for the next three years while pursuing the first half of his secondary education (*Untertertia, Obertertia,* and *Untersekunda,* corresponding to the lower and upper fourth forms and the lower fifth form in the British system).[24] We should note that at this point Heidegger was *not* studying to become a Jesuit priest. That brief adventure would begin in the fall of 1909, after he had completed high school, and it would last only two weeks.

In 1903 the rector of Konradihaus was the 32-year-old Father Conrad Gröber (1872–1948), who had taken the position in August of 1901 and who would remain in close touch with the school and its students even after being appointed pastor of Trinity Church in Constance in 1905.[25] He was a native of Messkirch and a graduate (1891) of the very Gymnasium that Heidegger was entering. As the fall term began, Father Gröber was just beginning to write his book on the history of the city's Jesuit Gymnasium and Collegium, in celebration of the up-coming tricentennial of their founding in 1604.[26] But neither the Collegium nor the Gymnasium were Jesuit schools any longer. In 1774, a year after Pope Clement XIV had suppressed the Society of Jesus, both the Collegium and the Gymnasium had been secularized, and they remained so thereafter. And Konradihaus, the seminary where Heidegger lived while attending the State Gymnasium, was under the direction of the archdiocesan clergy, not the Jesuits.

The question of how Heidegger's fees at the seminary would be paid was not a simple matter, for the Heidegger family, while not impoverished, was also not rich. Martin's father, Friedrich, at that time fifty-two years of age and the sexton of the parish church at Messkirch, had a total net worth of only 2000 marks and a yearly income tax assessment of 960 marks. (In American dollars at that time those amounts would be, respectively, about $475 and $230.) Occasionally he supplemented his income by exercising his old trade of barrel-making.[27] In any case, as Father Gröber told the archdiocesan chancellery office in Freiburg, Herr Heidegger could afford nothing towards the feeding and housing of his son at Konradihaus. The chancellery office nonetheless insisted on a yearly fee of 100 marks (about $24). In response Gröber wrote to the chancellery office on Saturday, October 10, 1903:

> Pastor C[amillo] Brandhuber in Messkirch and the undersigned request a change in the cost of maintenance [at Konradihaus] in the case of Martin Heidegger, of freshman class 'B.' From familiarity with the financial situation of the family, the undersigned knows for a fact that Heidegger's father can contribute not much more than 75 marks [$18]. The student is upright and talented.[28]

The chancellery office accepted this proposal. To subsidize this cost, Brandhuber approached the local Weiss Foundation[29] in Messkirch and obtained a grant for Heidegger of 100 marks for the year 1903–1904. But when the Church official in Freiburg heard that Heidegger had received the Weiss grant, he again wrote Gröber, this time to insist that the rector set an even higher fee.[30] Gröber responded proposing a fee of 150 marks ($36) per year, fifty of which, of course, would have to come from Friedrich Heidegger's pocket. The official accepted the proposal. A year or two later, when the Weiss Foundation increased Heidegger's annual award to 300 marks (about $71), the archdiocese raised the student's yearly assessment so as to equal that amount. But at least Friedrich Heidegger no longer had to pay anything to maintain his son at Konradihaus.

In the normal course of events, the young Heidegger would have completed all six years of high school in Constance. However, during his third year at the Gymnasium, that is, in the *Untersekunda,* Heidegger received yet another award, an Eliner Grant, for eventual studies at Freiburg University leading to the doctorate in theology. The grant, which at that time had a ceiling of 400 marks ($95) per year, had been initiated in the sixteenth century by Fr. Christoph Eliner (1538–1575), a theologian from Messkirch, and in fact it tended to favor young men from that town. The grant was properly intended for university students, but it could be applied as well to an upper-division Gymnasium student so long as he enrolled in the Berthold Gymnasium in Freiburg and later matriculated in the Theology Department of the university there.[31] And so in the fall of 1906 the 17-year-old Heidegger transferred to Freiburg to complete his final three years of Gymnasium and to prepare for university studies in theology.[32]

High school in Freiburg, 1906–1909, age 17–19. In Freiburg as in Constance, Heidegger took up residence at the *Gymnasialkonvikt* or *Internat,* the minor seminary, in this case located in the northern section of Freiburg at no. 11 Zähringenstrasse.[33] For his high school courses he attended the Berthold Gymnasium, which at that time was located in the center of the city on the northwest corner of Bertoldstrasse and Rotteckstrasse (now Rotteckring), kitty-corner from the local synagogue.[34] (The buildings were destroyed during a bombing attack on the night of Monday, November 27, 1944.) This Gymnasium too, like the one in Constance, was a state school. Here Heidegger would complete the *Obersekunda,* the *Unterprima,* and the *Oberprima,* corresponding to the upper fifth form and the lower and upper sixth forms of the British system. Photographs of Heidegger during each of these three school years have been published in Walter Biemel's *Martin Heidegger.*[35]

In CV-1915 Heidegger mentions that during his first year at the Berthold Gymnasium, 1906–1907, he got caught up in the study of mathematics, a subject that he would continue to pursue during his university career.[36] But his interests during that first year also extended to physics and even, via fairly liberal classes in religion, to evolution.

> During *Obersekunda,* when instruction in mathematics got away from merely solving problems and moved more onto theoretical tracks, my preference for this discipline became a really focussed interest, which extended to physics as well. Incentives for this came from religion classes, which led me to do extensive reading in the theory of biological evolution.

All this was happening at a time when the Catholic Pontifical Biblical Commission was issuing hopelessly conservative rulings on the historicity of the Pentateuch and just a few months before the Vatican would launch its campaign against 'Modernism.'[37]

The man who provided the incentives for the young student's interest in evolution was apparently Father Leonhard Schanzenbach (1852–1938), the rector of the minor seminary on Zähringsenstrasse where Heidegger lived, and at the same time Heidegger's teacher of religion and Hebrew at Berthold Gymnasium during his three years at the state school.[38] The course of religious studies at Berthold Gymnasium followed the program laid out in the theological manuals for high school students written by Father Theodor Dreher (1836–1916), then a canon of Freiburg Cathedral. Thus, in his first year at the Gymnasium Heidegger studied Catholic apologetics, followed in the second year by the Catholic doctrine of faith, modern Church history, and the Gospel of St. John, and in last year by Catholic moral doctrine.[39] It may well have been during his years at the Berthold Gymnasium that the young student began reading the controversial works of the famous but suspect Catholic theologian, Father Herman Schell, who had died just a few months before Heidegger transferred from Constance to Freiburg. We shall return to this matter later.

During the summer of 1907, after he had completed this first year at Freiburg, Heidegger, seventeen years of age, discovered Aristotle.[40] Heidegger was on vacation, and Father Gröber, who at that point had been pastor of Trinity Church in Constance for two years, presented his former student with a published copy of Franz Brentano's 1862 doctoral dissertation *On the several senses of 'Being' in Aristotle,*[41] thereby stirring up in him what would later become the question about the meaning of being.[42]

Whatever may have transpired during Heidegger's second year at the Berthold Gymnasium, this third or senior year (*Oberprima,* 1908–1909) was particularly fruitful for him in four distinct areas.

First, having worked his way time and again through the Brentano dissertation, Heidegger finally went to the source. As a senior high school student Heidegger checked out of the library Aristotle's collected works – presumably the whole set – and began, as he says, to puzzle over them at his reading desk.

Second, Heidegger exhibited an intense interest in German literature. The year before coming to Berthold Gymnasium he had already discovered the works of Adelbert Stifter (see note 32 above). Now during his senior year he began studying the major works of Lessing, Goethe, and Schiller under the guidance of Professor Friedrich Widder, his teacher of German. Moreover, outside of class he organized a private circle of students for the purpose of reading and discussing works of literature. This high school literary circle was still in existence eight years later, when the young Franz Josef Brecht – eventually professor of philosophy and rector at the University of Mannheim – became its head.[43] And during 1908, perhaps in the spring, Heidegger discovered a paperback edition of Hölderlin's poems, which in fact he brought with him to the front in World War One and continued to cherish well into his later years.[44] The young student must have exhibited a deep passion for these works, for in evaluating him at the end of his high school career (the text is provided below) Father Schanzenbach would write that Heidegger's other courses tended to suffer from his over-zealous interest in German literature.

Third, during that same academic year Professor Widder also introduced Heidegger to Plato during an advanced course in Greek. In CV-1915 Heidegger writes:

> In the senior year of high school it was above all the Plato classes of Gymnasium Professor Widder, who died some years ago, that introduced me to philosophical problems more consciously, but not yet with theoretical rigor.

Professor Hugo Ott has provided a list of the authors treated in Widder's Greek course. Only one dialogue of Plato, the *Euthyphro,* was studied during the course. The other works read were: Thucydides, *History of the Peloponnesian War,* Books VI and VII, Homer, *The Iliad,* Books XIII–XXIV, Sophocles, *Oedipus Tyrannus,* and Euripides, *Iphigeneia in Tauris* read in conjuction with Goethe's *Iphigenie auf Tauris.*[45]

Fourth and finally, yet another philosophical influence, one that would carry over into his university studies, affected the young Heidegger during his *Oberprima* year:

> In my last year at the Gymnasium I stumbled upon the book of Carl Braig, then professor of dogmatics at Freiburg University, *Vom Sein. Abriss der Ontologie* ['On Being: An Outline of Ontology']. It had been published in 1896, at the time when the author had been an associate professor of philosophy in the Freiburg theology department. At the end of the larger sections of the work there are always extensive passages from Aristotle, Thomas Aquinas, and Suarez, as well as the etymology of the words for basic ontological concepts.[46]

Almost fifty years later, it was with great fondness that Heidegger recalled those six years of high school. In a speech delivered when he was received into the Heidelberg Academy of Sciences in 1957 he said:

> At the liberal arts high schools in Constance and Freiburg in Breisgau, between 1903 and 1909, I enjoyed fruitful learning under excellent teachers of Greek, Latin, and German. Besides my formal schooling, during this period, I came upon that which would abide.[47]

Those years came to a successful conclusion on Tuesday, July 13, 1909, when

Heidegger passed the requisite *Abitur* or baccalaureate examination. Twenty-eight students were graduated from the high school that year, and Heidegger along with four others came out in the first category. Both in deportment (*Betragen*) and in application or diligence (*Fleiss*) he received grades of *gut*. In his academic subjects, on a scale of 1 = *sehr gut,* 2 = *gut,* and 3 = *befriedigt* ('satisfactory'), he received the following grades:

religion:	$1^1/_2$	mathematics:	2 (overall)
German:	$1^1/_2$	algebra:	$1^1/_2$ and 3
German essay:	2	geometry:	2 (overall)
Latin:	2	history:	1. 2, $1^1/_2$
Greek:	2	physics:	3
French:	2	philosophy:	2
Hebrew:	2	singing:	2
English:	no grade recorded	gymnastics:	1

Heidegger's overall evaluation (*'Notesumme bzw. Durchschnitts oder Gesamtprädikat'*) is listed as 'I', that is, the highest level. Under *Bemerkungen* ('Remarks') in his examination record there is written simply the name of the subject that Heidegger intended to pursue in his university studies: 'Theol.'[48]

Two months after graduation, on Saturday, September 10, 1909, Father Schanzenbach drafted his own report on Heidegger's years at the Berthold Gymnasium:

> Martin Heidegger, born in Messkirch on September 26, [18]89 as the son of the sacristan there, entered the *Obersekunda* in this city from the Gymnasium and seminary in Constance because his reception of an Eliner Grant required that he change institutions. His natural talent as well as his diligence and moral comportment are good. His character already has a certain maturity, and even in his studies he was independent; in fact, at times he pursued German literature – in which he is very well read – a bit too much, to the detriment of other disciplines.
>
> Definite in his choice of a theological vocation and inclined to life in a religious order, he probably will apply for acceptance into the Society of Jesus.
>
> Freiburg, September 10, 1909 Schanzenbach, Rector.

II. 1909–1911, age 20–21: Theological studies at Freiburg University

The Jesuit influence: Fall, 1909ff.: age 19ff. The fourth paragraph of CV-1915 begins: 'After completing the Gymnasium, I entered the University of Freiburg in Breisgau in the winter semester of 1909 . . .' But that is not entirely correct. Rather, on Thursday, September 30, 1909, Martin Heidegger interrupted his training for the secular or archdiocesan priesthood and entered the Jesuit novitiate of Tisis in Feldkirch. There he remained only two weeks, until Wednesday, October 13.[50] Rev. J.A. McDowell, S.J., reports:

> Having finished his high school studies, Heidegger in 1909 entered the Novitiate of the German Province of the Society of Jesus, at that time located in Feldkirch, (Austria) [near the border with Lichtenstein]. But his stay with the Jesuits was of brief duration. After some weeks he was dismissed for reasons of health.[51]

After his fortnight as a Jesuit novice Heidegger returned to Freiburg and resumed his studies towards the archdiocesan priesthood. For his academic courses he enrolled in the Theology Department of Freiburg University.[52] But for the purposes of his spiritual training he moved into the Archdiocesan Theological Seminary, officially known as the *Erzbischöfliches Theologische Konvikt* or *Grossherzliches Collegium Theologicum,* but popularly called the Sapientia or Sapienz from the name of the original institution founded in 1497, the Collegium Sapientiae.[53] Rebuilt after being bombed in World War II, it is still at the same location as in 1909, on Burgerstrasse (now Schoferstrasse) near Herrenstrasse, a block east of the Freiburg Cathedral; and then, as now, it stood cheek by jowl with the Freiburg's Protestant Seminary, founded in 1859.

Although from the fall of 1909 onwards Heidegger was no longer training for the Jesuit priesthood, he did not entirely escape the religious and intellectual influence of the Jesuits, for as Father McDowell points out:

> in the [arch]diocesan seminary of Freiburg in Breisgau, where Heidegger lived for two years [1909–1911], the spiritual direction of the students was put in the hands of the Jesuits. In those circumstances Heidegger would have made the *Spiritual Exercises* [of St. Ignatius of Loyola] more than once.[54]

When he was at Feldkirch Heidegger of course could not have made the full thirty-day retreat using St. Ignatius' treatise. Nonetheless, it is likely that once a year he did make a four- or five-day retreat at the Sapientia, using the *Spiritual Exercises.*

The theology years: 1909 to 1911, age 20–21. In the four paragraphs of CV-1915 that are devoted to his theology years, Heidegger mentions that

1. his course work in philosophy, which was specially programmed for theology students, did not satisfy him;
2. his extracurricular reading included:
   a) Scholastic textbooks, which gave him training in formal logic but likewise did not satisfy him;
   b) the works of Herman Schell, which let him find what he was looking for in the area of apologetics;

c) Thomas Aquinas' *Compendium Theologiae* ('the *Small Summa*') and certain works of Bonaventure;
d) Edmund Husserl's *Logical Investigations* and *The Philosophy of Arithmetic,* both of which influenced him considerably, if in different degrees;

3. his health had seriously deteriorated by the spring of 1911, and the recurrence of a chronic heart problem caused him to abandon his studies for the priesthood by the summer of that year.

Regarding Heidegger's extracurricular readings in medieval texts, CV-1915 does not mention which treatises of Bonaventure he read, but it is likely that among them was the *Itinerarium mentis in Deum* ('The Journey of the Mind to God,' 1259), selections from which Heidegger had first encountered when he read Braig's *Vom Sein* in the last year of high school. When he mentions the *Small Summa,* he is referring to the 256 questions of the incomplete *Compendium Theologiae* that Aquinas wrote in his mature years and devoted to such questions as God as one and triune, creation, and the humanity of Christ. (Heidegger would later call Aquinas' full *Summa Theologiae,* like all medieval *Summae,* 'a manual for beginners.'[55]) Thomas Aquinas was, it would seem, a natural choice for someone living at the Sapientia. Almost two decades later, on May 18, 1927, Heidegger remarked in his course *Die Grundprobleme der Phänomenologie:*

> Since Thomas [Aquinas] is taken before all others to be the authoritative Scholastic, and is also given ecclesiastical preference, the Jesuits, who side in their doctrine [of essence and existence] with Suarez (who himself doubtless saw the problem most acutely and correctly), at the same time have an interest in associating their view with that of Thomas.[56]

As regards Heidegger's course work, Dr. Bernhard Casper has recently generated a list of the theology and philosophy lectures for which Heidegger was officially registered during his four semesters of theology at Freiburg University, and from that list we note that over those two years Heidegger was formally enrolled in only two philosophy courses, one in logic and one in metaphysics.[57] In the paragraphs that follow I provide a translation of Casper's list, with some notes of my own interspersed. The number of hours indicated after each professor's name indicates academic hours per week. Winter semesters officially began on October 15 and ran through late February, whereas summer semesters began on April 15 and ran until the middle or end of July. Classes usually started a week or two after the official opening date of the semester.

First semester: winter 1909–1910, age 20.

1. An Encyclopaedia of Theological Sciences, [Rev. Julius Mayer,[58] two hours.]

2. Introduction to the Sacred Scripture of the Old Testament. [Rev. Gottfried Hoberg,[59] four hours.]
3. Exegesis of Paul's Letter to the Romans. [Rev. Simon Weber,[60] four hours.]
4. General History of the Church, Part One, with particular consideration of the period following [the Council of] Nicea (in A.D. 325). [Rev. Georg Pfeilschifter,[61] four hours.]
5. Theory of Religion [Rev. Heinrich Straubinger,[62] three hours.]
6. Logic. [Prof. Johann Uebinger[63] (Philosophy Department), four hours.]

Elsewhere Heidegger has mentioned that his interest in Husserl went back to this first semester at Freiburg University. In those early years, he says, he continued to rely on Brentano's book on Aristotle as 'the "rod and staff" of my first awkward attempts to penetrate into philosophy.' Therefore, having 'learned from many references in philosophy journals that Husserl's thought was determined by Brentano,' Heidegger 'expected from Husserl's *Logische Untersuchungen* [1900, 1901] a decisive advance into the questions stimulated by Brentano's dissertation,' especially the question about the meaning of being.

> The major academic work for theology still left enough time for philosophy, which belonged to the curriculum anyway. So it was that from my first semester [at the university] the two volumes of Husserl's *Logische Untersuchungen* stood on my desk in the Theological Seminary. These volumes belonged to the university library. The due date could be easily renewed again and again. The work was obviously of little interest to the students.[64]

But although he poured over Husserl's work, Heidegger got no help for the question about the meaning of being. He writes: '[M]y efforts were in vain because I was not searching in the right way. I realized this only very much later.'[65] As he reports in paragraph 8 of CV-1915, Heidegger's philosophical orientation was, and for another four or five years would remain, that of an Aristotelian Scholastic, and no doubt that orientation impeded his appropriation of the radicalness of Husserl's thought. 'My understanding of the term "phenomenological" was', he admits, 'limited and vacillating . . .' It could well be that, given his convictions about Aristotelian and neo-Scholastic realism, the young Heidegger misread Husserl in a way that Edith Stein later described as common among Husserl's disciples:

> The *Logische Untersuchungen* had caused a sensation primarily because it appeared to be a radical departure from the critical idealism of the Kantian and neo-Kantian variety. People saw in it a 'new Scholasticism' because it turned attention away from the 'subject' and toward 'things' [*Sachen*]. *Knowledge* again appeared as a *receiving* that took its laws from objects and

> not, as criticism would have it, as an act of *determining* that imposes its laws upon things. All the young phenomenologists were confirmed realists.[66]

Heidegger himself would certainly evidence his preference for a modified form of such realism in his first philosophy article, published two years later, 'Das Realitätsproblem in der modernen Philosophie' (1912).

Second semester: summer 1910, age 20.

1. Messianic Prophesies. [Hoberg, three hours.]
2. Hermeneutics, with the History of Exegesis. [Hoberg, two hours.]
3. Introduction to the Sacred Scripture of the New Testament. [Weber, four hours.]
4. General History of the Church, Part Two, with particular consideration of the sixteenth century. [Pfeilschifter, six hours.]
5. Theory of Revelation and of the Church. [Straubinger, three hours.]
6. Metaphysics. [Uebinger, four hours.]

It was during his second semester at the university that Heidegger took his first and only course in hermeneutics. Some four decades later, in 1953–1954, when he was reflecting on *Sein und Zeit,* Heidegger recalled those studies.

> The term 'hermeneutics' was familiar to me from my theological studies. At that time I was particularly agitated over the question of the relation between the word of Holy Scripture and theological-speculative thinking. It was, if you will, the same relation, namely, between language and being, only that it was veiled and inaccessible to me, so that through many deviations and false starts I sought in vain for a clue. [. . .] Without this theological origin I never would have reached the path of thinking. But origins always remain future.

In CV-1915 Heidegger also alludes to his reading of the then recently deceased but still controversial Catholic theologian, Father Herman Schell (1850–1906).[68] Schell, a student of Brentano's and Professor of Catholic Apologetics at Würzburg University from 1884 until his death, was associated with the heated polemic that broke out over *Reformkatholizismus* in the late nineteenth century and over Modernism in the early twentieth. On December 15, 1898, he had the distinction of seeing all his theological works and *Reformschriften* put on the Roman Index of Forbidden Books, principally but not exclusively because of his interpretation of the divine Trinity. Under the influence of the Catholic Tübingen School and ultimately of German Idealism, Schell had described the positive aseity of God in terms of a dynamic, self-actuating, and self-positing *causa sui* rather than simply as a static *ratio sui;* and he had offered a reading of the Trinity as the supreme expression of such self-production and self-realization.

On March 1, 1899 Schell submitted to the Vatican's censure of his books. Nonetheless, over the next seven years he remained the very active center of a heated controversy over the relation of Catholicism and modernity. Schell's express purpose was to overcome what he saw as the inferiority complex of German Catholics in the face of modern culture. Against Pope Pius IX's implied condemnation of 'progress, liberalism, and modern civilization' in the *Syllabus of Errors* (December 8, 1864),[69] Schell argued that the Church, without compromising her nature, could and should overcome her provincialism and engage in dialogue with the contemporary world.

In philosophy Schell tended to shun the papally legislated neo-Thomistic revival (Leo XIII's *Aeterni Patris,* October 4, 1879), and in apologetics he favored, with some reservations, the moral-psychological orientation of the 'immanence apologetics' of French Catholic philosophers Leon Ollé-Laprune (1839–1898) and Maurice Blondel (1861–1949). During his life, and even after his death, he was viciously attacked and maligned by such Vatican hacks as the German neo-Thomist Monsignor Ernst Commer (1847–1928).

The year after Schell died, Pope Pius X launched his attack against 'Modernism' (the word had been coined by Carl Braig in 1889) and began one of the Church's darkest and most repressive periods. The Holy Office decree *Lamentabili* (July 3, 1907) and the papal encyclical *Pascendi* (September 8, 1907) condemned the alleged program of Modernism both in general and in detail and effectively retarded the development of Catholic scholarship for decades.[70]

The fare of the theology courses that Heidegger took between 1909 and 1911 was almost certainly well within Roman guidelines, for the Theology Department of Freiburg University was generally quite conservative and correspondently compliant with the anti-Modernist crusade.[71] It may have been in reaction to such conservatism that Heidegger had already turned to the writings of Herman Schell. When he writes in CV-1915 that Schell's works helped him to find 'what [he] was looking for' in the area of apologetics, Heidegger is signaling, I think, a somewhat liberal attitude toward the Modernism that was then under such severe attack. The works he is referring to could have been Schell's two-volume *Apologie des Christentums* (1901 and 1905), which had not suffered ecclesiastical censure. But it is also not inconceivable that the young seminarian managed to get access to those works of Schell that had been put on the Index, both the theological books and such *Reformschriften* as *Katholizismus als Prinzip des Fortschritts* (1897) and *Die neue Zeit und die alte Glaube* (1898).

What is more, Schell's appropriation of the French 'immanence apologetics' may also have sparked Heidegger's interest in Maurice Blondel, at that time professor of philosophy at Aix-en-Provence. In his controversial *L'action* (1893) Blondel had argued for an orientation towards God from within the immanent exigencies of the human subject, specifically through a phenomenology of the will's dynamic relation to the supernatural. Blondel remained a devoted Roman Catholic throughout his life, but his focus on immanence caused conservative theologians to call his orthodoxy into question during the Modernist crisis. Caution about Blondel's work was certainly in order in 'arch-Catholic Freiburg' (as Husserl would later characterize the city[72]), especially among students for the priesthood. Nonetheless, as he himself told Henry Duméry in 1950, Heidegger read *L'action* 'secretly while with the Jesuits' at the Sapientia.[73]

Third semester: winter 1910–1911, age 21.

1. Introduction to Catholic Dogmatics: The Doctrine of God. [Rev. Carl Braig,[74] four hours.]
2. Exegesis of the Holy Gospel According to John. [Weber, four hours.]
3. General Moral Theology, Parts One through Three. [Mayer, three hours.]
4. The Doctrine of Property. [Mayer, one hour.]
5. Catholic Canon Law, Part One: Introduction, Sources, and Constitution. [Rev. Emil Göller,[75] four hours.]
6. General History of the Church, Part Three, The Age of the Enlightenment. [Pfeilschifter, one hour.]
7. History of the German state from the sixteenth century to the present. [Prof. Georg von Below[76] (Philosophy Department), four hours.]
8. The History of Medieval Mysticism. [Rev. Joseph Sauer,[77] two hours.]

During this, his third semester in theology, Heidegger took his only course on medieval mysticism, and no doubt among the readings for Prof. Sauer's course were the works of Meister Eckhart. The impression this course made on Heidegger was no doubt very great, for over the next eight years we find him proposing various projects connected with medieval mysticism. Five years after the course, in the conclusion to his book on *Duns Scotus' Doctrine of Categories and Meaning,* Heidegger announced his intention to write a book on the philosophical value of Eckhart's mysticism in connection with the metaphysical problem of truth.[78] And in mid-1919, as a Privatdozent, he projected a lecture course on the philosophical foundations of medieval mysticism.

But neither of these two projects came to fruition. The book was never written, and, contrary to widespread belief,[79] the course was never taught. It is true that in the *Vorlesungsverzeichnis* for the winter semester, 1919–1920, Heidegger did announce a two-hour lecture course entitled *Die philosophischen Grundlagen der mittelalterlichen Mystik.*[80] However, on Saturday, August 30, 1919, two months before the course was to begin, Heidegger wrote to the Philosophy Department from Constance in order to request, first, that the course on mysticism be dropped because he lacked time to prepare his lectures adequately; and, second, that his other announced lecture course

'Ausgewählte Probleme der neueren Phänomenologie' be increased from one to two hours per week and have its title changed to *'Grundprobleme der Phänomenologie.'*[81] Thus, in place of his reflections on mysticism Heidegger's students that semester were treated to his very first public analyses of the *Umwelt* and the hermeneutics of facticity. In place of Meister Eckhart, they got the first glimpse into what would become *Sein und Zeit.*[82]

By the end of his third semester at the university the young Heidegger found himself in a state of severe exhaustion brought on, as he says in CV-1915, by his 'intense engagement with philosophical problems, along with the tasks of [his] own professional studies.' Nonetheless, he registered for another semester of theology – his last, as it would turn out.

Fourth semester: summer, 1911, age 21.

1. Theological Cosmology: The Creation, Preservation, and Governance of the World. [Braig, four hours.]
2. Special Moral Theology, Parts One and Two. [Mayer, four hours.]
3. The Christian Art of the Nineteenth Century and the Present. [Sauer, one hour.]
4. The Age of the Renaissance (History of the Later Middle Ages). [Prof. Heinrich Finke[83] (Philosophy Department), four hours.]

But Heidegger was not well. In the middle of February – two months before this semester began – he left Freiburg and went home to Messkirch to rest. He returned in April to resume his studies, but his health continued to deteriorate, with negative consequences for his ecclesiastical plans.[84] In CV-1915 he writes: 'My heart-trouble, which had come about earlier from too much sports, broke out so severely that any later employment in the service of the Church was taken to be extremely questionable.'

Heidegger spent much of the spring, summer and fall 1911 recuperating in Messkirch; and at least some of those days he spent walking along his favorite pathway, the one he celebrated in his 1947–1948 reflection *Der Feldweg*:

> [The path] runs through the park gate and out towards Ehnried. The old linden trees in the castle garden gaze after it from behind the wall. . . On the bench there occasionally lay one or another of the great thinkers' books, which a youth was clumsily trying to decipher. When the puzzles crowded into each other and there seemed no way out, the pathway was a help. It quietly escorts ones' steps along the winding trail through the expanse of untilled land.[85]

In a 1969 letter Heidegger's younger brother Fritz reminded Martin of that summer:

> Once during the long holidays (1911) you managed to read and master in a

single day – walking along your usual path in the shade of the linden trees in the park – a philosophical work. It was a book by the philosophy professor Joseph Geyser.[86]

The book Heidegger was reading could well have been *Grundlagen der Logik und Erkenntnislehre* by Joseph Geyser (1869–1948) – not the work of a particularly great thinker, but nonetheless a book that the young Heidegger would favorably review in the fall of 1912 and mention again in his volume on Duns Scotus.[87]

And Heidegger read other things that spring and summer. Husserl's programmatic essay 'Philosophie als strenge Wissenschaft' had just been published in March 1911 in the journal *Logos,*[88] and Heidegger read it closely and in fact critically. Towards the end of the essay, next to Husserl's words 'The impulse to research must take its start not from philosophies but from issues and problems,' Heidegger scratched in the margin: *'Wir nehmen Husserl beim Wort'* – 'We take Husserl at his word.'[89]

By the fall of 1911, when he returned to Freiburg University, Heidegger had moved out of the theological seminary and into an apartment at #1 Hohenzollernstrasse on the northwest edge of the city. He had also transferred out of theology. His preference at this point was to study with Husserl at the University of Göttingen, but as he later told Prof. Herbert Spiegelberg, 'financial necessities prevented this and forced him to complete his studies at the University of Freiburg in his native state of Baden.'[90] Those financial difficulties had to do, at least in part, with the fact that upon leaving theology in the summer of 1911, Heidegger was required to surrender his Eliner Grant of 400 marks per year. And it would be over a year before he would receive any other financial assistance.

In any case, as he writes in CV-1915, 'in the winter semester of 1911–1912 I had myself enrolled in the Department of Natural Sciences and Mathematics.'

III. 1911–1913, age 22–23: Towards the doctorate in philosophy

Candidatus mathematicus. Until 1910 the Philosophy Department at Freiburg University was divided into two sections: the *philologisch-historische Abteilung,* which was made up of philosophy, history, art history, philology, and archeology, as well as a psychological laboratory (of which, in fact, Heidegger would be the head at least from 1933 through 1936); and the *mathematisch-naturwissenschaftliche Abteilung,* which included mathematics, chemistry, physics, biology, botany, and so on. Moreover, within the Philological-Historical Section, philosophy was (and still is) divided into Seminar I and Seminar II, the latter having the 'denominational' or Catholic chair that had been established in the nineteenth century.[91]

However, on October 15, 1910, one year before Heidegger left the seminary, the professors of natural science and mathematics split off from philosophy and formed an independent department, the *naturwissenschaftlich-mathematische Fakultät.* And it was in this department, not in philosophy, that Heidegger registered when he left his theological studies in the middle of 1911. It would seem, then, that Heidegger now intended to take a doctorate in mathematics and the sciences. Nonetheless, two years later, on June 30, 1913, we will find him, upon completion of his university course work, petitioning the Philosophy Department for the Ph.D., even though he signed the petitionary letter 'Martin Heidegger, Cand. math.,' that is, *Candidatus mathematicus.* The shift in the young scholar's interests goes unexplained. The most we have is his statement – half a promise and perhaps half an *apologia* – in the preface to the published version of his doctoral dissertation: 'Later investigations will show what I owe to my esteemed teachers in mathematics and physics.'[92]

In CV-1914 – the *Lebenslauf* published at the end of the book version of *Die Lehre vom Urteil im Psychologismus* – Heidegger wrote that from 1911 through 1913 he attended lecture courses 'above all in philosophy, mathematics, and the natural sciences. . . .'[93] CV-1913 (the earlier, handwritten draft of that *Lebenslauf*) puts it a bit differently:

> In 1911 I changed departments and was enrolled in the Department of Natural Sciences and Mathematics. I attended lecture courses in mathematics, physics, chemistry, and botany. Throughout the entire period of my university studies [1909–1913] I attended lecture courses in philosophy.[94]

These were pivotal years in the development of the young scholar, and CV-1915 gives the impression that during this period he discovered how to philosophize. While he remained a convinced Aristotelian Scholastic during those years, he says he also (1) learned 'to understand philosophical problems as problems'; (2) acquired 'insight into the essence of logic,' the subject in which he remained most interested; (3) developed 'a correct understanding of modern philosophy from Kant on' (he mentions 'the study of Fichte and Hegel'); (4) overcame his 'aversion to history' and understood how 'the history of ideas can fructify philosophy,' and (5) saw the need for an 'exploitation and utilization' of 'the intellectual wealth' and 'theoretical content' of classical medieval philosophers, in the interest of exploiting the resources of Scholasticism. Looking back on his university days some forty-five years later, he would remark:

> What the exciting years between 1910 and 1914 meant for me cannot be adequately expressed. I can only indicate it by a selective enumeration: the second edition of Nietzsche's *Wille zur Macht,* [reprinted with scholarly notes in 1911], expanded to twice the size of the original [1906] edition; the

> works of Kierkegaard and Dostoevsky in translation; my awakening interest in Hegel and Schelling; Rilke's works and Trakl's poems; Dilthey's *Gesammelte Schriften* [1914ff.].[95]

Heidegger spent basically three semesters in the Department of Natural Sciences and Mathematics; in his fourth and last semester he took only one course, in Renaissance history, and in fact, it seems to be the same course that Heidegger had started to take in the summer semester of 1911 but had been required to abandon for reasons of health. Again thanks to Dr. Casper we now possess a list of the courses in which Heidegger was officially enrolled between 1911 and 1913.[96] In CV-1915 Heidegger declares that he took 'a great quantity of lecture courses in philosophy' (Casper's list mentions six philosophy courses), and he emphasizes 'the seminar exercises with Herr Geheimrat Rickert' (Casper mentions only one, in 1912, although Heidegger was present in at least one more, in the summer semester of 1914). Casper's list does not include more courses that Heidegger would later mention: one or more courses in botany (cf. CV-1913 cited just above), one or more in art history with Professor Wilhelm Vöge[97] (1868–1952), and one in theology with Carl Braig (1853–1923), who seems to have been a major catalyst for Heidegger's interest in German Idealism and in the onto-theological structure of metaphysics.

> I did attend one lecture course in theology even in the years after 1911, the course on dogmatic theology by Carl Braig. I was led to do this by my interest in speculative theology and above all by the penetrating kind of thinking that this teacher evidenced in every lecture hour. On a few walks that I was allowed to take with him I heard for the first time about the significance of Schelling and Hegel for speculative theology as contrasted with the doctrinal system of Scholasticism. Thus the tension between ontology and speculative theology, as the structure of metaphysics, entered the field of my search.[98]

However, the majority of Heidegger's courses between the fall of 1911 and the summer of 1913 were in mathematics and the natural sciences. In what follows I translate Casper's list, interspersed with some additional information.

Fifth semester: winter, 1911–1912, age 22.

1. The Analytic Geometry of Space. [Prof. Lothar Heffter,[99] one hour.]
2. Exercises in Analytic Geometry. [Heffter, one hour.]
3. Differential Calculus. [Prof. Alfred Loewy, four hours.]
4. Exercises in Differential Calculus. [Loewy, one hour.]
5. Experimental Physics. [Prof. Wilhelm Himstedt, two hours.]
6. Experimental Inorganic Chemistry. [Prof. Ludwig Gatterman, five hours.]

7. Logic and Epistemology. [Prof. Arthur Schneider,[100] four hours.]
8. Seminar: Spinoza's Ethics. [Schneider, no hours listed.]

Heidegger's took his two philosophy courses this semester with Professor Arthur Schneider (1976–1945). Schneider, a specialist in medieval philosophy who had taken over the Catholic chair of philosophy (*Lehrstuhl der christlichen Philosophie*) only that fall, would direct Heidegger's Ph.D. dissertation just before leaving for a new position at Strassburg in November, 1913. Upon Schneider's departure the Catholic chair would remain vacant from 1913 to 1917, and, as we shall see below, Heidegger would consider himself a serious candidate for it.

As the next semester was just getting underway Heidegger, who had gone a full year without financial assistance, received word that on Monday, April 22, 1912, the Senate of Freiburg University, in its decision No. 1985, had awarded him a Grieshaber-Pino Grant of 400 marks per year, with the beginning of the stipend rendered retroactive to February 15.[101] The grant was renewed three times and ran out on May 15, 1916, almost a year after Heidegger had completed his *Habilitation*.

Sixth semester: summer, 1912, age 22.

1. Algebraic Analysis. [Heffter, three hours.]
2. Exercises in [Algebraic] Analysis. [Heffter, one hour.]
3. Integral Calculus. [Loewy, four hours.]
4. Exercises in Integral Calculus. [Loewy, one hour.]
5. Experimental Physics. [Himstedt, five hours.]
6. Introduction to Epistemology and Metaphysics.[102] [Rickert, two hours.]
7. Seminar: Epistemological Exercises in the Doctrine of Judgment. [Rickert, no hours listed.]

During these university years Husserl's *Logical Investigations* continued to stand at the center of Heidegger's interests. But now Heidegger was beginning to read Husserl through the eyes of Heinrich Rickert (1863–1936), the Neo-Kantian philosopher of values who held the chair of philosophy in Seminar I from 1894 until 1916, and above all through the eyes of Rickert's most famous pupil, Emil Lask (1875–1915).

In the Preface to *Die Lehre vom Urteil im Psychologismus* (1914) Heidegger acknowledged his indebtedness to Rickert for helping him 'see and understand the modern problem of logic,' and indeed this seems to have been the area of Rickert's major positive influence on him.[103] However, Rickert's value philosophy was another matter, and Heidegger's relation to it seems to have always been ambivalent. In a 1913 book review Heidegger wrote: 'In my opinion value theory, at least in its current form, remains caught in psychologism.'[104]

And in the Preface to his book on Duns Scotus (September, 1916) Heidegger expressed his conviction that Rickert's value to philosophy:

> is being called upon to take decisive steps forward and to deepen its work on philosophical problems. Its orientation to the *history of the spirit* provides a fruitful basis for creatively shaping philosophical problems from out of strong personal experience. Proof of that is given by the philosophical works of someone like Emil Lask. . . .[105]

By the fall of 1917 Heidegger would let it be known that he had begun to take a clear critical distance from Rickert.[106] The break was finalized in the summer semester of 1919 in Heidegger's lecture course *Phänomenologie und transzendentale Wertphilosophie* and was summarized in Heidegger's brief but definitive rejection of *Geltungslogik* in *Sein und Zeit,* § 33.[107] Nonetheless, during Heidegger's student days Rickert had a strong and positive effect on the young scholar. For all the defects of Rickert's value-philosophy, Heidegger was convinced that it kept the door open to the realm of the ontological under the rubric of 'validity.' In 1951, when he was asked about Rickert's (and, earlier, Windelband's) distinction of the historical and the natural sciences in terms of individualizing-ideographic judgments vs. generalizing-nomothetic judgments, Heidegger replied:

> I grew up on that distinction. In no way would I want to impugn the reputation of my esteemed teacher, but that distinction is really quite primitive. This kind of thinking is miles behind Schelling, Hegel, or Leibniz. And yet in 1900–1910 this was a liberating issue for us at a time when experimental psychology was attempting to become *the* scientific philosophy. In those days the school of value-philosophy was an essential and decisive support for philosophy as it had been known in the great tradition.[108]

The importance of Emil Lask for the young Heidegger in those years can scarsely be exaggerated, even though, as with Rickert, it would be a transitory influence. In 1957 Heidegger said it was 'through Rickert's seminar exercises' that he first came to know the works of Lask, 'who also tried to listen to the Greek thinkers as he mediated between [Rickert and Husserl].'[109] For Heidegger, the important thing about Lask was Husserl. In *Sein und Zeit* Heidegger would praise Lask for his unique role in appropriating Husserl's *Logical Investigations*. Most commentators, he writes there, stress Husserl's negative achievement, his refutation of psychologism in the first volume of that work, but they neglect the positive contributions Husserl made in the six investigations that comprise the second volume. However:

> The only person who has taken up these investigations [in volume two]

> positively from outside the main stream of phenomenological research has been E. Lask, whose *Logik der Philosophie* (1911) was as strongly influenced by the Sixth Investigation ('On Sensuous and Categorial Intuitions,' pp. 128 ff. [in the separate, 1922 edition]) as his *Lehre vom Urteil* (1912) was influenced by the sections [of that same Investigation] on evidence and truth.[110]

In his two major works, *Die Logik der Philosophie und die Kategorienlehre* (1911) and *Die Logik vom Urteil* (1912),[111] Lask sought to overcome the limitations of Kant's transcendental logic by giving it an ontological grounding, not, however, in the suprasensible, noumenal realm of traditional metaphysics but rather in the area of transcendental intelligible validity (*das Gelten*). Lask continued the Husserlian critique of psychologism and the assertation of the autonomy of the sense (*Sinn;* for Lask, the objectively valid linking of the formal and the material[112]) which is performed in acts of judgment. But Lask delved further into the categorial than had Husserl; and even though Heidegger would finally adjudge the results of this effort to be empty, nonetheless Lask opened Heidegger's own eyes to the crucial role of the categorial intuition of beingness in Husserlian phenomenology.

In the broadest sense Lask's efforts were not unlike those of Pierre Rousselot (1878–1915) and Joseph Maréchal (1878–1944), namely, to discover within the structure of predicative synthesis a reference to an objective, ontological in-itself-ness.[113] But Lask, steeped in Neo-Kantianism, took the path that led from logical formalism toward a static *Gelten,* whereas Rousselot and Maréchal, influenced by Augustine and Fichte, followed out the dynamism of the human spirit in its movement towards mystery. In 1927 Heidegger commented:

> If Lask, too, treats things for the most part formalistically and within the conceptual schemata of neo-Kantianism, nevertheless he consciously pushes on toward a philosophical understanding of logic and in so doing is compelled under pressure from the subject matter itself to return to the ontological problems. Still, Lask was unable to free himself from the conviction of his contemporaries that Neo-Kantianism had the vocation of renovating philosophy.[114]

Seventh semester: winter, 1912–1913, age 23.

1. Higher Algebra. [Heffter, four hours.]
2. Theory of Differential Equations. [Loewy, four hours.]
3. General History of Philosophy. [Schneider, four hours.]
4. Exercises in Epistemology. [Schneider, no hours listed.]

In 1912 Heidegger made his debut as a publishing philosopher with two articles. His first article, 'Das Realitätsproblem in der modernen Philosophie,' appeared in the lay Catholic journal, *Philosophisches Jahrbuch der Görresgesellschaft.*[115] Heidegger, true to his Aristotelian-Scholastic orientation, defended the critical realism of Oswald Külpe (1862–1915), which was summarized in the notion of *Realisierung,* the 'positing and determining of transsubjective objects'[116] (or rather, material data: *das Gegebene, Vorgefundene*) as they are in themselves. Heidegger supported this critical realism first against the 'conscientialism' (= immanentism) of David Hume, Ernst Schuppe, Richard Avenarius, and Ernst Mach, according to whom, he alleges, the proper object of knowledge is the consciousness of the knower; and then against Kantian phenomenalism, in which 'the object of knowledge undergoes an increased subjectivization via the categories, and knowing distances itself even further from its own object.'[117] In the process of arguing for a critical epistemology in which 'empirical and rational moments work together,' Heidegger summarized Husserl's anti-psychologistic argument that 'the mental existence of a concept and the ideal being of the content of that concept are totally different things' and that the principles of logic are not 'inductively grounded (and for that reason valid) causal laws of subjective mental processes' but rather 'immediately evident, objective, ideal principles.'[118]

Heidegger's second article, a three-part review-essay on recent works in logic and epistemology, 'Neuere Forschungen über Logik,' was published in the October, November, and December issues of *Literarische Rundschau für das katholische Deutschland,* 1912, a Catholic journal then edited by Heidegger's former teacher, Rev. Joseph Sauer.[119] The article offered a wide-ranging discussion of books and articles by Emil Lask, Alexius Meinong, and Joseph Geyser, with honorable mentions of Frege, Russell, Whitehead, and Husserl. At the beginning of the review-essay the young Heidegger announced his guiding issue: 'What is logic? Here we stand before a problem whose solution is reserved for the future.'[120] Peering into that future, Heidegger still hoped for help from Husserl, whose *Logical Investigations,* he wrote, 'probes the *meaning,* the *sense* of acts and thus becomes a doctrine of meaning [*Bedeutungslehre*], a *phenomenology* of consciousness.'[121] Fifteen years later, in *Sein und Zeit,* Heidegger radicalized the *Bedeutungslehre* that Husserl had elaborated in Investigations IV-VI of *Logical Investigations,* by tracing it back to the existential essence of human being: 'The doctrine of meaning,' Heidegger wrote, 'is rooted in the ontology of *Dasein.* Whether it prospers or decays depends on the fate of this ontology.'[122]

Early in 1913 Heidegger published his first two book reviews, brief notices that appeared in the February and the April issues of Sauer's *Literarische Rundschau.*[123] In the second review Heidegger suggested (without elaborating) that the correct way to approach the problem of bridging the gap between the atemporal reality of abstract thoughts and the temporal reality of sense perception was 'through a sharp separation of the logical, the epistemological, and the metaphysical sides of the question.'[124]

Eighth and last semester: summer, 1913, age 23.

1. The Age of the Renaissance. [Finke, four hours.]

In late April, as Heidegger's final semester of university studies was just getting underway and as he was finishing his doctoral dissertation on the doctrine of judgment in psychologism, a new journal appeared, *Jahrbuch für Philosophie und phänomenologische Forschung,* and the first issue (a double number) featured the groundbreaking treatise of its editor, Edmund Husserl: *Ideas for a Pure Phenomenology and a Phenomenological Philosophy.*[125] Husserl, who was still at Göttingen (he would not begin teaching at Freiburg until the spring of 1916) introduced the new journal with a manifesto of the phenomenological movement, in which he expressed high hopes for 'a fundamental transformation of philosophy via a securely founded and constantly progressing science.' He promised that what would unite the collaborators on this journal would be not a 'scholastic system' but

> the common conviction that we must return to the originary sources of intuition and to the essential unities that are to be drawn from them if we are to evaluate the great traditions of philosophy according to concepts and problems; and that only in this way can we clarify concepts intuitively and pose problems anew on intuitive grounds and thus be able to solve them on the basis of principles.[126]

As we saw above, from the time Heidegger first opened Husserl's *Logical Investigations* four years before, he had encountered insurmountable difficulties with the work itself and with the new method of thinking it proposed. Even now, when Lask's work on logic forced him to go back to Husserl's volumes with renewed interest, Heidegger still could not overcome those difficulties and in fact would not be able to do so until he began working closely with Husserl after the war.

Heidegger's first and major problem was about methodology. 'It concerned how to carry out the process of thinking that is called "phenomenology".'[127] For one thing, when Husserl did make programmatic or methodological statements, he seemed to claim that phenomenology was a new beginning 'which denied all previous thinking' and that 'one had to renounce introducing the authority of the great thinkers into the conversation.'[128] In any case Heidegger began to suspect that it was impossible 'to learn to do the kind of thinking called "phenomenology" simply by reading the philosophical literature.'[129]

This first difficulty with phenomenological procedures was connected with a second one: it seemed to Heidegger that Husserl had caught himself in a contradiction concerning the very nature of phenomenology. Whereas the first volume (1900) was devoted to refuting psychologism,

> the second volume, which was published the following year and which was three times as long, contains the description of the acts of consciousness essential for the constitution of knowledge. So it is a psychology after all . . . Accordingly, [it would seem that] with his phenomenological description of the phenomena of consciousness Husserl falls back into the position of psychologism that he has just refuted. But if such a gross error cannot be attributed to Husserl's work, what then is the phenomenological description of the acts of consciousness? If phenomenology is neither logic nor psychology, what is its proper characteristic? Has an entirely new discipline appeared here, with its own status and priority?[130]

But those were problems that went back as far as Heidegger's first reading of *Logical Investigations* in 1909. But now in 1913, with the publication of *Ideas,* it seemed to Heidegger that Husserl had provided an answer at least to the second problem. What indeed was phenomenology? In the tradition of Neo-Kantian thought, Husserl now declared phenomenology to be a 'pure' – that is, a *transcendental* – reflection, focused on transcendental rather than psychological consciousness, 'an investigation of the structure of acts of experience together with the investigation of the objects experienced in those acts with regard to their objectivity.'[131] While this might have seemed to be only an extension of Neo-Kantianism's investigation of the transcendental subject, Husserl now claimed, in Heidegger's words, 'that "transcendental subjectivity" attains a more original and universal determination' through 'the systematically planned and secured' investigations of phenomenology.[132]

But none of this satisfied Heidegger. 'Even after the *Ideas* was published, I was still captivated by the never-ceasing spell of the *Logical Investigations,* a spell that again stirred up an unrest that could not comprehend its own cause.'[133] Heidegger was convinced that something decisive had happened in the *Logical Investigations,* but he could not grasp exactly what it was. 'It remained unarticulated and even today can hardly be expressed.'[134] It had a lot to do with the categorial intuition and the givenness of entities that occurs in that intuition. Husserl's Sixth Investigation argued that in knowledge one intuitively and thus immediately knows not only a given entity (let us call it the 'what') but above all the categorial *givenness* of that entity (the 'how' of the 'what'). This intelligible givenness of entities was what the tradition had called *ousia* or 'being[ness]' and what the Greeks also knew as *alétheia.* As far as Heidegger was concerned, Husserl's rediscovery that all cognitive comportment is based on the intuition of beingness – that is, on the ineluctable fact that the 'how', the noetic *alétheia* or givenness of entities, is immediately present in human awareness – marked phenomenology's crucial breakthrough. 'What phenomenological investigations had recently discovered to be the underlying posture of thinking turns out to be the basic trait of Greek thinking, indeed of philosophy as such.'[135] But this insight still lay in the future. And even further in the future lay the question that would lead Heidegger beyond not only Husserl but the entire tradition of metaphysics: How does the 'how' come about?

The Rigorosum, July 26, 1913, age 23. By early summer of 1913 Heidegger, working under the direction of Professor Arthur Schneider, had finished his doctoral dissertation on the doctrine of judgment in psychologism and was prepared to defend it. In CV-1915 he writes:

> [I]n the dissertation on *Die Lehre vom Urteil im Psychologismus* I took my bearings both from modern logic and from basic Aristotelian-Scholastic views and attempted to find a foundation for further investigations regarding a central problem of logic and epistemology.

If Heidegger followed custom, he first sought out the university's Beadle (*Pedell*), a minor administrative official (usually a clerk) who for a tip would help guarantee that the candidate got the board of examiners that he or she wanted.[136] Then, on Monday, June 30, Heidegger officially petitioned the Philosophy Department, through his disseration director, to award him the doctorate.

> Freiburg in Breisgau
> June 30, 1913
>
> To the esteemed Philosophy Department of the Albert Ludwig University of Freiburg in Breisgau:
>
> Concerning the petition of Martin Heidegger, candidate in mathematics, that he be graduated with the doctorate:
>
> On the basis of the enclosed manuscript and the requisite testimonies, the undersigned respectfully lays before the esteemed Philosophy Department his respectful request that he be permitted to be graduated with the doctorate. The undersigned respectfully wishes to be examined in his major subject (philosophy) by Prof. Dr. Schneider, and in his minor subjects by Prof. Dr. Heffter (mathematics) and by Herr Geheimenhofrat Prof. Dr. Finke (medieval history).
>
> With highest regards, he remains the esteemed Philosophy Department's most respectful
>
> Martin Heidegger
> Cand. math.[137]

Along with this letter Heidegger submitted his manuscript as well as the requisite handwritten testimony that the manuscript was indeed his own work:

Declaration:

> The undersigned herewith gives his word of honor, in lieu of an oath, that he and he alone has authored the work that he hereby presents to the esteemed Philosophy Department.
>
> Freiburg in Breisgau, June 30, 1913
> Martin Heidegger, Cand. Math.

And finally he enclosed a brief, handwritten *Lebenslauf,* the one we have been calling 'CV-1913.' The text differs only slightly from the published version, CV-1914.

Curriculum Vitae
1913

> I, Martin Heidegger, was born in Messkirch (Baden) on September 26, 1889, the son of the sexton and master cooper Friedrich Heidegger and of Johanna, née Kempf, both of them citizens of Baden and members of the Catholic Church. From 1899 to 1903 I attended the middle school of my hometown, and in the fall of 1903 I entered the first year of the Gymnasium in Constance. Since 1906, beginning with the third year of high school, I attended the Berthold Gymnasium in Freiburg in Breisgau, and there in the summer of 1909 I passed the final comprehensive examination. In the fall of the same year I matriculated at the University of Freiburg in Breisgau as a theology student. In the winter semester of 1911 I changed departments and enrolled in the Department of Natural Sciences and Mathematics. I attended lecture courses in mathematics, physics, chemistry, and botany. Throughout the entire period of my university studies I attended lecture courses in philosophy.[139]

On Thursday, July 10, Professor Arthur Schneider drew up his report (*Gutachten*) on Heidegger's manuscript, a somewhat brief text that summarized the dissertation in one paragraph and evaluated it in another.[140] Although Schneider did not agree with everything in the last chapter of the work (he does not specify his disagreements), he finds the dissertation 'an outstanding achievement' and therefore forwards to the Philosophy Department Heidegger's petition for the *Rigorosum,* the oral examination. On Saturday, July 12, 1913, the Philosophy Department voted 11 to 0 to admit Heidegger to the examination with the board he had requested.

Two weeks later, on Saturday, July 26, Heidegger met the board in the Philosophy Department at 9:30 A.M. Schneider questioned him on philosophy until 10:30, then Finke and Heffter questioned him on medieval history and mathematics respectively, each for thirty minutes. Heidegger passed the examination with the grade that usually was reserved for those who would go on for the license to teach: *summa cum laude.*[141]

IV. 1913–1915, age 23–25
Preparation for the Habilitation

The months between the fall of 1913 and the fall of 1914 mark a significant turning point in Heidegger's development. Up to this time, as we have seen, Heidegger's main philosophical interests lay in logic and the philosophy of mathematics. In fact, when he started research on his *Habilitation* in the fall of 1913, the topic he chose to write on was *'das logische Wesen des Zahlbegriffs,'* the logical essence of the concept of number.[142] However, Heidegger never completed that work. Instead, by the fall of 1914 he had radically shifted his interests towards the areas of history in general and medieval philosophy in particular, and the qualifying dissertation that he finally defended in the summer of 1915 was the one on Duns Scotus.

In the last three paragraphs of CV-1915 Heidegger describes this shift as an intellectual conversion. Sometime after the doctorate, he tells us, he woke up from a mathematician's dogmatic slumber and for the first time saw the value of history; and this newly awakened interest finally led him to what he thought would be his philosophical mission: to bring together medieval thought and Husserlian phenomenology. As he puts it in CV-1915, his post-doctoral studies in Fichte, Hegel, Rickert,[143] and Dilthey, as well as his post-doctoral history courses with Professor Finke, 'resulted in the fact that my aversion to history, nurtured in me by my predilection for mathematics, was thoroughly destroyed.' His growing interest in history led him to what he calls 'an intense engagement' with medieval philosophy and culminated two years later in his qualifying dissertation, *Duns Scotus' Doctrine of Meaning and Categories.* In fact, he pledges that if he is given the license to teach, his life's work will be devoted to

> a comprehensive presentation of medieval logic and psychology in the light of modern phenomenology, with equal consideration of the historical position of individual medieval thinkers.

What happened to change Heidegger's mind from logic and mathematics to history? Answer: the vacating of the chair of Christian philosophy in the fall of 1913, when Professor Arthur Schneider (who had directed Heidegger's dissertation) left for the University of Strassburg. From mid-1913 through early 1917 Heidegger was intensely involved in an unsuccessful attempt to succeed Schneider in the chair, and he actively promoted himself around Freiburg as a Christian philosopher in the tradition of Thomas Aquinas. His unsuccessful attempt to win the position may also help to explain the eventual souring of the young Heidegger's relation to the Catholic Church and its vision of philosophy; but that topic lies beyond the scope of the present essay.[144] We shall follow Heidegger only up to the end of his *Lehrjahre* in mid-1915, when his chances of winning the chair still looked quite promising.

Summer and fall, 1913, age 23–24. Until the end of the nineteenth century the Chair of Christian Philosophy had been part of the *Theology* Department and had always been held by a priest. However, when Professor Baumgartner left the position in 1901, the University Senate decided to move the chair to the Philosophy Department and to appoint, from then on, only lay Catholic philosophers to the position. The first such lay professor was Adolf Dyroff (1866–1943), who held the position from 1901 to 1903, followed by Johann Uebinger from 1903 to 1911, and Arthur Schneider from 1911 to 1913.[145]

The problem, however, was that at the time there was a shortage of good lay Catholic philosophers in Germany with strong foundations in Scholasticism. In fact, in 1903 when Dyroff left Freiburg for the University of Bonn, Professor Heinrich Finke, who held the denominational chair of history within the Philosophy Department, had taken aside one of his better students, a bright young seminarian named Engelbert Krebs who had just completed his doctorate in philosophy under Finke's direction, and tried to convince him not to be ordained a priest so that instead he might go on to take the vacant chair. Krebs declined the suggestion, and the position was given to Johann Uebinger. Nonetheless, ten years later Krebs began to figure prominently in Heidegger's own designs on that chair.

Only eight years older than Heidegger, Engelbert Krebs held doctorates in both philosophy (1903) and theology (1909) from the University of Freiburg.[146] Ordained a priest in 1906, he received the *venia legendi* in theology in February of 1911, and that spring, just as Heidegger was withdrawing from theology for reasons of health, he began teaching as a Privatdozent in the Theology Department. But Krebs continued his research in philosophy, and on October 8, 1912, he read a paper on epistemology and natural theology at the meeting of the Catholic Görres Society in Freiburg.[147] Heidegger, who had just published his first philosophy article on a related topic in the Görres Society's *Philosophisches Jahrbuch,* may well have heard the lecture. But he did not meet Krebs personally until nine months later, in mid-July of 1913, only a few days before he defended his own doctoral dissertation.

According to Krebs' own notes, the discussion on the day of that first meeting ranged from Krebs' lecture, through Husserl's *Logische Untersuchungen,* to Heidegger's three-part article on logic that had been published the previous year. Krebs was quite impressed with Heidegger ('A bright fellow, modest but self-assured in the ways he bears himself,' he noted later[148]). And given the fact that Schneider was about to vacate the chair of Christian philosophy, Krebs regretted that Heidegger was not yet far enough along to take the position: 'Too bad he's not a couple years down the road. We could really use him now.'[149]

But in fact Schneider was already making plans for Heidegger to succeed him in the Catholic chair. Soon after Heidegger's doctoral defence of July 26, 1913, Schneider approached the auxiliary bishop of Freiburg, Friedrich Justus Knecht (1839–1921)[150] and through him petitioned the archdiocese to award Heidegger one of its grants from the von Schaezler Foundation for the study of Thomistic philosophy, an award that carried a yearly stipend of 1000 marks ($ 238). Recipients of the grant were obliged to study at institutions where 'philosophy and theology are taught according to the doctrine of St. Thomas Aquinas' (but Heidegger had already completed his requisite course work) and were expected to 'remain true to the spirit of Thomistic philosophy.'[151]

With the road paved for him, Heidegger wrote to the Freiburg chancellery office from Messkirch on Wednesday, August 20, 1913, to apply for the grant to help defray expenses while he was preparing the qualifying dissertation. Part of his letter read: 'The undersigned intends to dedicate himself to the study of Christian philosophy and to pursue an academic career.'[152] He was awarded the grant on September 29, 1913.

Presumably Engelbert Krebs – who was nurturing his own designs on the chair of Christian philosophy[153] – was unaware of all this until one day in early September, when he happened to run into Arthur Schneider on campus. Krebs kept a record of the conversation:

> Today (Tuesday, September 2, 1913) in the university library, when for the first I was drawn into an academic conversation by Arthur Schneider, I brought up the subject of Heidegger. Schneider told me that he had urged Heidegger at all costs to do the *Habilitation.* I [said]: Finke has advised him to take the State examination for secondary school teachers. Schneider: He must get the *Habilitation.* While working on the qualifying dissertation he will get (I have spoken to the auxiliary bishop on his behalf) a 1000-mark stipend from the Schaezler Foundation. Then the Görres Society's budget for Privatdozenten will take care of him. I am happy Heidegger will be looked after in this way. But Schneider thinks that while it is all to the good that he does systematic philosophy, he now still must work his way into the medieval philosophers.[154]

However, matters would not be that simple. A month later, on Friday,

October 10, 1913, Professor Thiersch, dean of the Philosophy Department, called up Krebs and asked him, now that Schneider was gone, to assume the teaching obligations of the Catholic chair at least on a temporary basis. Krebs was happy to accept, and on October 27 he was given a contract.[155]

But not without protest. Heinrich Finke, a staunch and very conservative Catholic layman, was determined that no priest should hold the denominational chair in philosophy, not even Father Krebs, whose doctoral dissertation he had directed and whose work he respected. Other faculty members objected that Privatdozent Krebs – besides being a priest and not being a professor, much less a member of the Philosophy Department – had in fact a year earlier taken the anti-modernist oath required of Catholic theology professors by Pope Pius X's decree *Sacrorum antistitum* (September 1, 1910).[156] This oath, which bound one to adhere to certain Catholic propositions on God, miracles, the founding of the Church, and the nature of faith, was the subject of great controversy in German universities at the time, so much so that in October of 1911 the organization of German university professors, meeting in Dresden, passed a motion excluding from its ranks anyone who swore the anti-modernist oath. Some professors in the group even demanded, unsuccessfully, that oath-takers be expelled from the university.[157]

Feelings against Krebs' appointment ran high. In the company of the philosophy dean Thiersch, Finke went to the Grand Duchy of Baden's Ministry of Education in Karlsruhe in mid-October to settle the matter. The result was that both the Philosophy and the Theology Departments agreed that even though the Philosophy Department would recognize the courses he taught, Krebs himself would remain a member of the Theology Department only. The Philosophy Department also voted down Heinrich Rickert's proposal that Krebs be allowed to sit on philosophy doctoral boards.[158]

At the start of November Krebs began his first two lecture courses in Christian philosophy, 'Geschichte der aristotelischen scholastischen Philosophie' and 'Einführung in die Philosophie, Logik und Erkenntnistheorie.'[159] However, Krebs was not entirely sure of himself in his new role as philosophy teacher, and therefore he sought out the help of his younger friend Martin Heidegger. The two were on close terms now, and on Friday, November 7, at the end of his first week of lecturing, Krebs jotted a memo to himself:

> For ten days now I have been entrusted with the professorship of [Christian] philosophy. Under Heidegger's influence I have studied chiefly Husserl as well as Heidegger's own little work ['Neuere Forschungen über Logik'] in the *Literarische Rundschau,* 1912, and Geyser's *Grundlagen [der Logik und Erkenntnis],* and I talk with him frequently in the Philosophy Department in order to get greater clarity on problems. I deliver to him the lecture that I intend to give in the course, and I talk over the content of the lecture with him. He helps me more than perhaps he himself realizes.[160]

The situation was not without a certain irony. Here was a young doctor Heidegger, recipient of a grant to write a dissertation that would qualify him to take the Catholic chair in philosophy, quietly helping a supposedly more seasoned scholar, who held that chair temporarily (but dearly hoped to keep it), to prepare his classroom lectures. Perhaps Finke had been right after all to oppose Kreb's appointment.

In any case Finke, in his determination to block any priest from holding the chair, changed his mind about Heidegger. Whereas in early September he had thought the young doctor should teach high school rather than prepare the *Habilitation,* at the beginning of November Finke reversed himself. He approached Heidegger and strongly urged him, if he wanted to have Schneider's chair, to work up a suitable qualifying dissertation in the history of philosophy and to present himself as soon as possible for the *Habilitation.*[161] Finke invited the young doctor to attend Finke's own seminars in order to learn historical method.[162]

For the content of Finke's conversation with Heidegger we are indebted to two memos that Engelbert Krebs wrote on Friday, November 14, on the basis of information from Heidegger. First, the shorter memo:

> This afternoon [November 14, 1913] between five and six [Heidegger] visited me and reported how *Finke* had stopped him and urged him to get the *Habilitation* with a dissertation in the history of philosophy, and that Finke had spoken to him in a way that made it clear that, given the current vacancy of the chair, *Heidegger* should *hasten* to make himself available soon, as a Privatdozent, for a possible appointment. So it could be that the provisional appointment that I now have is only to keep the chair warm for Heidegger, a schoolmate of my brother Hans.[163]

In his diary Krebs also wrote a longer version, in which he recorded Finke's comments on some of the other possible candidates for the chair.

> Today just after five o'clock Dr. Heidegger came to see me and said: Finke had spoken to him and had said: You must write a dissertation in the history of philosophy. Come see me in the Department. Then [Finke] had spoken about filling the chair and indicated that probably, or at least maybe, nothing would come of Dr. [Max] Ettlinger, for it was doubtful whether he would get anywhere with his proposal on Martin Deutinger, and it was equally questionable whether Rickert could work up any interest in a work on Martin Deutinger. [Finke said] Rickert had spoken in a very derogatory way about [Joseph] Geyser: Natorp had written [Rickert] about Geyser's *Grundlagen zur Logik und Erkenntnistheorie:* Absolutely nobody reads a book like that (!), and Husserl had written him: It is a meaningless compilation, even if Geyser had learned something from him. So see to it that you do

a dissertation in the history of philosophy. [Heidegger said] Finke had then expressed praise for my lecture courses, about which he had heard good reports, and when Heidegger intentionally made a slightly negative comment about me, [Finke] called me one of his most gifted students and insisted that I was entirely capable of controlling the area of the courses I had taken over. In brief, Heidegger was surprised to hear him speak of me with nothing but approval . . . If Finke now wants to bring Heidegger to the professorship – after advising him last summer to take his State examination in languages – that's fine by me.[164]

The news came as something of a blow to Krebs, and in both memos we can sense his disappointment. Krebs certainly did want the chair; in fact that very day on which Heidegger informed him of Finke's suggestion, Krebs had been officially named interim director of the Seminar of Christian Philosophy[165] (and he would retain that position through the summer of 1917). But from the report Heidegger brought him and from what he already knew about Finke's opposition to a cleric holding the position, it was clear, at least to Krebs, that his younger friend would soon supercede him in the chair.

Nonetheless, Krebs tried to be helpful. In line with Finke's proposal he suggested that Heidegger switch the topic of his qualifying dissertation to a text by the medieval Dominican philosopher Magister Dietrich of Freiburg (ca. 1250 to 1310) – the 'De origine rerum praedicamentalium,' which Krebs himself had studied a decade earlier when preparing his doctorate in philosophy.[166]

1914–1915, age 24–25. But Heidegger did not follow Krebs' advice, and despite Finke's urgings and strong support, he was reluctant to give up his work in the philosophy of mathematics. It is true that in the published version of his doctoral dissertation (1914) Heidegger would refer to Finke as the one 'who, with the most willing and obliging kindness awakened in the unhistorical mathematician a love for and understanding of history.'[167] But that awakening must have taken a while, for in a letter that Krebs wrote to Privatdozent Friedrich Nauen of Strassburg on January 2, 1914, Krebs reported not only that Heidegger was continuing to work on 'the logic of the concept of number' but also:

At this time it is unclear (1) whether Heidegger even can get the *Habilitation* before the summer of 1915; (2) whether he will get it with a historical or a logical work; the second is coming along excellently; the first he doesn't really want to work on; (3) what the unpredictable Mssrs. Finke and Rickert want in the meantime. The only thing clear is that Rickert intends to prolong the interim situation for a good while – on this I have statements from him in writing – and it is also clear that Finke wants it to end soon now and wants to see a layman in the picture.[168]

Besides Finke's history seminar, Heidegger during the summer semester of 1914 participated in Rickert's seminar as well, and at least one other student in that class thought it was clear what Heidegger's professional plans were. Years later Professor Julius Ebbinghaus recalled his first encounter with Heidegger:

> I first met Heidegger in a seminar I took under Rickert in the summer of 1914, and he was still dressed in the uniform of an alumnus of the Freiburg seminary for future priests (the so-called 'Sapienz'). As far as I recall, he intended to get the teaching license in the Philosophy Department as an aspirant for the 'denominational' chair of philosophy that the State had granted to the Catholic Church via the Concordat.[169]

It is possible that by the end of that same semester Heidegger *may* have settled on a new topic for his qualifying dissertation, and it is probable that he had asked Rickert to direct the work. But it is not sure that the topic was yet the *De modis significandi* of Thomas of Erfurt (alias Duns Scotus). An extraordinary letter that Heidegger wrote to Krebs on Saturday, July 19, 1914, allows us a glimpse of the young scholar hard at work on *something* having to do with Husserl just as the summer semester comes to an end.[170]

> Cordial thanks for your card. I've pulled back because I get bothered too much in the [philosophy] department. Last week I got caught up once again in my work. Wednesday [July 23] I will see Rickert to get his opinion. I have to sacrifice my holidays because Husserl's phenomenology is causing me a lot of trouble in the final passages, and I don't want to bring down on myself the accusation of misunderstanding [him], the way Messer and Cohn recently [did].[171] I hope to be able to send off my essay 'Über die Frage' at the end of the month.[172] In my leisure time I pull out your lecture notes, but of course I have to familiarize myself with [your] current course lest the two [seem to] run along on separate tracks without any connection at all.[173] Do we too belong to the 'neighboring islands?' We still don't have the *motu proprio* on philosophy.[174] Perhaps as an 'academic' you could apply for better treatment: all who succumb to having independent thoughts could have their brains taken out and replaced with spaghetti.
>
> Philosophical demand could be met by setting up vending machines in the train station (free of charge for the poor). I have a dispensation that covers the period of my studies. But would you be so kind as to put my name on the list too?
>
> Before long now you will develope into a *homo phaenomopius* and will demonstrate the metaphysics of movement *ad oculos*. Maybe before long there will be an occasion to take a walk and discuss your logic course a bit. With thanks and best regards,
>
> Cordially yours,
> M. Heidegger

Two weeks later the war broke out, and Heidegger did his best to be a part of it. However, both as a volunteer (at the beginning of August) and as a draftee (in mid-October) he was dismissed from active duty for reasons of health. He then devoted himself full-time to work on the qualifying dissertation. The first clear indication that the work was on medieval philosophy comes in a letter that Heidegger wrote to the Freiburg chancellery office on Sunday, September 20, 1914, to request a renewal of his von Schaezler grant. He wrote: 'The undersigned is busy with the elaboration and completion of his qualifying dissertation on Duns Scotus' theory of meaning and knowledge.'[175] In this statement we can clearly recognize for the first time what Heidegger in CV-1915 would refer to as his 'intense engagement with the philosophy of the Middle Ages,'

> an engagement that I recognized as necessary for a basic building up of Scholasticism. For me this engagement consists not primarily in a presentation of the historical relations between individual thinkers but rather in an interpretative understanding of the theoretical content of their philosophy.

Before 1914 was over Heidegger had published his doctoral dissertation on psychologism as a book and turned out three book reviews.[176] In the longest of the reviews, dedicated to Charles Sentroul's *Kant und Aristoteles,* Heidegger, among other things, praised the Marburg and Baden Neo-Kantians for helping to clear the way to 'a correct understanding of Kant,'[177] and he continued to uphold Rickert's and Lask's position on judgment and the categorial without yet breaking through to the crucial issue of the *Logical Investigations*: the meaning of the categorial intuition of beingness. In the review Heidegger gave the distinct impression that the Aristotelian Scholastic in him was learning more and more from Kant. But he was not yet a phenomenologist.

However, according to his own declarations he was certainly a Catholic philosopher. In petitioning the archdiocesan chancellery office to renew his von Schaezler grant (September 20, 1914) he spoke of his intention to pursue a 'career in the service of researching and teaching Christian-Scholastic philosophy', and in thanking the office (November 23) he spoke of his dedication to the 'Catholic Weltanschauung.'[178]

By the spring of 1915 Heidegger handed in the finished manuscript of his dissertation on Duns Scotus' doctrine of categories and meaning to his director, Heinrich Rickert.[179] Because he was not particularly familiar with the area, Rickert asked Krebs to read the work and offer an evaluation. Krebs' response to Heidegger's work was quite positive.[180] Everything was now in place for the mathematician-turned-medievalist to take the next and crucial step towards an appointment to the chair of Christian philosophy. By July of

1915 the young Dr. Martin Heidegger was ready to apply for a license to teach at Freiburg University.

Appendices

Appendix I

Martin Heidegger
Lebenslauf
[1913]

Geboren bin ich, Martin Heidegger, in Messkirch (Baden) am 26. September 1889 als Sohn des Mesners und Küfermeisters Friedrich Heidegger und der Johanna geborene Kempf, beide Badische Stadtsangehöriger und katholischer Konfession. Von 1899 bis 1903 besuchte ich die Bürgerschule meiner Vaterstadt, und trat im Herbst 1903 in die Untertetia des Gymnasiums Konstanz ein. Seit 1906 von Obersecundar an, besuchte ich das Bertholdsgymnasium in Freiburg-im-Breisgau und bestand eben da Sommer 1909 die Reifeprüfung. Im Herbst desselben Jahres wurde ich an der Universität Freiburg-im-Breisgau als Studierender der Theologie immatrikuliert. Im Winter-Semester 1911 wechselte ich die Fakultät und wurde bei der naturwissenschaftlich-mathematischen Fakultät inskribiert. Ich hörte Vorlesungen über Mathematik, Physik, Chemie und Botanik. Während der ganzen Zeit meiner Universitätsstudien hörte ich philosophische Vorlesungen.

Appendix II

Arthur Schneider
Gutachten
[re: Martin Heidegger's Inaugural Dissertation]
[July 10, 1913]

In ihrem ersten historisch-kritischen Teil zeigt die vorliegende Arbeit einen wie grossen Einfluss der Psychologismus in den logischen Urteilstheorie in der Gegenwart – gewollt und noch auch das ungewollt – auch jetzt noch, trotz aller erfolgten Bekämpfung, ausübt. Als charakteristische Belege hierfür werden die Theorien von Lipps, Meyer und Wundt herangezogen, in eingehender Analyse der hier vorhandene psychologistische Einschlag aufgezeigt, und vermittelst immanenter und transzendenter Kritik auf seinen Erklärungswert hin untersucht. Das Resultat ist ein negatives. Es wird dagetan, dass das Wesen des logischen Urteils durch jene ausgesprochen-psychologistischen Auffassungen in keiner Weise getroffen wird. Der zweite, positive Teil der Arbeit enthält sodann die Grundlinien einer eigenen Theorie des Verfassers, dem das Urteil der Logik vor allem Sinn ist.

Das ganze Problem, welches der Verfasser behandelt, ist ein schwieriges. Nichts weniger als ein Durchschnittsthema. Es setzt ausserumfassende Kenntnis der neueren Logik und nicht geringen Scharfsinn, vor allem schon eine gewisse Reife philosophischer Urteilskraft voraus. Diese Eigenschaften begrundet der Verfasser, der sich in wissenschaftlichen Zeitschriften mit logischen Ausführungen eingeführt hat, in hohem Masse. Bin ich auch mit dem positiven Teil der Darlegungen durchaus nicht in allen Punkten einverstanden, so handelt es sich doch auch hier um philosophisch interessante und bedeutsame Gedankengänge. Die ganze Arbeit muss als eine ausgezeichnete Leistung bezeichnet werden.

Ich erlaube mir darher den Antrag auf Zulassung des Verfassers zum mündlichen Examen der Fakultät zu unterbreiten. 10. Juli 1913 Schneider

Appendix III

Martin Heidegger
Lebenslauf
[1915]

Ich, Martin Heidegger, geboren den 26. September 1889 zu Messkirch (Baden), als Sohn des Mesners und Küperfermeisters Friedrich Heidegger und seiner Ehefrau Johanna, geb. Kempf, besuchte bis 1903 die Volks- und Bürgerschule in Messkirch. Seit 1900 erhielt ich Privatunterricht in Latein, so dass ich 1903 in die Untertertia des Gymnasiums in Konstanz eintreten konnte. Entscheidenden geistigen Einfluss verdanke ich dem damaligen Rektor des Knabenkonvikts, dem jetzigen Stadtpfarrer Dr. Konrad Gröber in Konstanz. Nach Absolvierung der Untersekunda (1906) besuchte ich bis zur Erlangung des Reifezeugnisses (Sommer 1909) das Bertholdsgymnasium in Freiburg-im-Breisgau.

Als in der Obersekunda der mathematische Unterricht vom blossen Aufgabenlösen mehr in theoretische Bahnen einbog, wurde meine blosse Vorliebe zu dieser Disziplin zu einem wirklichen sachlichen Interesse, das sich nun auch auf die Physik erstreckte. Dazu kamen Anregungen aus der Religionsstunde, die mir eine ausgedehntere Lektüre der Literatur über die biologische Entwicklungslehre nahelegten.

In der Oberprima waren es vor allem die Platostunden bei dem vor einigen Jahren verstorbenen Gymnasialprofessor Widder, die mich mehr bewusst, wenn auch noch nicht mit theoretischer Strenge in philosophische Probleme einführten.

Nach Absolvierung des Gymnasium bezog ich im Wintersemester 1909 die Universität Freiburg-im-Breisgau, wo ich ununterbrochen bis 1913 blieb. Zunächst studierte ich Theologie. Die damals vorgeschriebenen philosophischen Vorlesungen befriedigten mich wenig, so dass ich mich auf das Selbststudium der scholastischen Lehrbücher verlegte. Sie verschafften mir eine gewisse formale logische Schulung, gaben mir aber in philosophischer Hinsicht nicht das, was ich suchte, und auf apologetischem Gebiet durch die Werke von Herman Schell gefunden hatte.

Neben der kleinen *Summa* des Thomas von Aquin und einzelnen Werken von Bonaventura waren es die *Logischen Untersuchungen* von Edmund Husserl, die entscheidend wurden für meinen wissenschaftlichen Entwicklungsgang. Das frühere Werk desselben Verfassers, die *Philosophie der Arithmetik,* setzte mir zugleich die Mathematik in ein ganz neues Licht.

Die eingehende Beschäftigung mit philosophischen Problemen neben den Aufgaben des eigentlichen Berufsstudiums, hatte nach drei Semestern eine starke Überarbeitung zur Folge.

Mein früher durch zuviel Sport entstandenes Herzleiden brach so stark aus, dass mir eine spätere Verwendung im kirchlichen Dienst als äusserst fraglich hingestellt wurde. Daher liess ich mich im Wintersemester 1911 auf 1912 bei der naturwissenschaftlich-mathematischen Fakultät inskribieren.

Mein philosophisches Interesse wurde durch das mathematische Studium nicht vermindert, im Gegenteil, da ich mich nicht mehr an die vorgeschriebenen Vorlesungen in der Philosophie zu halten brauchte, konnte ich philosophische Vorlesungen in ausgedehnterem Masse besuchen und vor allem an den Seminarübungen bei Herrn Geheimrat Rickert teilnehmen. In der neuen Schule lernte ich allererst die philosophischen Probleme als Probleme kennen und bekam den Einblick in das Wesen der Logik, der mich bis heute vor allem mich [sic] interessierenden philosophischen Disziplin. Zugleich bekam ich ein richtiges Verständnis der neueren Philosophie seit Kant, die ich in der scholastischen Literatur allzuwenig und ungenügend berücksichtigt fand. Meine philosophischen Grundüberzeugungen blieben die der aristotelisch-scholastischen Philosophie. Mit der Zeit erkannte ich, dass das in ihr niedergelegte Gedankengut eine weit fruchtbarere Auswertung und Verwendung zulassen müsse und fordere. So suchte ich in meiner Dissertation über 'Die Lehre vom Urteil im Psychologismus' bezüglich eines Zentralproblems der Logik und Erkenntnistheorie unter gleichzeitiger Orientierung an der modernen Logik und den aristotelisch-scholastischen Grundurteilen für weitere Untersuchungen ein Fundament zu finden. Aufgrund dieser Arbeit wurde ich von der philosophischen Fakultät der Universität Freiburg zum Rigorosum zugelassen, das ich am 26. Juli 1913 bestand.

Das Studium von Fichte und Hegel, die eingehende Beschäftigung mit Rickerts *Grenzen der naturwissenschaftlichen Begriffsbildung* und den Untersuchungen Diltheys, nicht zuletzt Vorlesungen und Seminarübungen bei Herrn Geheimrat Finke, hatten zur Folge, dass die bei mir durch die Vorliebe für Mathematik genährte Abneigung gegen die Geschichte gründlich zerstört wurde. Ich erkannte, dass die Philosophie sich nicht einseitig weder an der Mathematik und der Naturwissenschaft noch an der Geschichte orientieren dürfte, dass letztere zwar als Geistesgeschichte die Philosophen ungleich mehr befruchten kann.

Das nun sich steigernde historische Interesse erleichterte mir so die für einen gründlichen Ausbau der Scholastik als notwendig erkannte eingehendere Beschäftigung mit der Philosophie des Mittelalters. Diese bestand für mich vorerst weniger in einem Herausstellen der historischen Beziehungen unter den einzelnen Denkern, als in einem deutenden Verstehen des theoretischen Gehaltes ihrer Philosophie mit den Mitteln der modernen Philosophie. So entstand meine Untersuchung über die Kategorien und Bedeutungslehre des Duns Scotus.

Sie zeitigte in mir zugleich den Plan einer umfassenden Darstellung der mittelalterlichen Logik und Psychologie im Lichte der modernen Phänomenologie mit gleichzeitiger Berücksichtigung der historischen Stellung der einzelnen mittelalterlichen Denker. Sollte es mir vergönnt sein, in den Dienst der wissenschaftlichen Forschung und Lehre treten zu dürfen, dann soll der Verwirklichung dieser Pläne meine Lebensarbeit gewidmet sein.

Appendix IV

Heinrich Rickert
Gutachten über die Habilitationsschrift des Herrn Dr. Heidegger
[July 19, 1915]

Die Schrift behandelt einen berühmten Scholastiker, über den eine verhältnismässig grosse Literatur existiert, und der trotzdem zum Teil so gut wie unbekannt zu sein scheint. Auch über die 'Sprachlogik' des Duns Scotus, die in der vorliegenden Studie das Hauptthema bildet, ist zwar schon von K. Werner bearbeitet, aber es fehlt bisher der Versuch, diese Gedanken in grössere logische Zusammenhänge in eins zu stellen und sie so wahrhaft philosophisch zu würdigen. Deshalb muss es als ein glücklicher Gedanke des Herrn Dr. Heidegger bezeichnet werden, die 'Bedeutungslehre' des Duns Scotus zum Gegenstand einer besonderen Abhandlung zu machen und ihr aus systematische Grundlegung des Verständnisses Ausführungen über die Kategorienlehre dieses Denkers voranzuschicken. So wird dem Begriff der 'Bedeutung' zunächst der logische Ort im All des Denkbaren angewiesen und damit die Beziehung einer 'spekulativen Grammatik' zu dem Grundprobleme der Logik klargelegt.

Zu einer *geschichtlichen* Behandlung des Themas ist es dabei jedoch noch nicht gekommen. Sie ist auch mit grossen Schwierigkeiten verknüpft und hätte die Kräfte des Verfassers wohl noch überstiegen. Es wäre dabei vor Allem auf den Einfluss Plotins zurückzugehen, der immer über den Aristotelismus hinausgetrieben hat, und den auch Prantl in seinem grossen Werk viel zuwenig würdigt. Die historische Einleitung, die Dr. Heidegger versucht hat, ist verfehlt und muss ganz weg bleiben. Vollends ist von jeder Verknüpfung dieser Studie mit einer beabsichtigten Darstellung der historischen Entwicklung der Anschauungen über Wesen und Aufgabe der Grammatik in Mittelalter abzusehen. Dr. Heidegger ist rein *systematisch* an modernen Problemstellungen orientiert, und seine Arbeit bleibt nur dann unangreifbar, wenn sie ausdrücklich auf eine historische Einreihung des Duns Scotus verzichtet. Der Verfasser hat einige Schriften des grossen Scholastikers studiert, ohne danach zu fragen, was dieser Autor von andern übernimmt, und was ihm eigentümlich ist, und er sucht nun zu zeigen, wie weit Duns Scotus sich den Gedanken von Logikern unserer Zeit nähert. Dieser Unternehmen ist durchaus verdienstlich und führt zu einigen recht interessanten Ergebnissen. Besonders die Ausführungen im Anschluss an das 'unum' und das 'verum,' also zwei der bekannten vier mittelalterlichen 'transcendentia,' zeigen unzweideutig, dass Duns Scotus Probleme gesehen hat, die heute im Mittelpunkt des logischen Interesse stehen, und sie dürfen manchen überraschen. Dadurch gewinnt Dr. Heidegger den Boden, auf dem sich das Problem des Verhältnisses von Wort und Bedeutung oder Sprache und logischen 'Sinn' in Angriff nehmen und verstehen lässt, was der Traktat 'De modis significandi sive Grammatica speculativa' der theoretischen Philosophie zu sagen hat. Auch in den einzeln Ausführungen über diese Schrift, auf die ich hier nicht näher einzugehen brauche, findet Dr. Heidegger Beziehungen zu modernen Autoren, besonders zu der bedeutsamen 'metagrammatischen Subjekts-Prädikats-Theorie' von Lask, dessen Schriften der Verfasser für seine philosophische Orientierung und auch für seine Terminologie ganz besonders viel verdankt, vielleicht mehr als ihm selbst zu Bewusstsein gekommen ist.

Da ich wie die Meisten meiner Fachgenossen auf dem Gebiet der mittelalterlichen Philosophie niemals selbstständig gearbeitet habe, hielt [sic] ich es für Wünschenswert, das Urteil unseres Kollegen Krebs über die Schrift kennenzulernen. Es stimmt mit dem meinigen in Wesentlichen überein. Krebs findet, dass die Studie, obwohl sie von jeder historischen Einreihung absieht, auch unser geschichtliches Wissen um die tatsächlich erreichte Höhe des logischen Denkens im Mittelalter bereichert und eine neue Betrachtungsweise und Würdigung der mittelalterlichen Geistesarbeit eröffnet. Die Texte, welche der Schrift zu Grunde gelegt sind, sind die der Pariser Ausgabe. Sie lässt wohl noch manches zu wünschen übrig, doch sind nach der Meinung des Kollegen Krebs die Textverderbnisse in den in Frage kommenden Schriften so geringfügig, dass die Arbeit als Ganzes völlig auf die Pariser Ausgabe aufgebaut werden kann. Einige Rezensionen, wie sie der Sinn erfordert an Stellen, die offenkundig verderbt sind, sollen durch Schiefdruck kenntlich gemacht und in Anmerkungen die Lesarten der Pariser Ausgabe angegeben werden, so dass auch in dieser Hinsicht die Schrift den wissenschaftlichen Ansprüchen genügen wird, wenn sie gedruckt vorliegt.

Alles in Allem ist die Arbeit zwar noch keine Studie zur *Geschichte* der mittelalterlichen Logik, aber eine wertvolle *Vorstudie* dazu. Und es wird noch manche solche Vorstudien bedürfen, ehe an einer geschichtlichen Darstellung selbst gegangen werden kann, die den 'Geist' der mittelalterlichen Logik wirklich durchdringt. Wir besitzen davon noch recht wenig, und der Verfasser kann sich hier grosse Verdienste erwerben. Er steht noch in den Anfängen seiner wissenschaftlichen Entwicklung, aber er vermag schon jetzt recht schwierige Gedankengänge früherer Jahrhunderte in sich aufzunehmen und besitzt auch genug moderne philosophische Bildung, um die Zusammenhänge von Vergangenheit und Gegenwart zu sehen. Da er auch mathematisch geschult ist und eine ausgesprochene Begabung für abstraktes Denken hat, darf man beim Fleiss und der Gründlichkeit, mit der er vorgeht, Erfreuliches von seinen späteren wissenschaftlichen Arbeiten erhoffen. Ich kann daher seine Zulassung zur Habilitation nur empfehlen.

Freiburg i. Br. 19. Juli 1915 Rickert

Notes

1. Much of the research for the present article was conducted in Freiburg and Messkirch in late August, 1977 (it was then that I discovered Heidegger's handwritten 1915 *Lebenslauf,* herein called 'CV-1915'), although a first draft of the article was completed only in April of 1987. In July of 1987 I discovered for the first time Professor Hugo Ott's two invaluable articles on the

young Heidegger: 'Der junge Martin Heidegger. Gymnasial-Konviktszeit und Studium,' *Freiburger Diözesanarchiv,* 104 (1984), 315–325, and 'Der Habilitand Martin Heidegger und das von Schaezler'sche Stipendium. Ein Beitrag zur Wissenschaftsförderung der katholischen Kirche,' *Freiburger Diözesanarchiv* 108 (1986), 141–160. I have drawn heavily on these articles for the present version of the article, completed in December of 1987.

2. This information on Heidegger's military service is compiled from two *Standeslisten* (records of personal and professional information) that Heidegger drafted in his own hand and submitted to the University of Freiburg: Universitätsarchiv, 'Heidegger. / Grossherzogl. Badische Universität Freiburg / PVS PER-NT. 056983.' The first one (hereinafter' Standesliste-1915) was completed on or just before Wednesday, October 27, 1915. (The Academic Senate forwarded Standesliste-1915 to the Ministry of Education in Karlsruhe on that date, accompanied by memo no. 2068: 'Grossherzoglichem Ministerium des Kultus und Unterrichts legen wir die Standesliste des Privatdozenten Dr. Martin Heidegger von Messkirch ergebenst vor.') The second *Standesliste* (hereinafter: Standesliste-1928) was drawn up in the fall of 1928. In Standesliste-1915, under 'Militärverhältnisse,' Heidegger says that he volunteered 'Im August 1914' without specifying the day, and continues: 'am 10. August 1914 entlassen.' (In Standesliste-1928, under 'Militär- und Kriegsdienstzeit,' Heidegger specifies that he volunteered on August 2, i.e., the day after the war began.) The 1915 text goes on: 'Vom 9. Oktober bis zum 20. Oktober eingezogen und wieder entlassen.' These and other documents that will be mentioned later in the present essay are, unless otherwise noted, in the Heidegger files in the Archives of the Albert-Ludwigs-Universität, Freiburg in Breisgau.
3. The work that Heidegger commented on in his dissertation, *Tractatus de modis significandi* (or *Grammatica speculativa*) was later shown to have been authored not by Duns Scotus (1266–1308) but by the late-thirteenth century follower of Scotus, Magister Thomas of Erfurt (Thomas de Erfordia, Thomas Erfordiensis), ca. 1379. See Martin Grabmann, 'De Thoma Erfordiensi auctore Grammaticae quae Ioanni Duns Scoto adscribitur Speculativae,' *Archivum Franciscanum Historicum,* 15 (1922), 273–277: 'Novissime cum codices *De modo significandi* seu *Grammatica speculativa* diversorum scholasticorum perscrutarer, verus huius Grammaticae auctor ex Bibliothecarum latebris prodiit, nempe Magister Thomas de Erfordia. Hanc thesim, ea quae in iis materiis litterariis possibilis est, certitudine gaudere, testimonio codicum manuscriptorum confirmatur' (275). Concerning Heidegger's published volume Grabmann writes: 'Martinus Heidegger, qui in opere perdocto *Grammaticam speculativam* explicat et cum modernorum philosophorum praeprimis E. Husserl confert, quaestionem et dubium de authenticitate movere praetermittit' (274). See also John D. Caputo, 'Phenomenology, Mysticism and the "Grammatica Speculativa": A Study of Heidegger's "Habilitationsschrift,"' *Journal of the British Society for Phenomenology,* 5, 2 (May, 1974), 101–117; also his *Heidegger and Aquinas: An Essay on Overcoming Metaphysics* (New York: Fordham University Press, 1982), 36–45. Throughout the present essay I shall mention Heidegger's dissertation by reference to its presumed subject, Duns Scotus.
4. Victor Farias, *Heidegger et le nazisme,* translated from the Spanish and the German by Myriam Benarroch and Jean-Baptiste Grasset (Lagrasse: Verdier, 1987), 58, makes the startling claim that Heidegger's qualifying dissertation 'fut lui aussi dirigé par A. Schneider, du moins si l'on en croit un rapport de Heidegger adressé à Georg Misch, dans le cadre d'un appel d'offres pour l'université de Göttingen. ...' Farias, without having seen such a document addressed by Heidegger to Misch, postulates (pp. 62 and 68) that it must underlie a report that Misch drew up on or soon after November 2, 1923 (see p. 67) that dealt with possible candidates for a position at Göttingen University and that is found in the university archives. At 312, n. 130, Farias cites the location of the report as 'Archives de l'université de Göttingen XIV. IV. 13.7. Bd. II Ersatzvorschläge für Professoren 28.10. 1920–1930. 9. 1933' [sic; perhaps: '28.10.1920–30.9.1933'?].
5. 'Einer hohen philosophischen Fakultät der Universität Freiburg i. Br. / Bewerbung des Dr.

Phil. Martin Heidegger aus Messkirch (Baden) um die Habilitation betreffend. / Der gehorsamst Unterzeichnete gestattet sich einer hohen philosophischen Fakultät der Universität Freiburg i. Br. seine Abhandlung über 'Die Kategorien- und Bedeutungslehre des Duns Scotus' vorzulegen. / Sollte diese für wissenschaftlich genügend befunden werden, dann gestattet sich der gehorsamst Unterzeichnete einer hohen philosophischen Fakultät zu ersuchen ihm die venia legendi für Philosophie zu erteilen. / Als Themata für den im Falle der Zulassung notwendigen Probevortrag erlaubt sich der Unterzeichnete folgende drei einer hohen philosophischen Fakultät zu unterbreiten: / erstens, der Zeitbegriff in der Geschichte / zweitens, das logische Problem der Frage / drittens, der Zahlbegriff. / In vorzüglichste Hochachtung verhart einer hohen philosophischen Fakultät gehorsamster / Martin Heidegger.'

6. See 'Exkurse XIX. Habilitationsordnung der philosophischen Fakultät der Universität Freiburg 1894,' in E. Th. Nauck, *Die Privatdozenten der Universität Freiburg i. Br. 1818–1955* (Freiburg im Breisgau: Verlag Eberhard Albert Universitätsbuchhandlung, 1956), 142–143; here, 143.
7. CV-1914 appears in Martin Heidegger, *Die Lehre vom Urteil im Psychologismus. Ein kritisch-positiver Beitrag zur Logik* [the title page continues: 'Inaugural-Dissertation zu Erlangung der Doktorwürde der hohen philosophischen Fakultät der Albert Ludwigs-Universität zu Freiburg i. Breisgau vorgelegt von Martin Heidegger aus Messkirch, Baden'] (Leipzig: Johann Ambrosius Barth, 1914), 111. An English translation by Therese Schrynemakers appears in Joseph J. Kockelmans, *Martin Heidegger: A first Introduction to his Philosophy* (Pittsburgh: Duquesne University Press; and Louvain: Editions E. Nauwelaerts, 1965), 1f., and is reprinted in *Listening,* 12, 3 (Fall, 1977), 110.
8. The German text of Heidegger's original five-page, handwritten CV-1915, which I discovered in the Archives of the University of Freiburg on August 31, 1977, is found in Appendix III. This is the copy that Heidegger submitted for the files of the Philosophy Department. In Appendix No. 2 (pp. 323–325) of his 'Der junge Martin Heidegger' Ott has reproduced yet another handwritten version of CV-1915 (with only insignificant differences with regard to the first vision), the one that Heidegger had the Philosophy Department forward to the Academic Senate of the University of Freiburg, which in turn forwarded it to the Grand Ducal Ministry of Education in Karlsruhe on Wednesday, July 28, 1915 (see below, n. 11). This second version is now in Stuttgart at the Hauptstaatsarchiv of the Kultusministerium of Baden-Württemberg, under the listing: 'EA III/1 Universität Freiburg, Heidegger Martin.'
9. The text of Rickert's *Gutachten* appears in Appendix IV.
10. A text based on the lecture was published as 'Der Zeitbegriff in der Geschichtswissenschaft,' *Zeitschrift für Philosophie und philosophische Kritik,* 161 (1916), 173–188; the first footnote, keyed to the title, reads: 'Das Folgende fällt *inhaltlich* mit der Probevorlesung zusammen, die der Verfasser am 27. Juli 1915 vor der philosophischen Fakultät der Universität Freiburg i. Br. hielt zur Erlangung der venia legendi. Die *Form* ist hier mehr dem Charakter eines Aufsatzes angepasst' (173, n. 1). The text has been republished in Martin Heidegger, *Frühe Schriften* (Frankfurt am Main: Vittorio Klostermann, 1972), 358–375, with the footnote recorded in Friedrich-Wilhelm von Herrmann's 'Bibliographischer Nachweis,' 376; reprinted in his *Gesamtausgabe,* I/1, edited by Friedrich-Wilhelm von Herrmann (Frankfurt am Main: Vittorio Klostermann, 1978), 415–433, with the footnote at 436. English translation by Harry S. Taylor and Hans W. Uffelmann, 'The Concept of Time in the Science of History,' *Journal of the British Society for Phenomenology,* 9, 1 (January, 1978), 3–10.
11. 'Philosophische Fakultät der Universität Freiburg i. Br. / Freiburg, den 27. Juli 1915 / Die Habilitation des Dr. Martin Heidegger aus Messkirch betreffend: / Dem Akademischen Senat beehre ich mich mitzuteilen, dass die philosophische Fakultät beschlossen hat, dem am 26. September 1889 zu Messkirch geborenen und am 26. Juli 1913 zum Doktor Phil. promovierten Martin Heidegger, der die für die Habilitation vorgeschriebenen Leistungen

erfüllt hat, die venia legendi für Philosophie zu erteilen und bittet den Senat, die Bestätigung der Habilitation durch das Grossherzogliche Unterrichtsministerium befürworten zu wollen. Das Gutachten über die Habilitationsschrift und den Lebenslauf des Dr. Heidegger füge ich bei. / Finke, Dekan.' The *Lebenslauf* that Finke mentions is the one that I have called the 'second version' (n. 8 above, ad fin.).

12. The Academic Senate of Freiburg University confirmed the Philosophy Department's decision and in memo no. 1641, dated Wednesday, July 28, 1915, recommended to the Grand Ducal Ministry of Education that it confirm the decision: 'Die philosophische Fakultät hat beschlossen, dem Dr. Phil. Martin Heidegger aus Messkirch die venia legendi für Philosophie zu erteilen. Der Senat beantragt, die Habilitation des Genannten für das gedachte Fach bestätigen zu wollen.' On Saturday, July 31, 1915, Dr. Schmidt, the Director of the Ministry, responded with memo no. A. 6624: 'An den Senat der Universität Freiburg / wir erteilen die Genehmigung zur Habilitation des Dr. Phil. Martin Heidegger aus Messkirch der philosophischen Fakultät für das Fach der Philosophie.' Memo no. 1685 (August 5, 1915), addressed to Finke from the Akademisches Directorium of the University, read: 'An die philosophische Fakultät zur gefl[älligen] Kenntnisnahme: Privatdozent Dr. Heidegger hat von hieraus Nachricht halten.'
13. The conscription date of August 18, 1915, is from Heidegger's Standesliste-1915 under 'Militärverhältnisse' ('Seit 18.VIII.1915 als Rekrut beim 2. Regr. E.B. 142, Müllheim, Berlin). The dates of September 18 and October 16, 1915, are from Farias, 59, with the source given as: 'Les documents que nous avons pu consulter au Krankenbuchlager der Berlin . . .' The date of November 1 is from Standesliste-1928 under 'Militär- und Kriegsdienstzeit.' (And in a letter dated December 13, 1915, and addressed to the chancellery office of the archdiocese of Freiburg, Heidegger described himself as 'z. Z. bei der Überwachungsstelle Freiburg i. Br. militärisch verwendet': cited in Ott, 'Der Habilitand,' 159.) But in a letter to Hermann Köstler, dated Friday, May 11, 1979, Mrs. Elfriede Heidegger provided the following (in part conflicting) information (the text is Köstler's): 'Martin Heidegger stand mit Ausnahme von sechs Wochen, in denen er nach einem langen Lazarettaufenthalt in Müllheim nach Hause entlassen wurde, *vom Frühjahr 1915* bis zum Frühjahr 1918 ununterbrochen in Militärdienst als Landsturmmann bei der Postüberwachungsstelle Freiburg . . .' Hermann Köstler, 'Heidegger schreibt an Grabmann,' *Philosophisches Jahrbuch,* 83 (1980), 96–109, here 98 (emphasis added). During the last year of the war Heidegger was drafted once again (according to Standesliste-1928, on January 1; but Husserl wrote to him at Lerchenstrasse in Freiburg on January 30, 1918: R I Heidegger, 30.I.18, Husserl-Archives, Leuven). According to Standesliste-1928, Heidegger spent from January 1 through May 15, 1918, in training with Ersatz-Bataillon [Infantry Reserve Batallion] 113, Fourth Company (at the Truppenübungsplatz in Heuberg, southern Germany: information, August 1977, from the late Prof. Franz Josef Brecht, who served in the army with Heidegger, and confirmed by Husserl's letter, R I Heidegger, 28.III.18; but Heidegger was in Freiburg on Friday, April 26, 1918: Husserl, R I Heidegger 11 [?].V.18). Standesliste-1928 says that from May 15 through July 20 he served at the main meteorological station (Hauptwetterwarte) in Berlin-Charlotty, and from the beginning of August of 1918 'bis Waffenstillstand, Frontwetterwarte 414. Stellungskämpfe vor Verdun [until the cease-fire, at Weather Station 414 at the Front. Combat in the trenches at Verdun].' However, Ott, in 'Der Habilitand,' 156 and n. 42, reports that according to the Hauptstaatsarchiv Stuttgart EA 3/1, Heidegger was already transferred to the front – to Frontwetterwarte 414 of the Third Army – on July 8, 1918. In any case it is sure that on Tuesday, July 2, 1918 Heidegger was still in Charlotty, for on that date he wrote to Husserl from there (cf. Husserl, R I Heidegger, 10.IX.18). On August 11, 1977, Mrs. Elfriede Heidegger informed me orally that Heidegger arrived back in Freiburg from military service in December of 1918.
14. During the war it was common for professors to maintain their academic post while serving

in a military capacity; see Köstler, 98, n. 14; also the remarks of Edith Stein (1891–1942): 'While the war lasted, he [Professor Körte of classical studies, at that time dean of the Philosophy Department] was a Captain of the Reserves and drilled recruits in Freiburg; in his free time, he discharged his duties as Dean. That is why he was wearing his field gray uniform when he received me.' Edith Stein, *Aus dem Leben einer jüdischen Familie. Das Leben Edith Steins: Kindheit und Jugend,* vol. 7 of *Edith Steins Werke,* L. Gelber and Romaeus Leuven, eds. (Louvain: E. Nauwelaerts, and Freiburg im Breisgau: Herder, 1965), 284; English translation by Josephine Koeppel, *Life in a Jewish Family: Her Unfinished Autobiographical Account,* vol. 1 of *The Collected Works of Edith Stein,* L. Gelber and Romaeus Leuven, eds., (Washington, D.C.: ICS Publications, 1986), 404.

15. For information on the course see Bernhard Casper, 'Martin Heidegger und die Theologische Fakultät Freiburg 1909–1923,' in Remigius Bäumer, Karl Suso Frank, and Hugo Ott, eds., *Kirche am Oberrhein. Beiträge zur Geschichte der Bistümer Konstanz und Freiburg* (Freiburg im Breisgau: Verlag Herder, 1980), 534–541, here, 539 and n. 14. (The article is also printed in *Freiburger Diözesanarchiv,* 100 [1980] 534–541.) In the 1915 Bursar's Record Book (Quästur-Journal) of Freiburg University the course bears the title 'Geschichte der antiken Philosophie.' Heidegger himself in his letter of December 13, 1915, addressed to the chancellery office of the archdiocese of Freiburg speaks of his course 'über Geschichte der antiken und scholastischen Philosophie': Ott, 'Der Habilitand,' 157 and 159. The title 'Grundlinien der antiken und scholastischen Philosophie' is found in Heinrich Finke's memo of November 20, 1915 (see n. 17 below) as well as in the Kollegienbuch of Fräulein Elfriede Petri. Because Heidegger was expected to be on active duty at the time, this course does not appear in the university catalogue of that year (*Ankündigung der Vorlesungen der Grossherzoglich Badischen Albert-Ludwigs-Universität zu Freiburg im Breisgau für das Winter-Halbjahr 1915/16* [Freiburg i. B.: Universitäts-Buchdruckerei U. Hochreuther, 1915]), and therefore it is not found in the list given in William J. Richardson, S.J. *Heidegger: Through Phenomenology to Thought* (The Hague: Martinus Nijhoff, 1963), 663–671.

16. On Engelbert Gustav Hans Krebs, see Albert Junghanns' doctoral dissertation, *Der Freiburger Dogmatiker Engelbert Krebs (1881–1950): Ein Beitrag zur Theologiegeschichte,* Albert-Ludwigs-Universität, Freiburg im Breisgau (Altendorf: D. Gräbner, 1979), especially 'Der 'Supplementauftrag' und das Tauziehen um die Professor für christliche Philosophie' and 'Engelbert Krebs und Martin Heidegger – Begegnung mit Edith Stein,' pp. 50–60, and the bibliography of Krebs' works, 318–36. The archives of the Dogmatics Seminar of the Theology Department at Freiburg University possesses relevant, unpublished materials of Krebs, which I have not seen. Junghanns, 318, lists some of them as follows: (1) 'Tagebuchnotizen in Taschenkalendern 1910–1914 (5 Kalender [sic]),' (2) 'Tagebücher 1914–1932 (11 Mappen),' and (3) 'Stichworte A-Z (4-Mappen).' Ott, 'Der Habilitand,' refers simply to Krebs' 'Tagebuch' and usually cites it by date (142ff.). Casper (538, n. 10, etc.) refers to Stichworte 'H' as 'Notizbücher, Buchstab H.' At 539, n. 14, he cites that source: 'Im Winter 1915/16 las er [= Heidegger] auf meinem Rat Geschichte der griechischen und mittelalterlichen Philosophie im Überblick.

17. On Saturday, November 20, 1915, Professor Heinrick Finke, who was dean of the Philosophy Department that year, wrote to the Academic Senate to ask permission for Heidegger to teach the course, which in fact was already underway: 'An den Akademischen Senat. / Privatdozent Dr. Heidegger, der zu Ende des Sommer-Semesters 1915 zugelassen worden ist, war zu Beginn des laufenden Winter-Semesters im Heeresdienst beschäftigt und ist zu Anfang November nach Freiburg überwiesen worden. So war ihm die Möglichkeit zu Vorlesungen geboten. Er hat nun in der vorigen Woche [i.e., in the week beginning Monday, November 8] mit einer jede zweite Woche zu haltenden vierstündigen Vorlesung über: 'Die Grundlinien der antiken und scholastischen Philosophie' begonnen. / Im Namen

der Fakultät bitte ich, die nachträglich Genehmigung bei Grossh. Ministerium des Kultus und Unterrichts erwirken zu wollen. / Dekan, Finke.' The Senate petitioned the Ministry of Education and received approval from Dr. Hübsch of the Ministry in memo no. A. 11027, dated Thursday, November 25, 1915: 'Die Abhaltung von Vorlesungen durch Privatdozent Dr. Heidegger betr. / An das Akademische Direktorium der Universität Freiburg. / Wir erteilen die Genehmigung dazu, dass Privatdozent Dr. Heidegger eine jede zweite Woche zu haltende vierstündige Vorlesung über 'Die Grundlinien der antiken und scholastischen Philosophie' liest.' In memo no. 2351, dated Tuesday, November 30, 1915, the Akademisches Direktorium informed Finke: 'An die philosophische Fakultät zur gefl. Kenntnisnahme. / Herr Privatdozent Dr. Heidegger hat von hieraus Nachricht erhalten.'

18. Heidegger and Elfriede Petri (born July 3, 1893, the daughter of Richard Petri, a German army colonel from Saxony) were married by Father Engelbert Krebs in the University chapel of Freiburg cathedral on Tuesday, March 20, 1917. (The date is from Heidegger's Standesliste-1928; Junghanns, 56, dates it to March 21, 1917, and says Ms. Petri 'damals beabsichtigte, zu konvertieren.') Their first son, Jörg, was born on January 1, 1919, and their second son, Hermann, on August 20, 1920. Edith Stein recalled that in 1916 '[t]he future Frau Heidegger, then still Fräulein Petri, was in Husserl's seminar, and she used to put up some lively opposition. / Husserl himself had told us about it, remarking: 'When a woman is that obstinate, there's sure to be a man in the background somewhere [Wenn ein Weibsbild so widerspenstig ist, dann steckt ein Mannsbild dahinter].' *Aus dem Leben,* 288; *Life,* 409.
19. On the history of Messkirch see Farias, 23–26. The name Mösskirch appears in a sixteenth century document cited by Ott, 'Der junge Martin Heidegger,' 320.
20. Henry Barnard, ed., *Memoirs of Eminent Teachers and Educators with Contributions to the History of Education in Germany* [Republished from *The American Journal of Education*'] (Hartford: Brown & Gross, 1878), 644, notes that in the late nineteenth century the ten years of *Volksschule* (which Barnard calls 'common' school) were divided into four 'periods,' each two years long, with admission to the first period at the age of six. According to CV-1913, Heidegger would have left the *Volksschule* after the second period (at ten years of age) and completed the remaining years in the *Bürgerschule* (but see n. 23). For further information on elementary schooling and middle schools see G.J. Tamson, *A General View of the History and Organisation of Public Education in the German Empire,* translated by Wilhelm Lexis (Berlin: A. Asher & Co., 1904), 89–106, with mention of the Grand Duchy of Baden on p. 105; Friedrich Paulsen, *German Education Past and Present,* translated by T. Lorenz (London and Leipsic [sic]: T. Fisher Unwin, 1908, reprinted, New York: AMS Press, 1976), 236ff., and especially the translator's 'Terminological Notes,' xi-xix; I.L. Kandel's chapter, 'Germany,' in Peter Sandiford, ed., *Comparative Education: Studies of the Educational Systems of Six Modern Nations* (London: Dent and Sons; New York: E.P. Dutton, 1918), esp. 121–130 and 140–155; Alina M. Lindegren, *Education in Germany,* United States Department of the Interior, Office of Education, Bulletin 1938, No. 15 (Washington, D.C.: United States Government Printing Office, 1939), 1–7. On the development of the *höhere Bürgerschule* in Baden see Mary Jo Maynes, *Schooling for the People: Comparative Local Studies of Schooling History in France and Germany, 1750–1850* (New York and London: Holmes & Meier, 1985), 161–178. The *Bürgerschule* system that Heidegger went through was discontinued in the educational reform of 1918.
21. In *Martin Heidegger. Zum 80. Geburtstag von seiner Heimatstadt Messkirch* (Frankfurt am Main: Vittorio Kostermann, 1969), facing 29; reprinted in Walter Biemel, *Martin Heidegger in Selbstzeugnissen und Bilddokumenten* Reinbeck bei Hamburg: Rowohlt, 1973), 15; English translation by J.L. Mehta, *Martin Heidegger: An Illustrated Study* (New York and London: Harcourt Brace Jovanovich/Original Harvest, 1976), 17, no. 4.
22. Professor Ott, 'Der junge Heidegger,' 316f., is, as far as I know, the first to mention Father Brandhuber, assistant pastor (1898–1900) and then pastor (1900–1906) at St. Martin's

Church, Messkirch. For a biographical note on Brandhuber see the unsigned, one-paragraph obituary 'Brandhuber Camillus' in 'Necrologium Friburgense 1931–1935' in *Freiburger Diözesanarchiv,* 64 (1936), 2.

23. 'Martin Heidegger, 26. IX. 1889 Messkirch. Vorbildung: Hat die 3. Klasse der dortigen Realschule absolviert und will nach Untertertia.' Erzbischöfliches Archiv Freiburg, Ordinariat Freiburg, Generalia. B 2–32/44–45: I cite the text and reference from Ott, 'Der junge Martin Heidegger,' 328 n. 12. There may (or may not) be a discrepancy between (1) CV-1913, in which Heidegger indicates that he spent *four* years in the *Bürgerschule,* and (2) the archival text we have just cited, which states that Heidegger had completed the *third* year by 1903. Heidegger may have started the *Sexta* (sixth German form, first British form) in 1900, at the age of eleven, after a preparatory year at the *Bürgerschule.* See the chart in Lindegren, p. 11 (but it would be one year off for Heidegger).
24. On Konradihaus and the teachers at the State Gymnasium in Constance (the Protestants Wilhelm Martens in history and Otto Kimming in Greek, Latin and German, and the free thinker Pacius in modern languages) see Farias, 27–32. For Heidegger's remark on the quality of instruction at Constance, see n. 47 below.
25. On Gröber see Erwin Keller, *Conrad Gröber, 1872–1948: Erzbischof in schwerer Zeit,* second edition (Freiburg, Basel, Wien: Herder, 1981). Also Hugo Ott, 'Gröber, Conrad,' in Bernd Ottnad, ed., *Badische Biographien,* Neue Folge (Stuttgart: W. Kohlhammer, 1982), I. 144–148. For the period of Gröber's rectorate of the minor seminary see Keller, Chapter VII, esp. pp. 55–59. Konradihaus, which had reopened in 1884, was rebuilt and expanded in 1901 in order to accommodate over a hundred young seminarians, many of whom otherwise would have attended school in Rastatt, Sigmaringen, or Sasbach. Gröber was appointed the first rector of the new building with its increased studentbody. His reputation as a teacher was eminent; however, in the summer of 1905, while Heidegger was still a student there, Archbishop Thomas Nörber of Freiburg visited Konradihaus and came away with the unfavorable impression that there were 'manche Lausbubengesichter darunter' (cited in Keller, 58). Gröber was soon removed and appointed pastor of Trinity Church, where it was felt his administrative talents would be better employed.
26. Konrad Gröber, *Geschichte des Jesuitenkollegs und -Gymnasiums in Konstanz* (Constance: A. Streicher, 1904). For the date of the beginning of his book ('im Oktober vergangenen Jahres') see p. iii.
27. Information from Ott, 'Der junge Martin Heidegger,' 318 and 319. Ott, 319, also discovered the information about Friedrich Heidegger's occasional work as a cooper; see Georg Wöhrle, 'Die Lage des Handwerks in Messkirch, mit besonderer Berücksichtigung der Schmiede, Wagner und Sattler,' in *Schriften des Vereins für Sozialpolitik* (published in Leibniz by Duncker and Humblot from 1873 to 1939), 69 (1897) 1–55; concerning Friedrich Heidegger, p. 51, end of the first paragraph: 'Ein weiterer Küfer [in Messkirch] ist Messner [sic Wöhrle in the original; Ott, in citing the text, corrects it to 'Mesner']. Er macht nur nebenbei etwas Küferarbeit,' ('Another cooper [in Messkirch] is a sacristan. He only occasionally does some cooperage.') The conversion of marks into American dollars is based on the then official exchange rate of $ .238 per mark, which in 1924 was officially reconfirmed for the Weimar Republic's Reichsmark.
28. 'Eine Änderung des Pensionsbeitrags erbitten sich Herr Stadtpfarrer C. Brandhuber in Messkirch und der Unterzeichnete bei Martin Heidegger III b. Wie der Unterzeichnete sicher aus Kenntnis der Familienverhältnisse weiss, kann der Vater des Heidegger kaum mehr als 75 Mk. aufbringen. Der Zögling ist brav und talentiert.' Erzbischöfliches Archiv Freiburg, Ordinariat Freiburg, Generalia. B 2–32/44–45. I cite the text and reference as given on p. 318 of Ott, 'Der junge Martin Heidegger,' to which I am indebted for all the information concerning Heidegger's fees at the Constance seminary.
29. Ott, 'Der junge Martin Heidegger, 319. The foundation was established by the Fürstenberg

family (whose ancestors had ruled Messkirch from 1627 to 1806) and was named for Catholic historian and theologian Father Johann Baptist Weiss (1820–1899), author of the 22-volume *Lehrbuch der Weltgeschichte* (Vienna: W. Braumüller, 1859–1898): Farias, 24, 27, 55, 311, n. 103 (but Farias' bibliographical data are incorrect).

30. The text of the official's letter is given in Ott, 'Der junge Martin Heidegger,' 319: 'Hohes Rektorat des Erzbischöflichen Gymnasialkonvikts Konstanz setzen wir in Kenntnis, dass laut Mitteilung des Grossherzoglichen Oberschulrats der Zögling Martin Heidegger (U III [= Untertertia]) pro 1903/04 ein Stipendium Weiss aus Messkirch im Betrag von 100 Mk. erhalten hat, und sehen wir einem Antrag auf Erhöhung seines Verpflegungsgeldes entgegen. Dabei bemerken wir . . . Ew. Hochwürden wollen, sofern dies nicht schon geschehen ist, allen Zöglingen verkünden (welche Verkündigung jährlich zu wiederholen ist), dass jeder, der ein Stipendium oder eine Unterstützung aus einem Lokalfond erhält, verpflichtet ist, diess unverzüglich dem Rektor anzuzeigen. Wer diese Anzeige schuldbar unterlässt, wird mit grösserer Erhöhung seines Verpflegungsbeitrags bestraft.' That is: 'We inform the esteemed Rectorat of the archdiocesan high-school seminary that according to a communication from the Grand Ducal Supreme Educational Council, the pupil Martin Heidegger (U III [= Untertertia]) has received a Weiss Grant from Messkirch for 1903/04 in the amount of 100 marks, and we are awaiting a proposal [from you] to raise the charge for his room and board. Thus we observe . . .: If it has not already been done, would Your Reverence please announce to all the pupils (and the announcement is to be repeated each year) that everyone who receives a grant or assistance from a local foundation is obliged to report this without delay to the rector. Anyone who culpably neglects to make this report will be penalized by a[n even] greater increase in his obligatory contribution.'
31. The source of the information on Heidegger's reception of the Eliner Grant is a brief, 111-word document (cited later in our text) written on Friday, September 10, 1909, by Father Leonhard Schanzenbach (see n. 49 below), rector of the minor seminary in Freiburg and professor of religion and Hebrew at Freiburg's Bertholdsgymnasium. The letter concerned the candidacy of the recently graduated Heidegger for university-level studies in theology. Professor Ott has discovered the document (Erzbischöfliches Archiv Freiburg, Ordinariat Freiburg, Generalia. B 2–32/157) and published it in 'Der junge Heidegger,' 323. Ott provides further information on the history and conditions of the grant, ibid., 320–321.
32. Concerning his last full year at Constance, Heidegger reports that in 1905 (therefore, either during the second half of his *Obertertia* or the first half of his *Untersekunda*) he discovered the Austrian author Adelbert Stifter and first read his collection of stories, *Bunte Steine* ('Colored Stones'): *Frühe Schriften,* x; *Gesamtausgabe,* I/1, 56; English translation by Hans Seigfried, 'A Recollection,' in Thomas Sheehan, ed., *Heidegger, the Man and the Thinker* (Chicago: Precedent Press, 1981), 22.
33. The (old) minor seminary in Freiburg had been closed in 1874 during the Kulturkampf (in Baden, from 1871 to ca. 1886) and was reopened in 1881 under the directorship of Father Leonhard Schanzenbach (concerning whom see n. 38 below). In 1889 the seminary moved into a newly constructed building at #11 Zähringenstrasse.
34. On the Berthold-Gymnasium see *Freiburg im Breisgau. Stadtkreis und Landkreis. Amtliche Kreisbeschreibung,* vol. I/2 (Freiburg im Breisgau: Rombach & Co., 1965), 801 and 936–938.
35. Biemel, 18–19 in both the German and English editions.
36. In 'Der junge Martin Heidegger,' 322, Ott mentions that during Heidegger's last two years at the Gymnasium it was a Professor Mühlhäusser who taught him mathematics; but the teacher who inspired Heidegger's interests in this discipline during the *Obersekunda* remains unnamed.
37. The rulings on the Pentateuch are given in Conrad Louis, ed., *Rome and the Study of Scripture: A Collection of Papal Enactments on the Study of Holy Scripture together with the*

Decisions of the Biblical Commission, 6th revised and enlarged edition (St. Meinrad, Indiana: Grail Publications, 1958), 115–122.

38. For biographical information on Schanzenbach see the obituary 'Schanzenbach Leonhard' (signed 'A.') in 'Necrologium Friburgense, 1936–1940' in *Freiburger Diözesanarchiv,* 68 (1941), 27–28. Schanzenbach became director of the (old) minor seminary in Freiburg in 1881, but he officially became 'rector' only in 1889 when the seminary moved into its new quarters on Zähringenstrasse. He retired from teaching in 1919 but remained rector until 1934.
39. Heidegger's education was to be very much under the influence of Father Dreher's works, including his *Kleine Grammatik der hebräischen Sprache mit Übungs- und Lesestücke für Obergymnasien bearbeitet* (Freiburg: Herder, 1898), which Father Schanzenbach used in teaching Heidegger Hebrew. Father Dreher's work on apologetics, which Heidegger studied during *Obersekunda,* was the 67-page *Kleine katholische Apologetik für reifere Schüler höherer Lehranstalten* (Freiburg: Herder, various years and editions). During the *Unterprima* and *Oberprima* he used the four-part *Lehrbuch der katholischen Religion für Obergymnasium,* originally published in Sigmarigen by M. Liehner, 1876, but in later editions published by R. Oldenbourg in Munich. For the *Unterprima* course in modern Church history there was Dreher's 108-page *Abriss der Kirchengeschichte für Obergymnasium* (Sigmarigen: M. Liehner, 1882; adapted also as Part IV of his *Lehrbuch*), adapted and translated into English by Bonaventure Hammer, *Outlines of Church History* (St. Louis: Herder, 1896). Dreher's interest in the Collegium Sapientiae, the major seminary where Heidegger lived from 1909 to 1911, is mentioned by Wolfgang Müller, 'Dreher, Theodor' in Bernd Ottnad, ed., *Badische Biographien,* Neue Folge (Stuttgart: Kohlhammer, 1982), I, 102. See also L. Bopp, 'Dreher, Theodor,' in *Lexikon für Theologie und Kirche,* III (1959), 543.
40. Martin Heidegger, *Zur Sache des Denkens* (Tübingen: Max Niemeyer, 1969), 81; English translation by Joan Stambaugh, *On Time and Being* (New York: Harper & Row, 1972), 74.
41. Franz Brentano, *Von der mannigfachen Bedeutung des Seienden nach Aristoteles* (Freiburg: Herder, 1862; reprinted, Darmstadt: Wissenschaftliche Buchgesellschaft, 1960); in English: *On the Several Senses of Being in Aristotle,* trans. Rolf George (Berkeley: University of California Press, 1975).
42. *Frühe Schriften,* x; *Gesamtausgabe,* I/1, 56; 'A Recollection,' 22.
43. I am grateful to the late Professor Franz Josef Brecht of Mannheim for communicating to me (August 9, 1977) this information about the literary circle.
44. On Heidegger's discovery of Hölderlin's poems: *Frühe Schriften,* x; *Gesamtausgabe,* I/1, 56; 'A Recollection,' 22.
45. Ott, 'Der junge Heidegger,' 322.
46. *Zur Sache des Denkens,* 81f.; *On Time and Being,* 74f. Heidegger uses the alternate spelling: *Carl* rather than Karl. On Braig, see n. 74 below.
47. *Frühe Schriften* x; *Gesamtausgabe,* I/1, 56; 'A Recollection,' 22.
48. *Notentabelle für das Abiturientenexamen am Gymnasium in 1909,* Berthold-Gymnasium, Freiburg im Breisgau, unpublished; cited with the kind permission that Mrs. Elfriede Heidegger communicated verbally on Saturday morning, July 30, 1977. A photograph of Heidegger upon completion of the Abitur (his feet not touching the ground) is found in *Martin Heidegger. Zum 80. Geburtstag,* facing 37. Farias reports (51) that Messkirch's Catholic newspaper, *Heuberger Volksblatt,* carried a note on July 21, 1909: 'The young Martin Heidegger, the studious and talented son of sacristan Friedrich Heidegger, received his baccalaureate in Freiburg with the highest honors. He intends to devote himself to the study of theology.' On September 10, 1909, the same newspaper reported (Farias, 51–52) that on Monday, September 6, 1909, in Hausen im Tal near Messkirch, the 19-year-old Heidegger had acted as president of and speaker at a celebration in honor of the Augustinian

priest-orator Abraham a Sancta Clara (Johann Ulrich Mergerle, 1644–1709), author of frequently anti-semitic sermons (see also n. 73 below). In his speech Heidegger discussed the heated conflict between two journals, the *Hochland,* with its Modernist Catholic reputation, and the *Gral,* edited by the anti-Modernist and arch-conservative Richard von Kralik of Vienna. Heidegger urged the youths in the audience to subscribe to *Gral* and to join its organization, the *Gralbund.* (Did Heidegger change his mind on this matter while studying theology at the university? See the discussion of Herman Schell, below.)

49. I translate from the German text given in Ott, 'Der junge Heidegger,' 323, from the Erzbischöfliches Archiv Freiburg, Ordinariat Freiburg, Generalia. B 2–32/157. Rektoratszeugnisse für die Abiturienten (Kandidaten der Theologie): 'Martin Heidegger, geboren in Messkirch am 26. September 89 als Sohn des dortigen Stadtmesners, trat vom Gymnasium und Konvikt in Konstanz in die hiesige Obersekunda ein, weil der Bezug eines Eliner'schen Stipendiums den Wechsel der Anstalt verlangte. Seine Begabung sowie sein Fleiss und seine sittliche Haltung sind gut. Sein Charakter hatte schon eine gewisse Reife, und auch in seinem Studium war er selbständig, betrief sogar auf Kosten anderer Fächer zuweilen etwas zu viel deutsche Literatur, in welcher er eine grosse Belesenheit zeigte. / In der Wahl des theologischen Berufs sicher und zum Ordensleben geneigt, wird er sich wahrscheinlich um Aufnahme in die Gesellschaft Jesu melden. / Freiburg , den 10. September 1909 / Schanzenbach, Rektor.'
50. Farias, 33. See also Gerd Haeffner, 'Martin Heidegger (1889–1976)' in Otfried Höffe, ed., *Klassiker der Philosophie* (Munich: C.H. Beck, 1981), II, 361–362.
51. J.A. McDowell, *A Genese da Ontologia Fundamental de Martin Heidegger: Ensaio de caracterização do modo de pensar de 'Sein und Zeit* (São Paulo: Herder, 1970), 155 n. 116.
52. On the Theology Department of Freiburg University, see Bernhard Welte, 'Die Theologie zwischen Erbe und Neubeginn,' in *Festschrift der Universität Freiburg zur Eröffnung des zweiten Kollegiengebäudes,* Johannes Vincke, ed., (Freiburg im Breisgau: Verlag Eberhard Albert Universitätsbuchhandlung, 1961) 9–30. The Theology Department at the time was composed of eleven professors, all priests, and had about 225 students out of the 2600 registered at the university; see Joseph Lins, 'Freiburg,' *The Catholic Encyclopaedia,* VI (1909), 266 and 269, and his 'Baden, Grand Duchy of,' ibid., II (1907) 199.
53. On Heidegger's entry into the Sapientia, Farias, 309, n. 26, refers to documentation in: 'Erzbischöfliches Archiv Freiburg. Generalia. Rubrik: Klerus, betr. Theologisches Konvikt. Volume 7, 1908/1909/1910/1911. B 2–32/174.' On the Collegium Sapientiae see Adolf Weisbrod, *Die Freiburger Sapienz und ihr Stifter Johannes Kerer von Wertheim* (Freiburg im Breisgau: Verlag Eberhard Albert Universitätsbuchhandlung, 1966). On its modern use as a theology seminary see *Freiburg im Breisgau. Stadtkreis und Landkreis,* 791 and 929; on the Protestant seminary (mentioned just below in the text), ibid., 798.
54. McDowell, 155 n. 116.
55. Martin Heidegger, *Schellings Abhandlung Über das Wesen der menschlichen Freiheit (1809),* Hildegard Feick, ed. (Tübingen: Max Niemeyer, 1971), 33; English translation by Joan Stambaugh, *Schelling's Treatise on the Essence of Human Freedom* (Athens, Ohio and London: Ohio University Press, 1985), 27.
56. Martin Heidegger, *Die Grundprobleme der Phänomenologie, Gesamtausgabe,* II/24, Friedrich-Wilhelm von Herrmann, ed. (Frankfurt am Main: Vittorio Klostermann, 1975), 113; English translation by Albert Hofstadter, *The Basic Problems of Phenomenology* (Bloomington, Indiana: Indiana University Press, 1982), 80.
57. Casper, 535f. Some of the information I have added to Casper's list comes from various editions of the *Ankündigung der Vorlesungen* (1909–1918), usually abbreviated as the *Vorlesungenverzeichnis.* These pamphlets can be misleading about which courses were offered, especially during the years of World War I when some members of the university faculty were unexpectedly called to military service.

58. Julius Mayer (1857–1926) was the author of *Geschichte der Benediktinerabtei St. Peter auf dem Schwartzwald* (1893), *Die christliche Ascese* (1894), and *Predigten von Alban Stolz. Aus dessen Nachlass zu seinem hundertsten Geburtstag herausgegeben* (1908), all published by Herder in Freiburg.
59. Gottfried Hoberg (1857–1924), an arch-conservative Old Testament exegete and, beginning in 1903, consultor to the Pontifical Biblical Commission, taught at Freiburg University from 1890 to 1919 and wrote widely on the Pentateuch. His works include (all the following were published by Herder in Freiburg) *Die Genesis nach dem Literalsinn erklärt* (1899), *Moses und der Pentateuch* (1905), two short lectures published as *Über die Pentateuchfrage. Mit Berücksichtigung der Entscheidung der Bibel-Kommission 'De mosaica authentia pentateuchi' vom Jahre 1906* (1906), *Exegetisches Handbuch zum Pentateuch, mit hebräischem und lateinischem Text* (Freiburg: Herder, 1908ff.). On Hoberg see Raimondo Köbert, 'Hoberg, Gottfried,' *Enciclopedia Cattolica* (Città del Vaticano, 1948–54), VI, 1452–3, and Alfons Diessler, 'Hoberg, Gottfried,' *Lexikon für Theologie und Kirche* V (1960), 397.
60. Simon Weber (1866–1929), a conservative theologian, came to Freiburg in 1898 as professor of apologetics and from 1908 to 1916 was professor of New Testament exegesis. He authored the monumental, 532-page *Die katholische Kirche in Armenian, ihre Begründung und Entwicklung vor der Trennung. Ein Beitrag zur christlichen Kirchen- und Kulturgeschichte* (Freiburg: Herder, 1903) and *Christliche Apologetik* (Freiburg: Herder, 1907); see S. Hirt's obituary in 'Necrologium Friburgense' in *Freiburger Diözesanarchiv,* 59 (1931), 22–27; and H. Riedlinger, 'Weber, Simon,' in *Lexikon für Theologie and Kirche,* X (1965), 973.
61. The noted church historian Georg Pfeilschifter (1870–1936) held the chair of church history at Freiburg from 1903 to 1917 (when he was succeeded by Emil Göller; cf. infra) and in 1925, while at Munich, founded the Deutsche Akademie. See J. Oswald, 'Georg Pfeilschifter 1870–1936,' *Historisches Jahrbuch,* 56 (1936), 437–440.
62. Heinrich Straubinger had just taken over the chair of apologetics (which had been separated off from the chair of dogmatics and bestowed on Andreas Schill in 1889) that autumn of 1909, and he held it until 1949. See Welte, 'Die Theologie,' 14f.
63. Johann Uebinger (1854–1912) held the chair of Christian philosophy (Lehrstuhl der christlichen Philosophie) in Seminar I of the Philosophy Department from 1903 to 1911 as the successor of Adolf Dyroff (1866–1943), who held it from 1901–1903. He took the doctorate at Würzburg with the dissertation *Philosophie des Nikolaus Cusanus* (Würzburg: J.B. Fleischmann, 1880) and went on to publish *Die Gotteslehre des Nikolaus Cusanus* (Münster and Paderborn: Ferdinand Schöningh, 1888) and to edit various works of Cusanus in *Zeitschrift für Philosophie* (1894–96).
64. For all the citations in this paragraph: *Zur Sache des Denkens,* 81f.; *On Time and Being,* 74f.
65. *Ibid.,* 82 = 75 for this and the following citation.
66. Stein, *Aus dem Leben,* 174; *Life,* 250. Koeppel's translation is misleading at this point and has been corrected here.
67. Martin Heidegger, *Unterwegs zur Sprache* (Pfullingen: Günther Neske, 1959), 96; English translation by Peter D. Hertz, *On the Way to Language* (New York: Harper & Row, 1971), 9f. Hoberg, who taught the course on hermeneutics, published *Katechismus der biblischen Hermeneutik* (Freiburg: Herder, 1914; but Köbert, in 'Hoberg,' 1452, lists its first publication as 1904).
68. Schell's major works include:
    1. *Die Einheit des Seelenlebens aus den Principien der Aristotelischen Philosophie entwickelt,* (Freiburg im Breisgau: F.J. Schenble, 1873; reprinted unchanged, Frankfurt am Main: Minerva, 1967). This is Schell's doctoral dissertation in philosophy, done under Brentano at Würzburg.
    2. *Das Wirken des Dreieinigen Gottes* (Mainz: Kirchheim, 1885). This is Schell's doctoral dissertation in theology.

3. *Katholische Dogmatik,* 4 vols. (Paderborn: Ferdinand Schöningh, 1889–1893).
4. *Die Göttliche Wahrheit des Christentums.* This work was projected in four books; the first book (which, as far as I know, was the only one of the four to be published) is in two volumes: *Gott und Geist,* 2 vols, Erster Teil, Grundfragen (Paderborn, Ferdinand Schöningh, 1895), Zweiter Teil, Beweisführung (ibid., 1896).
5. *Der Katholizismus als Princip* [sic] *des Fortschritts* (Würzburg: Andreas Göbel, 1897).
6. *Die neue Zeit und die alte Glaube* (Würzburg: Andreas Göbel, 1898).
7. *Apologie des Christentums,* 2. vols., I. Religion und Offenbarung (Paderborn: Ferdinand Schöningh, 1901 [3rd ed.: 1907]); II. Jahwe und Christus (*ibid.* 1905 [2nd ed., 1908]).
8. *Christus: Das Evangelium und seine weltgeschichtliche Bedeutung* (Mainz: Kirchheim 1903); English translation, translator not listed, *The New Ideals in the Gospel* (London: K. Paul, Trench, Trübner, 1913).
9. *Kleineren Schriften,* Karl Hennemann, ed. (Paderborn: Ferdinand Schöningh, 1908).

On Schell see Josef Hasenfuss, 'H. Schells Synthese von scholastischem und modernem Denken und Glauben im Sinne eines christlichen Personalismus,' in Joseph Ratzinger and Heinrich Fries, eds., *Einsicht und Glaube* [Festschrift for Gottlieb Söhngen] (Freiburg: Herder, 1962), 377–398. Also: Thomas Franklin O'Meara, *Romantic Idealism and Roman Catholicism: Schelling and the Theologians* (Notre Dame, Indiana, and London: University of Notre Dame Press, 1982), 194–196.

69. In Section X the *Syllabus* condemned what it called 'errors regarding contemporary liberalism,' such as: 'LXXX. Romanus Pontifex potest ac debet cum progressu, cum liberalismo et cum recenti civiltate sese reconciliare et componere.'
70. See Norbert Trippen, *Theologie und Lehramt im Konflikt. Die kirchlichen Massnahmen gegen den Modernismus im Jahre 1907 und ihre Auswirkungen in Deutschland* (Freiburg: Herder, 1977). For Schell, see 189–220.
71. See Welte, 'Die Theologie,' 23f. Also Junghanns, *Der Freiburger Dogmatiker,* 41–46.
72. 'In arch-Catholic Freiburg I do not want to stand out as a corrupter of the youth, as a proselytizer, as an enemy of the Catholic Church.' Edmund Husserl, R I Otto 5.III.19, Husserl-Archives, Leuven. An English translation of the entire text is published as: Edmund Husserl, 'Letter to Rudolf Otto (1919),' in Sheehan, ed., *Heidegger,* 23–26; here, 24. 'Arch-Catholic': According to the census of December 1, 1905, Freiburg had a population of 76,286, of whom 53,133 (70%) were Catholic: Lins, 'Freiburg,' *The Catholic Encyclopaedia,* VI (1909), 264.
73. Henry Duméry, 'Blondel et la philosophie contemporaine (Etude critique),' *Etudes blondeliennes,* 2 (1952), 92 n. 1 *ad fin.* During the summer of 1910 Heidegger published a brief article, his first, in the journal *Allgemeine Rundschau,* vol. 7, about the inauguration of a monument to Abraham a Sancta Clara (see n. 48 above) on Monday, August 15, 1910, in Abraham's native town of Kreenheinstetten near Messkirch: Farias, 39, 47–49, and 309, n. 45. Farias claims that the brief article 'articulates all the determining elements' of 'Martin Heidegger's early ideological and spiritual evolution' (39).
74. Braig (1853–1923) was a student of the last of the great Catholic Tübinger theologians, J. Kuhn, and an outstanding Leibniz scholar. He began teaching at Freiburg University in 1893 and held the chair in dogmatic theology from 1897 to 1919, when he was succeeded by Engelbert Krebs. Under the general title of *Die Grundzüge der Philosophie* he published (all with Herder in Freiburg) *Vom Denken. Abriss der Logik* (1896), *Vom Sein. Abriss der Ontologie* (1896) and *Vom Erkennen. Abriss der Noetik* (1897). See Friedrich Stegmüller, 'Braig, Carl,' *Lexikon für Theologie und Kirche,* II (1958), 642; Welte, 'Die Theologie zwischen Erbe and Neubeginn,' 13f.; and Farias, 63.
75. Emil Göller (1874–1933), professor of church history and canon law, came to the University of Freiburg in 1909. He succeeded Pfeilschifter in the chair of church history in 1917 and held it until 1933. His publications dealt mostly with the history and finances of the Roman Curia.

76. See Farias, 36–37.
77. Archeologist and historian of ecclesiastical art Joseph Sauer (1872–1949), a student of church historian Franz Xaver Fraus at Freiburg, wrote his qualifying dissertation under Pfeilschifter and was appointed *Privatdozent* for church history in 1902. In 1905 he was named *ausserordentlicher* Professor with a contract to teach the history of Christian literature and theological science in the Middle Ages, and his lecture courses were on the Council of Trent, the history of mysticism and scholasticism, and the church and theology in pre-Reformation Europe. See Johannes Vincke, 'Joseph Sauer, 1872–1949,' in Johannes Vincke, ed., *Freiburger Professoren des 19. und 20. Jahrhunderts* (Freiburg im Breisgau: Verlag Eberhard Albert Universitätsbuchhandlung, 1957), 109–119, with excerpts from his diary (1924–1939), 119–137, and a photograph of Sauer facing 128.
78. *Frühe Schriften,* 344 n. 2; *Gesamtausgabe,* I/1, 402 n. 2. In his letter to Grabmann, dated January 7, 1917, Heidegger mentions his enthusiasm 'für weitere Arbeiten auf dem Gebiet der mittelalterl. Scholastik u. Mystik.' Cited in Köstler, 102 and 104.
79. For example, Casper, 540, Köstler, 98, and (following Casper) Farias, 63.
80. The course was announced on p. 23 of *Ankündigung der Vorlesungen der Badischen Albert Ludwigs-Universität zu Freiburg im Breisgau für das Winterhalbjahr 1919/1920* (Freiburg im Breisgau: Universitäts-Buchdruckerei Emil Gross, 1919).
81. 'Konstanz / 30 August 1919 / Einer hohen philosophischen Fakultät der Universität Freiburg i. Br. / Vorlesungsänderung des Privatdozenten Dr. Martin Heidegger für Wintersemester 1919/1920 betr. / Der Unterzeichnete gestattet sich, eine hohe philosophische Fakultät zu bitten seine für das Wintersemester 1919/1920 angekündigten Vorlesungen ändern zu dürfen. / Bei der Aufstellung des Planes rechnetet der Unterzeichnete mit langeren Herbstferien. Under den jetzigen Umständen wird aber eine strengen Anforderungen genügende Durcharbeitung des Materials für die angekundigte Vorlesung: "Die philosophischen Grundlagen der mittelalterlichen Mystik" unmöglich. Der Unterzeichnete bittet daher um die Erlaubnis an Stelle der genannnten Vorlesung die ausserdem angekündigte einstündige Vorlesung über "Ausgewählte Probleme der reinen Phänomenologie" in eine zweistündige umwandeln zu dürfen unter dem Titel: "Grundprobleme der Phänomenologie," Dienstag und Freitag von 4 bis 5 Uhr (für Anfänger) mit anschliessendem Kolloquium Dienstag 6 bis 7 einhalb. / Mit vorzüglichste Hochachtung / Dr. Martin Heidegger Privatdozent.'
82. Cf. *Sein und Zeit,* 11th ed. (Tübingen: Max Niemeyer, 1967), 72 n. 1; English translation by John Macquarrie and Edward Robinson, *Being and Time* (New York: Harper & Row, 1962), 490 n. H. 72.
83. On Heinrich Finke see 'Heinrich Finke' in Sigfrid Steinberg, ed., *Die Geschichtswissenschaft der Gegenwart in Selbstdarstellungen* (Leipzig: Felix Meiner, 1925), I, 1–34, with bibliography 34–38; Johannes Spörl, 'Heinrich Finke 1855–1938,' *Historisches Jahrbuch,* 58 (1938), 241–248; G. Schreiber, 'Finke, Heinrich' in *Lexikon für Theologie und Kirche,* X (1965), 140–141, with further secondary sources.
84. Farias, 33.
85. Martin Heidegger, 'Der Feldweg' in *Martin Heidegger. Zum 80. Geburtstag,* 11–15, here 11; English translation by Thomas F. O'Meara, revised by Thomas Sheehan, *Listening,* 8 (1973), 33–39, here 33; reprinted in Thomas Frick, ed., *The Sacred Theory of the Earth* (Berkeley; North Atlantic Books, 1986), 45–48, here 45.
86. Fritz Heidegger, 'Ein Geburtstagsbrief des Bruders,' in *Martin Heidegger. Zum 80. Geburtstag,* 60.
87. Joseph Geyser, *Grundlagen der Logik und Erkenntnislehre. Eine Untersuchung der Formen und Prinzipien objektiv wahrer Erkenntnis* (Münster: H. Schöningh, 1909). At this time Geyser held the chair in Christian philosophy at Münster. He would hold the comparable chair at Freiburg from 1917 until 1924, when he left for Munich. See Fritz-Joachim von Rintelen, 'Joseph Geyser zum Gedächtnis,' *Philosophisches Jahrbuch,* 58 (1948), 307–311.

88. Edmund Husserl, 'Philosophie als strenge Wissenschaft,' *Logos,* 1, 3 (1910–1911), 289–341. On the appearance of the article in March, 1911: Karl Schuhmann, *Husserl-Chronik. Denk- und Lebensweg Edmund Husserls* (The Hague: Martinus Nijhoff, 1977), 154.
89. According to students' notes, on Wednesday, July 4, 1951, during his three-semester course 'Übungen im Lesen,' Heidegger cited Husserl's sentence, 'Nicht von den Philosophien sondern von den Sachen und Problemen muss der Antrieb zur Forschung ausgehen,' and then continued: 'Der Satz steht gesperrt da. Aber es ist die Frage, woher die Sachen kommen, ob man im Jahr 1910 [sic] schon so ohne weiteres bei den Sachen war. Ich habe damals als Student daneben geschrieben: 'Wir nehmen Husserl beim Wort.' Es ist noch längst nicht entschieden, ob die Sache der Philosophie das Bewusstsein ist, und wenn, dann warum? Aber diese Fragen hat sich Husserl nicht gestellt. Bei ihm läuft der Weg anders.'
90. Herbert Spiegelberg, *The Phenomenological Movement: A Historical Introduction,* 2nd. edition, vol. 1 (The Hague: Martinus Nijhoff, 1971), 276. In a footnote Spiegelberg notes that this is an '[o]ral communication' from Heidegger.
91. On the history of the Philosophy Department as presented in this paragraph and the following one, see Siegfried Gutenbrunner, 'Die Philosophische Fakultät 1961' in Vincke, *Festschrift der Universität Freiburg,* 105–124. In 1909 the philological-historical section of philosophy had forty-three professors, and the mathematics-and-natural-sciences section had thirty: Lins, 'Freiburg,' *The Catholic Encyclopaedia,* VI (1909), 269. On the history of the teaching of mathematics at University of Freiburg see H. Gericke, *Zur Geschichte der Mathematik an der Universität Freiburg i. Br.* (Freiburg im Breisgau: Verlag Eberhard Albert Universitätsbuchhandlung, 1955). As late as the 1911 catalogue of courses, mathematics and the natural sciences were still listed under the Philosophy Department, although this changed thereafter. (The other three departments or *Fakultäten* in the university after the split remained the same: theology, law and political science, and medicine, with, respectively, eleven, sixteen, and fifty lecturers.)
92. *Frühe Schriften,* 3; *Gesamtausgabe,* I/1, 61. In the original 1914 edition: vii. In a letter to Dr. Fr. Nauen, dated January 2, 1914, Engelbert Krebs wrote: 'Im Sommer 1913 promovierte hier bei Schneider ein junger *Mathematiker und Philosoph* Martin Heidegger, ein sehr tüchtiger Mensch.' Cited in Hugo Ott, 'Der Habilitand,' 147 (emphasis added). A somewhat inaccurate description of his studies is given in *Zur Sache des Denkens,* 82; *On Time and Being,* 75: 'After four semesters I gave up my theological studies and dedicated myself entirely to philosophy.'
93. *Die Lehre vom Urteil* (1914), 111; English translation by Therese Schrynemakers in Kockelmans, 2; in *Listening,* 110.
94. See Section III for the complete text.
95. Heidegger, *Frühe Schriften,* x; *Gesamtausgabe,* I/1, 56; 'A Recollection,' 22. Heidegger remarks a misinterpretation of Nietzsche that was current at that time: *Nietzsche,* 2 vols (Pfullingen: Neske, 1961) I, 252–253; English trans. by David Krell, *Nietzsche,* 4 vols. (New York: Harper & Row, 1979ff.), I, 218–219.
96. Caspers, 538 n. 9.
97. Heidegger mentions his course or courses with Vöge in *Frühe Schriften,* xi; *Gesamtausgabe,* I/1, 57; 'A Recollection,' 22. See Karl Bauch, 'Wilhelm Vöge,' in Vincke, *Freiburger Professoren,* 183–190, with a photograph of Vöge facing 184.
98. *Zur Sache des Denkens,* 82; *On Time and Being,* 75. Heidegger frequently mentions Braig; e.g.: *Frühe Schriften,* xi; *Gesamtausgabe,* I/1, 57; 'A Recollection,' 22. See also O'Meara, 195. The structure of metaphysics that Heidegger refers to here is what he later called 'ontotheology.' That word was first used by Kant, but in a different sense, in his lectures on philosophy of religion: 'Philosophische Religionslehre nach Pölitz,' in *Kants gesammelte Schriften,* ed., Deutsche Akademie der Wissenschaften zu Berlin (Berlin: de Gruyter, 1972), XXVIII. 2, 2 (Vorlesungen 5, 2/2), 1003, 1004, 1013; English trans. by Allen W. Wood

and Gertrude M. Clark: Immanuel Kant, *Lectures on Philosophical Theology* (Ithaca and London: Cornell University Press, 1978), 31, 33, 44.

99. On Heidegger's teachers of mathematics, Alfred Loewy and Lothar Heffter, see Gericke, *Zur Geschichte der Mathematik,* 69–72. Also on Loewy see E.Th. Nauck, *Die Privatdozenten,* 113. A list of teachers in the natural sciences during Heidegger's student days is given in E.Th. Nauck, *Zur Vorgeschichte der naturwissenschaftlich-mathematischen Fakultät der Albert-Ludwigs-Universität Freiburg i. Br. Die Vertretung der Naturwissenschaften durch Freiburger Medizinprofessoren* (Freiburg im Breisau: Verlag Eberhard Albert Universitätsbuchhandlung, 1954), 62f.

100. Arthur Carl August Schneider, who took the doctorate in philosophy at the University of Breslau in 1900, had studied for a while under Husserl, as he mentions (without giving the exact period) in the *Lebenslauf* printed at the end of the excerpt from his doctoral dissertation, *Beiträge zur Psychologie Alberts des Grossen* (Münster: Aschendorff, 1900) 41; Prof. Karl Schuhmann has suggested (see Ott, 'Der Habilitand,' 144, n. 12) that 'Schneider habe vermutlich Heidegger auf Husserl aufmerksam gemacht.' (But did Husserl share Johannes Daubert's opinion that Schneider was a 'dolt'? Cf. '*dieses Kamel,*' in Daubert's letter to Husserl, dated Tuesday, October 29, 1907, printed in Reinhold N. Smid, 'Zwei Briefe von Johannes Daubert an Edmund Husserl aus dem Jahr 1907,' *Husserl Studies,* 1 [1984], 143–156; the letter is given at 151–153, and the cited phrase is on 153.) Schneider was a Privatdozent at Munich from 1903 until 1908, when he was appointed *ausserordentlicher* Professor for Catholic philosophy there, taking the place of Georg Freiherrn von Hertling. He held the chair of Catholic philosophy at Freiburg from the fall of 1911 until the fall of 1913, when he left for Strassburg. In 1920 he went to Frankfurt and in 1921 to Cologne. Before coming to Freiburg he published *Die Psychologie Alberts des Grossen. Nach den Quellen dargestellt,* 2 vols. (Münster: Aschendorff, 1903–06).

101. Heidegger provides this information about the Grieshaber-Pino Grant in Standeslist-1928 under the category 'Stipendium (während der Ausbildungszeit und Beihelfen aus staatlichen Mitteln.' Ott too mentions the grant ('ein Stipendium aus der Stiftung Grieshaber . . . ca. 400 Mk. jährlich') in 'Der junge Martin Heidegger,' 321, n. 20, as well as in 'Der Habilitand,' 141 ('das sogenannte Grieshaber'sche Stipendium . . .').

102. Farias, 58, mistakenly cites the title of Rickert's course as 'Introduction to Logic and Metaphysics.'

103. *Frühe Schriften,* 3.; *Gesamtausgabe,* I/1, 61. In the original 1914 edition: vii. In CV-1915 Heidegger also credits Rickert with helping to open his eyes to history.

104. *Literarische Rundschau,* 39, 4 (April 1, 1913), col. 179; *Gesamtausgabe,* I/1, 46. For a roughly contemporaneous reading of value philosophy see Joseph Fischer, 'Die Philosophie der Werte bei Wilhelm Windelband und Heinrich Rickert' in Joseph Geyser et al., eds., *Festgabe zum 60. Geburtstag Clemens Bauemker* (Münster: Aschendorff, 1913), 449–466.

105. *Frühe Schriften,* 133; *Gesamtausgabe,* I/1, 191.

106. On October 8, 1917, in a letter to Professor Paul Natorp of Marburg Edmund Husserl could report that Heidegger was no longer satisfied with the philosophy of Rickert: Husserl-Archives, R I Natorp 8.X.17; partial translation in Sheehan, 'Heidegger's Early Years: Fragments for a Philosophical Biography' in Sheehan, ed., *Heidegger,* 8. On August 9, 1977, the late Professor Franz Josef Brecht of Mannheim informed me that Heidegger himself frequently communicated the same dissatisfaction to Brecht while the two were on military guard duty in southern Germany in January of 1918.

107. *Sein und Zeit,* 155f.; *Being and Time,* 198f.

108. 'Gespräch mit M. Heidegger im Rahmen des Pro-Seminars von Prof. Spoerri. Zürich, den 6. November 1951,' *ad fin,* unpublished.

109. *Frühe Schriften,* x; *Gesamtausgabe,* I/1, 56; 'A Recollection,' 22.

110. *Sein und Zeit,* 218 n.; *Being and Time,* 493f. n. H. 218.

111. Both works have been reprinted by the original publisher in Emil Lask, *Gesammelte Schriften,* Eugen Herrigel, ed., vol. 2 (Tübingen: J.C.B.Mohr [Paul Siebeck]), 1923, 1–282 and 283–463 respectively. Rickert's attempt to reconcile his own 'subjective' approach with Lask's 'objective' approach – especially as expressed in Lask's critique of Rickert mentioned in his 1908 lecture 'Gibt es einen 'Primat der praktischen Vernunft' in der Logik?' At the Third International Congress for Philosophy in Heidelberg – is found in Rickert, 'Zwei Wege der Erkenntnistheorie. Transscendentalpsychologie und Transscendentallogik' *Kant Studien,* 14(1909), 169–228; cf. 210. On Lask see Georg von Lukacs, 'Emil Lask,' *Kantstudien* 22 (1918), 349–370; Georges Gurvitch, *Les tendances actuelles de la philosophie allemande: E. Husserl, M. Scheler, E. Lask, M. Heidegger* (Paris: J. Vrin, 1949), 153–186; Hans Peter Sommerhäuser, *Emil Lask in der Auseinandersetzung mit Heinrich Rickert* (Berlin: Ernst-Reuter-Gesellschaft, 1965), as well as his 'Emil Lask, 1875–1915: Zum neunzigsten Geburtstag des Denkers,' *Zeitschrift für philosophische Forschung,* 21 (1967), 136–145.
112. See Heidegger, 'Neuere Forschungen über Logik,' *Literarische Rundschau für das katholische Deutschland,* 38, 10 (October 1, 1912), col. 471; also in *Gesamtausgabe,* I/1, 24–25.
113. On Rousselot and Maréchal see Thomas Sheehan, *Karl Rahner: The Philosophical Foundations* (Athens, Ohio: Ohio University Press, 1987), 55–102. Rousselot was killed at Les Eparges, near Verdun, on April 25, 1915. Lask was killed in the Carpathians at Turza-Mala (Galicia, now in southern Poland) one month later, on May 26, 1915.
114. *Die Grundprobleme,* 253; *Basic Problems,* 178. Heidegger earlier offered similar criticisms of Lask in his courses: summer semester, 1922: 'Phänomenologische Interpretation ausgewählter Abhandlungen des Aristoteles zur Ontologie und Logik' (on Friday, July 21, and Monday, July 24, 1922); and summer semester, 1923: 'Ontologie. Hermeneutik der Faktizität,' (on Wednesday, June 13, 1923).
115. Martin Heidegger, 'Das Realitätsproblem in der modernen Philosophie,' *Philosophisches Jahrbuch,* 25 (1912), 353–363; reprinted in Heidegger, *Gesamtausgabe,* I/1, 1–15; English translation by Philip J. Bossert, 'The Problem of Reality in Modern Philosophy,' *Journal of the British Society for Phenomenology,* 4, 1 (January, 1973), 64–71. On this article see Karl Lehmann, 'Metaphysik, Transzendentalphilosophie und Phänomenologie in den ersten Schriften Martin Heideggers (1912–1916),' *Philosophisches Jahrbuch,* 71 (1963), 331–357, here 334. Also Philip J. Bossert, 'A Note on Heidegger's 'Opus One',' *Journal of the British Society for Phenomenology,* 4, 1 (January, 1973), 61–63. In 1916 Martin Grabmann sent Heidegger a copy of Grabmann's own article on Külpe, 'Der kritische Realismus Oswald Külpes und der Standpunkt der aristotelisch-scholastischen Philosophie,' *Philosophisches Jahrbuch,* 29 (1916), 333–369 – perhaps because Heidegger had sent Grabmann a copy of his Duns Scotus book (which appeared in late 1916) and maybe even his own 1912 article on Külpe. In his return letter to Grabmann dated January 7, 1917, Heidegger mentions Külpe both favorably and somewhat critically; see Köstler, 'Heidegger schreibt an Grabmann,' 98 (99), 103, and 104 *ad fin.*
116. 'Das Realitätsproblem,' 356; *Gesamtausgabe,* I/1, 5; 'The Problem of Reality,' 66.
117. 'Das Realitätsproblem,' 360; *Gesamtausgabe,* I/1, 10; 'The Problem of Reality,' 68.
118. 'Das Realitätsproblem,' 362, 357, and 358; *Gesamtausgabe,* I/1, 13, 7, and 8; 'The Problem of Reality,' 13, 7, and 8.
119. *Literarische Rundschau,* 38, 10 (October 1, 1912), cols. 465–472; 38, 11 (November 1, 1912), cols. 517–524; 38, 12 (December 1, 1912), cols. 565–570. The article appeared under the rubric of 'Übersichten' rather than 'Rezensionen und Referate.' It is reprinted in *Gesamtausgabe,* I/1, 17–43. Sauer was the chief editor of the *Rundschau* from 1905 to 1914: Vincke, 'Joseph Sauer,' 114.
120. *Literarische Rundschau,* 38, 10 (October 1, 1912), col. 466; *Gesamtausgabe,* I/1, 18.
121. *Literarische Rundschau,* 38, 11 (November 1, 1912), col. 520; *Gesamtausgabe,* I/1, 30.
122. *Sein und Zeit,* 166, cf. note 1; *Being and Time,* 209; cf. 492, note x.

123. A review of F. Ohmann, ed., *Kants Briefe in Auswahl* (Leipzig: Insel-Verlag, 1911): *Literarische Rundschau,* 39, 2 (February 1, 1912), col. 74; and a review of Nikolai von Bubnoff's qualifying dissertation, *Zeitlichkeit und Zeitlosigkeit*, (Heidelberg, 1911): *Literarische Rundschau,* 39, 4 (April 1, 1913), cols. 178–179; both reprinted in *Gesamtausgabe,* I/1, 45–46. On von Bubnoff, with a bibliography of his works, see Erich Th. Hock, 'von Bubnoff, Nicolai, Religionsphilosoph' in Bernd Ottnad, ed., *Badische Biographien,* I, 83–85.
124. *Literarische Rundschau,* 39, 4 (April 1, 1913), col. 179; *Gesamtausgabe,* I/1, 46.
125. *Ideen zu einer reinen Phänomenologie und phänomenologischen Philosophie, I. Buch,* in *Jahrbuch für Philosophie und phänomenologische Forschung,* 1/1 (1913), 1–323. The journal appeared irregularly, e.g.: 2 (1916); 3 (1916); 4 (1921).
126. Untitled first and second pages in *Jahrbuch für Philosophie und phänomenologische Forschung,* 1/1 (1913).
127. *Zur Sache des Denkens,* 83; *On Time and Being,* 76.
128. *Ibid.,* German, 85 and 86; English, 78.
129. *Ibid.,* German, 86; English, 78.
130. *Ibid.,* German, 83f.; English, 76.
131. *Ibid.,* German, 84; English, 77.
132. *Loc. cit.*
133. *Ibid.,* German, 85; English, 78.
134. *Ibid.,* German, 85; English, 77f.
135. *Ibid.,* German, 87; English, 79. On the categorial intuition and Heidegger's later insight into the meaning of being, see Sheehan, *Karl Rahner,* 291–294.
136. See Stein, *Aus dem Leben,* 284; *Life,* 404; cf. (only in the English edition) 505 n. 194.
137. 'Freiburg-im-Breisgau, den 30. Juni 1913 / Einer hohen philosophischen Fakultät der Albert-Ludwigs-Universität zu Freiburg i. Breisgau / Gesuch des Kand. Math. Martin Heidegger um Zulassung zur Doktorpromotion betr. / Der gehorsamst Unterzeichnete gestattet sich auf der beilegenden Arbeit und der erforderlichen Zeugnisse einer hohen philosophischen Fakultät die gehorsamste Bitte um Zulassung zur Doktorpromotion vorzutragen. Der gehorsamst Unterzeichnete wünscht geprüft zu werden im Hauptfach (Philosophie) durch Herrn Prof. Dr. Schneider, in der Nebenfächern (Mathematik) durch Herrn Professor Dr. Heffter und (Mittlerergeschichte) durch Herrn Geheimenhofrat Prof. Dr. Finke. / In vollkommenste Hochachtung verhart einer hohen philosophischen Fakultät gehorsamster / Martin Heidegger Cand. math. [= Candidatus mathematicus.]
138. 'Erklärung. / Der Unterzeichnete gibt hiermit sein Ehrenwort an Eides Statt, das derselbe die an einer hohen philosophischen Fakultät vorgelegte Arbeit selbsständig verfasst hat. / Freiburg in Breisgau, 30. Juni 1913 / Martin Heidegger, Cand. Math.'
139. The text of CV-1913 appears in Appendix I.
140. The text of Schneider's *Gutachten* appears in Appendix II.
141. The grade of *summa cum laude* is noted in Standesliste-1915: 'Promoviert, Prädikat: Summa cum laude.' (Ott, 'Der Habilitand,' 143, n. 10, has also found this information in the archdiocesan archives: Erzbischöfliches Ordinariatsarchiv Nr. 7247, 229–231.) Husserl's remark that this grade is reserved for those going on to the *Habilitation* is found in Stein, *Aus dem Leben,* 288; *Life,* 408.
142. The source of this information is the note made on November 14, 1913 (either in Taschenkalender 1913 or under Stichworte 'H') by Krebs, who, according to Ott's report ('Der Habilitand,' 145–6; Casper, 538, also alludes to the information) wrote that Heidegger felt 'ganz zu Hause' with the topic 'das logische Wesen des Zahlbegriffs . . . weil er die höhere Mathematik ganz beherrscht (Infinitesimal-, Integralrechnung, Gruppenordungen [??] und dergleichen mehr).' (The material in brackets is added by Ott.) The topic was probably suggested in part by Rickert's essay that greatly influenced the young Heidegger, 'Das Eine, die Einheit und die Eins. Bemerkungen zur Logik des Zahlbegriffs,' *Logos* 2 (1911–12);

indeed it is probable that from 1913 on, Heidegger wanted Rickert to direct the qualifying dissertation. In his letter of July 2, 1915, addressed to the Philosophy Department (see n. 5 above) Heidegger included 'der Zahlbegriff' as the third possible topic for his *Probevortrag*.

143. In CV-1915 Heidegger refers to Rickert's *Die Grenzen der naturwissenschaftlichen Begriffsbildung* (Tübingen: Mohr, [2nd. ed.] 1913). About one third of the work is translated as: Heinrich Rickert, *The Limits of Concept Formation in Natural Science: A Logical Introduction to the Historical Sciences (abridged edition),* ed. and trans. by Guy Oakes (London and New York: Cambridge University Press, 1986).
144. See Casper, 540–541.
145. For the information in this and the following two paragraphs see Junghanns, 38–54. Farias (58 and 62) wrongly thinks the chair was a *theology* position after 1901, whereas on January 5, 1917, when he left his temporary position in the chair of Christian philosophy, Krebs wrote to Grabmann; '... während ich selber – Gottlob – zur dogmatischen Theologie zurückkehren darf.' Cited in Köstler, 97.
146. On Krebs see n. 16 above.
147. The lecture of October 8, 1912, was published in 1913 as 'Erkenntniskritik und Gotteserkenntnis, mit besonderer Berücksichtigung von Vaihingers Als-Ob-Philosophie,' in Geyser et al., eds., *Festgabe zum 60. Geburtstag Clemens Baeumker,* 467–491. Krebs' general thesis (cf. 469, 491, etc.) was that human knowledge cannot be adequately explained if epistemology excludes a concept of God as the grounding unity of the relation of finite subjects and objects. For details on Krebs' lecture and the circumstances leading to this meeting with Heidegger see Ott, 'Der Habilitand,' 143–4.
148. 'Ein scharfer Kopf, bescheiden, aber sicher in Auftreten,' cited in Ott, 'Der Habilitand,' 143, without date; presumably from either Krebs' Taschenkalender, 1913, or his Stichworte 'H.'
149. 'Schade, dass er nicht schon seit zwei Jahren soweit ist. Jetzt hätten wir ihm nötig,' Stichworte 'H,' cited in Junghanns, 54, and Ott, 'Der Habilitand,' 144 (with Ott's reference: 'wenige Tage nach Heideggers Promotion'); but Ott transcribes the last German word as 'not.'
150. See R. Padberg, 'Knecht, Friedrich Justus,' in *Lexikon für Theologie und Kirche,* VI (1961), 356–7.
151. '... dem Geiste der thomistischen Philosophie getreu bleiben ...': Knecht's letter to Heidegger, September 29, 1913, cited in Ott, 'Der Habilitand,' 154. For information on the von Schaezler Foundation (the 'Constantin und Olga von Schaezler'sche Stiftung zu Ehren des hl. Thomas von Aquin') see ibid., 151–154. Only theologians and priests were supposed to be eligible for awards; Heidegger seems to have been the only layman ever to receive one. To the best of my knowledge, Heidegger does not mention the von Schaezler grant in either the 1915 or the 1928 Standesliste.
152. 'Der gehorsamst Unterzeichnete gedenkt sich dem Studium der christlichen Philosophie zu widmen und die akademische Laufbahn einzuschlagen.' In his letter of acceptance of the grant (October 10, 1913) Heidegger wrote: 'Nach Kräften werde ich mich bemühen, durch mein wissenschaftliches Arbeiten das in mich gesetzte Vertrauen zu erfüllen.' Both texts are found in Ott, 'Der Habilitand,' 154. The grant was renewed again on November 18, 1914 (but with the archdiocese's advice that, for financial security, Heidegger get certified for high-school teaching while pursuing the *Habilitation*) and (with only a half-award) on January 12, 1916: ibid., 155–159.
153. Ott, 'Der Habilitand,' 147.
154. The German text is in Ott, 'Der Habilitand,' 145; from Stichworte 'H' (as noted in Junghanns, 54), dated September 2, 1913.
155. For information in this and the following paragraph, see Junghanns, 51.
156. See Junghanns, 41–46, and 52; Ott, 'Der Habilitand,' 150. The text of the oath is in the *Acta*

Apostolicae Sedis 2 (1910), 655–680; an English translation is found in *American Catholic Quarterly Review,* 35 (1910), 712–731.

157. Farias, 62.
158. Junghanns, 51f.
159. Junghanns, 52.
160. Krebs' note dated November 7, 1913, cited partially in Junghanns, 55, and partially in Ott, 'Der Habilitand,' 145; from either Krebs' Taschenkalender, 1913, or his Stichworte 'H.' Heidegger continued to help Krebs with the course throughout the semester. On December 15, 1913, Krebs noted: 'Ich war manchmal ganz ab und fertig mit meiner Weisheit, und doch kam noch immer rechtzeitig Licht. Viel verdanke ich Gesprächen, die ich über das zu präparierende Thema mit Dr. Heidegger . . . hielt.' Cited in Ott, 'Der Habilitand,' 147.
161. Krebs is the source of our information on the meeting of Finke and Heidegger; see notes 163 and 164. Finke continued to support Heidegger at least through the fall of 1916 (and probably until Joseph Geyser's appointment to the chair in the spring of 1917), as we learn from Husserl's letter R I Natorp 8.X.17, cited in part in Sheehan, ed., *Heidegger*, 7.
162. In a letter to Privatdozent Friedrich Nauen, dated January 2, 1914, Krebs wrote: 'Er [Finke] hat ihn [Heidegger] nun aufgefordert, . . . für die Erlernung der Methode das Historische Seminar Finkes zu besuchen.' Cited in Ott, 'Der Habilitand,' 147.
163. Krebs, Stichworte 'H,' November 14, 1913, cited in Casper, 538, n. 10, and partially in Junghanns, 55. (Farias, 57–8, misquotes the entry slightly.)
164. Krebs, Taschenkalender, November 14, 1913, cited in Ott, 'Der Habilitand,' 146.
165. Junghanns, 52.
166. Ott, 'Der Habilitand,' 146, where the text is called 'De origine Praedicamentorum.' On Krebs' doctoral studies in philosophy see Junghanns, 16–20. Krebs passed the *rigorosum* on July 23, 1903, and later that year published the 79-page third chapter ('Meister Dietrichs Philosophie') of his doctoral dissertation as *Studien über Meister Dietrich* (Freiburg: Herder, 1903). A longer (385-page) version of his work was published in Münster three years later as *Meister Dietrich (Theodoricus Teutonicus de Vriberg). Sein Leben, seine Werke, seine Wissenschaft* (Münster: Aschendorff, 1906). Krebs provides the bibliographical information on and the contents of 'De origine rerum praedicamentalium,' ibid., 10*–11*.
167. *Die Lehre vom Urteil* (1914), vii; *Frühe Schriften,* 3; *Gesamtausgabe,* I/1, 61.
168. Part of Krebs' letter to Nauen is cited in Ott, 'Der Habilitand,' 147.
169. Julius Ebbinghaus, in *Philosophie in Selbstdarstellungen,* Ludwig J. Pongratz, ed. vol. 3 (Hamburg: Felix Meiner, 1977), 31.
170. For the German text of Heidegger's letter see Ott, 'Der Habilitand,' 148.
171. In *Ideen* (Section 79), 158, n. 2, Husserl criticized two articles, by August Messer and Jonas Cohn, that appeared in the first volume of *Jahrbücher der Philosophie:* 'Beiden haben . . . *den Sinn* meiner Darstellungen missverstanden . . .'
172. Heidegger is referring to his unpublished work on 'the logical problem of the question' ('das logische Problem der Frage'), which he eventually used towards his *Habilitation* defense. In his letter of July 2, 1915 (see n. 5 above) he mentions this topic as the second of the possible themes of his *Probevortrag,* or trial lecture.
173. Having begun the cycle of instruction in Scholastic philosophy with his introduction to logic and epistemology the previous semester, Krebs continued the cycle during the summer semester (April to July) 1914 with a four-hour lecture course on ontology and cosmology: 'Metaphysik: Grundfragen der Ontologie und Naturphilosophie' (cited in Ott, 'Der Habilitand,' 148, n. 21). Heidegger refers to the course later in the letter when he mentions 'the metaphysics of movement.'
174. Heidegger is referring to the Church's anti-modernist campaign of the times. A 'motu proprio' (literally, 'on her/his own initiative') is a document issued by the pope supposedly without the counsel of others. Pope Pius X's motu proprio 'Doctoris angelici' issued on the

feast of Sts. Peter and Paul, June 29, 1914, mandated that by mid-1917 all Catholic *theology* schools in 'Italy and the adjacent islands' (Sicily, Sardegna, etc.) that conferred church degrees would have to use Aquinas' *Summa Theologiae* in their dogma courses (and lectures would have to be in Latin) or else lose the right to confer those degrees.

175. '[D]ie Bedeutungs- und Erkenntnislehre des Duns Scotus': Ott, 'Der Habilitand,' 155. In his letter requesting a renewal of the von Schaezler grant, Heidegger claimed that he had no other means of support ('Da der Unterzeichnete auch heute nicht auf irgendwelche Unterstützung und Erwerbsquelle Hoffnung und Anspruch hat, ...') and yet it seems from Standesliste-1928 that he did have the Grieshaber-Pino grant of 400 marks ($95) per year until May 15, 1916.

176. The book version of the dissertation has been noted above, n. 7. Heidegger also published much of the dissertation as an article: 'Die Lehre vom Urteil im Psychologismus,' *Zeitschrift für Philosophie und philosophische Kritik,* 155 (1914), 148–172; and 156 (1915), 41–78. In the first footnote Heidegger refers to the publication as 'Abschnitte' of his dissertation; the 'V. Abschnitt' of the book-version is omitted. The three book reviews were of: Franz Brentano, *Von der Klassifikation der psychischen Phänomene* (Leipzig: Duncker & Humblot, 1911): *Literarische Rundschau,* 40, (May 1, 1914), cols. 233–234; Charles Sentroul, *Kant und Aristoteles,* trans. L. Heinrichs (Kempten and Munich: Kösel, 1911): ibid., 40, 7 (July 1, 1914), cols. 330–332; and F. Gross, ed., *Kant – Laienbrevier* (Munich: Bruckmann, 1912): ibid., 40, 8 (August 1, 1914), cols 376–377. These reviews are reprinted in *Gesamtausgabe,* I/1, 47–54.

177. *Literarische Rundschau,* 40, 7 (July 1, 1914), col. 331; *Gesamtausgabe,* I/1, 51.

178. '... im Dienste der Erforschung und Lehre der christlich-scholastischen Philosophie ...' (September 20, 1914) and 'im Dienste der christlich-scholastischen Philosophie und der katholischen Weltanschauung' (November 23, 1914). In a letter addressed to the chancellery office on December 13, 1915, and requesting a final renewal of the von Schaezler grant Heidegger said he hoped to be able to thank the archdiocese for the fact 'dass er seine wissenschaftliche Lebensarbeit einstellt auf die Flüssigmachung des in der Scholastik niedergelegten Gedankengutes für den geistigen Kampf der Zukunft um das christlich-katholische Lebensideal.' Texts in Ott, 'Der Habilitand,' 155, 156, 159. In Standesliste-1915 Heidegger had declared his religious affiliation to be Catholic, but he omits this from Standesliste-1928. See also Junghanns, 57–58, and Farias, 63–64.

179. *Frühe Schriften,* 133; *Gesamtausgabe,* I/1, 191.

180. Ott, 'Der Habilitand,' 149, cites Krebs' note ('im Tagebuch,' without date) that 'las ich sie [the Duns Scotus dissertation] auf Rickerts Wunsch für diesen durch und schrieb ihm ein Referat darüber, aufgrund dessen sie akzeptiert wurde.' Heidegger mentions this also in his letter to Martin Grabmann, dated January 7, 1917: '... Professor Krebs ..., der die Arbeit im Ms. gelesen, ...' cited in Köstler, 100 and 103, lines 5–6. Rickert acknowledges Krebs' assistance in the Gutachten he wrote on Heidegger's work; see Appendix IV.

Time Out ...

JOHN SALLIS
Loyola University of Chicago

It suspends the flow of time, stops the incessant drive into the future, and yet keeps the clock running. It clips the wings of temporal ecstasy, but only temporarily, only by a certain deferral, a postponement. It can suspend time only by being itself a definite, carefully regulated interval of time, time at a standstill even while remaining time, almost a kind of space of time inserted into time, suspending time, almost as if it were a bit of eternity. Also, then, an intense time, a time of intense preparation, a time of decision.

Heidegger arrived in Marburg in the autumn of 1923. Gadamer tells of the summer evening's celebration that had preceded Heidegger's departure from Freiburg: friends, colleagues, students invited to Todnauberg, a bonfire, Heidegger's speech beginning with the words, 'Be awake to the fire of the night'.[1] Heidegger was to remain in Marburg for five years, years unmatched, it would seem, by any others in their intensity. These were the years in which *Being and Time* was prepared and published. In 1928 he returned to Freiburg, writing to Gadamer at the time that only when he began 'to sense the power of the old ground' did he realize how – in the project of fundamental ontology – 'everything began to get slippery'.[2] The time of that project would prove to have been a temporary suspension, a certain postponement of the abysmal drive of questioning. And yet, also a time of intense questioning, a postponement of questioning effected only by a certain intensification of questioning.

Less than a year after he arrived in Marburg, Heidegger presented a lecture to the Marburger Theologenschaft. To this lecture, 'The Concept of Time' (July 1924),[3] there have been repeated references. First of all, by Heidegger himself in a footnote in *Being and Time*, remarking that certain of the analyses there being presented – the note occurs near the beginning of the Second Chapter of the Second Division – were communicated in the 1924 lecture.[4] Then by Gadamer, who describes the lecture as the 'original form' (*Urform*) of *Being and Time*.[5] Also by Michel Haar, who (with Marc de Launay) has translated the lecture into French and who calls it 'a first epitome, already very

J.C. Sallis, G. Moneta and J. Taminiaux (eds.), The Collegium Phaenomenologicum, 139–147.
© Kluwer Academic Publishers.

complex, of . . . *Being and Time*'.[6] Also by Thomas Sheehan, who provides a precise account of the lecture, concluding that it is 'an essential but partial step along the way to the writing of *Being and Time*'.[7]

The lecture is indeed an essential step, the decisive moment in which a certain prehistory is gathered from out of, and into, the unity of the future project. Recall some moments of that prehistory, some of the texts of the early Freiburg period. For instance, the review of Jaspers' *Psychology of World-Views*, begun by Heidegger in 1919 though published only much later:[8] here one finds an engagement with the analysis of death; also Dasein characterized as having one's own self in a way quite irreducible to immanent acts of consciousness; an insistence, too, in criticism of Jaspers, on developing the problem of access to Dasein, on what is already termed hermeneutics.[9] Then, the lecture-course (winter semester 1920–21) 'Introduction to the Phenomenology of Religion', in which one finds developed the questions of facticity and of primordial temporality.[10] The essay sent to Natorp in Marburg in support of Heidegger's nomination there: a philosophical interpretation of Aristotle introduced by an analysis of the 'hermeneutic situation'.[11] And the course just preceding his departure from Freiburg, 'Hermeneutics of Facticity': by this time a number of the characteristic terms of *Being and Time* have appeared (*in-der-Welt-sein, Alltäglichkeit, Bedeutsamkeit, Vorhandenheit*); also the threefold articulation (*Welt, In, Wer*) that will structure the First Division of *Being and Time*; and, throughout, a call for a certain return to the Greeks, coupled with a demand for the destruction of tradition.[12]

And yet, it seems that it was only after the move to Marburg, specifically, in the lecture 'The Concept of Time', that this prehistory crystallized into a systematic presentation of what was to become the project of *Being and Time*.[13] A year later (summer semester 1925) the lecture course *History of the Concept of Time*[14] presents in almost fully developed form what will become the First Division of *Being and Time*. In the following year the book – its first two Divisions – is completed. In February 1927 *Being and Time* – all that Heidegger was ever to publish of it – appears.

The 1924 lecture marks, then, the beginning of the Marburg period. Perhaps also something more. Perhaps the text in which Heidegger will have begun to write not only *Being and Time* but also the texts of those courses that immediately follow, in which the slippage of the project will, even if almost imperceptibly, have begun to operate.

'The Concept of Time' begins in a manner appropriate to the theological audience by referring time to eternity – or, rather, by introducing such a referral only to disavow it. In the abrupt disavowal there is not only a decision regarding the ground of time but also a question of the very appropriateness of grounding to time.

The question is: What is time? It is as a way of broaching the problem of access to time that Heidegger begins with the opposition between time and eternity. If the meaning (*Sinn*) of time lies in eternity, in a being out of time, utterly outside of time, then time must be understood on the basis of eternity, from out of eternity. Thereby a way out (*Ausgang*) into the investigation is prescribed: from eternity to time. The difficulty is that philosophy, unlike theology, can make no claim to understand eternity. This difficulty cannot be removed for the philosopher: 'If the philosopher questions about time, then he is resolved to understand it from out of time [*aus der Zeit*]'. The philosopher would understand time not by taking time out of time toward an eternity from which it would be understood. Rather, he would understand time out of time in precisely such a way as to forego referring it to anything else, would understand it from out of itself. Only the slightest move is required to convert this resolve into the project of understanding time without reference to infinity – that is, the project of understanding the radical finitude of time.[15]

Heidegger is emphatic: the considerations voiced in 'The Concept of Time' are not theological. From a theological point of view, they are considerations that can only serve to make the question of eternity *more difficult*.

Indeed, he adds with equal emphasis, they are not even philosophical. For they do not claim to give a general systematic determination of time; such a determination 'would have to question back behind time into the involvement of other categories in it'. Over against such a philosophical consideration of time, Heidegger poses his as belonging to prescience (*Vorwissenschaft*). It is the concern of such prescience to consider, for example, how time shows itself for physics, that is, what kind of self-showing is operative in the way that time is preunderstood in physics as clock-time. More generally, prescience undertakes to demonstrate whether 'an investigation is in touch with its matter [*bei ihrer Sache ist*] or is nourished by some traditional and worn-out word-knowledge'. Heidegger draws a curious analogy: prescience is like the police force at the parade of the sciences.

Here, too, it is a matter of investigating time from out of time, that is, of not questioning back behind time to something else, as would allegedly be required of a philosophical determination. Rather, what is to be undertaken is to attend to the way in which time shows itself, to enforce the bond of the sciences to their *Sachen*. Need it be said: pre-science is nothing other than phenomenology.

Moving quickly past Einstein's theory of time, back to Aristotle's, from which it is not fundamentally differrent, Heidegger observes how both regard time as essentially linked to measurement and, hence, as determined from the now-point. The question is: What about the now? The question is the one asked by Augustine: What about the relation of the now to spirit? Is spirit time? Am I the now? In a more precise and differentiated formulation:

Am I myself the now and my Dasein time?
Or is it, in the end, time itself that provides the clock in us?

The question is that of the *identity of time and Dasein.* In raising the question Heidegger is also introducing a difference between time as determined by the now (clock-time, but also what *Being and Time* will call *die besorgte Zeit*) *and* time itself. The sense of the identity will prove to require such differentiation: it is an identity of Dasein with time itself, not with the now, not with the clock that time itself provides us for measuring everything in time. This question of the identity of time and Dasein will prove, in a sense, to have been the sole question of Heidegger's lecture.

The development of the question requires that Dasein be characterized. Heidegger begins with a general character: Dasein is the being that each of us ourselves are, the being that each of us touches upon in the basic assertion 'I am'. The question of time has quickly become a question not of *what* time is but of *who* it is; more closely, it has become a question not only of how we – say, as spirit – are time but of how I am time, of how I am myself as time, of how I am time as myself, of how I am my time. I am myself from out of time, and I am time from out of myself – *'in der Jeweiligkeit als meiniges'*.

The characterization is expanded, Heidegger enumerating eight basic structures of Dasein: (1) Dasein is *Being-in-the-world*, in distinction from a subject of the sort that would need somehow to escape from its own immanence into the world; Dasein is in-the-world in the sense of dealing with it (*umgehen*), as concern (*Besorgen*). (2) Dasein is *Being-with-one-another (Miteinandersein)*, a being with others in the same world. (3) Dasein's being in the world with others occurs for the most part in *speaking (Sprechen)*. (4) Dasein is a being for which the '*I am*' is constitutive; Dasein is my own. (5) Yet, in its everydayness, Dasein is not itself but is the nobody that is called '*das Man*'. (6) This being is such that its *Being is at issue (ein solches, dem es in seinem . . . In-der-Welt-sein auf sein Sein ankommt);* all its concernful dealings in the world are such as to be, at the same time, a matter of concern with its own Being. (7) In everydayness Dasein does not reflect on the I and the self but rather *finds itself (befindet sich)* there in its dealings in the world. (8) Dasein is not something that we can observe or prove but rather something that we *are*; thus to speak interpretively about the self is merely a distinctive way in which Dasein itself is.

Thus Heidegger assembles in the lecture most of the existential structures that will be elucidated in the First Division of *Being and Time,* assembles them in much the same language that will be in play there. In the final term of the enumeration – in contrast to the others – it is a matter not so much of an existential structure as, rather, of the distinctive methodological structure of the analysis of Dasein, of the precise way in which such analysis itself belongs to Dasein as a distinctive possibility. It is not a matter of observing Dasein, of analyzing it as though it were something other than the one carrying out the analysis. Rather, the interrogator and the interrogated are the same, and everything depends on the remarkable relatedness back and forth between them.[16] In being Dasein I have always already understood and interpreted myself; the analysis of Dasein would, then, draw out that already operative self-disclosure, would, as it were, listen in on it and elevate it to the level of conceptual comprehension.[17]

The posing of the question of primordial access to Dasein, the development of this question and of a strategy responsive to it – it is perhaps this complex of issues opening the Second Division of *Being and Time* that the lecture will have unfolded most rigorously. The opening paradox will already have been in place: How is it possible ever to get access to Dasein as a whole, since as long as it has not reached its end, it is still incomplete, whereas once it reaches that end, it is no longer Dasein at all. The paradox leads into an analysis of Dasein's *end*, that is, of death. Heidegger will prove almost already to have written, in the lecture, the existential analysis of death: Death is Dasein's ownmost possibility, a possibility that is most extreme (*äusserste*), impending (*bevorstehende*), certain yet indefinite.

One formulation responds to the question: What is it for Dasein to have its own death? What is this having? Heidegger answers: 'It is Dasein's running-ahead (*Vorlaufen*) to its goneness (*Vorbei*) as its most extreme possibility, which impends with certainty and complete indefiniteness'.

To have its own death, to comport itself to its own death, is, then, to be toward its own goneness, *das Vorbei*. When I comport myself, to *das Vorbei*, there is, Heidegger says, a certain uncovering. One could say: *das Vorbei* is such that, when I cast ahead toward it, there is reflected back from it a certain self-disclosure. Specifically, it reveals my Dasein as sometime no longer there (*als einmal nicht mehr da*), no longer there with such and such things and with these and those persons. In short: '*Das Vorbei* draws everything along with it into the nothing'. It is, then, not some event that befalls me, not a 'what' (*Was*) at all but rather a 'how' (*Wie*); it is, in the end, as the proper end, the authentic 'how' of my 'there' (*da*).

To have its own death is, then, to run ahead to *das Vorbei*, to run up against one's own goneness. Such movement is authentic Being-toward-death and, as such, is the authentic future. As authentic future it involves, in turn, a return to past and present, and thus forms, unfolds, time itself: 'Being-futural gives time [*Zukunftigsein gibt Zeit*], forms the present and lets the past [*Vergangenheit* – not yet *Gewesenheit*] be repeated in the how of its being-lived'.

Death is the end, the final possibility, the most extreme possibility, the possibility beyond which one cannot cast oneself, *das Vorbei*. It is, one may say, the suspending of time, of the time as which I am myself. It is *a future that will never be present*, that will never have become present: 'As the authentic future, *das Vorbei* can never become present'. With death my time will have stopped, come to a standstill; death is as much out(side) of my time as is eternity. And yet, it is precisely from *das Vorbei* that authentic time is formed, that is, proper time, time itself, or, rather, the time that I myself am. Death, *das Vorbei*, suspends time and yet grants time, lets it unfold. It is not something other than time but is, rather, something that one might almost call a time out of time; it is the limit of time, itself neither time nor not time, the limit too of the *itself*, as well as of my *own* self. It is a limit that delimits without being simply delimitable, an elusive and self-effacing limit – impending with certainty and complete indefiniteness.

Indeed, when *das Vorbei* ceases to be elusive, that is, when – always already – one begins to arm oneself against its complete indefiniteness by bringing measure to bear on the not-yet onto which one is thrown back in running up against death as possibility, then it ceases even to be future, becoming only a part measured from the present (the goneness of the no-longer-present). One says now: The past is what is gone, what is irretrievable, so that *das Vorbei* comes to name the past rather than the future. It is with just this gigantic ambiguity that the word occurs in Heidegger's lecture. One might well wonder whether the disappearance of the word in *Being and Time* does not have to do with precisely this ambiguity, that is, with the difficulty that one all too easily regards what is gone as the mere opposite of what is present, thus taking *das Vorbei* as an absence that would be only the privation of *die Gegenwart*. But death is a future that can never be present – that is, the task is to think death as absolute, as absolved from being determined by opposition to presence, as the most extreme limit of presence.

The past too is to be won back, thought in its 'how' and not just as what is gone. It is to be thought by casting *das Vorbei* in(to) the future, casting oneself toward it, running ahead. In the language of Heidegger's lecture: The possibility of access to history is grounded in the possibility of being-futural. That, Heidegger says, 'is the first principle of hermeneutics'.

Without that casting, time is determined from the now of the present, from the 'what' of the present rather than the 'how' of the future, from what is present, from the now of the things with which it is presently concerned. Time becomes empty, becomes *langweilig*, a long and boring while that must be filled up with the ever new. Another suspending of time by time, by setting time out of time, by drawing out the now of presence, engaging it in what is present. Or, rather, or suspending of time by inserting into it a now of presence, a definite, carefully regulated, measurable time, almost a kind of space of time, an empty space that one cannot but seek to fill up. Yet, even in this interval, this time out, one keeps the clock running.

The lecture culminates in the assertion of the identity: Dasein is time. Or, in Heidegger's formulation: 'Dasein, comprehended in its most extreme possibility of Being, is time itself, not in time'. One could add: only because Dasein is time is there open to Dasein the authentic and inauthentic limiting of time, the suspending of time in a certain time out of time.

The lecture concludes by turning back to the initial question – What is time? – and making explicit the transformation that the question has undergone as a result of the analyses. It has become: Who is time? Then: Are we ourselves time? Then: Am I time? And finally: Am I my time? The transformation is also one by which a question of 'what' becomes a question not only of 'who' but of 'how'. This final turn exhibits the interplay of question and *Sache* that will prove methodologically distinctive in *Being and Time* and that effectively fills out the merely preliminary concept of phenomenology: formulation of the question leads into disclosure of *die Sache*, that disclosure, in turn, reflecting back upon the question so as to require its reformulation.

But what of the future already projected, the future from which there will have been a return, the future in the return from which the lecture text will have been written? To what extent will Heidegger in the 1924 lecture text already have written the two Divisions of *Being and Time* that will be published in 1927? To what extent will he also have begun writing the texts of those courses in which a certain torsion will, quite unobtrusively, begin twisting the project out of shape, in which the slippage of the project will begin coming into play, in which perhaps already, even if still almost imperceptibly, everything will have begun to get slippery.

The lecture culminates in the assertion of the identity: Dasein is time, time is Dasein. In *Being and Time* this identity will be opened up, difference inscribed in it; it is such difference that will not yet have been written in in Heidegger's writing of the lecture text. Indeed, he will insist in *Being and Time* that time is not anything other than Dasein; thus the identity will remain, as such, intact. But it will come to be expressed with a certain differentiation: *Time is the meaning of the Being of Dasein*. The words thus inscribed, *meaning* and *Being*, serve to indicate what will come to mediate (I use this word cautiously, erasure in hand) the identity of time and Dasein. *Being and Time* will bring to the determination of the identity, on the one hand, an ontologicall reflection establishing the difference between Being and beings, hence, the difference between Dasein and the Being of Dasein (i.e., care); on the other hand, a significational reflection establishing the difference between a being (or Being) and its meaning (*Bedeutung* or, more broadly, *Sinn*), meaning as *das Woraufhin* of a certain operation of projective understanding. In the lecture these differences will not yet have been inscribed in the identity.

Time remains thus identical with my Dasein, with what could be called each individual Dasein, were it not that such a designation tends to neutralize the mineness, the ownness, of Dasein and its time, thus broaching the inauthentic suspending of time. Time, which will prove to be original dispersion, is dispersed amongst what could – granted the reservation – be called the multiplicity of individual Daseins. Time will not yet have been, within the identity, sufficiently differentiated from Dasein to function as a meaning-horizon not simply dispersed amongst Daseins. In the words of the lecture: 'Insofar as time is ever mine, there are many times. *D i e Zeit ist sinnlos*'. It will have been (in this text) meaningless (*sinnlos*) because dispersed; it will be (in *Being and Time*) meaningless because it proves to be the meaning-horizon within which, from which, everything else becomes meaningful, comes to have meaning.

But it is from another future that Heidegger will have begun writing about understanding time (from) out of time. Taken in the most radical sense, such a project would involve understanding time without referring it to a being, without, for example, grounding it in a being. Indeed, in the project of *Being and Time*, time will be taken as that to which all beings are referred, as the meaning of Being (*Sinn vom Sein*) – *hence as beyond Being* (ἐπέκεινα τῆς οὐσίας), in the phrase that will recur in the texts immediately following *Being and Time*.[18] The question will be: How is one to think together the character of time as beyond Being *and* its being brought back to a being, Dasein, with which it would be identical? Thus, the apparently simple identity of time and Dasein – their identity with one another, not their self-identity, which is anything but simple, proving even in the lecture to be subject to suspensions and interruptions – will prove to be extremely complex and recurrently questionable. Thus is anticipated in the lecture a twisting of the identity, the move beyond being turning, as it were, against the move back to Dasein – preparing a certain twisting loose, a slippage, a separation that will no longer be merely differentiation, broaching a crisis of the identity. Eventually – drastically telescoping a very complex and extensive history – Heidegger will come to think identity as such from the belonging-together (*Zusammengehörigkeit*) of Dasein and that which will have been, but will no longer be, called *time*.

Notes

1. Hans-Georg Gadamer, *Philosophical Apprenticeships*, trans. Robert R. Sullivan (Cambridge: MIT Press, 1985), 47–48.
2. *Ibid.*, 50.
3. The lecture is to appear in a volume of the III. Abteilung of the *Gesamtausgabe* entitled *Der Begriff der Zeit*.
4. *Sein und Zeit*, 9th Edition (Tübingen: Max Niemeyer Verlag, 1960), 268.
5. Gadamer, 'Martin Heidegger and Marburg Theology', *Philosophical Hermeneutics*, trans. David E. Linge (Berkeley: University of California Press, 1976), 199.
6. Michel Haar (ed.), *Heidegger* (Paris: L'Herne, 1983), 36.
7. Thomas J. Sheehan, 'The "Original Form" of Sein und Zeit: Heidegger's Der Begriff der Zeit (1924),' *Journal of the British Society for Phenomenology*, vol. 10 (1979), 83.

8. 'Anmerkungen zu Karl Jaspers "Psychologie der Weltanschauung'," in *Karl Jaspers in der Diskussion*, ed. Hans Saner (Munich: R. Piper, 1973), 70–100. Reprinted in Heidegger, *Wegmarken, Gesamtausgabe*, vol 9 (Frankfurt a. M.: Vittorio Klostermann, 1976), 1–44.
9. See David Farrell Krell, *Intimations of Mortality* (University Park: Pennsylvania State University Press, 1986), chap. 1.
10. These questions are developed in relation to the original Christian experience expressed in St. Paul's Letters to the Thessalonians. See Thomas J. Sheehan, 'Heidegger's "Introduction to the Phenomenology of Religion",' *A Companion to Martin Heidegger's 'Being and Time'*, ed. Joseph J. Kockelmans, *Current Continental Research* 550 (1986), 40–62.
11. See Thomas J. Sheehan, 'Heidegger's Early Years: Fragment for a Philosophical Biography', in *Heidegger: The Man and the Thinker*, ed. Thomas J. Sheehan (Chicago: Precedent Publishing, 1981), 11–12; Gadamer, 'Martin Heidegger and Marburg Theology', 200–201; Gadamer, *Philosophical Apprenticeships*, 46–47.
12. See Sheehan, 'Heidegger's Early Years', 13.
13. A degree of reservation is required here, since many of the texts of the early Freiburg period are not yet available. There is even, at the present time, some uncertainty regarding the list of Heidegger's courses during this period. See Theodore J. Kisiel, 'Heidegger's Early Lecture Courses', *A Companion to Martin Heidegger's 'Being and Time'*, Ed. Joseph Kockelmans, 22–39.
14. *Prolegomena zur Geschichte des Zeitbegriffs, Gesamtausgabe*, vol. 20 (Frankfurt a.M.: Vittorio Klostermann, 1979). English translation: *History of the Concept of Time: Prolegomena*, trans. Theodore Kisiel (Bloomington: Indiana University Press, 1985).
15. See *Sein und Ziet*, § 65.
16. Thus, in *Being and Time* (§ 2) Heidegger will refer to 'a remarkable "relatedness backward or forward" which what we are asking about (Being) bears to the questioning itself as a mode of Being of a being'.
17. Thus, in Being and Time (§ 29): 'Like any ontological interpretation whatsoever, this analytic can only, so to speak, listen in [*abzuhören*] to some already disclosed being regarding its Being. And it will attach itself to Dasein's distinctive and most far-reaching possibilities of disclosure, in order from these to get information [*Aufschluss*] about this being. Phenomenological interpretation must give to Dasein itself the possibility of primordial disclosure and, as it were, let it interpret itself. Such interpretation takes part in this disclosure only in order to raise existentially into the concept the phenomenal content of what has been disclosed'.
18. *Die Grundprobleme der Phänomenologie, Gesamtausgabe* 24 (Frankfurt a.M.: Vittorio Klostermann, 1975), 400–402; English translation: *The Basic Problems of Phenomenology*, trans. Albert Hofstadter (Bloomington: Indiana University Press, 1982), 283–84. *Metaphysische Anfangsgründe der Logik, Gesamtausgabe* 26 (Frankfurt a.M.: Vittorio Klostermann, 1978), 237; English translation: *The Metaphysical Foundations of Logic,* trans. Michael Heim (Bloomington: Indiana University Press, 1984), 184.

Heidegger's 'Searching Suggestion' Concerning Nietzsche

WALTER BROGAN
Villanova University

I

It is often difficult in reading a text of Heidegger's on another thinker to distinguish between Heidegger's thought and that of the person he is interpreting. Despite Heidegger's insistence that we need only Nietzsche's texts and should put to the side secondary sources in reading Nietzsche, we often find in reading Heidegger's *Nietzsche* that it is as important to understand Heidegger's own thought as it is to meditate on Nietzsche's thought. Perhaps this is because Heidegger's *Nietzsche* is not a secondary source but a primary philosophical text requiring that we confront it on its own terms as a matter for thought. Does a confrontation between two thinkers, such as is going on in this work, move in its own orbit and open up something essential that moves between them and belongs to neither of them? If so, then Heidegger's *Nietzsche* cannot be read and critically evaluated according to the standards established for faithful commentaries. What then are the methodological requirements that govern a confrontation of this sort and prevent the conversation from becoming either a one-sided taking over of another's thought or a one-sided repetition of what was said? If we assume that Heidegger's *Nietzsche* is such a dialogue, what are some of the conditions Heidegger says are necessary for such an event to take place? Heidegger says in the beginning of his *Nietzsche*: 'We can never succeed in arriving at Nietzsche's philosophy proper if we have not in our own questioning conceived of Nietzsche as the end of Western metaphysics and proceeded to the entirely different question of the truth of Being'.[1] This movement from the essence of metaphysics seen in its completeness beyond and back to the truth of Being hidden from all metaphysical thinking provides the framework for Heidegger's reading of Nietzsche. Only from within this movement, Heidegger says, can a *proper* reading of Nietzsche's philosophy take place. This genuine attunement to Nietzsche's thought, then, places demands upon us that a mere study of Nietzsche's work – even if philologically accurate and adhering to standards of correctness – may

J.C. Sallis, G. Moneta and J. Taminiaux (eds.), The Collegium Phaenomenologicum, 149–158.
© Kluwer Academic Publishers.

occasion but cannot guarantee. The interpretation of Nietzsche's text is determined in advance by the direction of the thinker's inquiry. Nietzsche's philosophy is to be drawn up into the movement of a questioning that goes beyond any expression of the thought of Nietzsche as *expressed*. Nietzsche's style of writing encourages this dialogical approach to his text. He masks his thinking in aphorisms and contradictions in order to prevent a mere following of his thought and in an effort to release the issues *to be thought* from their concealment in the language of metaphysics. Zarathustra says: 'Whoever writes in blood and aphorisms does not want to be read but to be learned by heart. In the mountains the shortest way is from peak to peak: but for that one must have long legs'.[2] Heidegger says in *What Is Called Thinking*?, a book that can be read on one level as a justification of his Nietzsche interpretation:

> We take (the philosophers') language to be mere expression, setting forth philosophers' views. But the thinker's language tells what is. To hear it is in no case easy. Hearing it presupposes that we meet certain requirements, and we do so only on rare occasions. We must acknowledge and respect it. To acknowledge and respect consists in letting every thinker's thought come to us as in each case unique, never to be repeated, inexhaustible – and to be shaken to the depths by what is unthought in his thought . . . The unthought is the greatest gift that thinking can bestow.[3]

The unthought is that which is to be thought, that which needs to be thought, the gift of one thinker to another. This gift, we are told, in no way limits the inexhaustible richness and uniqueness of each thinker. The 'gift-giving virtue', as Nietzsche calls it, belongs to neither thinker alone. Zarathustra says in discussing this gift: 'You say you believe in Zarathustra? But what matters Zarathustra? . . . Now I bid you lose me and find yourselves; and only when you have all denied me will I return to you'.[4] The task of thinking, imposed as a criterion for a genuine dialogue and confrontation with Nietzsche, cannot, according to Heidegger, be viewed as a willful activity originating entirely within the one who wishes to think. Heidegger says: 'No thinking creates for itself the element in which it operates. But all thinking strives, as if automatically, to stay within the element assigned to it'.[5] The destiny of thought 'takes *its way* already *within* the total relation of Being and man's essence, or else it is not thinking at all'.[6]

To read Nietzsche properly requires thinking. All thinking, and most especially Nietzsche's thought, is, Heidegger says, a transition, a movement within the history of Being and beyond to the origin of that history. The thinker stands decisively in this movement. The decisive transition that Nietzsche's thinking brings about leads to the *Untergang* of metaphysics. If Heidegger's dialogue with Nietzsche is also transitional, then it must, so to speak, leap ahead of this accomplishment. But in the case of a dialogue with Nietzsche, who brings metaphysics as a whole into its end, the thinker who confronts him in dialogue must step back from metaphysics and enter into a more originary thinking than is possible within metaphysics. This character of transitional thinking as a decision that guides the thinker's interpretation is, I believe, what Heidegger means when he says that 'every thinker thinks one thought only'.[7] The strictness and rigor of a thinker's thought, Heidegger says, does not deny a multiplicity of meanings, nor even a multiplicity of possible interpretations of his thought. Heidegger discredits any misunderstanding of this point that would assume he wishes to impose a universal schema onto Nietzsche's philosophy or that he intends to reduce the multivocity of Nietzsche's work to 'a formal-logical univocity'.[8] Zarathustra says: 'When your heart flows broad and full like a river ... When you will with a single will, there is the origin of your virtue'.[9]

In *Eperons*, Derrida speaks of Heidegger's 'hermeneutic hold' which assumes there is a single true meaning to Nietzsche's text to be discovered by one who meditates on and from within the Truth of Being.[10] But Heidegger's insistence on the singularity of a thinker's thought is not meant in the sense of a ground to which all his thoughts must be referred. It is much more the *Ab-grund* which frees thinking to first of all open up a ground for thought. Thus we must be careful to distinguish two issues here. Heidegger's claim that every thinker thinks one thought only is not to be equated with his charge that Nietzsche's fundamental metaphysical concept is the eternal return of the same; nor is his insistence that eternal recurrence, the will to power, the revaluation of values, and the overman all must be thought as the Same in Nietzsche's philosophy to be equated with the singularity of his thought as a thinker. The latter claims arise out of Heidegger's conviction that Nietzsche is the last metaphysician and that he thus gathers the previous history of metaphysics into a whole. It is a claim that he argues for carefully on the basis of his confrontation with Nietzsche's texts and by a rigorous questioning of the meaning of Nietzsche's basic positions, all of which arise out of a long history of metaphysics and can only be understood by subjecting them to a dialogue with that history. The claim that every thinker thinks one thought only is another matter, although not unrelated.

The approach through questioning, the thoughtful dialogue, the movement from the end of metaphysics back to the truth of Being, thinking in transition, listening to and for the unthought and unsaid in Nietzsche's works, the attunement to the one essential thought of Nietzsche and the element in which he thinks – these become the methodological requirements necessary, according to Heidegger, for a *proper* reading of Nietzsche. By a 'proper' reading of Nietzsche, Heidegger means a proper way of reading Nietzsche. In *What Is Called Thinking?*, Heidegger characterizes his own way as 'still as searching suggestion'.[11] At stake in our attempt to question Heidegger through questioning his interpretation of Nietzsche are some of the most important insights that

Heidegger achieved along the path of his own thinking. A judgment concerning the legitimacy of this *methodos* requires a thoughtful assessment of Heidegger's own thinking.

II

Having pointed to the realm of thought in which Heidegger's Nietzsche interpretation is operating, we can now move to his claim that it is only upon conceiving of Nietzsche as the end of Western metaphysics that we can properly question the meaning of his thought. It is important to note at the outset that this is not a conclusion that Heidegger reaches *after* his investigation, but the basis upon which his investigation proceeds. It also needs to be emphasized that Heidegger's persistent and pervasive charge that Nietzsche is a metaphysician is itself multifaceted. Indeed, Heidegger's most profound work on the essence of metaphysics emerged during the period of and out of his confrontation with Nietzsche. Heidegger's efforts to enclose Nietzsche within the metaphysical tradition parallel his efforts to think the closure of metaphysics. Thus his reading of Nietzsche is a strategy which also serves to disentangle Nietzsche's thinking from the tradition. For Nietzsche's thought is not viewed by Heidegger as just that of another metaphysician. Heidegger takes Nietzsche's own understanding of his project – to place man beyond the limits of metaphysics – very seriously. Thus Heidegger calls his reading of Nietzsche a *necessary* elucidation *to prepare* for a confrontation with Nietzsche.

Heidegger is, of course, aware of the fact that the claim that Nietzsche's philosophy is metaphysical runs counter to Nietzsche's frequently expressed conviction to the contrary. The basis of this charge lies in Heidegger's attempt to think through the essence of metaphysics, which he says Nietzsche failed to do. A rather large portion of Heidegger's *Nietzsche* is dedicated to the question: What is metaphysics? Thus the last three lectures in his work: 'Metaphysics as History of Being', 'Sketches for a History of Being as Metaphysics', and 'Recollection in Metaphysics', do not actually deal with Nietzsche or Nietzsche's texts *per se*. In fact, as Hannah Arendt points out,[12] the second volume on the whole operates at a level removed from the careful attention to Nietzsche's texts that is evident in the first volume of the *Nietzsche* work. It raises the question of the consummation of metaphysics as a matter for thought that Nietzsche's philosophy initiates. In view of Heidegger's basic claim that Nietzsche must be read in the context of the history of metaphysics, it is not inappropriate that Heidegger devotes himself in his Nietzsche lectures to an understanding of this history and to a discussion of the essence of metaphysics. It is the success of these efforts that lend weight to his understanding of Nietzsche.

One of the things that emerges out of his discussion of the essence and history of metaphysics is a different conception of metaphysics than the one under which Nietzsche was operating. It is important to recognize this because if one fails to do so and assumes that Nietzsche and Heidegger have the same understanding of metaphysics, then it will be impossible to make a judgment regarding Heidegger's assessment of Nietzsche's work. Heidegger says: 'In contrast to what Nietzsche has revealed as the history of metaphysics, it is necessary to take a *more original* look into the history of metaphysics'.[13] According to Heidegger, this more originary look reveals that Nietzsche did indeed bring about an overturning of metaphysics, but not its overcoming. For Nietzsche, metaphysics means primarily Platonism, the valuative projection of the suprasensory as a repository of meaning and truth. It is this expression of metaphysics that Nietzsche overcomes. Heidegger remarks:

> Nietzsche understands his own philosophy as the countermovement to metaphysics, and that means for him a movement in opposition to Platonism. Nevertheless, as a mere counter-movement, it necessarily remains, as does everything 'anti', held fast in the essence of that over against which it moves. Nietzsche's counter-movements against metaphysics, as the mere turning upside down of metaphysics, is an inextricable entanglement in metaphysics, in such a way, indeed, that metaphysics is cut off from its essence and, as metaphysics, is never able to think its own essence'.[14]

According to Nietzsche, the collapse of the suprasensory order requires a revaluation of the sensory. Thus Nietzsche's philosophy cannot be fully understood as a mere reversal of Platonism. It is the task of revaluation that is Nietzsche's central focus. The will to power, essentially the revaluating will emerges intact out of the ashes of metaphysics as Nietzsche understood it. Only the will to power can create meaning within the nihilism that has empowered metaphysics and brought it to its end. To do so, the revaluating will must embrace this lack of meaning and affirm it as its own. This is accomplished through the affirmation of the eternal recurrence, which is the will's positing of itself into view and re-presenting itself to itself as what is.

In his penetration of metaphysics, Nietzsche unmasks it inherent nihilism. He makes evident the centricity of will to power throughout metaphysical thinking, even when it is attempting to disown its willfullness. He sees how all metaphysical thinking is evaluative. Finally, Nietzsche recognizes that the fundamental issue in coming to grips with metaphysics is the issue of who man is and how his relation to beings is founded. He even makes clear that this issue is fundamentally related to time and thus he offers his discovery of the eternal return. In all of these ways, Nietzsche reaches into the very heart of metaphysics. Heidegger accepts these and other basic insights as essential. Indeed, Nietzsche thinks through to the core of metaphysics so successfully that his thinking displaces the movement of metaphysics and brings it to an end.

Heidegger says: 'all the themes of Western thought, though all of them transmuted, fatefully gather together in Nietzsche's thinking'.[15]

According to Heidegger, Nietzsche's incapacity to address the question of the nothing and its relation to Being, his failure to question the imposition of value as the meaning of beings, his proclamation of the eternal recurrence which leaves intact the rule of presence that dominates the metaphysical understanding of time, his declaration of the overman as will to power which radicalizes the dominance of subjective will that emerges in Descartes' philosophy – all of these indications point to Nietzsche's failure to think beyond metaphysics.

Heidegger's claim that Nietzsche is a metaphysician does not deny that Nietzsche abandons the priority of Being in the way it manifests itself in all previous metaphysics. Metaphysics is brought to an end by Nietzsche precisely in the active forgetting and the abandonment of this Being. The beingness of beings is nothing. Both Heidegger and the critics of his Nietzsche interpretation agree on this. What many critics do not accept is Heidegger's claim that this outcome of Nietzsche's thought is the final stage in the nihilistic history that Nietzsche uncovered.

According to Heidegger, neither Platonism, nor Christianity, nor Cartesian subjectivity is the essence of metaphysics. Rather these are epochs in the history of Being which conceal its essence. The essence of metaphysics lies in the thinking of Being as the beingness of beings, in thinking Being on the basis of beings, and thus in the oblivion of the question of Being as Being. Heidegger says: 'However extensively and from whatever point of view we prefer to interrogate Nietzsche, we do not find that his thought thinks Being from its truth as the essential occurrence of Being itself'.[16] Heidegger cautions that we should not assume that Nietzsche ought to have thought in this way or that not to have done so was an inadequacy in his thought; nor is it his intention, he says, to offer a more correct version of Nietzsche, more correct even than Nietzsche's own self-understanding. We live in an age where the label 'metaphysician' has become derogatory, largely due to the influence of Nietzsche and Heidegger. But Heidegger says: 'every thoughtful converse with him (Nietzsche) is constantly carried into other dimensions. This is why all formulas and labels fail in a special sense, and fall silent in the face of Nietzsche's thought'.[17]

Heidegger's reading of Nietzsche does place Nietzsche's thought in the context of Heidegger's own assessment of the history of Being as metaphysics. He does so explicitly to ask the question of Nietzsche's relation to that history and to ascertain how Nietzsche's essential insights develop in and beyond that history. But such a reading is certainly faithful to the level of Nietzsche's thinking, for Nietzsche is, above all, the one who penetrated this history to the core and carried it up into his own philosophy in an original vision. Zarathustra says: 'Not only the reason of millenia, but their madness too, breaks out in us. It is dangerous to be an heir'.[18] To naively ignore the enormous heritage of the questions Nietzsche raises and thus to trivialize them with shallow meanings and surface analysis is certainly not to do justice to Nietzsche's thought. As Zarathustra's journey makes evident, one cannot grapple with Nietzsche's thought without recognizing his persistent dialogue with the tradition of metaphysics. If one discovers by placing Nietzsche's thought in confrontation with metaphysics that this thought fails to free itself from that tradition, this cannot be viewed as an imposition on Nietzsche based on criteria that are external to his thought. Nor can one simply say that Nietzsche did not believe in the truth of being or that this Heideggerian discovery was not a problem *for him*. For it is precisely this that is symptomatic of metaphysics, and this position does not do justice to the proximity of Nietzsche's thought in the direction of posing such a question.

According to Nietzsche, beings are determined and constituted out of will to power. Willing is the indwelling structure of beings and the essence of man's being. As such, will to power is the way in which beings are, the Being of beings as a whole. In this, Nietzsche remains a metaphysician. He is a radical metaphysician in that his philosophy thinks wholly and completely of beings and remains faithful to this kind of thinking. But to say that Nietzsche is a metaphysician indicates the greatness of Nietzsche's thought. Heidegger says:

> The reference to the fact that Nietzsche moves in the orbit of the question of Western philosophy only serves to make clear that Nietzsche knew what philosophy is. Such knowledge is rare. Only great thinkers possess it. The greatest possess it most purely in the form of a persistent question.[19]

Heidegger says that he wishes to show that Nietzsche is a serious thinker, no less rigorous than Aristotle, for example. Heidegger clearly believes that we are only able to think beyond metaphysics, if at all, because Nietzsche has thought through metaphysics into its end. The need to understand the Being of beings is surely still an important aspect of Heidegger's own thinking; or else he would not have had to read Nietzsche and be 'shaken to the depth' by what he uncovers. Heidegger understands his own project of showing the metaphysics of Nietzsche in positive terms.

III

Heidegger's positive assessment of his claim that Nietzsche is a metaphysician shows that he considers such a reading of Nietzsche to be the only basis upon which to appraise the extent to which Nietzsche's philosophy opens up the possibility of non-metaphysical, meditative thinking:

> The essence of metaphysics, the fact that in concealing it shelters the

> unconcealment of Being and thus is the *secret* of the history of Being, first permits the experience of thinking the history of Being passage into the free region. The truth of Being itself essentially occurs as the free region.[20]

It is this contention that underlies Heidegger's rejection of a series of alternative interpretations of Nietzsche's philosophy that were prevalent at the time (and still are).

These alternative interpretations include the political and biologistic readings of Nietzsche in Nazi Germany during the period in which Heidegger was lecturing. Heidegger says, in his posthumously published article in *Der Spiegel*,[21] that anyone with ears to hear will recognize in his Nietzsche lectures a confrontation with Naziism. The Nazi political usurpation of Nietzsche viewed Nietzsche's idea of eternal recurrence as an aberration, a contradiction to his essential thought which was will to power. Nowadays, perhaps in reaction to this, the tendency is the reverse – to emphasize the free play that the eternal recurrence opens up and to ignore the will to power. Heidegger's insistence that we take the inner relatedness of will to power and eternal recurrence seriously prevents a selective reading of Nietzsche that arises only when there exists an incapacity to think along with Nietzsche at the level on which his thinking operates. Heidegger's resolute treatment, in the second lecture course, of the will to power in its contemporary expression as will to technological domination calls into question the supposition that Heidegger remains silent about politics after his rectorship of Freiburg University. What is significant is not the absence of politically relevant insight in Heidegger's later philosophy, but the realization that man's political life must be seen as arising out of his relation to Being, or, as in the case of technology, to the default of Being. No political philosophy, Heidegger would insist, which wishes to understand itself can sidestep its essential dependence on a response to this relation. Thus, the political meaning of Nietzsche's philosophy would be lost to or misappropriated by anyone who cannot sustain this level of inquiry. This lesson is drilled home time and again by Heidegger in the course of his lectures.

But Heidegger also repudiates, on similar grounds, the existential-humanistic interpretation of Nietzsche by such philosophers as Jaspers, and the seemingly irreconcilable debate between cosmological and psychological accounts of Nietzsche's thought.[22] Likewise, he dismisses the view of Nietzsche's thought as primarily a philosophy of value. All of these accounts are seen to be operating out of empty, left-over structures of metaphysics while disclaiming their dependency on this way of thinking. Nietzsche himself cautions against such approaches to the event of his thinking in his characterization of the activities of the last men.

Those who offer an account of Nietzsche as an existentialist criticize Heidegger for having ignored Nietzsche's emphasis on the creative will of the individual. But Heidegger addresses this subject thoroughly in the context of a critique of subjectivity as the outcome of representational thinking. This leads him to criticize Nietzsche's 'I will' as the final stage of the metaphysical will to power in the age of technology. On a broader level, it is Heidegger's contention that no worthy assessment of an individual human being's existence can neglect to raise the question of the human being's relation to the truth of Being.

> Every humanism is founded on a metaphysics or makes itself that foundation. Every determination of the essence of man which already presupposes, consciously or not, the interpretation of beings without raising the question concerning the truth of Being is metaphysical.[23]

Heidegger acknowledges that Nietzsche thinks axiologically and ethically; he recognizes that Nietzsche operates on the basis of a psychological/genealogical critique, etc. But he tries to show that Nietzsche thinks these profoundly, and that is to say metaphysically. It is because man *is* will to power that the will to power is a psychological attitude that Nietzsche recommends. For Nietzsche, psychology and morality are no longer seen as separate regions along with metaphysics. Psychology and morality are rather the essence of metaphysics. Metaphysics is shown by Nietzsche to be nothing other than value-positing, and metaphysical man is seen as *positing* the Being of beings as Will. This is Nietzsche's essential disclosure. It is this insight that returns metaphysics to its essence and permits Heidegger to think through the *telos* of metaphysics and to pose the question of man's essence. In his essay 'The Ends of Man', Derrida acknowledges the seriousness of Heidegger's challenge to humanism and existentialism:

> Any questioning of humanism which is not coupled first of all with the archeological radicality of the questions outlined by Heidegger and which does not make use of the indications he gives the genesis of the concept and of the value of 'man', any metahumanist position not within the opening of those questions remains historically regional, periodic, and peripheral, juridically secondary and dependent, regardless of its interests and its necessity as such.[24]

This paper has tried to demonstrate that if proper attention is paid to the way Heidegger reads Nietzsche, then the claim that he offers a reductive interpretation aimed at forcing Nietzsche back into a bondage to traditional metaphysics is unfounded. An attempt to assess Nietzsche's relation to metaphysics requires that the question, What is Metaphysics?, be asked thoughtfully. In responding to this genuine questioning, Heidegger does claim that Nietzsche is a metaphysician. But the meaning of this 'searching suggestion' is the question that guides Heidegger's confrontation with Nietzsche throughout his lectures. Any attempt to assess Nietzsche's thought in the context of thinking beyond metaphysics requires the careful foundational approach to

Nietzsche that Heidegger has shown. Otherwise it will founder in confusions that do not do justice to the greatness of Nietzsche's thought.

Notes

1. Martin Heidegger, *Nietzsche,* vol. 1, *The Will to Power as Art,* trans. David F. Krell (New York: Harper and Row, 1979), p. 10.
2. Friedrich Nietzsche, *Thus Spoke Zarathustra,* in *The Portable Nietzsche,* trans. Walter Kaufmann (New York: The Viking Press, 1954), 1: 152.
3. Martin Heidegger, *What Is Called Thinking?*, trans. J. Glenn Gray (New York: Harper and Row, 1968), p. 76.
4. *Thus Spoke Zarathustra*, 1: 190.
5. *What Is Called Thinking?*, p. 65.
6. *Ibid.*, p. 80.
7. *Ibid.*, p. 50.
8. *Ibid.*, p. 71.
9. *Thus Spoke Zarathustra*, 1: 188.
10. Jacques Derrida, *Eperons*: *Les styles de Nietzsche*, trans. B. Harlow (Chicago: The University of Chicago Press, 1978), p. 98.
11. *What Is Called Thinking?* p. 56.
12. Hannah Arendt, *The Life of the Mind,* vol. 2, *Willing* (New York: Harcourt Brace Jovanovich, 1978).
13. Martin Heidegger, *Nietzsche,* vol. 4, *Nihilism* (Harper and Row, 1982), p. 83.
14. Martin Heidegger, 'The Word of Nietzsche: "God is Dead",' in *The Question Concerning Technology and Other Essays,* trans. W. Lovitt (New York: Harper and Row, 1977), p. 61.
15. *What Is Called Thinking?*, p. 51.
16. *Nietzsche*, vol. 4, *Nihilism*, p. 199.
17. *What Is Called Thinking?*, p. 52.
18. *Thus Spoke Zarathustra*, 1: 189.
19. *Nietzsche*, vol. 1, *The Will to Power as Art,* p. 4.
20. *Nietzsche*, vol. 4, *Nihilism*, p. 250.
21. *Der Spiegel* (1976), 30 (23). Eng. trans. in *Philosophy Today* (1976), 20(4–4), pp. 267–84.
22. This debate fails to think through the dichotomy of man and nature and presupposes an understanding of the Being of each that does not grasp the ontological difference.
23. Martin Heidegger, *Letter on Humanism* in *Basic Writings* ed. David F. Krell (New York: Harper and Row, 1977), p. 202.
24. Jacques Derrida, 'The Ends of Man' in *Philosophy and Phenomenological Research,* vol. 30, no. 1 (1969), p. 49.

The Middle Voice in *Being and Time*

CHARLES E. SCOTT
Vanderbilt University

The Function of the Middle Voice in the Book as a Whole

The task of thinking about Heidegger after Heidegger is not necessarily one of following the development and shaping of his various thoughts. We might also think back from where we are now or from one or another of his later works, reversing a forward, linear development, or we might follow the transformation of the question of being to something vaguely other than being that is both unknown and to be thought. We might depart from Heidegger and follow language and thought that have emerged from the impact of his work. Or we might follow his own language, its movements and developments. It often shows a way that Heidegger himself was not always clear about, a way that he found himself following as though something were emerging beyond his intentions and reflections, a language in which thinking changed as it felt the impact of other language and thought that were forgotten, set aside, or never quite articulated, but are now released in his writing. Heidegger's way of thinking is not simply the totality of his own careful efforts. It is a way that spawns beginnings and departures. His 'way' passes on a preoccupation with what is in its own lineage and is also beyond the reach of clarity in our inherited language and thought. The task of thinking in this language is governed by what is to be thought and is not quite thinkable, like an enticement, oblique and hidden, but received now with a sense of quiet urgency, drawing and perplexing, upsetting our satisfactions and our sense of rightness as we think. Heidegger's way of thinking at the very least involves dissatisfaction, uncertainty, and experimentation.

We shall address part of this task of thinking about Heidegger after Heidegger now as it emerges with regard to the language of *Being and Time* by following the function of the middle voice. It is an obscure and almost lost voice in our grammar and speech, and one that contributes significantly to the difficulty and awkwardness of Heidegger's first major book. Through the function of this voice an aspect of our history comes to bear. It is a voice that is

J.C. Sallis, G. Moneta and J. Taminiaux (eds.), The Collegium Phaenomenologicum, 159–173.
© Kluwer Academic Publishers.

still awkwardly accessible, but used obliquely primarily in reflexive constructions or in some classical Greek works and German expressions. It is one that in its recall unsettles the dominance of active and passive voices, one that obstructs the kind of clarity that we expect. It disrupts the ontological language of *Being and Time*. It makes doubtful straightforward descriptions and the active transcendental overtones that run through *Being and Time.* By paying attention to the function of this voice in that essay we are following an aspect of Heidegger's language that reorients thinking and calls into question Heidegger's own active purposes in his account of Dasein. This voice speaks and retrieves a part of our history and can say things in ways that are different from our customary articulations and our dominant philosophical expressions. Through this voice a history takes place that redirects thinking and, though obscure, seems to promise a kind of clearing different from our most refined clarity. In its recall a disquieting retrieval occurs in this voice's functions in *Being and Time,* one that provides a burst of possibilities for thinking that considerably exceeds Heidegger's own expectations for fundamental ontology.

Although I can only indicate the point here, we shall see the likelihood that through the functions of the middle voice in *Being and Time*, the project of fundamental ontology itself becomes far more provisional than Heidegger thought it to be when he conceived the essay. Fundamental ontology will not be a beginning for thinking as Heidegger at one time thought, but is rather an ending of a way of thinking. The middle voice puts our dominant voices in question and hence moves aside the fundamental ontological beginning. It is a voice that is more primordial in Heidegger's thought than the influence of, say, Husserl or the 'voice' of Aristotle. It is embedded in his language, recalled vaguely by reflexivity and also by the language of happening, e.g., Dasein is its own self-disclosure; but it is also a voice that is hard to think in and with. In both its possibilities and its lapses in our western grammars it speaks with an antiquity that exceeds that of our oldest philosophers. It is prephilosophical in our traditions, and its recall puts in question those ways of thought that think as though there were no middle voice.

In order to make manageable our discussion, I shall follow the function of rupture vis à vis the middle voice in *Being and Time*, as distinct to giving an account of specific claims in the book. We shall attend to how the occurrence of the middle voice has a rupturing effect in *Being and Time* and hence furthers a movement toward a way of thinking that is different from the thinking that Heidegger could carry out prior to the influence of *Being and Time*. Rupture is a part of the de-structuring process in the book's discourse, and that process is probably the book's most important effect in our culture. When one's thinking and speaking have been developed in a de-structuring process, for example, and not only by thinking about de-structuring, that process – de-structuring – is in the thinking, is a forming part of the thinking, a part that 'makes de-forming' as thinking goes on. The discourse does not simply emphasize rupture; it makes a process of rupturing thought. Desire for a neutral, tightly stitched language of observation, for example, desire for a language that accounts things with the expectation that its neutrality and power of observation will give it the power to say what is true or to speak on the basis of something that is universally true – desire for that kind of language probably can not exist in discourses that are developed in and through the de-structuring that develops in Heidegger's discourse, just as desire for thinking without dialectic can not exist in an Hegelean discourse. Fear of non-logical connections, horror over death, a sense of mystery related to rational coherence – those feelings fade in thinking that is developed through the ruptures of de-structuring. Interest in connections, powers, and ways of living that emerge from the gaps occasioned by de-structuring or from non-controlling attentiveness or from the strife of opposites: interest of those kinds develop through de-structuring thought instead of interests developed through experiences of monarchial order or of rational authority. *Being and Time* sets in motion ways of thinking that develop in and through de-structuring, and those ways of thinking were only beginning to be foreseeable during the time of the book's conception.

Because of our time constraints, I shall also exemplify the discursive, thought-forming function of rupture and de-struction rather than following that function through the entirety of *Being and Time*. The middle voice in Heidegger's approach to *phenomenon, speech,* and *hiding* has a de-structuring function throughout the book. Heidegger's discussion of 'phenomenon' is based on the Greek *phainesthai*, the middle voice of *phaino*. Since the middle voice is only traced in modern language, we resort to reflexive formations, such as 'what shows itself.' The reflexive structure, however, relies on pronouns and nouns in a fashion that distracts from and probably distorts what the middle voice could say with one verb form. We lack the voice to say conveniently 'the occurrence of self-showing.' We say, 'showing itself from itself.' The middle voice mutes the 'it' and does not need the reflective 'self.' It consequently could say an occurrence that was neither active nor passive nor even necessarily reflexive.[1] Bringing to daylight, i.e., daylighting or brightening, seems to be meant in *phainesthai*. Phenomena are beings, *ta onta*, that is being manifest and palpable indicate a middle voice process that we can best express as self-showing. That is a process of coming to light without action in the midst of all kinds of action. 'Beings show themselves from themselves', although we need to hear the middle voice alternative in this reflexive phrasing.

Heidegger's phenomenology thus speaks of things that are self-showing without agency in their occurrence qua self-showing. The logos of beings is not to be taken as the structure of constituting agency. Neither a 'who' nor a 'what' is intended when he speaks of self-showing. The 'founding' process of coming to light is middle voiced, and its structures, its logos, are not finally accessible to literal or figurative language. How are we to 'address' phenomena in light of their accessibility in the middle voice? Speaking may let something come to light. *Logos*, taken in its meaning of speech (*apophansis*), is self-showing (*apophainesthai*) as it is spoken about. Words let something be seen in self-showing occurrences. The *phainesthai* occurs as something is spoken about and shows. The speaker, says Heidegger, is a medium, while the speaking '"lets us see," from itself, *apo* . . ., what is being talked about' (7.b). Two kinds of things happen: as *apophansis* speaking shows what is spoken of; as *apophainesthai* speaking shows itself coming to light as its own occurrence, an occurrence keyed by the *apophainesthai* of the addressed. Heidegger is proposing in his phenomenology a way of speaking that is alert to both functions. If *apophansis* is taken without *apophainesthai* – if the showing activity of speaking is taken without the middle voice process of self-showing – speaking will be interpreted as making present or as presencing. But if both functions are held together, speaking will be interpreted as addressing not only *what* is shown but a showing itself with the self-showing of what is shown. The middle voice function is not primarily one of representing or designating. It shows out of itself. The '*what*' that is shown is not central or peripheral. The atomic imagery behind 'central' and 'peripheral' is dropped. What is shown is in self-showing. And since self-showing is not a what or who or an action, the present time as a determinant now does not dominate the concept. Further, since self-showing is not agency-centered and can not be thought of as constitution or synthesis, its communication can not be conceived adequately in terms of literal or figurative language.

How to speak otherwise is a continuing issue for Heidegger. Since he has not posed the issue in terms of power, but rather in terms of release, opening up, and disclosing, a primary emphasis on domination, submission, and transvaluation is foreign to his way of speaking. 'De-struction', although involving a release of subordinated and subjected ways of thinking, puts emphasis on release of words and ideas that are not power oriented. There is also considerable conflict among terms and ideas in *Being and Time* as they are changed by its different and changing discourse. But what is to be let seen, through the descriptions and conflicts, is a submerged aspect of Dasein – its self-disclosive world-related openness – that will reorient Dasein around the self-disclosure of being. In this preparatory essay Heidegger needs to let Dasein overcome its ignorance of its own coverup, its not knowing that it has developed itself by putting derived aspects of its being in front of something else that it is but can hardly speak of. Its '*pseudesthai,*' its 'being false,' needs to come into the open. That opening out of being false into the *phainesthai* of its being might yield the significantly different way of speaking and thinking that *Being and Time* forecasts. The kind of language that Heidegger consequently needs in the essay is one that maintains the question of Being and puts in question everything that is unquestioned or not really in question in Dasein's tradition. If he can put in question the literal and symbolic certainties of a tradition by another description that can be taken literally as accurate about Dasein and if he can also develop that account in the question of Being which the Daseins-analysis can not resolve or adequately answer in any literal terms, then he will have maintained the question of Being. He will have developed a discourse in which that question de-structures the essay's own seeming certainty. The book will be a 'medium' that shows something other than the totality of its contents and other than what it speaks directly about. A remarkable combination of *phainesthai* and *pseudesthai* would occur.

If *Being and Time* is successful in holding together *apophansis* and *apophainesthai*, its literal, descriptive claims will be offset by a process that it embodies, that it 'says,' with and beyond its accounts and that lets self-showing be seen in and through what is described. In that way it will hold in question its descriptions, interpretations, judgments, and syntheses. Their adequacy and manner of speech will not circumscribe or justify their own occurrence. Their active voice will not be sufficient for their own self-evidence. The *apophainesthai* of the discourse will be in the questionableness of its fully developed and established speech. The question of Being will thereby be allowed and seen in a discourse that shows in detail how Dasein shows itself.

The question of Being that is beginning to be shown in the questionableness of Heidegger's language shifts the meaning of 'founding' and 'foundation.' In this context, causation language clearly misleads. The ideas of agency, extratemporal process, and substance are being set aside.[2] 'Standing' in question, which we will find associated with 'ex-sistence,' rather than present endurance, is the 'foundation' of Dasein, and this understanding has begun to undercut the constructive use of 'foundation.' The concept of foundation in relation to Dasein is moving toward an interpretation of Being without foundation by virtue of its use in the context of Dasein's question of Being.

When Heidegger makes the expression 'to the things themselves' the motto of his phenomenology, he has no objects in mind. That phrase in his context means '*apophainesthai ta phainomena*': 'to *let* what shows itself be seen from itself, just as it shows itself from itself' (7c). The *let* is affiliated with 'shows' itself from 'itself' and with 'how.' *How* things show themselves will be *let* seen. That means that the discourse itself, by making the *how* of self-disclosure its guiding principle, will develop an ear for its own middle voice: a way of thinking Being as self-disclosiveness is being developed in the texture of this discourse. Coming to light, rather than apparent objects, guides this understanding. When descriptions of things coming to light and the self-disclosure of discourse itself are held together in the essay's speaking and thinking, Heidegger's phenomenology will have achieved its preliminary goal. He will have shown by paying attention primarily to how things show themselves, and by casting a descriptive effort in the question of Being, how language becomes alert to: 1) the covering up of the question of Being that is pervasive of how things show themselves and 2) the pervasiveness of the uncovering self-disclosure of discourse. This language participates in the cover-up and also recognizes it. Being thematically guides this discourse as the pervasive commonality of all beings. It is let be as question in Dasein's covering-up and self-disclosing. The discourse, as a process, gives space and thematic effectiveness to Being in the middle voice, lets Being be the phenomenon of this *aphophainesthai*, this speaking situation that speaks itself as other things are spoken of.

The interpretive work of *Being and Time* is thus a field of conflict between metaphysical thinking and the disclosure of Being. The interpretation is carried out as ontology, cast now in the question of Being, not in the presence, atemporality, or definability of Being. The ontological orientation carried with it an emphasis on structure: Heidegger's Daseins-analysis is a description of the 'basic *structures*' of Dasein's self-disclosure. These basic structures put the question of Being as the question of the *meaning* of Being. On the one hand, Heidegger by seeing the question of Being as the issue of the meaning of Being is showing how Being has been concealed-revealed in Dasein's way of being: an historical, developmental investigation that shows how the meaning of Being has been a concealing factor for human being. The analysis develops this way of concealing by transforming 'meaning' from propositional and systematic language into a language of existential insufficiency, mortality, and disclosure without substantive basis. On the other hand, *this* investigation is part of that history: it is moved by the issue of meaning in relation to Being. It names the meaning of Being and pursues the question of meaning at the same time that it transforms that question. By determining the meaning of Being Heidegger will have shown how Dasein has been constituted, how it has come to be as it is in the context of its history with Being. As a part of de-structuring metaphysical thinking, the determination of the meaning of Being is conceived in the concealment of Being by metaphysical language and thought. As an investigation of the meaning of Being, however, the essay itself is conceived in a language of structure, whole/part, imminence/transcendence, meaning/non-meaning – a language that is doubtful to the extent that the concealment and self-disclosure of Being become apparent in the discourse.

In *Being and Time* Being is conceived as 'transcendence pure and simple' because Dasein in its active and passive voices lacks a language for it. Its 'transcendence' offsets all of its determinations. But as language and thinking appropriate the occurring concealment of Being in Dasein, the 'transcendence' of Being will look less and less like transcendence. Being's 'transcendence' will be overcome by its recall when the discourse is disclosive of Being in its middle voiced concealment. This disclosure will make phenomenological ontology and its focus on 'the cardinal problem, the question of the meaning of Being in general' (7.c), a part of a passing era. The middle voiced, disclosive occurrence of this phenomenological discourse makes obsolete its own method and problematic. A different language is coming to speech.

Through the function of the middle voice Heidegger has allowed part of our language's history to break the dominance in language of objectification and subjective constitution and the multiple problems and polarity that that dominance has spawned. If we followed it carefully through *Being and Time* we would find that the middle voice functions in a de-structuring way in association with the question of Being in most of the book's sections. The middle voice's absence in modern linguistic functions and its memory both in the question of Being as Heidegger develops it and in our grammar's reflexive functions allow it to disrupt the unconscious assumption in speech that self-showing involves constituting acts and relies on subjective reflexivity. In its rupture of our conventions, the middle voice creates a need for revised language and thinking. It suggests that ways of being different from Dasein's, in its domination by activity and passivity, may be necessary for people to think and live through the question of Being. That question, repressed and overlaid as it is, is *the* formative power of Dasein. *Being and Time* is struggling with the rupture of its own language occasioned by the question of Being in its middle voice, and as we think with the book we undergo the effects of this rupturing process.

An example: Historicity in the Middle Voice

The issue of historicity, of the ontological basis for historical occurrences, is set in the context of Heidegger's preoccupation with Dasein's finite unity. Only after that unity is demarcated, named, and explicated in terms of care, temporality, and mortality does Heidegger turn to the way the unity of Dasein is shown in historical processes. Just as he has shown how all of Dasein's ways of being in the world manifest the mortality of Dasein's occurrence, he will now show how all historical happenings manifest Dasein's historicity. He will found historical realities and possibilities in Dasein's being. But just as Dasein's finite being destabilized the configuration of foundation, ground, Being, and unity, historicity will further destabilize the idea of transcendental unity, will eliminate subject-object pairing in thinking about history, and will recast the question of history into a nonlinear conception of historical happening. *Historicity* functions as an elaboration of mortal temporality, and only when Dasein has come to a free and open relation with its own deathliness is it prepared to reinterpret history and historicity with primary reference to its own being. Authenticity, Heidegger shows, is Dasein's opening to its essentially historical being.[3]

Dasein is not essentially a subjective occurrence. Its middle voiced happening – its being its own phenomenon – and its being essentially world-relational rather than a subject that relates to the world, means that the activity and structures of subjectivity are utterly misleading when one begins to think about human being and the meaning of Being. Heidegger uses 'disclosure' to de-structure the dominance of subject-terms for interpreting human being and Being – hence his beginning of his discussion of phenomenological method with the middle voice of *phainesthai* and *pseudesthai*. Neither showing nor concealing is active or passive. Authentic Dasein yields to its disclosure, its self-showing, in its unprotected and bare deathliness. A thorough concealing continues in traditional and everyday ways. Dasein's open, nonresisting acceptance of its being makes clear that concealing goes on, that it *is* a concealing occurrence, and that concealing need not be the basis for interpretative thinking. When historicity and deathliness come together in Dasein's resolved openness with its being, the dominance of the subject has already been de-structured. The question of unity is clearly not a question of unity of subjectivity. Any idea of history and historicity that cover over Dasein's deathliness, thrown fragmentariness, the question of Being, or the deep and structural sense of its own instability – such ideas will not attract authentic Dasein.

If history is not interpreted against a backdrop of subjectivity or of objective reality, how is it to be thought out? How is Dasein's finite middle voice to be rendered into active interpretation and thinking? What happens to Dasein-the-foundation in this process that appears relentless in its destructuring of inherited patterns of thought?

Heidegger's intention to ground historical occurrences and their study in Dasein leads him to formulations taken from transcendental phenomenology. He replaces talk of consciousness with discussions of understanding, interpretation, and state of mind and casts his discussion out of the problematic of consciousness. But he establishes the unity of Dasein in the transcendental terms of ontological conditions for the possibility of ontic states.[4] Historicity, which is 'basically a more concrete development of temporality', consequently functions in this discussion as the steady structure that grounds 'the endless multiplicity of possibilities' for historical occurrences (74). Heidegger is convinced that without an ontological structure, particular occurrences would lack ordered identity. So he emphasizes the transcendental-like structures. The historical status of historicity itself is uncertain in this way of posing the problem. Historicity can be taken to be trans-historical in the sense that it grounds all temporal events, or it can be taken to be thoroughly historical, i.e., itself generated in a developing process. If historicity, belonging as it does to the being of Dasein, makes history possible, then it would appear to be transhistorical. If historicity is itself historical, then it would be a finite structure and a process characterized by birth and death. Heidegger probably means both of these possibilities at different times. Regardless of his intentions, the struggle which takes place in the context of deathliness and finitude between the transhistorical and the historical elements in his language moves this discourse toward a way of thinking in which history is seen as the way all necessary conditions occur, so that the question of history is posed in exclusive reference to history itself and not in reference to the conditions for the possibility of history. Histories become their own conditions. This way of thinking, however, becomes viable in the context of Heidegger's thought only when the issue of unity and conditions is de-structured. This begins in *Being and Time*, but the book was not written in the full impact of that process.

Historicity, as we shall see in the following section, is conceived in nonlinear terms, and whether Dasein has a specific, developmental beginning – a birth into history – is not a primary concern. Finitude and historicity are not to be conceived in a quasi-explanatory context, e.g., that Dasein did in fact have a beginning in a natural or world-historical process. Doubtlessly it did. But Dasein's historicity is already assumed by the concern reflected in that claim. We are not looking for origins or originary developments. We are attempting to pose the issue of historicity in terms of Dasein's self-disclosure as a temporal, finite being. The account needs to begin in Dasein's appropriation of its thrown mortality: it needs to begin with an effort to think from and toward its appropriation of self-showing, without explanation, and without any traditional guides for speaking and thinking. If Dasein can hold itself in its mortality and in the question of the meaning of Being, perhaps the transcendentally oriented language will discover something that it cannot handle. Perhaps the awkwardness of finding through the metaphysical and phenomenological traditions something that is covered over by them will make possible a different and less encumbered way of speaking and thinking.

Heidegger uses the expression 'temporality temporalizes' in showing how Dasein's being relates to everyday experiences and schemes of time (cf. 75, 78, 80). He wants to show that Dasein's understanding of its being is embedded in the casual, everyday manner of experiencing time. He further wants to show that care and Dasein's essential caring for its being in its being are indicated even by everyday life in which one could not care less for ontological issues. Our interest, however, is in Heidegger's use of an expression that recalls the middle voice. Temporality temporalizes: that is one way to interpret Dasein's historicity.[5] Dasein's 'stretch' between birth and death, the occurrence of 'primordial temporality,' reveals the whole of Dasein and its 'constancy and steadiness' (75). Dasein is its historical constancy and is the basis for the particular constants that we find in history and everyday life. Heidegger looks for a way to say that something unfolds out of itself and throughout the human world without indicating dialectical development or objective 'world-historical processes.' The 'foundation' of temporal occurrences is itself an occurrence, and 'time is neither objectively present nor in the subject nor in the object, neither "inside" nor "outside," it is "prior" to every subjectivity or objectivity, *because it presents the condition of the very possibility of this "prior"*' (80, emphasis added). Time as the condition for temporal subjectivity and objectivity is neither active nor passive. It does not simply reflect back on itself. It temporalizes. Temporality shows temporality in and as it occurs.

When the fundamental condition for all subjective and objective temporal relations is thought out in this middle voiced way, subjectivity falls away in relation to 'condition.' Temporality does not occur like subjectivity or subjects occur, nor does it receive action. Temporal 'there' takes place. Everyday time emerges and develops. Birth and death stretch out together in a finite process that in its self-showing does not allow reduction. Dasein is its own occurring. In this process of coming to be and ceasing to be, always, as not subjective and not objective, but in a middle voice, Dasein's being is in question. As time 'times,' meanings both show time and cover it (*phainesthai* and *pseudesthai* happen together). History takes place not as a story or as a complicated world-historical process, but as Dasein 'times' out. Dasein is not 'in' history by being historical. It is historical in its self-showing. Since it is self-showing in the birth-death stretch, it is more radically historical than can be conveyed by an evolutionary, developmental idea. Every objective explanation expresses Dasein's concern for its being, shows Dasein as care in the process of birth and dying, and fades in its promise of certainty as Dasein experientally recalls its being. In its middle voice, all of Dasein's certainties fade out. Such fading is one more instance of temporality temporalizing.

When one holds in mind Heidegger's insistence on a unity of structures and a unified process of temporality with this middle voice aspect of his thinking, the discourse-developing tension in *Being and Time* is clear. As temporality is thought through it becomes clear that Dasein's historicity means that no objective or subjective stance for Dasein as such can withstand the fading-out process. Dasein is not an occurrence that begins in time. It care-fully 'times' and therefore can tell itself of real, objective origin. Its occurrence excists in the sense that timing stands out (*ecstatis* is Heidegger's term) from all factual standing. Dasein's constancy is ex-standing: the middle voice will not be absorbed into the active or passive voices that provide continuity by stances, connections, and receptions. Dasein begins to appear as historicity in the strong sense that historical explanations of it fall short and conceal its finitude – its originating and dying time. The constancy promised by Heidegger's transcendental, phenomenological language has been turned into a radically finite event by a middle voice in the midst of an otherwise objective description of human occurrence.

There are two emphases in the way Heidegger thinks of history in *Being and Time*. They may well be complementary, although either's dominance of the other will lead to considerably different ways of thinking.

The first emphasis thinks of Dasein as having come to be and as mortal. It combines this thought with the question of the meaning of Being. Dasein is not only the 'stretch between birth and death' in its throwness. Dasein is also a history that manifests beginning without meta-historical meaning or grounding. Meaning occurs *in* Dasein's history and finds no transhistorical reverberation. The 'stretch' of the individual is like Dasein itself, the finite stretch between birth and death. Always aborning, always dying, always witness to beginning and end, Dasein is its own basis for believing that as a way of being it is subject to beginning and ending. Not only is history as such consequently finite (since history is the stretch of Dasein's being), but historical segments have only Dasein as their continuing ground. For Heidegger the transcendental thinker, Dasein is the condition for the possibility of history and histories. For Heidegger the de-structionist of transcendental thinking, Dasein does not mean its own continuing. It is a passing away that has no preestablished directedness toward some type of eternity or toward long endurance.

Within this emphasis the question of Being looks like a defining aspect of Dasein's being. The history of this question completes and exhausts its meaning. If Being is desubstantialized by making it the questionableness of the question, Being, and not only the meaning of Being, is thought as finite. Being is then taken to be the question of Dasein's finitude. It is 'beyond' any grasp, formulation, or way of life. It is the ground of Dasein's thinking and doing. It is the strange, fading, and revealing basis of being-in-the-world. But it does not appear to be outside the occurrence of its own history. In *Being and Time* Heidegger does not think of Being as intrinsically historical. Dasein is intrinsically historical. The possibility that Being itself is historical as the question of Dasein's historical being, however, is not far removed from the essay's way of thinking. It often seems to be only one de-structuring step away.

The second emphasis sets aside the imagery of beginning and end. Historicity becomes the dominant word. It names the way finite Dasein shows itself. This approach asks us to recast the issue of history as the question of how Dasein shows itself, of how temporality temporalizes. We begin to forget the problems of relative versus nonrelative grounding as we appropriate our own finite temporality. This part of Heidegger's de-structuring process thinks outside of the context of universal-particular and relative-absolute, although his opposing terms *ontic-ontological* and *existentielle-existential*, as well as his overriding concern for unity and ontological continuity, are in tension with historicity as middle voiced, nonnormative occurrence.

Within this second emphasis one can easily think of Being as a self-showing, self-concealing mystery that is not circumscribed by Dasein's linear procession. Temporality is like a mysterious emission of being, and the problem is to learn to think of emission or the *Schicht of Geschichte* in substance-free language. The history of Being is how it is lived out in its arriving-withdrawing. Does Dasein highlight, as it were, Being's withdrawal? Its self-showing? Does it live as though Being were not there at all? Does it learn to hear Being's occurrence in its own historicity? Its question arises from its mystery, its continual escape from meaning and from the temporality that reveals it. Dasein's historicity is the occurrence of Being's questionableness in existence. And Being's difference from Dasein, which is shown through Dasein's own mortal, fragmentlike quality, is able continually to incite existential doubt and wonder: Being's withdrawal is hinted at in the absence of meaning and existential incompleteness that pervade Dasein's meaning and undermine all momentary fulfillment.

The difference of Being is essentially shrouded in Dasein. Dasein's own self-showing, its difference from subjectivity and objectivity, shows nothing exactly. Certainly not something other. But it does show a dimension of occurrence that escapes our grammars, words, and syntax. Thinking in acceptance of such mystery partakes of the mystical in the sense that the thinker is in touch with, it in the hearing of, unsayable, unspecifiable difference that occurs in the ground of Dasein's own occurrence. Meditative discipline, attitudes similar to reverence, and the affections of noninterference and noninsistence are appropriate.

Within both of these emphases difference pervades relations of similarity, continuity and contiguity. Whether thought in terms of the finiteness of history as such or of Dasein's occurrence as historicity, our thinking Being and time together in this essay shows that beings in their definitive relations are 'gapped' by nothing definitive or sayable. Heidegger thinks of this difference as that between Being and beings: in the 'is' Being happens in a strange intimacy or closeness with Dasein that disrupts continuity in mortal 'timing'. *Being and Time* leaves the reader (and Heidegger too) with the question of how to think our mortal 'timing,' and the question holds multiple possibilities for ways of thinking that emerge from and leave behind the de-structuring that has gone on in *Being and Time*. Is human history to be thought in reference to its gaps and fissures that make intelligible in terms of self-defining historical regions and demarcated spans of time the indwelling absence of definition and identity? Is thoughtful speaking to take place by plays of differences that disrupt totalities of meaning and the sense of grammatical connections? Is the acceptance of finite temporality to be developed by studies of ways in which our languages remember and forget temporality temporalizing? Such projects assume the de-struction of Dasein as it is thought in association with transcendental grounding and indicate that at least an initial phase of the de-structuring process worked: the unity of Dasein turns out to be unthinkable in terms of a unitary continuity for differences. That 'unity' appears rather to be *phainesthai* and *pseudesthai* at once, i.e., no unity at all. That is not what Heidegger intended. But that is what his discourse accomplished.

In the penultimate paragraph of *Being and Time* Heidegger says that 'we must look for a way to illuminate the fundamental ontological question, and follow it'. In the margin of his copy of *Being and Time* he noted the words 'a way' and wrote 'not "the" sole way.'[6] The essay is the result of his intention to pursue the question of Being by 'the understanding of Being that belongs to existing Dasein'. He has tried to show how Dasein's understanding of Being is articulated in formative, traditional ideas about Being. At best such a study will have instigated a 'strife in relation to the interpretation of Being.' This strife for which the essay has served as preparation will bring out the question of Being.[7] Once initiated, the strife takes priority over the way Heidegger presents his investigation, i.e., he has started a process that he suspects will not be controlled by *Being and Time* and probably will not support his own way of developing its question. He is in a question that is not his, one that he knows to have made possible his own work and the continuing work of the book that he has brought to a close. But he is not sure how this possibility for raising the question of Being is to be interpreted. At the conclusion of his investigation of Dasein as the 'place' of this question he asks, 'How is the disclosive understanding of Being belonging to Dasein possible at all?' By 'going back to the primordial constitution of the being of Dasein that understands Being' he has initiated strife around the question of Being. That strife puts his work in question and articulates both the question of Being and an understanding of Being to which Heidegger knows that he has not done justice. Should it happen that the strife of this question were also its Logos, its gathering, then we would expect Heidegger's discourse to have initiated a process of investigating and questioning that goes far beyond the constraints of his triggering analysis. The strife would be disclosive of a discursive history that produced a dominant way of being – Dasein – which has as its future continuing strife. Should the strife end, Dasein would no longer exist. By initiating this process *Being and Time* has anticipated its own demise and has been true to its own unresolved conflicts. Both non-resolution and conflict will continue in this discursive strand in the dominance of difference.

Notes

1. In Old Sanskrit as well as in Greek, the middle voice could express reflexive action, such as 'he washed his hands'. Even then, however, in Old Sanskrit, for example, only two words were needed – pănt nĕniktĕ – so that the nominal and pronominal functions are expressed in the verb, and the inherence of the nominal in the verbal is indicated. In non-reflective instances, however, such as the middle voice of *die* – mriyáte – or of *born* – ayáte – a different situation is stated. The German 'es wird gestorben' or 'es wird geboren' are probably close to the intended, middle voice meaning. In these cases no one forms an action or conceives an action, and the situation itself does not refer back to itself in a way that allows a noun or pronoun to act or be acted on. Dying or borning is going on. In the cases of *phainesthai*, like the *gegonesthei* (becoming becomes), no one and no thing is acting or receiving action.
2. Many *sta* words, derived from the Sanskrit *stha*, to stand, undergo rethinking in *Being and Time* as well as in post-*Being and Time* works. They include not only history, stance, substance, and understanding, but also consist, constancy, constitution, destiny, ecstasy, existence, subsist, and system. *Dastehen, entstehen, Gestalt, Stelle, stellen, stehen, Stand, Verständnis, Verstehen, vorstellen* are also prominent in this family. Generally these words are destabilized in Heidegger's discourse relative to the traditional metaphysical uses. Insofar as the question of Being is the '*Stelle*' of thinking, for example, and the temporal occurrence of being is the 'stance' of *Being and Time*, an 'understanding' emerges in the discourse in which there is no *sub*-stance. 'To come to stand' is of a larger non-standing event, and the tradition's intuitive correlation of 'stand', 'found', and 'ground' is changed. 'Stand' no longer addresses the question of how things are together in common.
3. 'When Dasein, anticipating, lets death become powerful in itself, as free for death, it understands itself in its own *higher power*, the power of its finite freedom, and takes over the *powerlessness* being abandoned to itself in that freedom, which only *is* in having chosen the choice, and becomes clear about the chance elements in the disclosed situation.' When he says that 'authentic being-to-death, i.e., the finitude of temporality, is the concealed ground of the historicity of Dasein' he means that mortality is the meaning of all events. He is showing that Dasein's wholeness is centered in mortality, and not, for example, in presence. Finitude and mortality immediately mean the up-coming end, i.e., authentic futurity (74).
4. For example: 'Only if death, guilt, conscience, freedom, and finitude live together equiprimordially in the being of a being as they do in care, *can* that being exist in the mode of fate, i.e., be historical in the ground of its existence' (emphasis added). 'Only authentic temporality that is at the same time finite makes something like fate, i.e., authentic historicity, possible' (974). In these examples, the transcendental overtone has been so qualified by the ideas of finitude and mortality, as we have seen, that speaking of the transcendental status of Dasein's ontological structures has become awkward and counterintuitive. But these types of formulation point out that Heidegger's de-structuring of transcendental phenomenology involves his reliance on that way of thinking.
5. 'The historicity of Dasein is essentially the historicity of the world which on the basis of the ecstatic and horizonal temporality belongs to the temporalizing of that temporality' (75).
6. Heidegger wrote to a young and anxious Karl Löwith, when the student feared that his departure from his Doktor-Vater's ideas in *Being and Time* might prevent his advancing, that he, Heidegger, had no interest in schools of agreement. His work, he said, prevented such a traditional desire. Rather, difference and disagreement are to be developed. Thinking has its many ways. 'My work is unique in a limited way and can only be done by me – on account of the uniqueness of this constellation.' Further, 'whether one goes along with *Being and Time* is a matter of complete indifference to me . . .' His indifference came from the recognition that misunderstanding and trivialization are inevitable and that agreement and disagreement are

incidental to the work of thinking with and through the essay. His recognition of the limits of his own way in the context of Dasein's history with Being means that strife, departure, and difference are recognized by him as welcomed. 'The Nature of Man and The World of Nature: For Heidegger's 80th birthday,' Karl Löwith, in *Martin Heidegger: In Europe and America,* eds. Ballard and Scott, (Nijhoff, 1973), pp. 37–8.

Reference, Sign, and Language: *Being and Time*, Section 17

PARVIS EMAD
De Paul University

> The measure of discoveredness which has gone into a language can be preserved, or renewed beyond the 'death' of a language.
>
> Heidegger,
> *Prolegomena zur Geschichte des Zeitbegriffs*

Introduction

The beginning of the unfolding of the Preparatory Fundamental Analysis of Dasein is marked by the effort to unroll the discussion of the familiar but as yet uncomprehended phenomenon of the world. The issue which sustains this discussion throughout, and distinguishes it from philosophy's concern with the world is called reference (*Verweisung*). Although this issue is specifically dealt with in section 17 of *Being and Time*, reference so pervades the entire discussion of the world as to extend its influence far beyond this section. Without the involvement of reference overall in the discussion, Preparatory Fundamental Analysis could not *de facto* demonstrate that the dominion of 'relation' and 'object' is brought to an end and a new understanding of the world is attained. Henceforth it makes no sense to talk about being *related* to the world. The phenomenon of reference provides the primary indication that we are *in* the world. Composed of references of all kinds, referential contexts are indicators of our being *in* the world. Subsequent to the discovery of the world in *Being and Time*, 'object' too loses its primacy along with 'relation.' Now we realize that the confrontation with objects happens only when we do not heed the flexible referential contexts which give rise to something entirely different from an object. This is so because referential contexts do not have the constancy which supports something as immutable as an object. The novel understanding of the world, attained in *Being and Time*, the insight into the ontological zone which is there prior to the confrontation with objects – such understanding and insight are foreshadowed in the phenomenon of reference.

Entitled 'Reference and Sign,' section 17 deals with reference in conjunction with sign (*Zeichen*). Reference and sign are considered together because reference is an essential structure of being in the world and can be studied in an

J.C. Sallis, G. Moneta and J. Taminiaux (eds.), The Collegium Phaenomenologicum, 175–189.
© Kluwer Academic Publishers.

exemplary fashion in the sign. The clearer this structure becomes, the better the phenomenon of the world is understood. Reference as it occurs in the sign gives us a unique opportunity for seeing world's elusive proximity to things. Through reference, sign has a proximity to the world which can be seen in referential relations which give rise to the sign.

The joint discussion of reference and sign makes an indirect contribution to a fuller and more rounded account of the world. By examining reference as it occurs in the sign, this discussion indicates that world is not only disclosed in *Da* (here/there) but also in referential relations to things. Thus this discussion prevents us from misunderstanding the world as an occurrence which takes place in the isolation of a *Da*. This means that the occurrence of the world in *Da* is not detached from referential contexts and from referential relations to things. The phenomenon which already prevents a detachment of the world from things, is the phenomenon of reference. The key for understanding how this detachment cannot occur lies in language which keeps world and things together.

According to the analyses of *Being and Time,* world is disclosed in disposition, understanding *and* language. But what about language as concerns referential relations? These, too, reveal world. Can we say of referential relations that whenever references occur they involve language? By following the role which reference assumes in the discussion of the world, and by paying close attention to the discussion of language in *Being and Time* we shall respond to this question. We shall work out the relation between reference and language by attending closely to the role which reference plays throughout the Preparatory Fundamental Analysis of Dasein. In the end we shall see that the proximity of the world to things as well as world's disclosure (*Erschlossenheit*) in *Da* are occurrences which fall in the domain of language as this domain is elaborated upon in *Being and Time*.

The expression 'domain of language' must be taken seriously because while, as we shall show, referential relations fall in the domain of language, their status with regard to essential distinctions within this domain is unclear. To shed some light on the status of references within the domain of language, we must first demonstrate by way of a fairly straightforward reading of the text that referential relations do in fact fall in the domain of language. Once this is accomplished, it is not too difficult to show that the fact that referential relations fall in the domain of language is confirmed by the case of the sign. Subsequently, we will have to work out the exact sense in which referential relations are situated within the essential distinctions made in the domain of language. Thus the course which the following discussion will take is laid out. (1) We must show that reference and referential relations fall in the domain of language, (2) we must show that this is borne out by the analysis of the sign, and (3) we must show which position reference and referential relations take in respect to the distinctions that are intrinsic to the domain of language.

1. Reference, Meaning and Signification

In order to show that referential relations fall in the domain of language, it is necessary to find out how these relations are involved with phenomena called meaning (*Bedeutung*) and signification (*Bedeutsamkeit*). How do these relations show their proximity to meaning? In order to respond to this question we must carefully go through the analysis of referential relations as presented in *Being and Time*.[1]

Phenomenologically, referential contexts and referential relations are distinguished from the ordinary background of objects in that these contexts and relations do not have the stability which characterizes the background of objects. Thus the referential contexts and referential relations which give rise to the crystal vase as the container of the rose, differ significantly from the stable background against which the crystal vase appears as the object of a crystalographical study. Prior to being reduced to such a stable background, referential contexts and relations are those in which we primarily 'live.' Accordingly, what they give rise to is what we primarily deal with. We deal primarily with what is at hand (*zuhanden*) and not with objects. What is at hand is, above all else, distinguished by its close ties, via reference, to the world. This means that what is at hand has a 'worldly' character. Let us see what this 'worldly' character is all about.

If we examine referential contexts and relations, we find a nexus of references which operate within these contexts and which are oriented toward certain destinations (*Bewandtnis*).[2] These destinations *in toto* hold the key for grasping the 'worldly' character of what is at hand in a particular reference. In the destinations preceding it, what is at hand bears the stamp of the world. We see this by examining the destinations of referential relations.

What is striking about these destinations is that their totality lights up before referential contexts are formed. As *Being and Time* puts it:

> The totality of destinations which for instance constitutes the handiness (*Zuhandenheit*) of what is handy in a workshop is 'earlier' than the individual tool. Likewise the totality of destinations is earlier than the farmstead with all its tools and its landed properties (SZ 112).

The totality of destinations of references lights up 'earlier' and has an ontological character quite different from what arises out of a particular referential context. What so arises, what is at hand, is discovered in the light of destinations of references. Hence, these destinations are seen *before* what is at hand is discovered. Put more precisely, the prediscovered destinations provide the references with the perspective they need for finding what should be put at hand in a given referential context. These destinations are 'essentially not discoverable (*entdeckbar*)' (SZ 115) because they are already in view, i.e., discovered.

Accordingly we can say that because destinations *in toto* are viewed in advance, certain things emerge from within a given referential context. Whether what thus emerges is suitable or not is determined with regard to the destinations as a totality already placed in view. The specific ontological character of destinations consists in the inapplicability to them of the criteria of suitability or unsuitability. The inapplicability to the totality of destinations of something like a criterion of suitability, is the first indication we get of the formation of these destinations in accord with meaning. While what is at hand may or may not be suitable for a particular purpose, totality of destinations is neither suitable nor unsuitable but only *meaningful*. We shall return to this point a bit later.

Destinations are characterized as pre-discovered. However, this characterization does not mean that destinations must be thought to represent a configuration of extraneous relations which lie before us like a blueprint. They are said to be pre-discovered because we are already familiar with them, know them and exist in them. But as Dasein we exist already *in* the world and are familiar with it. This means that the *a priori* character of the destinations within a referential context must be understood as collateral with the *a priori* character of being-in-the-world. This, of course, is another way of saying that destinations point to the world. And this is indeed what *Being and Time* explicitly maintains:

> This pre-disclosed totality of destinations entails an ontological relation with the world (SZ 114).

Thus destinations which form the referential contexts are indicators of our existence in the world. Moreover, they also circumscribe the 'worldly' character of the handy. In what way?

What is present as a handy tool has close ties with a particular referential context and thereby is intimately bound to destinations which form that context in advance. Thus when something emerges as a handy tool from within a particular referential context, it shows the convergence of a variety of references and their destinations. Since we exist in these destinations and are familiar with them and since 'wherein' we exist is the world, therefore the handy as the point of convergence of destinations has a 'worldly' character.

However, at this point we cannot overlook a significant question. Are we not suggesting the identity of destinations *in toto* with the world when we bring together our existence in the destinations with the world as 'wherein' we exist? Are we not suggesting the identity of the world with the familiar destinations within a given context? To show that such identification does not occur, we let ourselves be guided by the following fundamental questions.

What does occur when we find a particular 'handy' suitable for a particular purpose? Moreover, what is it exactly that guides us toward this particular 'handy' and not toward another one? What sort of 'look' (*Sicht*) is the one most appropriate to that 'in view of which' (*Woraufhin*) a reference is a reference? We combine all these questions when we ask: What sort of *look* guides the discovery of the handy? It is clear from the preceding discussion that our existence within the matrix of familiar destinations means our familiarity with them or with their 'already-discoveredness.' Thus when we ask what sort of look leads us to the discovery of the handy, we mean how do we go about discovering the handy in the light of what is already discovered, i.e., destinations. The answer is that we embark upon the discovery of the handy by taking our guidance from a signifying which occurs in Dasein. This signifying is an occurrence in Dasein by which referential contexts and relations are understood as Dasein's possibility, its potentiality for being. Existing in the familiarity with the destinations that form a particular referential context,

> Dasein 'signifies' (*bedeutet*) to itself and originally gives itself to understand its own being and potentiality for being in regard to its being-in-the-world (SZ 116).

We avoid identifying the destinations *in toto* with the world, when we bear in mind that however close signifying may be to the world, signifying never exhausts the world. Rather, as an occurrence in Dasein the signifying of destinations reveals Dasein's ability to build world. For signifying shows that Dasein is not merely passively in the world but builds it. (This is such a crucial ability that Heidegger devotes a large portion of a lecture course after *Being and Time* to interpret it in greater detail.)[3] The ability of Dasein to build world comes about due to the accessibility in advance of what is called signification (*Bedeutsamkeit*) (Cf., SZ 116). Signification is the 'source' of Dasein's 'natural creativity.' The signifying of signification in Dasein reveals Dasein as the ontic condition for the discovery of the handy that is most suitable to a particular purpose:

> *In its familiarity with signification, Dasein is the ontic condition for the possibility of discoveredness of beings which are encountered in a world in the mode of being destined to . . .* (SZ 117). (Heidegger's emphasis)

Accordingly, we must distinguish between signification and the handy which may prove to be suitable or unsuitable. When we simply 'put away or change the unsuitable tool' (SZ 209) without thinking about it twice, we indicate that signifying of signification is an independent phenomenon beyond the criteria of suitability and unsuitability.

To sum up and to achieve a sharper focus, we can say that when we choose this and not that tool we give ourselves to understand (1) that we exist within a referential context composed of references aimed at certain destinations, (2) that the totality of destinations is signified, and (3) that this signifying is what accounts for Dasein's ability to build a world. In short, the choice of such and such a tool indicates that we have 'actively' put into words a signification in order to 'terminate' a reference. Saying 'not this hammer, the other one,' we put to word a signified meaning. This means signifying of meaning occurs in the utmost proximity to language. In order for Dasein to 'actively project' a signification and thus to 'terminate' a reference, Dasein must already have an access to meanings and must use words. *Being and Time* formulates the intricate proximity of Dasein, signifying, meaning, and word as follows:

> ... the signifying itself, with which Dasein is always familiar, entails the ontological condition for the possibility that Dasein, which understands and interprets, can disclose something like 'meanings' upon which is founded in turn the possible being of word and language[4] (SZ 117).

Thus signifying, meaning and word go together. The meaning which is already there is signified and put into word. And this means that the mere existence within the referential contexts and referential relations is indicative of the accessibility in advance of meaning and words. It is thus clear that referential contexts and relations fall in the domain of language. Before we determine how referential relations are situated with respect to the distinctions that are intrinsic to the domain of language, we must take a look at the sign. We must do so because our findings about reference will be corroborated by the reference which occurs in the sign.

2. Reference, Sign and Meaning

If anything, the preceding discussion makes it clear that reference and referential relations fall in the domain of language. The outcome of our examination of reference and of referential relations will be confirmed by studying reference as it occurs in the sign. As far as the entirety of *Being and Time* is concerned, section 17 of this work offers the only possibility for such a study.

It is the activity of hammering to which *Being and Time* frequently refers as an activity which shows a referential context and the point of convergence of all references within that context. But what is interesting about the hammer (no less than other tools we use) is that at first glance the referential contexts and relations which give rise to the hammer are inconspicuous. The detailed attention paid to sign in section 17 shows a tool which is highly suited for making conspicuous the referential contexts and relations. The gathering together in this tool of referential relations and meaning is such as to make the sign strikingly noticeable. This striking noticeability is called for because the sign is distinguished from other tools by its function of drawing attention to tools and their respective referential context. We see this by examining the reference as it occurs in a sign. Our examination of reference as it occurs in the sign begins by addressing a widespread misconception about the sign.

This misconception consists in taking signs as tools which are only produced. The phenomenological analysis of sign, however, shows that all signs are signs inasmuch as they are *taken* as signs. Even when they are produced and set up, their production is guided by something being taken as a sign. It is in taking something as a sign (*Zum-Zeichen-nehmen*) that 'a more original sense' (SZ, 107) of sign becomes manifest. Taking something as a sign sometimes proves to be an activity by which 'we may discover something for the first time' (SZ 108). To see this we focus on that occurrence in the sign which constitutes the sign's being. This occurrence is none other than the coalescing in sign of reference and indicating (*Zeigen*). It is also this occurrence which accounts for the sign's striking noticeability. To see this occurrence, we must begin by briefly discussing the indicating of the sign.

Signs are tools which indicate something. However, this indicating does not constitute the ontological structure of a sign *as a tool*. The ontological structure of a tool consists of a reference, a serviceability for something. *Being and Time* invites us to note the subtle difference between reference (serviceability) and indicating in a sign:

> The tool called hammer too is constituted by a serviceability. However, this does not turn the hammer into a sign (SZ 105).

On the one hand, a sign is a sign because it indicates something, on the other hand, sign is a tool and is ontologically constituted by reference. What is it then that distinguishes a sign *as a tool* from other tools like a hammer? Nothing but the coalescing in the sign of reference and indicating. Unlike the hammer, which shows only the structure of 'in-order-to,' serviceability, or reference, sign is a tool in which reference and indicating coalesce. *Being and Time* draws our attention to the coalescing in sign of reference and indicating by calling the latter a

> 'referring' ('*Verweisung*') which is the ontic concretization of the purpose to which serviceability is directed (*Wozu einer Dienlichkeit*) and in terms of which a tool is determined (SZ 105).

By contrast,

> the referring of 'serviceability' is an ontological categorial determination of tool *as* tool (SZ 105).

It should be pointed out parenthetically that Heidegger distinguishes the first usage of the word *Verweisung*, (as equivalent to indicating) from its second use (as equivalent to reference), by putting the former in quotation marks. What this passage calls 'ontic concretization' of the purpose served by a sign, is precisely what we call the coalescing in sign of reference and indicating. We see this coalescing better when we note that signs do not result from supplementing an already existing thing with the function or 'value' of indicating. Taking a thing as a sign does not mean we have

> made an addition (*Dreingabe*) [of the 'value' of indicating] to something which is already present (*Vorhanden*) (SZ 108).

Such addition is unnecessary because the indicating of a sign can neither be separated from a sign nor added to it. Such addition is not necessary because the ontological structure of the sign, namely reference, already indicates something. That is why *Being and Time* states that

> indicating is grounded in the ontological structure of the tool, in its serviceability for something, (SZ 105)

i.e., in a reference. Put slightly differently, reference and indicating in a sign are indistinguishable because sign is a tool in which serviceability (reference) is concretized as indicating. But why should there be something like a sign where such concertization occurs?

If our environing world would consist of only one single referential context, there would be no need for signs. However, since the environing world confronts us with a variety of referential contexts and with tools arising from within them and since not all these tools are conspicuous to the same extent, there is need for a sign that would call attention to the multifaceted environing world. If tools that arise from various referential contexts were all equally conspicuous, if 'they did not hold back and step forward (*ansichhaltendes Nichtheraustreten*)' (SZ 107), there would be no need for signs. The concretization in sign of the purpose it serves as a tool (the coalescing of reference and indicating) occurs in sign because we need a tool with the specific function of raising the handy and the referential contexts and relations to the level of explicit circumspection (*Umsicht*).

If the south wind is taken as the sign of approaching rain, the referential contexts and relations within which rain is significant and is endowed with meaning, are brought to the level of explicit circumspection. Likewise, when the turn signal of the automobile is taken as a sign which indicates direction, the vehicle, respective referential contexts, and the meaning signified within these contexts are brought to the level of explicit circumspection. Thus a sign brings certain segments of the environing world to explicit circumspection because through the coalescing in sign of reference and indicating, a sign *indicates* the meaning which is only *signified* in a reference.

Considering the coalescing in sign of reference and indicating, sign indicates the meaning which is signified in a referential context and in the destinations of references which compose that context. The indicating of the sign shows its proximity to meaning. How does this indicating relate to meaning *and* language? In order to respond to this question, we must closely examine the indicating of the sign and the sign's referential character as a tool. Can the reference in the sign be separated from the sign's indicating in spite of coalescing of reference and indicating?

Although coalescing in the sign, reference and indicating each continue to do what each is supposed to do 'individually.' Concretization of reference in indicating does not mean the disappearance of one in the other. Were this to occur, i.e., were the reference to be disappearing in indicating and vice versa, then a hammer would be indistinguishable from a sign. This means that as a tool with the structure of reference, the sign *signifies* a meaning and as a tool which indicates something, the sign *indicates* a meaning. With this finding we touch the heart of the relation between sign and meaning.

The indicating of a sign indicates the meaning which is signified by references and by the accessibility in advance of their destinations. Thus the signifying of meaning through reference must be kept apart from the indicating of the same meaning through the sign's specific function. As a tool sign arises out of a referential context *and* brings to the fore the meaning which is signified in that context. A sign's indicating occurs *after* the referential contexts, totality of references, their destinations, and the signifying of meaning have occurred. This means that the sign indicates referentiality, handiness of the handy, and its 'worldly' character – or what *Being and Time* calls worldhood:

> Sign is something ontically handy, which as this definite tool functions as something which indicates (*anzeigt*) the ontological structure of handiness, totality of reference and worldhood (SZ 110). (Heidegger emphasizes the entire quotation)

This means that as a tool with referential and indicating capabilities a sign *refers* to and indicates a meaning. How does this meaning stand with respect to the word and language?

When a sign indicates the direction which is to be taken or to be avoided, the sign indicates a meaning already signified in a reference and already put into words. Indicating 'stop' or 'turn to the left,' a sign indicates a meaning already signified and put to word in the reference which occurs in the referential context known as transportation. Since the meaning so indicated is already put to word, sign's indicating, no less than the purpose the sign serves, fall in the domain of language. Thus our study of sign corroborates our initial finding with regard to referential relation and language. The sign's indicating indicates the meaning already signified and put into word by a reference. How is the signifying of a reference (which may also be indicated in a sign) situated in respect to the distinctions that are intrinsic to the domain of language? We can respond to this question by turning to section 34 of *Being and Time*.

3. Reference, Meaning and Language

From the beginning Heidegger is interested in pointing out something about language which, while sustaining language through and through, remains withdrawn and removed from the realm of spoken word. The later distinctions between the essence of language and language and between the essence of language and saying (*die Sage*) are initially thought as an existential foundation, a sustaining ground of language which is different from the spoken word. (However, we should hasten to add that this sustaining ground is not related to language as 'ground' is to 'consequence.' For the foundation of language does not exist in a metaphysical realm *beyond* the spoken word. Rather, what sustains the spoken word is present in this word.)

The distinctions we referred to earlier as intrinsic to the domain of language are those that involve this foundation or ground. It is in respect to this ground that we must try to situate referential relations. Are these relations occurrences which happen in the domain of the spoken word or is it in the realm of the ground or foundation of language that they originally take place? To shed some light on this question we must look at the context in *Being and Time* in which the relation between reference and assertion is discussed.

In order to delineate the relation of reference to assertion we recall that the word *reference* brings to mind referential contexts, referential relations as well as signified meaning. How is assertion related to these phenomena? Let us consider a familiar tool: the door as door. A tool comes to view because destinations of references are already accessible in accord with the meaning already signified; the door as viewed from within the signifying pre-view of building a shelter is no longer experienced immediately *as* a door when it becomes the subject of an assertion. The door *as* door is present differently when we exist in a nexus of references (when we receive the meaning which signifies building a shelter) than when we make the door subject of an assertion. While existing in that nexus, we experience the door *as* door. To make the door subject of an assertion, we do not need to experience the nexus of references and all that they imply. This shows that assertion is cut off from the nexus of references and from destinations which signify meaning. Thus when we designate something *as* something by considering in advance the destinations which signify meaning, we do something quite different from what we do when we make something subject to a predication.

Considering the immediate experience of something from within the destinations of references which signify meaning, and considering the subjection of the same thing to an assertion, we must distinguish between the original *as* of interpretation, and the non-original derivative *as* of assertion. The 'as' of interpretation, the hermeneutical 'as,' indicates the silent coming forth of something from within a referential context and in accord with the meaning which is signified. By contrast, the 'as' of assertion, the apophantical 'as,' indicates that the referential context and the signified meaning are no longer originally accessible. Passing a judgment on something only dimly reflects the original emergence of that thing from within a referential context and in accord with a signified meaning. This means that the apophantic 'as' results from the modification of the hermeneutical 'as.' This modification occurs when the referential context and signified meaning are no longer originally accessible. This modification occurs when we see that the apophantic 'as' is one which

> no longer reaches out into a totality of destinations. Regarding its possibilities of articulating referential relations (*Verweisungsbezüge*), this 'as' is cut off from the signification which constitutes the worldly character of the environment (SZ 210).

This means that the relation between reference and assertion is basically one of lack and deprivation. Taken by itself, assertion is removed from the original referential contexts and from signified meaning. In short, assertion indicates severance from references, their destinations, and from signified meaning.

What do we learn from discussing the relation of assertion to referential relations and to references? We learn that as an original phenomenon, reference does not fall in the domain of the spoken word, in the field of asserted language. Does this mean that reference originally occurs in that domain which sustains language, is its ground and foundation? To answer this question, we must briefly discuss what is the ground and foundation of language according to section 34 of *Being and Time*.[5]

The view on language expressed in section 34 is decisively determined by a crucial distinction made between *Rede* (a term which, for reasons soon to become clear, should be left untranslated) and language. This distinction which articulates an ontological priority of *Rede* over language is initially merely indicated in the lecture courses of the Marburg period. The Logic course of 1925/26 simply expresses this priority as follows:

> The fundamental movement is not from language to *Rede* but from *Rede* to language.[6]

The same priority builds the conclusion of the discussion of language in another Marburg lecture course:

> We have now the phenomenon of *Rede* which underlies (*zugrundeliegt*) language so that we can say *there is language only because there is Rede.*[7]

However, it is in *Being and Time* that *Rede's* ontological priority vis-à-vis language is, for the first time, explicated as the sustaining ground and foundation of language. We call *Rede* the sustaining ground of language because section 34 distinguishes between *Rede* as 'the existential-ontological foundation of language' (SZ 213) and language as 'the uttering forth (*Hinausgesprochenheit*) of *Rede*.' (SZ 214) *Rede* is not a ground which in a metaphysical manner resides *beyond* language. Since language represents the uttering forth of Rede, since language comes forth from Rede, the latter is the ground which sustains language. Therefore, this ground is present in the spoken language without being entirely identical with the spoken language. The sustaining ground of language, *Rede* is present in the activities of uttering, speaking, asserting and the like. But none of these activities represents exhaustively the ground which sustains language. The distinction made in *Being and Time* between *Rede*, the foundation or the ground of language, and the uttering forth of this ground, indicates that discussion of language in this work is under the sway of the tension and the difference between utterance and the presence in this utterance of its ground.

Insofar as *Rede* comes so close to utterance, to assertion, to talk and discourse, and insofar as *Rede* nevertheless remains withdrawn from these activities, we should refrain from translating *Rede* with terms like 'talk,' 'discourse,' or 'speech.' For such translations inevitably pull *Rede* into a realm to which it is only partially related. However, it should also be clear that much more is involved here than merely keeping intact another Heideggerian term. For even in the original German the term *Rede* is liable to gross misunderstanding – reason enough for F.-W. von Herrmann to point out that

> the term *Rede* is not originally a philosophical and ontological term. In the natural language we use the term *Reden* as synonymous with speaking. An address or a lecture is a *Rede* held about a theme. What we originally designate as *Reden* is exactly such as to remain within the activity of uttering (*Verlautbarung*). We speak in words that are uttered. In natural speaking there is no difference between *Reden* and speaking, between *Rede* and language.[8]

This is to suggest that in order to take the term *Rede* as Heidegger intended it,

> we must in the first place bracket all the meanings which we associate with the word *Rede* and *Reden* . . . Only when we set aside the familiar meanings of the word *Rede* shall we be free for the specifically ontological meaning of this word which will then be a term which designates the ontological existential essence of what we otherwise call *Rede* or language.[9]

We grasp the ontological import of the term *Rede* when we transcend the ordinary connotations of it as are indicated in talk, speech, discourse, and the like. The choice of the term *Rede* invites us to ponder about that 'element' in *Reden*, in speaking which while still residing in the realm of speaking is not identical with this realm. What is it about this realm that remains withdrawn from this realm and nonetheless goes on to address us and claim us as *Rede*, as speech? What so claims us and addresses us is the existential-ontological foundation of language, its sustaining ground, i.e., *Rede*.

Having attended to the essential distinctions that are intrinsic to the realm of language, we may now deal with the issue as to how reference and referential relations are to be situated with respect to these distinctions. How is reference, which falls outside of the realm of assertion, related to the ground and foundation of language called *Rede*? We have already prepared the ground for responding to this question. Since assertion is removed from the originally accessible referential relations and from originally signified meaning and since assertion presents a manner in which the uttering forth of the ground of language takes place, therefore reference, referential relations, and signified meaning which fall outside of assertion must inevitably fall within the ground which sustains language. The sign which indicates 'stop' or 'turn to the left' indicates a meaning already signified through a reference. Since this meaning does not fall in the domain of assertion it must fall in the domain of the ground which sustains language. Let us take a closer look at this domain.

The ground which sustains language is succinctly characterized in *Being and Time* as follows:

> *Rede* means organizing in terms of meaning the understandableness of being-in-the world, which is determined by disposition. [*Rede ist die bedeutungsmässige Gliederung der befindlichen Verständlichkeit des In-der-Welt-seins.*] (SZ 216)

Its brevity notwithstanding, this characterization indicates clearly that the sustaining ground of language is involved in the entirety of being-in-the world. But the entirety of being-in-the world means disclosure of the world as it occurs in *Da and* as it occurs in referential relations. This means that the ground of language is involved in the disclosure of the world as this disclosure occurs both in *Da* and in referential relations. By reading this characterization both in translation and in the original German, we see that the sustaining ground of language is involved in the disclosure of the world in terms of meaning, disposition, and understanding.

Now, even a cursory reading of the analysis of *Da* in *Being and Time* is enough for realizing that the *Da* is existentially structured in terms of understanding, disposition, and *Rede*. Accordingly, even a cursory reading of the characterization of the ground of language should be enough to ensure that what sustains language is involved in world's disclosure as it occurs in *Da*. But what about referential relations and the ground which sustains language? That this ground is also involved in the disclosure of the world as this disclosure occurs in referential relations is clearly indicated in the description of this involvement as being in accord with meaning (*bedeutungsmässig*). Then in what context do we come upon meaning other than the context of the analysis of reference?

What sustains language and is its foundation is not subsequently added to world's disclosure. This is borne out by the 'activity' which the sustaining ground of language initiates in the entirety of being-in-the world. The ground of language is said to be organizing the occurrence of disclosure of the world as it occurs in understanding, disposition, and meaning. (*Gliederung* from *Gliedern* should not be translated with articulation, because as a mode of utterance articulation is subsequent to the ground of language.)[10] We should point out that meaning is not separated from being-in-the world to be added to it by the ground which sustains language. Meaning, as we tried to show, is an essential event in the occurrence of references to the world. References and referential relations fall in the domain of language via meaning.

These references and relations fall in the domain of language insofar as the ground of language which lies in this domain initiates the 'activity' of organizing world's disclosure. But the initiation of this 'activity' is not an event which is extraneous to world's disclosure. This 'activity' is essentially a disclosing capability. (Otherwise the ground of language would be lying outside of the phenomenon of being-in-the world.) This shows how close the ground and foundation of language is to the event of disclosure as such.

The way in which references and referential relations fall in the domain of language further shows that the language of propositions and assertions is by a crucial distance removed from what sustains and enlivens the ordinary language. Thus the philosophical analysis of ordinary language is occupied with the language which is removed from references to the world. The philosophical analysis of language misses the essential occurrences which pertain to the relation of language and world. Heidegger has in mind these essential occurrences when in the early terminology of the Marburg period he speaks of a measure of discoveredness which survives the 'death' of a language.[11]

Notes

1. All references to *Being and Time* will be made, in the body of the text, to *Sein und Zeit*, Gesamtausgabe, vol. 2, edited by F.-W. von Herrmann (Frankfurt am Main, 1977) with the abbreviation SZ followed by page number.
2. *Bewandtnis* in its full ontological import is difficult to translate. It means 'always already being turned toward.' The term destination needs to be heard with this essential meaning in mind.
3. Cf., M. Heidegger, *Die Grundprobleme der Metaphysik, Welt-Endlichkeit-Einsamkeit*, Gesamtausgabe vol. 29/30, edited by F.-W. von Herrmann (Frankfurt am Main, 1983), p. 397f.
4. In a marginal note to the passage just quoted, Heidegger states: 'Unwahr. Sprache ist nicht aufgestockt, sondern *ist* das ursprüngliche Wesen der Wahrheit als *Da*' (Untrue. Language is not propped up but is the original essence of truth as *Da*.) The key for understanding this marginal note which certainly reflects Heidegger's thinking after the *Kehre*, lies in a remark he makes to his Japanese interlocutor in *On the Way to Language*: 'And ways of thinking protect and conceal the mysterious character that we can walk them forward and backward, and that indeed only the way back will lead us forward.' (P. 12. ET slightly modified, G. p. 99 Neske, 1959.) The note presents the attempt at taking 'the way back' which 'leads forward.' What emerges from this attempt is the statement that 'Sprache ist nicht aufgestockt' (language is not propped up). To what portion of this passage from *Being and Time* is this statement directed? Insofar as the passage in question articulates something like a layered structure upon which language rests, the statement 'Sprache ist nicht aufgestockt' is aimed at the term '*fundieren*' which expresses something like a layered structure. Thus after the '*Kehre*,' language can no longer be thought as resting on layers of meaning, word, etc. Rather what earlier appears as layered now is more appropriately seen as coming from the 'gathering power' of language itself. Thus this note does not indicate a rejection of the views on language expressed in *Being*

and Time but a re-thinking of these views. To what extent the views on language expressed in *Being and Time* are still, i.e., after the '*Kehre*' considered important and are not abandoned, can be seen from Heidegger's remarks on section 34 of *Being and Time* made in *On The Way to Language*. Cf. Et, p. 42, G. p. 137.

5. For a detailed analysis of section 34 of *Being and Time* and clarification of difficult issues related to this section, as well as a thorough going criticism of deepseated misconception of this section in the secondary literature, cf. F.-W. von Herrmann *Subjekt und Dasein*, zweite Auflage (Frankfurt am Main, 1985), pp. 92–224.
6. M. Heidegger, *Logik, Die Frage nach der Wahrheit*, Gesamtausgabe vol. 21. edited by Walter Biemel (Frankfurt am Main, 1976), p. 134.
7. M. Heidegger, *Prolegomena zur Geschichte des Zeitbegriffs,* Gesamtausgabe, vol. 20, edited by Petra Jaeger (Frankfurt am Main, 1979) p. 365.
8. F.-W. von Herrmann, *op. cit.* p. 102.
9. *Ibid.,* p. 103.
10. Cf. F.-W. von Herrmann, *op. cit.* p. 105.
11. Cf. M. Heidegger, *Prolegomena zur Geschichte des Zeitbegriffs,* Gesamtausgabe, vol. 20, edited by Petra Jaeger (Frankfurt am Main, 1979), p. 374.

Narrow and not Far-reaching Footpaths
Heidegger and Modern Art

ROBERT CREASE
State University of New York, Stony Brook

The art of our time, we often hear, is undergoing a period of crisis of a magnitude greater than ever before. For over half a century many artists simultaneously have felt that art has to break with its past and remake itself anew, and yet have been at a loss regarding the direction in which to take it. Or, when artists have chosen a direction and announced that art is at last on the right track, this judgment has proven to be premature. The problem is epitomized by the plight of the later Bauhaus movement. On the one hand, its followers felt the continuing need for a direction, for an ideology; on the other hand, they also felt that the Utopian idealism that had so inspired its founders is not what art is all about. Artists themselves have been uncertain about what art is, and this has given a unique face to the history of art in our time; our century has witnessed the rapid turnover of movements, the rise of the importance of manifestos, the periodic ransacking of the past in search of themes and styles, and the feeling that art is a frontier that has to be continually pushed forward. Rosenberg speaks of this as the age of the 'de-definition of art,' and of the modern art work as an 'anxious object,' for it does not know whether it is a work of art or not.[1] Greenberg writes of the 'crisis of the easel painting,'[2] others of crises in music and architecture.

Is this crisis merely an art-historical event? Have all the various threads of influence and innovation, revolution and reaction that weave together what we think are patterns in art history simply become momentarily entangled? Does art unravel of itself, unconnected with other essential activities of man, such as philosophy or political activity? Or is it no coincidence, for example, that the exploration of the possibilities of abstract art, our century's greatest contribution to art history, developed in the age that Martin Heidegger speaks of as the end of metaphysics, when what we call truth no longer is seen to have any firm ground?

Heidegger indeed seems to be a philosopher who might offer responses to these sorts of questions. For him, art and philosophy both have to do with truth, and our time is a critical one for the meaning of truth. In *Being and Time*,

J.C. Sallis, G. Moneta and J. Taminiaux (eds.), The Collegium Phaenomenologicum, 191–198.
© *Kluwer Academic Publishers.*

Heidegger speaks of a 'crisis of foundations' besetting mathematics, physics, biology, the human sciences and theology, and implied that this crisis might be the symptom of a more general problem concerning the meaning of Being to which the book was addressed. In 'The Age of the World Picture,' he writes of five phenomena of the modern age: modern science, machine technology, art's moving into the purview of aesthetics, the conception of human activity as culture, and the loss of the gods. 'What interpretation of truth,' Heidegger asks himself, 'lies at the foundation of these phenomena?'[3] In that essay, questioning was restricted to how a particular conception of the world establishes modern science and thrusts thinking into a time of crisis. Nevertheless, Heidegger's general approach indicates that he may be someone to whom we can turn for answers to questions about the crisis in modern art.

When we do, however, we find that Heidegger is strongly ambivalent about modern art. On the one hand, he gives art a central place in human existence; perhaps only in Nietzsche's philosophy is it as foundational. Art is an origin, one of the decisive ways that articulate historical existence. Not only that, it has a special destiny in our own time. At the end of metaphysics, when technology and the *Gestell* reign supreme, he writes at the conclusion to 'The Question Concerning Technology,' art is the domain where we are to await the 'saving power' against the menace of technology.[4]

So much for art in general; what about actual works of contemporary art? For them, Heidegger has nothing but words of reproach. Art, he thinks, has interpreted itself as somehow about subjectivity and the 'aesthetic experience,' and has become a routine cultural phenomenon. 'Experience is the element in which art dies,' he writes in the Epilogue to 'The Origin of the Work of Art,'[5] and notes in the margins, 'Is modern art delivered of the bond to what is given in experience? Or is the only change in what is experienced – indeed, so that now the experience is even more subjective than before?' In the *Spiegel* interview, he asserts that modern literature is 'by and large destructive,' and in *An Introduction to Metaphysics* he writes that 'for us moderns . . . the beautiful is what reposes and relaxes; it is intended for enjoyment and art is a matter for pastry cooks.'[8] There are a few other similar remarks, typically short, sweeping, disparaging.

How could someone who accorded such a grand destiny to art in such a destitute time have been so negative and pessimistic regarding its contemporary practices?

Before further pursuing this question, we should first consider the possibility that Heidegger has nothing particularly significant to say about modern art. We shall discover that we have little to learn from his scattered and tentative references to actual works of modern art. In fact, there is a danger of underestimating the significance of Heidegger's writings for art by seeking a basis for criticism in them and finding them inadequate for that purpose. They are not the product of a serious study of modern art. When he speaks of *die moderne Kunst* in the notes to 'The Origin of the Work of Art,' whom does he have in mind? Cezanne? Picasso? Pollock? When he speaks of *die heutige Literatur* as 'destructive' in the *Spiegel* interview, whom is he talking about? Joyce? Musil? Grass? Can his remarks be meaningfully applied to the works of these people? These remarks are brief, unspecific ventures which read as though he were uncertain about them. In the *Spiegel* interview, Augstein decides to press Heidegger about his statement that modern art is destructive. It does not know its place, its *Ort,* responds Heidegger. Augstein points out that this is also true of thinking, as Heidegger himself has just indicated; 'now you are asking something of art which you no longer ask of thinking.' '*Gut,*' is the reply, '*streichen Sie es*.'[9] We would only be fair to Heidegger, I think, if we extend this *Streich* to all of Heidegger's remarks about modern art.

In a sense, in fact, the entire essay, 'The Origin of the Work of Art,' is not so much an essay on art as it is an essay concerned with the overcoming of metaphysics. What governs the movement of the argument and dictates the questions asked, the paths of the replies, the terms used, and the choice of examples is not an independent meditation on art. The primary intention is to liberate thinking from metaphysical words such as 'usefulness,' 'material,' 'spectator,' and 'creation,' words that refer ultimately to man as origin, in favor of words such as 'reliability,' 'earth,' 'preserver,' and 'work,' words which refer to something other than man. This is a very important point, but I do not want to belabor it. I shall be content with citing Heidegger's own remark in the last paragraphs of the *Addendum*. 'The whole essay, "The Origin of the Work of Art," deliberately yet tacitly moves on the path of the question of the essence of Being. Reflection on what *art* may be is completely and decidedly determined only in regard to the question of *Being*. Art is considered neither an area of cultural achievement nor an appearance of spirit; it belongs to the disclosure of appropriation by way of which the "meaning of Being" can alone be defined. What art may be is one of the questions to which no answers are given in the essay.'[10]

This should give serious pause to anyone who is expecting to learn something about art from this essay. Not only are Heidegger's remarks on modern art not supported by an independent meditation on actual art works, but his major essay on art is guided, not by the question of art, but by the question of Being. What can we possibly have to learn about art from an essay which does not even attempt to answer the question of what art is?

The answer, I think, has to do with Heidegger's identification of art with truth. 'Beauty is truth' is one of the oldest maxims of Western philosophical thinking about art. At first glance it seems that Heidegger continues this tradition, for 'The Origin of the Work of Art,' too, arrives at the verdict that beauty is truth. But in fact, a revolution in the understanding of art is brought about when the conception of truth as unconcealedness is introduced into the tradition of beauty as truth. All senses of truth entail a disclosure, an uncovering of the object as it is. Tacitly presupposed by this, however, is a kind of openness in which something can be seen and can show itself. In *Being and Time* and 'The Essence of Ground,' this openness is called 'the world,' and it resembles a transcendental idea, a concept corresponding to a requirement of intelligibility in general. The notion of world is abstract, devoid of specific content and only incidentally related to anything similar to what he will later call 'earth.' But the world of an art work cannot be treated as a transcendental concept. What allows the peasant woman of the van Gogh painting to work and to live is not so much the abstract concept of world as the concrete reality of *her* world. The world spoken of in 'The Origin of the Work of Art' is a concrete, historical world, and it is established by the presence of a number of a certain kind of being Heidegger calls a 'work.' There are a small number of autonomous, creative possibilities that are at the same time necessities of historical *Dasein*. Art is one of them, but there are others; in 'The Origin of the Work of Art' Heidegger mentions in addition the founding political act, religious activity, the essential sacrifice, and philosophical thinking. Whenever one speaks or thinks or acts alongside others – whenever one is *human* – one does so inside a world established by works of these types. These works are not first and foremost objects in the world, but are the institutions that give shape to the world.

The essential relation of a work of each of these kinds is not a historiographical one to a preceding succession of works, but to the open area, to truth in its most primary meaning. Heidegger is fond of quoting Hölderlin's words that the poet and the thinker 'dwell near on mountains far apart.' Heidegger does not assimilate art to philosophy the way philosophers often do. The philosopher and the artist are concerned, not with different forms of symbolic mediation between man and truth, but with the same event – with truth as the open area in which things show themselves that precedes all consciousness, collective consciousness, personal sensibility, or any other thing which has been held to be the origin of the work of art. A work of art *is* the happening of truth, not a symbol or form of it. A founding political act *is* the happening of truth, not a symbol or form of it. And so on. Truth only happens in concrete works, and is not something different works share or have in common. Each of these ways is an originary happening of truth in its own right.

The distinctively artistic character of art's revelation of truth is something not addressed in 'The Origin of the Work of Art' – this much is acknowledged in the Addendum and also in one of the marginal notes. And there are problems with Heidegger's view. While Heidegger mentions five 'essential activities' in 'The Origin of the Work of Art,' no justification for this particular number of fundamental activities is given, nor for these particular choices.

Indeed, it is hard to see how such a justification *could* be given. Heidegger, in fact, seems unsure on this point. In *An Introduction to Metaphysics*, written at the same time, he refers at one place to poetry and philosophy as belonging uniquely to the same order, at another place to 'the energies of the spiritual process, poetry and art, statesmanship and religion,' and at still another place to 'the gods, the temples, the priests, the festivals, the games, the poets, the thinkers, the ruler, the council of elders, the assembly of the people, the army and the fleet.'

This problem, however, does not detract from Heidegger's insight that art has to do with truth understood not as imitation, representation, or expression but with something implicit in these – with unconcealedness within an open area established by works. This insight, together with Heidegger's remarks on the particularly modern understanding of beings which he addresses in the writings on technology, begin to reveal a possible answer to our questions about modern art.

By technology, we know, Heidegger means more than the stepped-up acquisition of knowledge about the physical world and the advanced machines that are the fruit of this knowledge. Though technology at first appears to be no more than an instrument for our projects, it actually signifies a particular way beings become present to us, a way so fundamental to our age that there is no question of being able to choose or decline it. The Greeks understood method as a path (*odos*) that comes after (*meta*) the object of study, an approach to a thing dictated by what the thing itself is. The modern conception of method, however, involves a procedure established in advance of any project whatsoever, and involves anticipations about the objects as well as about the results of its inquiry. The modern conception of method accordingly consists of a representation projected into nature. Codified by Descartes in the 17th century, the modern age has consolidated and extended this view, beyond the specific comportment of the scientist towards nature to the meaning of what it is to be in general. The result is a wholesale instrumentalization of man and beings, so that what is does not reveal itself of itself but is laid hold of and grasped by a project which has already anticipated what it will find. This technological understanding of beings – the *Gestell* (enframing) is Heidegger's famous name for it – involves the obliteration of the open area, of truth in the primary sense. Man is no longer aware of it, forgets it the way a forgotten memory becomes not even an image that cannot be recalled but something that does not so much as disturb us by its absence.

Because the *Gestell* involves the forgetting of the open area as a whole, it is not primarily a philosophical phenomenon. It has to do with truth as such, with revealing, with *phainesthai*, unconcealment of any sort. It is the understanding of truth underlying the five phenomena of the modern world Heidegger was seeking in 'The Age of The World-Picture.' The phenomenon of the world becoming suppressed by the technological understanding of beings is one and the same with the world becoming picture and thinking becoming calculation.

A certain approach to art is also directly affiliated with the phenomenon of the suppression of the world, which Heidegger refers to as 'aesthetics.' Man's relation to art becomes a subject-object relation, distinguished from other such relations as a different kind of 'experience.' Yet this is to dissociate it from any foundational role in human life and to reduce it to the level of an artifact. 'Perhaps experience is the element in which art dies,' Heidegger writes in the Epilogue to 'The Origin of the Work of Art.'

When thinking responds to the challenge it faces from the *Gestell*, it cannot pretend to 'stand outside' technology; attempts to evade, deny, or reform calculation all remain determined by it. Thinking can manage to achieve a certain measure of distance and freedom only by turning its attention to the nature of technology, by taking its orientation from the challenge to it, by trying to reawaken first the sense of amnesia, of something missing, and then seek to make its way into the enigmas involved in truth as unconcealedness.

Frequently he poses this as an 'either-or' decision. Either thinking will remain merely calculation and the nature of truth will continue to be obscured, or thinking will set itself to the task of confronting technology and address the nature of revealing.

Considering the affiliation mentioned above between 'The Origin of the Work of Art' and Heidegger's project of overcoming metaphysics, it is no surprise that at the end of this text Heidegger sees art as faced with a similar 'either-or' decision. Either art will remain a mere cultural phenomenon or the decision will be made to restore to art its foundational role through meditation on its nature as an origin. Heidegger selects the concluding exergue from Hölderlin's poem, 'Die Wanderung,' to underscore the exclusive nature of this choice. The ending of 'The Origin of the Work of Art' is unequivocal inasmuch as it points to this decision as the critical one; it is ambiguous inasmuch as it leaves up in the air which way he thinks this decision will fall.

We know about the 'either' from Heidegger's disparaging comments; what about the 'or'? Here it is not a question of making a prediction about future movements and styles, which would merely project a representation of the present into the future. 'All mere chasing after the future so as to work out a picture of it through calculation in order to extend what is present and half-thought in what, now veiled, is yet to come, itself still moves within the prevailing attitude belonging to technological, calculating representation.'[11] This much is clear if we remember the parallel 'or' of thinking. One of the most fundamental of Heidegger's themes is the emerging of truth from untruth, *Rede* from *Gerede*, revealing from concealing. '*Das Man*' is an existential, part of *Dasein*'s positive constitution. Authentic Dasein is a clearing away of the concealments of '*das Man*'; it is not an exceptional or detached condition of a subject, but the modification of an existential without identifying criteria. In later writings, such as 'The Origin of the Work of Art,' the necessity for the work arises from the perpetual need to clear away dissimulations. Still, there is always an ambiguity regarding what is authentic and what not. In the language of 'The Origin of the Work of Art,' it is never finally certain what is *Verstellen* and what *Versagen*, what refusal and what dissembling. There is no talisman for authenticity. As far as the last judgment regarding the rank of greatness is concerned – despite Heidegger's maladroitly expressed remark at the beginning of the second lecture of this text about 'great art' – all artists are forever in purgatory, as are all philosophers. Just like the 'other beginning' which thinking is only now beginning to achieve, that of art is a long, slow process with no unambiguous avatars or prophets. This sets Heidegger apart from authors such as Schiller, Wagner, and Nietzsche, who did anticipate that a particular form of art would be the avant-garde of cultural revolution.

The 'either-or' decision of art cannot mean, therefore, the sudden appearance of new movements that are authentic responses to the *Gestell* while all the rest are mute. To say that art is faced with a 'decision' is to say only that art is oriented by the technological understanding of beings – its forms may range from wholesale surrender to the 'artistic experience' to genuine attempts to awaken the sense of a truth that transcends it.

This idea of orientation permits us, I think, to begin to make our way amid the field of styles and concerns of art ever since Cezanne began to explore the disharmony between being faithful to representation and being faithful to vision. The various forms of art that promote a different kind of 'experience,' that emphasize the uncanniness of what we take for granted (Rosenberg called Oldenburg the 'Columbus of the underfoot'), or that attempt to present truthfully without representation, can be mere reactions or more deliberate responses to the *Gestell*. Tinguely's machines are reactions; just like their Dada predecessors these machines indeed mock 'aesthetic experience,' but by substituting other experiences that are subjectivity still, such as surprise, shock, amusement, charm, and fright. A principle involved in some action painting, earth art, and conceptual art is that the actual product, the art 'object' itself, is of less significance than the methods or strategies of which it is or would be the remnant. Here, too, the 'artistic experience,' though discounted, is merely redirected. Perhaps there is something in Oldenburg's soft objects which sets them apart from Tinguely's anti-machines, in Pollock's use of automatic procedures which sets his paintings apart from those of the Surrealists; the point is that they are each oriented by a challenge that the *Gestell* has made to the possibility of art having any role at all in truth as unconcealedness. This orientation is one of the metamorphoses by which art resists allowing itself to become a collection of artifacts.

Philosophers have a nearly irrepressible tendency to impose an agenda on art, or to use art works as no more than illustrations of philosophical points – Heidegger himself did in *Being and Time*. This happens whenever philosophers ascribe the origin of the work of art to personal or collective expression, representation, the depiction of reality, or moral edification. Heidegger's notion that art is truth understood as unconcealedness avoids this kind of imposition. It is even less of an imposition, I believe, than art-historical interpretations of the history of works according to which they come in mainstreams with peripheral or secondary tributaries. It also permits us to avoid putting ourselves in the position of having to make definitive judgments about the rank of figures in this history, but instead allows us to view them with the same kind of ambiguity with which Heidegger views the rank of philosophers in the history of thought.

Heidegger's remarks on technology were motivated by the feeling that he had experienced in thinking the beginnings of a turn away from the technological understanding of beings. Art, too, has begun to make this 'other beginning,' however slowly and tentatively. What are we to make of Heidegger's pessimism? He was looking for evidence of a turn, but his eyes were not as sensitive to the terrain of art as they were to that of thinking. By his own words the most he could expect to see is only what in the *Spiegel* interview he says is visible in the region of thinking – not manifest landmarks but only 'narrow and not far-reaching footpaths.'[12]

Notes

1. Harold Rosenberg, *The Anxious Object* (New York: New American Library, 1966).
2. Clement Greenberg, *Art and Culture* (Boston: Beacon Press, 1965).
3. Martin Heidegger, 'The Age of the World Picture,' *The Question Concerning Technology*, trans. William Lovitt (New York: Garland, 1977), p. 117.
4. Martin Heidegger, 'The Question Concerning Technology,' *The Question Concerning Technology*, p. 35.
5. Martin Heidegger, 'The Origin of the Work of Art,' *Poetry, Language, Thought,* trans. Albert Hofstadter (New York: Harper & Row, 1971), p. 79.
6. Marginal notes are taken from Volume 5 of the Gesamtausgabe edition (*Holzwege* [Frankfurt am Main: Klostermann, 1978]), and are my translations.
7. *Der Spiegel* (31 May 1976), p. 209.
8. Martin Heidegger, *An Introduction to Metaphysics*, trans. Ralph Manheim (New Haven: Yale University Press, 1959), p. 131.
9. *Der Spiegel* (31 May 1976), p. 219.
10. Martin Heidegger, 'The Origin of the Work of Art,' p. 86.
11. Martin Heidegger, 'The Turning,' in *The Question Concerning Technology,* p. 48.
12. *Der Spiegel* (31 May 1976), p. 219.

Toward the Hermeneutic of *Der Satz Vom Grund*

REGINALD LILLY
University of New Hampshire

> And it demands a new accuracy for language rather than the invention of new terms, as I once thought; on the contrary, it demands a return to the original contents of our own constantly decaying language.
> Heidegger

Introduction

What we have in view is the hermeneutic of *Der Satz vom Grund*. However, in a text composed two years earlier (1954), Heidegger responds to the observation that he no longer uses the term 'hermeneutic', saying

> I have left an earlier standpoint, not in order to become ensconced in another one, rather because even the previous position was a station in being under way. What remains in thinking is the way. (*US* 98f.)[1]

If hermeneutics was a station on Heidegger's way, then clearly we must distinguish between hermeneutics and one's path of thinking, the latter of which is essential. But in the same conversation, Heidegger speaks of hermeneutics in a sense that seems synonymous with way-making, if to be on a path of thinking implies proffering what one finds on that path:

> The expression 'hermeneutic' is derived from the Greek verb *ἑϱμηεύειν*. This is related to the root word *ἐϱμηνεύς*, which one can bring together with the name of the god Hermes in a play of thought that is more binding than the rigor of science. ἑϱνῆς is the divine messenger. He brings the message of destiny; *ἑϱμηνεύιν* is that exhibiting that brings tidings, insofar as one is able to listen to the message. (*US* 121f.)

Here we apparently have two different senses of hermeneutics. How are we to understand this difference? In *SvG* Heidegger points to the essential relationship between what we encounter and the path upon which we encounter it when he says. 'Within the purview opened up by the path and through which the path leads, whatever can be caught sight of at any given time gathers itself from some point along the path' (*SvG,* 106). So, to encounter hermeneutics in Heidegger's thought means to understand it from the vantage point of a particular path. For our inquiry this means we must ourselves traverse those paths on which Heidegger 'caught sight' of hermeneutics, for then we can see in their essential unity both the particular path and the concept of hermeneut-

J.C. Sallis, G. Moneta and J. Taminiaux (eds.), The Collegium Phaenomenologicum, 199–224.
© Kluwer Academic Publishers.

ics that comes to light on the path. Accordingly different notions of hermeneutics will correspond to different notions of way-making.

Rather than immediately jumping into a speculation on *SvG*'s hermeneutic, we propose to take the long road. We propose first to traverse the path in which hermeneutics is embraced by Heidegger as an essential moment of that path. Fundamental ontology is such a path. Once we have come to grips with the sense of hermeneutics to be found there, we will be in a position to consider the hermeneutic of *SvG,* particularly insofar as it is different from Heidegger's earlier understanding of hermeneutics. This procedure implies a definite directionality in our reading. Rather than taking up the bird's-eye view of Heidegger's entire *Denkweg* – a viewpoint which invariably sees the beginning in light of the end, and from which it is easy, and perhaps popular today, to see in words and phrases of his earlier texts the tremors of his later thought (tremors which can be seen as always already propelling Heidegger beyond himself) – I propose to read Heidegger forward, that is, as a thinking arising out of the tradition of philosophy that, in an attempt to move beyond it, encountered crises arising from the way it sought to go beyond the tradition it took up. Hermeneutics was essential to this thinking's path.

So, we seek to grasp the path of Heidegger's early thinking not by explicit or implicit reference to where Heidegger 'ended up', but by entering into that project which Heidegger first staked out for himself, a project around which there gathers that which can be caught sight of. This path, and the issues belonging to it, bears the name 'fundamental ontology'. Our concern then is with that thinking engaged in the project of fundamental ontology, a project embodying a specific sense of way-making. This nonpanoptic way of reading seems the most faithful not only to the above citation from *SvG,* but also to the experience of thinking. In any case, any reading which seeks to see telltale signs of the later Heidegger already in the Marburg period presumes the sort of reading we carry out here.

Every interpretation risks violence, for even the most systematic of philosophical texts is marked by polysemy. Hence, though our reading of Heidegger as a fundamental ontologist is an important, even necessary reading, this should not be taken as a last reading, nor do we intend to 'reduce' Heidegger to this project. In fact our concern with the *projected* movement of fundamental ontology should underscore the *unprojected* movement of Heidegger's thought engaged in that project, a movement which, of course, carries Heidegger beyond the project of fundamental ontology.

We propose then to turn to a consideration of fundamental ontology, paying particular attention to the role hermeneutics plays. This will, of course, require bringing into view works which are in essential proximity to *SZ,* especially *GP, MAL, L, KPM,* and *WG.* Having established the nature of hermeneutics within the context of fundamental ontology, we will then turn to

SvG where, because of obvious restrictions, we will only be able to sketch some suggestions as to how the hermeneutic of *SvG* is to be understood.

Fundamental Ontology as Transcendental Philosophy

Though the texts that gather themselves around the project of fundamental ontology may be read in many ways, there is no doubt about the starting point of *SZ:* Being has fallen into oblivion, yet we nevertheless have a notion of what Being means, be it ever so vague. *This tension of oblivion versus understanding constitutes the essence of the fundamental ontological problematic* and indicates its solidarity with transcendental philosophy. It seems equally clear that Heidegger believed there is a genuine meaning of Being which could be brought forth from its oblivion and clarified. Thus the ultimate transcendental philosophical 'goal [is] the working out of the question of Being in general', so as to gain a 'clarified idea of Being in general' (*SZ,* 436). The clarification of the idea of Being in general is the specific task of a science of Being, ontology (Cf. *GP* § 3); it is the task of fundamental ontology as a preparation for ontology to raise the question of Being and show the horizon within which Being will be ontologically clarified.[2] For Heidegger, to clarify the meaning of Being means to clarify the ground of Being: meaning and ground are the same. Only when Being's meaning has been so clarified will a factically situated understanding of beings be transparent to itself, that is, grounded. Thus the transcendental project of raising and clarifying the meaning of Being is essentially a grounding project. We shall see that, as a response to the demand to raise from its oblivion and clarify the meaning of Being, this transcendental project is guided by the demand for providing sufficient grounds: the principle of sufficient reason.

The question of Being as the question of the ground or Being of beings is formulated within a transcendental, a priori framework in that it not only asks after the conditions for the possibility of the relation of beings to their ground in Being, but also after the conditions for the possibility (viz. ground) of Being.[3] As *the* question, that is, the *transcendental* question, 'the Being-question therefore aims at ascertaining the a priori conditions for the possibility not only of the sciences [. . .] but also the conditions for the possibility of those ontologies themselves which are prior to the ontical sciences which provide their foundations' (*SZ* 11). Only when the conditions for the possibility (viz. Being) of any being whatsoever have been clarified will the mode of Being of any particular being be grasped in its ground.[4]

Though Heidegger does not depart from the classical framework of transcendental philosophy, he does see that despite its concern with the ground of constituted beings, transcendental philosophy has failed to secure its own ground, that is, to provide an adequate transcendental ontology, for it has overlooked the Being of this ground, viewing it instead as simply another, albeit privileged, being.[5] Husserl's pure Ego is only one example of how the Being of the ground of beings, and consequently the synthesis of beings and their ground, remains veiled.[6] One can then see 'Husserl's phenomenology already presupposes what Heideggerian ontology first must investigate, namely the synthesis a priori'.[7] Ultimately what is at issue is not only the constituted being, nor only the constituted being in relation to its constituting ground, but the constitution of that through which beings are constituted, which is to say the constitution of that which constitutes what is constituted. Since Being constitutes beings in their beingness, for Heidegger '*the meaning of Being formally takes over the function of universal phenomenological constituting*';[8] the *meaning* of Being is the *ground* of Being and therefore what is at issue is what constitutes Being as such. Hence the task of transcendental philosophy is to clarify this ground of Being, and to do so in such a way that the conditions for the possibility of beings are grasped in their Being; or, in other words, transcendental philosophy must establish the conditions for the possibility – the ground – of the ontological difference.

However, it is precisely the meaning of Being which has fallen into oblivion. To try to get 'behind' beings in an attempt to determine Being would be merely to repeat the history of philosophy's oblivion of Being; and the names of these ventures are well known: *cogito, Geist,* pure Ego, Substance, etc. Here we face the aporia of transcendental philosophy: if one can not get behind beings to Being without, ironically, forgetting Being, how is one to gain access to the Being of beings and to Being as such? Clearly one cannot jump 'behind and beyond' beings, which means one cannot immediately assume a transcendental standpoint. Rather there must be, starting from *this side* of the transcendental standpoint, some way of working one's way *to* that standpoint.[9] But 'from what being can there be read off[10] the meaning of Being; from which being may the disclosure of Being take its point of departure?' (*SZ* 7). In the words of a priori, transcendental philosophy: How can one gain access to the conditions for the possibility of beings and Being as such – the transcendental ground – without implicitly conceiving of this ground/condition itself as a (highest) being always already constituted in its Being?[11] This is the methodological problem of transcendental philosophy which fundamental ontology confronts. As fundamental ontology's inaugural text, *SZ* must work out this methodological problem in such a way that the starting point of an a priori, transcendental meditation – whose goal is the working out of the genuine meaning of Being – will itself be grounded.

In response to the problem of access Heidegger introduces what one may call a *transcendental fact.* 'We always conduct ourselves within an understanding-of-Being. From out of this there grows the explicit question of the meaning of Being and the tendency towards its conception' (*SZ* 5). A transcendental fact is a being which *essentially* stands in relation to Being and the ground of Being – the transcendental ground, the condition for the possibility of any being whatsoever (*itself included*) – such that from its factuality (beingness) one can read off the meaning of Being. Such a being which is in essential proximity to its ground and the ground of Being is one in which the transcendental synthesis a priori comes to pass;[12] it is a being whose very Being is to have access to the transcendental ground: its Being *is* transcendence. This transcendental fact to which Heidegger appeals is, as intimated, understanding-of-Being (*Seinsverständnis*)[13] which is 'a determination of the Being of Dasein' (*SZ* 12), that being for which Being is always at issue. As a transcendence that always already grasps beings in their ground, in the ground of Being, understanding-of-Being thus offers Heidegger, at least formally, a solution to the aporia of finding a point of departure for the working out of a '*transcendental science of the universal synthesis of the constituted and the constituting*';[14] for this reason 'Dasein has a [. . .] priority as the ontico-ontological condition for the possibility of all ontologies' (*SZ* 13). Or as he says, 'With the existence of Dasein there is factually established the possibility of two fundamental types of science: the objectification of beings as positive science, and the objectification of Being as temporal, that is, transcendental science, ontology, philosophy' (*GP* 466). Since the principle issue for transcendental philosophy is the ground of Being (which itself constitutes beings in their beingness), 'Our question is about the objectification of Being as such, that is, about the second essential possibility of objectification in which philosophy as science is to be constituted' (*GP* 458). What cannot be stressed too strongly is that Dasein is formally defined as that being which is an understanding of the genuine meaning and ground of Being, and it is in virtue of this understanding – be it ever so vague to *factical* Dasein – that, through fundamental ontology's recovery of this understanding of Being, transcendental philosophy's project of formulating a science of Being can be fulfilled. One can even say that inasmuch as fundamental ontology – the hermeneutic of Dasein – is to establish the conditions for the possibility of ontology, fundamental ontology is from the start conceived of as 'passing over' into ontology; therefore everything depends on the starting point and exposition of fundamental ontology.

Therefore since, formally, Dasein as transcendental fact is that from out of which fundamental ontology is to raise the Being-question, one can see why 'the problem of obtaining and securing the kind of access which will lead to Dasein becomes even more a burning one' (*SZ* 16). Only if this access is firmly established and worked out concretely can Dasein fulfill its role in Heidegger's projected transcendental philosophy of providing access to the genuine meaning of Being. As Heidegger says, 'In the posing of its task, as well as in the commencement, procedure, and goal of carrying out this task, the grounding of metaphysics must solely and rigorously be lead by its basic question. This basic question is the problem of the inner possibility of understanding-of-Being, from out of which all explicit questioning of Being arises' (*KPM* 209). But on what path is one to encounter Dasein, the transcendental fact? If this fact is to be the 'transcendental clue' (*SZ* 39), then one must not import into it alien concepts in an attempt to 'make something of it', 'make it into' a means of access to Being. Rather this fact *must* offer one immediate access to itself *as* transcendental clue. It must be able to 'show itself in itself from itself' (*SZ* 16). This means that *in its very appearing* there must appear the synthesis a priori that constitutes it in *fact.*

However, one might ask, if there is such a transcendental fact whose very appearing offers one insight into the synthesis of the constituted and constituting and hence the possibility of answering the question of the meaning of Being, how is it that this has for so long escaped notice? This question again underscores the point of departure for Heidegger's transcendental meditation: there is a genuine meaning of Being and Dasein denotes that being which is an understanding of that meaning; *factical* Dasein, however, has 'proximally and for the most part' forgotten this meaning, and all previous ontologies are marked by this oblivion. The problem of gaining access to Dasein's understanding of this meaning is the problem of how these 'two Daseins' are to be understood as one, and how it is possible to begin with factical, forgetful Dasein and work one's way to that Dasein which 'always already' grasps the genuine meaning of Being. This tension, seen in the heart of the problem of transcendental philosophy as posed on the first page of *SZ,* permeates the exposition of fundamental ontology which hopes, through an analytic of factical Dasein, to arrive at the genuine meaning of Being. This meaning of Being and the understanding-of-Being which grasps it are not historical – indeed they are a priori. As such they are the condition for the possibility of every historical ontology and of factical Dasein's Being-a-whole, which in each case, marked as they are by forgetfulness, is grounded upon the understanding of the genuine meaning of Being. The project of ontology claims that this genuine meaning can be articulated as being such a basis.[15] But the specific problem of gaining access to Dasein's genuine understanding-of-Being as an access to ground is inseparable from the more general problem of access to any being whatsoever, to which we now turn.

Ground and λόγος

In Chapter 7 of *SZ* Heidegger presents his reflection on our access to beings. From this reflection he formulates the method transcendental philosophy must pursue in order to raise and answer the question of Being. He explains, at one and the same time, what makes this access possible, and how there arises the problem of gaining such access. The discussion revolves around two key terms: 'appearing'[16] and 'as'. Traditionally appearance has been conceived of as concealing something behind itself which does not appear, or does not 'appear as' what does appear. As such, 'appearing as' indicates a semblance. Semblance then signifies a certain disjunction between what appears and what does not appear but nevertheless has some relation to what appears. Philosophy has sought to grasp the relation between these two, perennially conceiving of this relation, at least implicitly, as one between beings.

Heidegger reminds us that if this view has any merit, dissembling 'appearing as' is possible only because beings *do show themselves,* even if as something other than what they are, for beings (*τα ὄντα*) are a shining forth (*φαίνεσθαι*), they are phenomena, that which in principle is accessible. Thus 'we must *keep in mind* that the expression 'phenomenon' signifies *that which shows itself in itself,* the manifest' (*SZ* 28). But, 'if we are to have any further understanding of the concept of phenomenon, everything depends on seeing how the two designations of *φαίνόμεηα* ('phenomenon' as that which shows itself and 'phenomenon' as semblance) are structurally connected' (*SZ* 29). To understand this structural connection is to understand both how access to beings is possible and what thwarts this access.

But if phenomena are always a self-showing, how can they ever deceive us? Needn't we simply turn our gaze (*νοεῖν*) to their self-showing in order to grasp them truly, that is, 'as they are'? No, for such gazing can never be true or false, only a perceiving or not perceiving.[17] Hence in such gazing there can be no question of semblance. But one cannot avoid the possibility of semblance. Whence does this possibility arise? 'When something no longer has the form of a pure letting-see but is always making recourse to something to which it points, thereby letting something be seen *as* something, it thus acquires a synthesis-structure, and with this the possibility of covering up' (*SZ* 34). In order for there to be a covering up (semblance) indeed there must first be a self-showing (phenomenon); however, that there is no 'simple' self-showing indicates that something else has always already come into play in this self-showing, namely a *letting be seen.* This is the function of *λόγος*, discourse.

> Discourse 'lets something be seen' (*ἀπό . . . from out of itself; it lets what is under discussion be seen. In discourse (απόφανσις*), to the extent that it is genuine, *what* is said is created [geschöpft] from out of that which is under discussion, so that discursive communication, in what it says, makes manifest what is under discussion and thus makes it accessible to others (*SZ* 32).

λόγος is, according to its basic function, *ἀπόφανσις* – discourse that points out and lets see. [. . .] The function of discourse is the *δηλοῦν* – the making manifest of beings' (*L* 142). As a speaking-pointing out, discourse – if it is genuine – lets be seen what is under discussion. If it is not genuine, access to what is under discussion is thwarted, it is not allowed to be seen 'as it is'. So access to beings in their Being (as well as the lack thereof) is a matter of a certain commensurability of discourse (*λόγος*) and phenomenon: phenomenology as the method of transcendental philosophy is predicated upon the possibility of this commensurability; phenomenological discourse is an apophantical discourse. This commensurability is seen in the synthesis-structure of discourse. Because discourse is both a speaking-pointing out and what this speaking is about – what it points out and lets be seen – *λόγος* has a synthesis-character in that it brings together what it at the same time keeps apart (daieresis), namely the speaking and what this speaking is about (*SZ* 33). If the synthesis of these two is lacking, so too is our access to what is under discussion – it is covered over. Everything depends on the commensurability of synthesis and daieresis (Cf. *L* 135f.).

How are we to understand this commensurability? The synthesis between speaking-pointing out and what is under discussion *can* mean the former *agrees* with the latter. In this case we have a 'correct judgment'; the absence of this synthesis/agreement – the separation of speaking-pointing out and what is under discussion – being 'false judgment'. This is the notion of commensurability as *adequatio*. But then how can this agreement or lack thereof be conceivable unless both the speaking-pointing out and what is under discussion have already been pointed out, allowed to be seen, in discourse (*SZ* 217)?[18] The relation between the speaking and what is spoken about cannot be taken as posterior to discourse, but must be taken as constitutive of it. Here we gain a further insight into discourse's synthesis-character. Discourse is not only a speaking-pointing out [*was geredet ist*], but, insofar as what is under discussion only is as something which has been allowed to be seen, discourse also *constitutes* in this speaking-pointing out what is under discussion (*das worüber geredet wird*). Discourse then encompasses both its *was* and *worüber*. The *was* is projected upon the *worüber* as its meaning, and the *worüber* as such first comes forth as the meaning and ground of the *was*. Discourse as daieretic must keep the two separate in order for there to be *ἀποφανσις*, as synthesis it must bring them together.

Since discourse is always a pointing out that lets be seen what is under discussion, since there is necessarily a commensurability between the two in the synthesis/daieresis-structure of discourse, it might seem that semblance is only the product of a malicious, sophistical word-play, an intentional obfuscation of the *worüber*. But how is such sophistry possible if discourse always is a letting be seen of what shows itself in itself from itself, namely what is under discussion? How can sophistry obfuscate what it constitutes in its speaking-pointing out (*das worüber*)? That clearly something like this is possible means there is an incommensurability, a disjunction that must be accounted for. This disjunction, a 'mis-speaking', is only possible because of the daieresis (separating) which essentially belongs to synthesis, to every speaking-pointing out (*SZ* 159; *L* 138–42). But how is it that this daieresis, which belongs to the synthesis-structure of every speaking-pointing out, introduces the possibility of a mis-speaking-(not)pointing out? How can the equilibrium in the synthesis-daieresis structure of speaking-pointing out be disrupted such that the daieresis becomes not just a separating, but a dispersion, so much so that synthesis is 'overwhelmed' and fails, such that the *was* is not commensurate to the *worüber*? What accounts for this disruptive difference in discourse? How can λόγος fail? What eludes discourse?

> Clearly such as what proximally and for the most part does *not* show itself, what, as opposed to that which proximally and for the most part shows itself, is *concealed,* but what at the same time so essentially belongs to that which proximally and for the most part shows itself, that it constitutes it in its meaning and ground.
>
> What in an exceptional sense remains *concealed,* or again falls back into *coveredness,* or only shows itself *'dissemblingly',* is not this or any particular being, rather (...) the *Being* of beings. (*SZ* 35)

We now can see how sophistry is possible, how discourse's synthesis of the *was* and *worüber* can fail to bring together the daieretic – even necessarily so. The 'failure' of this synthesis means not letting that which is under discussion show itself as what it is. For something to show itself 'as it is' means to show itself in itself, 'in its Being', in that which constitutes (the condition for the possibility of) the being as it is, that is, in its beingness. 'When a being appears to us in its 'genuine' mode of Being, when it appears to us 'the way it really is,' it appears to us from the perspective of the *transcendental* synthesis a priori, which consists in the meaning or the truth of Being'.[19] Though it constitutes 'the ground and meaning' of what shows itself, it is precisely this – Being – which does *not* show itself, and what does not show itself cannot be allowed to be seen, if letting-see only lets be seen what shows itself. Being escapes apophantical discourse. So the disjunction (viz. dispersive daieresis) between the *was* and *worüber* – a disjunction which accounts for the possibility of semblance, sophistry, and falsehood – is itself grounded in a deeper incommensurability between *λόγος ἀποφαντικος* (speaking-pointed out) and Being.[20] Therefore the disjunction between the *was* and *worüber* cannot be 'resolved' unless the deeper disjunction between discourse and Being is resolved, for so long as this disjunction persists, the *worüber* can never be 'truly' constituted in discourse, can never show itself 'as it is', 'in its Being', because Being will always already have eluded discourse.

Such a disjunction would be a fatal aporia to the project of ontology, for the task of phenomenological discourse – which is an apophantical discourse – is to bring forth Being from out of its oblivion, to point out and let it be seen in its ground. But insofar as Being eludes apophantical discourse, it cannot become the theme, the *worüber* of a discourse; it cannot be objectified. If so, then the transcendental project of grounding founders. In fact, transcendental philosophy would be 'stillborn' for, unlike ontical discourses which take beings as their theme and object (their *worüber*) and can 'get away' with vaguely presuming the meaning of Being, transcendental, ontological discourse has *Being* as its theme and object – its *worüber* – and therefore cannot utter a meaningful word so long as this disjunction persists. In order for transcendental philosophy to be possible, in order for Being to become the *worüber* of a discourse, it must show itself. Heidegger recognizes this crucial aporia when he proposes a nearly Sysiphean challenge: 'As its object, phenomenology has taken in its 'grasp' what therefore in an eminent sense requires, from out of its ownmost content, to *become* a phenomenon' (*SZ* 35, emphasis added). Only then will Being be something that discourse can let be seen. To shift our emphasis here, we can say that ontology seeks to clarify the *phenomenon* of Being (hence ontology is possible only as phenomenology), but the first step toward this science is to 'make' Being *become* a phenomenon. This is the (violent) task of fundamental ontology's phenomenological hermeneutic.

Transcendental Philosophy and Hermeneutics

The imperative that Being become a phenomenon reiterates the imperative we saw above: the transcendental fact (understanding-of-Being) must, in its very appearing, show itself *as* transcendental fact. Both imperatives essentially are informed by the transcendental problematic: though it is impossible to assume without further ado the transcendental standpoint, nevertheless what ultimately is called for is a self-evident, grounded starting point for moving from *this side* of the transcendental standpoint *to* that standpoint, alone from which the starting point of this movement can be shown to be grounded. Here we glimpse the importance of method for the fulfillment of the promise of transcendental philosophy, and herein we also see a significant paradox which transcendental philosophy faces. On the one hand transcendental philosophy is possible only on the basis of the adoption of a correct starting point and method, while on the other hand the correctness of the method and starting point is determinable only from the viewpoint of an attained transcendental standpoint. Starting point and method therefore are necessarily preparatory – *vorbereitend, vorläufig* – for their presentation and employment necessarily come before what they make possible, that means before the attainment of the (ontological) standpoint from which alone they can be shown to be grounded. It is only afterwards, through a certain recoil of the transcendental standpoint (ontology) made possible by this method back upon the starting point that what is preparatorily projected in the beginning can be shown to be grounded.

Thus there is an essential circularity that obtains between the point of departure and that at which the method aims: ontology. Speaking of this circle, one commentator writes:

> The method of ontology as the explication of transcendental-ontological truth is itself conditioned by this truth. This truth has the character of a ground [*Grund*]. Therefore the method is subordinated to the principle of reason [*Prinzip vom Grund*]. The ground is to be laid bare in accord with this principle of reason. The method thus has the task of grounding in the sense of explicating from the point of view of the ground. Methodologically, however, what is to be understood is Being as ground. Hence the ground is to be explicated from the point of view of the ground. The method of ontology must ground [*begründen*] from the point of view of the ground; neither what is to be grounded nor what grounds can be anything other than the ground. [...] That the ground is equally what grounds and what is to be grounded is nothing other than the definition of transcendental truth (a priori clearedness). [...] The difference is the distinction between the ground which is as yet not understood and is to be grounded, and the ground which is understood and grounds (hence which is understood only when it is understood as a self-grounding ground). Hence the difference is the difference in the understanding of ground; understanding describes the 'way' from a ground that is not understood to one that is.[21]

The imperative that the transcendental fact appear as it is in fact, that Being become a phenomenon; that the meaning of Being can be brought forth from its oblivion – these all say the movement from a ground not understood to one that is is a movement from an *implicit,* to an *explicit* grasp of the meaning of Being: ontology 'has the function of *explicitly* projecting [...] what is *already* projected in prescientific experience, that is, understanding' (*GP* 399). Below we will consider the nature of hermeneutics as an explicating discourse, but first it is important to appreciate the continuity of the moments of this circular movement within Heidegger's project.

Above all, Heidegger must show that the ontology springing from a pre-ontological source is not just *an* ontology – there are many of these – but that it is *the thematic explication of the genuine meaning of Being,* a meaning at the basis of, but 'passed over' by, all previous ontologies.[22] Ontology requires that its starting point and the method which undertakes its explication be grounded. This demand harbored *within* ontology to appropriate its source and origin leads Heidegger to project an *Umschlag* (turning around, enveloping), a recoiling of ontology on its fundamental ontological origin in pre-ontological understanding-of-Being.[23] In 1928 Heidegger named this recoiling movement *meta-ontology,* and though in *SZ* he had not yet so named this recoil, it is clear he conceived of it; indeed he says and *must* say, in accord with the transcendental requirement of providing sufficient, i.e., explicit grounds: 'Philosophy is universal phenomenological ontology proceeding from the hermeneutic of Dasein [viz. understanding-of-Being] which, as the analytic of existence, has firmly established the end of the guiding line of all philosophical questioning from out of which it *arises* and to which it *returns* (*SZ* 38, 436).

If for meta-ontology 'To think Being as the Being of beings and to radically and universally grasp the problem of Being likewise means to make beings *thematic* in their totality *in the light of ontology* (*MAL* 200, emphasis added), then we see meta-ontology's object – Being and beings in their totality – is not a different one from fundamental ontology's – Being-in-the-world – but it has this object in a specific sense or light, namely, it has it in view of its essential tendency (*SZ* 5)[24] or possibility to yield, from out of its latency, the explicit, ontological grasp of Being. Fundamental ontology's task is to raise the question of Being, which means to show the essential tendency/possibility of Being to become a phenomenon whereupon it can then be clarified in ontology. Meta-ontology too has the task of explicating this tendency, but presumes 'the idea of Being already [has been] clarified beforehand' (*SZ* 436; cf. *MAL* 186), and because it has the clarified idea of Being 'in hand' its explication, as opposed to that of fundamental ontology, is a grounded/grounding explication. It is the 'final response' to the demand expressed in the principle of sufficient reason. In meta-ontology we glimpse the relation between retrieval and ground.

Thus, though 'Fundamental ontology and meta-ontology make up, in their unity, the concept of metaphysics' (*MAL* 202; cf. note 2), we can, for the sake of precision, distinguish three moments in Heidegger's metaphysics: *fundamental ontology* takes factical Dasein as its point of departure for raising the question of Being; this leads to *ontology,* the explicit, thematic grasp of the idea of Being in general (which is the goal of philosophy); but the demand harbored within ontology for having a grounded starting point necessitates a recoil of ontology – viz. *meta-ontology* – onto this starting point which, from the point of view of meta-ontology, can then legitimately be called 'the metaphysical ontic'[25] (*MAL* 201), the origin and ground of ontology. Meta-ontology grasps the inseparability of implicit, pre-ontological understanding-of-Being and its passage over to an explicit, ontological understanding-of-Being as well as the leading back of the latter into the former. As such it is the *metaphysics of truth, logic* (*MAL* 275); in a sense it is nothing other than the explication of the necessity/validity of these 'leadings' or 'turnings'. It affirms understanding-of-Being as the be and end all.

Heidegger explicitly points both to the circularity of this movement of understanding-of-Being – a circling which is the closing of the transcendental circle à la meta-ontology – and to this circularity as a circle of grounding:

> This understanding-of-Being first makes possible the 'why'. However, this means it already contains the first and final primordial answer to all ques-

> tioning. Understanding-of-Being yields, as the absolutely most pre-cursive *answer,* the first and final grounding. In it transcendence is as such grounding. Because Being and the constitution of Being are therein uncovered, the transcendental grounding is called *ontological truth.* (*WG* 48f.)

Thus meta-ontology is the transcendental philosophy-grounding/grounded grasp of Dasein mediated by the clarified idea of Being (ontology); this mediation is, however, the mediation of what in (the transcendental) fact is immediate: understanding of the genuine meaning of Being. As the final moment of the transcendental movement, in meta-ontology all method is sublated,[26] for method is conceived only and always as the necessary way-making from and back to a beginning (Cf. *SZ* 38, 436).

Of utmost importance is to understand this recoil as the metaphysics of truth, or logic. Heidegger understands logic not in the ordinary sense of the science of judgments, or 'the rules and norms of statements' (*MAL* 282), rather 'the first fundamental principle of logic is the principle of reason [*Satz vom Grund*] [. . .] whose theme is the transcendental truth, transcendence' (ibid). Its concern is with metaphysical foundations: the occurrence of world, understanding-of-Being, transcendence, and the disclosure of beings – wherein one sees logic's fundamental concern with truth, *aletheia* (*MAL* 281). Fundamental ontology is also concerned with the occurrence of world, understanding-of-Being, transcendence, and truth, but meta-ontology – whose first concern is grounds – seeks to show these in their ground, a showing which can only be achieved on the basis of an explicated ontology.

The movement inaugurated in fundamental ontology from not-understanding to understanding thus must culminate in a meta-ontological explication of the ground of the movement such that the *movement of explication* itself will be intelligible in its ground. When we noted above the hermeneutical task of 'making Being become a phenomenon', clearly, within the framework of transcendental philosophy, the making Being become a phenomenon (hence the articulation of an ontology) therefore must be done in such a way that the path traversed in this movement toward ontology itself becomes explicit, thereby enabling the clarified meaning of Being to recoil upon and illuminate the correctness of the starting point and method of transcendental philosophy as well as the integrity of its execution.

Here comes forward the central place of λόγος, discourse, for meta-ontology. Specifically, the recoil in question is of the λόγος of ontology on the λόγος of fundamental ontology. One can say that in this recoil *both* fundamental ontology and ontology are shown to be grounded. Therefore, from the transcendental (viz. meta-ontological) point of view it is necessary that fundamental ontology carry out its analysis of Dasein not only in such a way that the concept of λόγος which emerges from that analysis can lead over to ontology but it must carry it out such that, in the meta-ontological recoil, ontology shows itself to be nothing but the explication of the meaning of Being as originally, but unthematically, grasped by that understanding-of-Being which is the object of fundamental ontology. Most simply put, in meta-ontology the *λόγοι* of ontology and of fundamental ontology must show themselves to be commensurate, for only then are the movements between them grounded. As a preparation for the meta-ontological recoil it is one of the primary tasks of the hermeneutic of Dasein to develop the concept of *λόγος* which will make a grounded ontology possibility.

Generally, the task of the hermeneutic of Dasein is to inaugurate the movement from out of the oblivion of Being in Dasein's everydayness, a movement which, in making Being become a phenomenon, makes its thematic grasp in ontology possible, a movement which meta-ontology's recoil completes and grounds.[27] Heidegger captures the archimedean character of hermeneutics in the Sysiphean challenge posed by a science of Being when he says 'the λόγος of the phenomenology of Dasein has the character of a *ἑϱμηνέύειν*, through which the genuine meaning of Being, as well as the fundamental structures of his Being, are *made known* to the understanding-of-Being that belongs to Dasein itself'; thus we are to understand "hermeneutics' in the sense of the working out of the conditions for the possibility of every ontological investigation' (*SZ* 37). If, as Heidegger is often wont to say, everything is determined in its beginning, then it falls to hermeneutics to establish from the outset the conditions for the possibility of phenomenological ontology and to inaugurate its fulfillment in metaphysics.

Here we grasp a *double origin*[28] in hermeneutics which allows us to characterize it as a meta-discourse in at least two senses. The origin is found on the one hand in that the beginning of transcendental philosophy is in an understanding-of-Being alienated from itself – a not-understanding-of-Being. On the other hand, without something like a genuine understanding-of-Being, transcendental philosophy would be impossible. Hermeneutics conceives of these origins within the unity of a movement: in making understanding-of-Being known to not-understanding-of-Being, it 'transforms' it into itself. As the discourse that carries this out, hermeneutics is a meta-discourse for in making the essential distinction – that of the double origin – it has always already passed beyond, is 'above' the beginning point (viz. oblivion of Being); it is already beyond the opposition of origins and in this regard always already has in view the fulfillment of the transcendental project. Nevertheless, hermeneutical discourse *must* make this distinction in order to set up the terms of the movement (which for it always already has been accomplished). Thus only hermeneutical, meta-discourse can describe this beginning point as not-understanding-of-Being, much less as an implicit grasp of the genuine meaning of Being; and it can only do so by taking recourse to a double origin. Furthermore, hermeneutics is a meta-discourse in the sense of the 'meta' in meta-ontology, for it is through the discourse of pointing-out not-understanding-of-Being that the movement from out of this beginning point to (genuine) understanding-of-Being is inaugurated. The continuity of the hermeneutical discourse thereby establishes not only the possibility of (the movement toward) a thematic grasp of Being, but equally the possibility of the recoil – meta-ontology – of ontology back upon the starting point. That hermeneutics is concerned to establish the possibility of undertaking this movement of departure *and* return is seen in the fact that an essential moment of the hermeneutic of facticity is to show that and how apophantical discourse – hermeneutical, phenomenological discourse is apophantical – is rooted in Dasein's Being-in-the-world, an issue to which we will return below.

Therefore, just as meta-ontology is a mediation of what (for fundamental ontology) is immediate – understanding-of-Being – so hermeneutical discourse provides a necessary mediation of what in (the transcendental) fact is immediate: the transcendental synthesis a priori. Its exposition must show Dasein is so constituted that in it there is performed the transcendental synthesis a priori, or more exactly, Dasein, despite its obliviousness to the meaning of Being, nevertheless has always already grasped its genuine meaning and can come to an explicit awareness of this meaning. Only because the transcendental synthesis is the grounding performance – that which underlies even Dasein's oblivion of Being – can the hermeneutic of facticity be the beginning point for a project that expects to yield grounds. If Dasein did not harbor within itself its ground, as obscure as it may be to factical Dasein, then terms like 'transcendental synthesis' and 'performance' as ways to describe the advent and presence of the meaning of Being themselves become strangely opaque and perhaps cover over the question of the relation between Being and ground.[29]

It is crucial to grasp the import of the performance of the transcendental synthesis a priori for the hermeneutic of facticity. From the hermeneutical viewpoint factical Dasein is "in the performance" (*GP* 454) of this synthesis – Dasein is Being-disclosing, world-projecting. The performance of this synthesis – or its daieretic pendant, the distinguishing between Being and beings – therefore is definitive of Dasein: 'Only a soul that can make this distinction has the capacity to become, over and above the soul of an animal, the soul of a human' (*GP* 454). This means Dasein (always already) grasps the genuine meaning of Being and, on the basis of this, projects a concrete meaning of Being in disclosing beings. However, though the genuine meaning of Being is the ground and meaning of factical Dasein's projection, it is this ground which, to the extent that factical Dasein is 'absorbed' in the beings it discloses, is forgotten. In other words, the oblivion of Being occurs when Dasein forgets that the meaning of Being it factically projects is a projection, one based on a primordial grasp of the genuine meaning of Being; it forgets that upon which its projection is based and, in a certain 'ontological inversion', thinks of Being in terms of beings. Here we again encounter the double origin in Dasein's Being: at one and the same time it is not-understanding-of-Being and understanding-of-Being; the movement from one to the other is inaugurated through a hermeneutical exposition which traces Dasein's factical projection back to its ground in the genuine meaning of Being. So, though indeed there is this double origin, hermeneutically, metaphysically regarded, one is prior to the other – it is a priori – namely, the understanding of the genuine meaning of Being, the ground and meaning of every factical projection of Being. Indeed by virtue of its priority it informs the essence of its geminate: facticity as not-understanding-of-Being.

> Factically existing Dasein has forgotten this Prior [*Früher*]. Therefore if Being, which is always already understood 'beforehand' [*früher*], is itself to become an *object,* then the objectification of this Prior – that which has been forgotten – must have the character of a coming back to what at one time and already in advance was understood [*das vormals schon und im vorhinein schon Verstandene*]. Plato, the discoverer of the apriori also saw this character of the objectification of Being when he characterized it as *αναμνησις*, recollection. (*GP* 463–4)

The hermeneutical movement from an origin in factical, forgetful Dasein to an a priori origin in a Dasein which always already grasps the meaning of Being is 'the self-retrieval [*Sichzurückholen*] from out of forgetfulness into the recollection of what is prior, wherein the empowering of the understanding of Being decisively lies' (*GP* 465). We see then that the movement hermeneutics inaugurates is a return to Dasein's 'pre-factical', a priori understanding-of-Being. Since this movement – one of crossing-overs, bindings (*λεγειν*) – is essential to hermeneutics as a meta-discourse it becomes clearer why *λόγος* is of central importance to it.

Before examining whether hermeneutic's conception of *λόγος* is sufficient for this task we must consider more explicitly what this discourse is to bring to language. We have seen that it must make Being become a phenomenon, it must bring Being to language. Since Being is always the Being of beings, to bring Being to language means to bring to language Being in its difference from beings. Though the term 'ontological difference' is not to be found in *SZ,* this is precisely what hermeneutics must articulate. If 'ontological difference' expresses the double origin of which we have spoken, and if the task of hermeneutics is to inaugurate the movement – whose first moment is the distinguishing between origins – between these origins such that, in meta-ontology, this movement itself will be explicable, i.e., grounded, then we see that hermeneutics must carry out its exposition such that Being in its difference from beings becomes explicit, *and* such that this movement of differencing *itself* can be thematically grasped in ontology. The latter is particularly important for Heidegger's grounding project, for its explication constitutes the ontological elucidation of the inaugural moment of the transcendental project: the hermeneutical distinguishing between the two origins of which we have spoken. Thus, though 'the distinction between Being and beings is *pre-ontologically* – that is, without any explicit concept of Being – *latent in the existence of Dasein's "da"*' (*GP* 454), this pre-ontological distinction *cannot* remain beyond ontological explication and the grounding illumination provided in the meta-ontological recoil. It cannot remain beyond apophantical discourse for then this pre-ontological distinction would not be what it is, the beginning for the working out of ontology. The necessity of hermeneutics bring this distinction as well as the distinguish*ing* from out of its abeyance is not lost on Heidegger: 'Because in making this distinction of Being and beings *explicit* both terms distinguished play off each other [*sich gegeneinander abheben*]. Being thereby becomes a possible theme of conceptualization (λόγος)' (*GP* 454, emphasis added; cf. *MAL* 193).

Here we see our origins in closest proximity: on the one hand it is necessary to make the distinction between Being and beings. On the other, lest this distinction be a 'disjunction', it is necessary to show this distinction is made from within a primordial unity. This is found in the fact that beings are only what they are *on the basis of* the prior understanding of Being; beings are disclosed in their Being. Ontologically expressed: though factically there are many modes of Being, it is necessary to distinguish between this manifold and the genuine meaning of Being; but lest this distinction be a 'disjunction', it is also necessary to show these derive from the genuine meaning of Being. Even more, it is necessary to show that and how Being, as grasped in its genuine meaning, gives rise to the factical projection of Being and the oblivion that belongs to this projection.

So the task of hermeneutics is two-fold: it must explicate the distinction between beings and Being, between the factical projection of Being and the genuine meaning of Being, and do so such that nevertheless a unity obtains, a unity of differencing. If hermeneutics can make this two-fold movement of distinguishing-grounding/unifying explicit such that this movement can be articulated in the idea of Being (ontology), then the hermeneutical process of bringing this movement forth (which is tantamount to making Being become a phenomenon) will prove, in the meta-ontological recoil, to be a grounded process. The circle of transcendental philosophy will be complete, the double origin will be shown in its essential unity.

Having always already made the distinction of Being and beings Heidegger goes about showing this primordial unity by focusing on the structure of understanding as *projection:*

> We understand beings only insofar as we project them upon Being; for its part Being must be understood in a certain way, that means, for its part

> Being must be projected upon something. We will not now touch upon the question of whether this retrogression of one project to another does not open a *progressus in infinitum.* (*GP* 396–7).

But he does come back to it, pointing to that in which the final unity of understanding lies: 'The series, we mentioned earlier, of projections inserted one after the other, as it were – understanding of being, projection upon Being; understanding of Being, projection upon time – has its end in the horizon of the ecstatical unity of temporality' (*GP* 437).

This series of projections is of great importance, for it reveals the structure of understanding: what is understood is only understood insofar as it is grasped in relation to something else – that upon which it is projected. Projection thereby sanctions the hermeneutical, recuperative movement from Dasein's Being-obliviating dispersion in beings to that upon which their understanding is based: understanding of Being. Thus for understanding there is a priority of the 'upon which' of projection, for the 'upon which' gathers the diversity of the projected, unifying it in its ground, its meaning. Ultimately we find that temporality makes understanding – the projective movement of understanding – and, *a fortiori,* transcendence, possible.

Here we gain a crucial insight. Temporality makes understanding possible: only by virtue of temporality's *ecstatic* nature can understanding be transcendental – '*ein darüber hinaus*' (*GP* 405), '*das Überschreitende als solches*' (*GP* 425) – and grasp both the projected *and* that upon which the projected is projected. Temporality is the ground and meaning of Being and the condition for the possibility of understanding-of-Being (*GP* § 20c, d). If this is the case, and if understanding Being means to grasp it in its ground, then understanding Being also requires grasping its 'upon which': temporality. It is here Heidegger sees the above noted danger of an infinite regression of grounds. This danger threatens most when considering the requirements of understanding: to understand Being one must also understand its 'upon which': temporality. And in turn, to understand temporality means to understand a priori *its* unity which, according to the structure of understanding, is provided by an 'upon which'. Heidegger calls this grounding 'upon which' of temporality *Temporalität.* Emphasizing the difference, so crucial to the structure of understanding, between temporality and *Temporalität,* he speaks of the present and its 'upon which' in *Temporalität: Praesenz:*

> Is *Praesenz* indeed indentical with the present? In no way. The *present,* the *enpresenting of* . . . we describe as one of the *ecstacies of temporality.* The name *Praesenz* already indicates that we do not mean any *ecstatical phenomenon* as we do with present and future, in any case not the ecstatic phenomenon of temporality in regards to its ecstatic structure. Nevertheless there subsists a relation between present and *Praesenz* that is not accidental. (*GP* 434–5).

This 'not accidental' relation is none other than that called for by projective understanding for an 'upon which'.

> Enpresenting is the ecstasis in the temporalizing of temporality which as such is familiar with *Praesenz* [*sich auf Praesenz versteht*]. As removal to . . . the present is a being open for *beings confronting us* which are thus understood in advance in terms of *Praesenz*. (*GP* 435–6).

Here we encounter two related paradoxes which resound in the heart of Heidegger's project. The first of these flows from Heidegger's attempt to avoid an infinite regress – one set in motion by the projective character of understanding – by saying the ground of grounds (*Temporalität*) is not ecstatic. If it were, it would be necessary to postulate a further ground or 'upon which' which would unify the ecstatic manifold. But by conceiving of the 'upon which' of temporality as non-ecstatic, he is plagued by the obverse problem. For Heidegger *Praesenz* is the 'upon which' of the present, its schema; there are similar schemata for the other temporal ecstacies. However, if *Praesenz* is not ecstatic – as presumably is the case with the other schemata – then how does it relate to them, i.e., how is it unified with them? Are we pushed back to a schema of schemata? Or even if *Praesenz* had a certain priority – as does the present as seen in the *Augenblick* – then how does it, being non-ecstatic, come to be differentiated into the three ecstacies of temporality? Secondly, if *Temporalität,* as the 'upon which' of temporality, is the condition for the possibility of temporality and is the unity of its ecstatic, inherently eccentric character, and if *Temporalität* as the ground and unity – the 'upon which' – of temporality must be understood a priori in order for ecstatic temporality to be possible, to be unified, to be grounded and intelligible,[30] and if understanding is essentially a temporal phenomenon – indeed is only possible on the basis of the *unity* of ecstatic temporality – then how does factical, ecstatic Dasein's understanding 'have' or grasp this 'upon which' (*Temporalität*) when it is what must be grasped prior to what (viz. temporality) makes understanding possible? To propose *Temporalität* is produced or projected by temporality not only does not answer these questions,[31] but runs counter to the thrust of understanding, for every bringing forth, every disclosure presumes a priori an understanding of the 'upon which' of disclosive projection; it requires a grasp of the horizontal unity of temporality.[32]

We see these two paradoxes are essentially related, for the problem of the relationship of *Temporalität* as unity and ground to ecstatic temporality is inseparable from the question of how understanding, as what is made possible by temporality, is to understand a priori the unity and ground of temporality, i.e., *Temporalität.* The problem is, most simply, the relation between two orders of understanding: a priori understanding and the (factical) understanding it makes possible. Since the hermeneutic of facticity in an important respect begins with the latter of these, what is at stake here is nothing less than the project of fundamental ontology, for the problem we face here is precisely the inaugural hermeneutical distinction of origins – not-understanding and understanding, projection and ground of projection – essential to the project of fundamental ontology.

In *MAL* § 10, Heidegger focuses on this distinction between a priori and factical understanding, (significantly, in reference to *SZ*). Specifically he points out an 'ambiguity' in the term 'Dasein', an ambiguity central to the formation of the transcendental project and which we have discussed in terms of a double origin. He speaks of *two* Daseins:

> This neutral Dasein is never the one that exists; Dasein always only exists in its factical concretion. However, neutral Dasein is indeed the source of the inner possibility which arises in every existing Dasein and is the inner enabling of existence. (*MAL* 172).

Presumably to neutral Dasein corresponds a priori understanding-of-Being and to factical Dasein the understanding of factically projected Being based on the a priori understanding. Though this apparent miosis of Dasein indeed corresponds to the basic structure of Heidegger's thinking – the relation of grounded and ground – it also underscores a problem in the fulfillment of a transcendental project seeking to clarify the idea of Being and show its meaning to be the basis for every factical, concrete projection, for what must be shown is not only the nature of 'neutral Dasein's' understanding of the genuine meaning of Being,[33] but its empowering the factical projection of Being. How does neutral Dasein relate to factical Dasein? The articulation of this relating is tantamount to the articulation of the performance of the distinction between the a priori and the factical, between Being and beings. This 'differencing' must be articulable in order for understanding's series of projections not to lead to a *progressus in infinitum,* but to testify to the unity of the genuine meaning of Being and its differentiating in factical projections, a unity whose recuperation in ontology hermeneutics initiates by taking recourse to the projective structure of understanding. As a problem of ontology, this differencing is none other than the problem of the 'principle of individuation' (*MAL* 270). As Heidegger remarks:

> The problem of the regional multiplicity of Being however includes, precisely when posed universally, the question of the unity of the general term 'Being', the question of the manner of the declension of the general meaning of 'Being' to the various regional meanings. That is the problem of the *unity of the idea of Being and its regional declensions.* [. . .] In any case, the problem is the unity and generality of the idea of Being. (*MAL* 192)

Heidegger recognizes this ontological problem is not simply categorical, i.e., the subsumption of a multiplicity under a unifying concept of Being. Rather – and especially since the hermeneutical movement is a retrieval – what is of utmost importance is how the unified idea of Being comes to be declined into regions, a declension which hermeneutics hopes to trace, in *λόγος*, back to its unity.

> Being not only means the multiplicity of regions and the *modi existendi* and *essendi* that belong to them, but the idea of Being is meant in reference to its essential *Gliederung* in *existentia* and *essentia*. This *Gliederung* is a basic problem of ontology – the problem of the *fundamental articulation [Grundartikulation] of Being*. (*MAL* 192–3).

We leave *Gliederung* untranslated, for it has an important polysemy. From the general ontological view, *'Gliederung'* means 'dividing', and thereby we face the fundamental ontological problem of Being's – and Temporalität's – principle of individuation. The other sense of *Gliederung* is *essentially* bound to individuation; *'Gliederung'* also means 'articulation' and we thereby confront the specific ontological problem – the relation of Being and *λόγος*. These two problems – the general and the specific – constitute the conundrum of transcendental philosophy.

Λόγος Αποφαντικος and Beyond

We have come full circle, again facing the problem of the relation of Being and *λόγος*. In my view this disjunction between Being and the *λόγος* of ontology brought Heidegger to an *unprojected* turn in his thinking away from apophantical discourse and, *a fortiori*, ontology. However, the full exposition of the importance of this problem for his abandonment of ontology and turn to the poets is, in the present context, neither possible nor necessary. For our purposes it suffices to have shown what 'hermeneutics' means within the context of the fundamental ontological project and what the basic problems are that it faces. In this section, which serves as a conclusion to our prior reflections and as an indication for the possible exposition of the hermeneutic of *SvG*, we intend merely to point out a feature that distinguishes Heidegger's earlier and later understandings of hermeneutics. This feature is the relative status of language and especially words, a feature of great importance for the apophantical discourse of fundamental ontology's hermeneutic.

As we have seen, in his Marburg period Heidegger conceived of hermeneutics from within the transcendental philosophical project of fundamental ontology. This project and its hermeneutic is a response to and an expression of the demand placed upon thought by the principle of sufficient reason, and as that faculty which is able to be addressed by and respond to this demand, understanding is given a privileged place by transcendental philosophy – Heidegger's included.[34]

In Heidegger's thought, understanding asserts its apriority by showing the projective character of all disclosure: beings are what they are only on the basis of an a priori understanding upon which they are disclosingly projected. However, we have seen the egregiousness of projective understanding brings Heidegger between the horns of a dilemma: on the one hand he faces an infinite regress of grounds. On the other he faces the problem of the unity and difference of transcendental philosophy's double origin, a problem he identifies but does not solve with terms such as 'the *Gliederung* of Being' and 'transcendental dissemination' (*MAL* 173ff.). The latter of these 'horns' is particularly important, for it penetrates a fundamental premise of ontology, namely that 'discourse is equiprimordial with understanding' (*SZ* 161) and, *mutatis mutandis,* Being. A corollary to this is that 'discourse is the articulation of intelligibility' (*SZ* 161). One would then expect discourse to always be intelligible, in and of itself meaningful.[35]

However the analysis of *Gerede* shows discourse not only has the possibility of being, but proximally and for the most part *is,* an oblivion of intelligibility, of understanding, and consequently a hermeneutic of factical discourse is necessary. This implies there are two distinct notions of discourse – one which is equiprimordial with understanding-of-Being and one which is not. Hermeneutics, guided by the structure of understanding, will show the former is the ground of the latter. Even further, discourse itself has a ground: 'discourse and hearing are grounded in understanding' (*SZ* 164). Most important is that not only must discourse be placed in an essential relation to (i.e., grounded in) understanding, but there is a sense in which discourse is *not* essentially an articulation of intelligibility, but only subsequently hermeneutically derives its meaning from understanding. Any difference between discourse and meaning or intelligibility – i.e., discourse and understanding – obviously presents at least a potential threat to the possibility of onto-logy. If discourse – say, an ontological one – is not the bearer of its meaning, but functions as a sign pointing to the site from which it derives its meaning (understanding), then ontological discourse would itself require a hermeneutic. Such a conception of language, which led Romantic hermeneutics to seek the meaning of written and spoken works in the intentions of the author/speaker, portends for ontology a similar regress.

What is this sense of discourse which of itself is *not* an articulation of intelligibility. It is a discourse embodied in *words.* Pointing to the relation between Dasein (viz. understanding-of-Being) and words Heidegger remarks:

> Because Dasein in its Being is meaningful [*bedeutend*], it lives in meanings and can express itself as this. And only because there is something like verbalization, that is words [*Worte*], that accrue to meanings, is there consequently vocabulary [*Wörte*]; that means that here, for the first time, the linguistic forms which coin themselves can be detached from meaning. Such an entirety of verbalizations, in which, after a certain manner, the

intelligibility of Dasein grows and is subsistent, we designate as *language*. (*L* 151; cf. *SZ* 151)

That words and language are subordinate to Dasein *qua* understanding-of-Being, especially when it is a question of meaning, is obvious: '*Only Dasein, therefore, can be meaningful or meaningless*' (*SZ* 151). This process of words accruing to meaning is a rather occult process Heidegger never explains, and, we should point out, denotes the same process denoted by 'the *Gliederung* of Being' and 'transcendental dissemination'. If the ontology Heidegger seeks is to be a concrete discourse – one employing words – then clearly the process of words accruing to meaning, i.e., words accruing to the meaning of Being, is the condition for the possibility of ontology. However this accruing is, as Heidegger points out, the incipient *self-alienation*[36] of intelligibility, i.e., understanding.

This ambivalent status of words sheds light on why Heidegger, as he indicates in the epigram that opens this essay, felt it necessary to coin new terms, words which, 'newly minted' so to speak, would most palpably manifest their being accretions of meaning, i.e., would most nearly, as 'non-words', be not words but meanings. In employing such non-words Heidegger is seeking a maximum transparency of language and words to meaning, a maximum which ontology calls for but, insofar as it employs words, can only approach asymptotically, for though the attainment of this maximum would be the closing of the difference between word and meaning, this closing can be achieved only on the basis of the *elimination of words: silence*. Silence then is the coincidence of the double origin: fallen Dasein and authentically resolute Dasein, the oblivion of Being and understanding-of-Being. This means the conditions for the possibility for fulfilling the project of fundamental ontology are, ironically, only met in silence. This is the phyrric victory of transcendental philosophy.

The dilemma then is that Being has fallen into oblivion, and the only means by which Heidegger can conceive to bring Being forth from this oblivion, i.e., to speak of Being, is through apophantical discourse. Apophantical discourse is, as we have seen, a pointing-out and letting see, a thematizing in which what is under discussion – Being – is objectified, defined. Yet this thematizing, apophantical discourse is precisely what, in the process of attempting to rescue Being from oblivion, nihilates Being. In other words: what ontology's hermeneutic seeks to bring forth is the transcendental synthesis – the 'hermeneutical as' – a structure which, though a (transcendental) fact constitutive of Being-in-the-world, has been 'forgotten'. But the very bringing forth of this 'hermeneutical as' in apophantical discourse flattens it out into an 'apophantical as'. As such apophantical discourse experiences an '*auto-défait*'. Heidegger traces this fate of apophantical discourse whose hallmark is a certain involution of language corresponding to a transformation of our comportment towards beings as ready-to-hand to beings as always already disclosed, i.e., present-at-hand

(Cf. *L* 153ff.). In this involution discourse is concerned with its embodiment, is concerned with defining its terms, and thus we see the essential connection between apophantical discourse, its self-undoing, and words.

Later in his career Heidegger rethinks the nature of words and language, both *vis-à-vis* man and Being, calling into question precisely the subordination of λόγος and thinking to the principle of sufficient reason. Such a rethinking enabled him to grant words and language an important autonomy *vis-à-vis* understanding and restores to words a fundamental polysemy which becomes central to the hermeneutic of *SvG*.[37] No longer ciphers in need of deriving their meaning from an a priori understanding but themselves being the play of the advent and withdrawal of Being, words provide Heidegger the possibility of a hermeneutic that seeks not to articulate the univocal and genuine meaning of Being, but that opens up the essential relation of Being and ground(lessness) through a multiplication of readings of the principle of sufficient reason: *Nihil est sine ratione*. The hermeneutic of *SvG* is an orchestration of readings and changes in emphases rather than an analytic of a transcendental fact. It is one which no longer dreams of a transparent, scientific λόγος of Being and ground, but has 'returned (*sic*) to the original contents of our own constantly decaying language' and its abysmal riches.

Notes

1. The following abbreviations will be used in our text to indicate works of Heidegger: *US* = *Unterwegs zur Sprache* (Pfullingen: Neske Verlag, 1957); *SZ* = *Sein und Zeit* (Tubingen: Niemeyer Verlag, 14th ed., 1977); *SvG* = *Der Satz vom Grund* (Pfullingen: Neske Verlag. 5th ed., 1978); *MAL* = *Gesamtausgabe, vol. 26: Metaphysische Anfangsgründe im Ausgang von Leibniz* (Frankfurt am Main: Vittorio Klostermann, 1978); *GP* = *Gesamtausgabe, vol. 24: Die Grundprobleme der Phänomonologie* (Frankfurt am Main: Vittorio Klostermann, 1975); *L* = *Gesamtausgabe, vol. 21: Logik: Die Frage nach der Wahrheit* (Frankfurt am Main: Vittorio Klostermann, 1976); *WG* = *Vom Wesen des Grundes* (Frankfurt am Main: Vittorio Klostermann, 6th ed., 1973); *KPM* = *Kant und das Problem der Metaphysik* (Frankfurt am Main: Vittorio Klostermann, 1951). All translations by the author.
2. The essential relation between fundamental ontology and ontology can be seen in the fact that at times Heidegger sees fundamental ontology as including ontology (the science of Being as such) (viz. *MAL*) and sometimes he sees the exposition of the science of Being as distinguishable from fundamental ontology (viz. *GP*). For the sake of precision, we will distinguish between fundamental ontology, ontology, and meta-ontology, though of course what is of utmost importance is their essential relation. We shall return to this below.
3. Cf. *SZ* p. 50, note 1. 'Apriorism' is the method of every scientific philosophy that understands itself'. This is only one of many instances in which Heidegger invokes the classical framework of transcendental philosophy. For further discussion of this issue, see Carl Friedrich Gethmann's *Verstehen und Auslegung: Das Methodenproblem in der Philosophie Martin Heideggers*. (Bonn: Bouvier Verlag Herbert Grundmann, 1974); also Joseph Kockelmans' 'Destructive Retrieve and Hermeneutic Phenomenology in *Being and Time*' in *Research in Phenomenology,* vol. 7 (1977). pp. 106–37.; and Ingeborg Koza's *Das Problem des Grundes in Heideggers Auseinandersetzung mit Kant* (Ratingen bei Düsseldorf: A. Henn Verlag, 1967).

4. On the theme of categorical-ontological and transcendental-ontological elements in *SZ* see Gethmann's *Verstehen,* pp. 31–41; also Kockelmans' 'Destructive Retrieve', pp. 114–16.
5. Even, and perhaps especially, the nature of this privilege has gone unquestioned, though it harbors an understanding of Being. See, for example, Heidegger's discussion of the *potius quam* in his *MAL,* pp. 135–45 and *WG,* especially the third part.
6. Cf. G. Moneta, *On Identity* (The Hague: Martinus Nijhoff, 1977), especially the chapter 'Transcendental Identity', pp. 30–36. Also p. 99.
7. Gethmann, *Verstehen,* p. 48.
8. Gethmann, *Verstehen,* p. 51.
9. To characterize the standpoint complementary to the transcendental, Manfred Brelage has coined the term 'Cizscendenz'. See his *Transzendentalphilosophie und konkrete Subjektivität: Eine Studie zur Geschichte der Erkenntnistheorie im 20. Jahrhundert.* (Berlin: de Gruyter, 1964) pp. 72–253. See also Gethmann, *Verstehen,* pp. 279f.
10. The word in Heidegger's text is '*ablesen*'. For an exposition of the problematic of *SZ* as one of textuality, see Thomas J. Wilson's *Sein als Text* (München: Alber Verlag, 1981).
11. Here we glimpse the regressus in infinitum that always threatens metaphysics.
12. Cf. Gethmann, *Verstehen,* pp. 121–24. See also *GP* p. § 13b.
13. *SZ,* p. 5. '*Seinsverständnis ist ein Faktum*'.
14. Gethmann, *Verstehen,* pp. 50f.
15. Here we glimpse the inner relation between the hermeneutic of facticity and the deconstructive retrieval of the history of philosophy.
16. With the term 'appearing' we are compressing Heidegger's discussion of *Schein* and *Erscheinung*.
17. In commenting on the passage to which we are referring (*SZ* p. 33, 1. 30–41), Thomas J. Wilson makes the following observation:

    However we must note that 'true' always stands in quotation marks, and that *noein* can remain an *agnoein.* By this procedure he wants to bring Aristotle's doctrine into accord with his own theory of truth in which the place of truth is to be found neither in sensible perception nor in judgment. The perception of colors can remain an unsuitable means of access to the given. Taken by itself it must remain so. Only when it is taken up into state-of-mind understanding [*das befindliche Verstehen*] can it provide such an access. That perception has always already occurred is to be understood as an a priori.

    Wilson, *Sein als Text,* p. 199. This means that the apophantical 'as' is always already the hermeneutical 'as'.
18. Here we see that there must be something like an a priori discourse, one which occurs 'prior to' any particular 'pointing out' and 'being under discussion'. Hermeneutics is such an a priori discourse, as we shall see.
19. Kockelmans, 'Destructive Retrieve', p. 129.
20. Heidegger accounts for this disjunction or lacunae in terms drawn from his later thought where there is no disjunction between Being and language. This disjunction is the default of Being, a default which is likewise the failure of a work to name the relation between Being and language.

    Because the meditation on language and Being determined my path of thinking from early on, their situating discussion therefore remains as much as possible in the background. Perhaps it is the fundamental deficiency of the book *Being and Time* that I ventured too much too soon. (. . .) Nevertheless, nearly a decade has passed until I am able to say what I thought – the appropriate word is today still lacking. (*US* 93).

    See also Joseph Kockelmans' 'Ontological Difference, Hermeneutics, and Language' in *On Heidegger and Language* (Evanston: Northwestern University Press, 1972), p. 210 and footnote 38.

21. Gethmann, *Verstehen,* pp. 229–30.
22. Here we see that Heidegger's retrieval of the history of metaphysics is concerned to show how and to what extent previous ontologies have failed to complete their task.
23. For a sketch of the general problem of the *Umschlag,* see my 'Umschläge: Nietzsche and Heidegger at the End of Philosophy', in *Research in Phenomenology.* vol. 15 (1985), especially pp. 99f.
24. Terms like 'essential tendency', 'essential possibility', 'immer schon vollzogene Möglichkeit' must be understood as necessities. What sort they may be is the problem of meta-ontology and the metaphysics of truth, i.e., logic.
25. Clearly Heidegger's use of the term 'metaphysics' means to stress, through the notion of 'meta', the *movement* from out of the ontic to the ontological and its meta-ontological recoil. As such metaphysics would be a philosophical path one must take to establish ontology, i.e., scientific philosophy.
26. Cf. Gethmann, *Verstehen,* pp. 285f. Here we must point out that Krell's advocacy of a hermeneutic of Dasein or mortals stands in need of a clarification of the term 'hermeneutic'. This constitutes our general task. See Krell's *Intimations,* pp. 43f.
27. We can see how, once Heidegger came to focus on this recoil, hermeneutics as a word and 'discipline' disappeared from his works in being absorbed or displaced by the more comprehensive concern of a metaphysics of truth, logic.
28. Though he does not use the term double origin, Jean-Luc Nancy's discussion of hermeneutics and interpretation in Heidegger focuses on the ambiguity of origin and is complementary to what we have in view here. See his *Le partage des voix* (Paris: Galilee, 1983).
29. This surely is Heidegger's position in *SvG.*
30. By connecting Being with understanding as we do in this clause, we recognize the full force of the principle of sufficient reason.
31. Heidegger seems to try to take this tact when he renames the schemata of *Temporalität 'Ekstemata'* (*MAL* 269–70).
32. Recourse cannot be simply taken to the world or its worlding to establish this unity for the unity of the horizons of temporality is the condition for the possibility of world (*MAL* 269–70). For a discussion of temporality, its schemata, and transcendence, see John Sallis' 'Imagination and the Meaning of Being', section 3, in *Heidegger et l'idée de la phénomènologie,* Dordrecht, Kluwer, 1988.
33. This understanding, to avoid an infinite regression, would seem to not be projective, but immediate, noetic.
34. For an analysis of the change in Heidegger's view of the principle of sufficient reason see John Caputo's 'The Principle of Sufficient Reason: A Study of Heideggerian Self-Criticism', in *The Southern Journal of Philosophy,* vol. 13 (Winter 1975), pp. 419–25.
35. This is the position of structuralists and even post-structuralists such as Derrida, Foucault, and Ricoeur. The later Heidegger would be counted among their ranks.
36. See H.-G. Gadamer, *Wahrheit und Methode* (Tübingen: J.C.B. Mohr [Paul Siebeck], 4th ed., 1975). pp. 368–71. For Gadamer this self-alienation only occurs in writing, not speech. He does not, however, adequately explain how the transition from speech to writing is an essential transformation of words.
37. The possibilities for a retrieval of traditional hermeneutical question opened up by the restitution of meaning to words have been partially explored by Jean Greisch in his 'Les mots et les roses' in *Revue des sciences philosophiques et theologiques,* vol. 57 (1973), pp. 433–55.

The Sensitive Flesh

ALPHONSO LINGIS
The Pennsylvania State University

The Things

First, what is it that we perceive? We perceive things – configurations against a background. From time to time, it is true, perceptions of the light, or the darkness, or fog, or sky, or rumble, or stench get mentioned in Merleau-Ponty's text, but they are perhaps moments of instability, or inachievement, not the normal case. For Merleau-Ponty finds there is such a thing as a norm, a finality, in perceptual consciousness; it is the positing of things. The phenomenon of perceptual constancies, of a sense of the real colors, the right lighting, the true size and shape, shows that there are norms within the perceptual flux; what determines the real and the true and the right is the possibility of a thing taking form. And the compossibility of things – there is a coherence, a consistency in the flowing field of perception; it is a world of coexisting, compossible things. That is why, despite the fog, despite the darkness, despite the rumble, Merleau-Ponty can say that a figure against a field is the essence of, the very definition of consciousness. We cannot explain the apparition of things by a subject of the perception which collates or synthesizes its sensations; it is rather the thing that polarizes and focuses and synthesizes the various surfaces and senses of the perceiving subject.

Things are wholes, which involve a multiplicity of parts or aspects. *Phenomenology of Perception* first sets out to argue that a perceived thing has the constitution of a Gestalt. It is not a simple assemblage or aggregate of simples, sense data, with only extrinsic relations of spatio-temporal juxtaposition, between them – the conception on which empiricism is based. It is also not a synthesis of spatio-temporal simples, predicated of a subject of predication posited by the understanding, or taken as signs of a signification which would be ideal and intuited or constituted by the intellect, or taken as particulars instantiating a universal as positive, as given, as they. Intellectualism is based on some variant of that idea – that the sensible, in order to be perceived as a thing, requires the addition of some universal or some ideality. Husserl, for

J.C. Sallis, G. Moneta and J. Taminiaux (eds.), The Collegium Phaenomenologicum, 225–240.
© Kluwer Academic Publishers.

example, conceived of perception as a kind of predication; for him a perceptual object involves an ideal essence, intuited or posited, or intuited in being posited, maintained the same, and a multiplicity of sense particulars which belong together because they each manifest or express it, function as a sign of it.

The concept of Gestalt would most correctly state the relationship of unity and multiplicity in the makeup of a sensible thing. There are parts, different sensuous aspects, and each does something in its own place and moment to contribute to the makeup of the thing. But they do not exist outside of the whole, which partitions them, gives them their role, makes them function. The soap molecule does not exert a force of cohesion in the directions it does to occupy its place when it is outside of the soap bubble, and the red of the brick is the red it is only when involved with this texture, this light, this expanse of more red or other colors. One cannot say what this red is, or see it, outside of this complex of the colors that intensify it, contrast with it, reverberate it, the textures that modulate it, the form that molds it, condenses it, or fragments it.

But this also means that what holds these different sensuous elements together is neither simple extrinsic relations of juxtaposition, nor some ideal factor to which they would be predicated, or some universal factor also intuited along with them. Their unity is not conceived, posited or intuited apart from them; it is in them, sensible and perceived with them and in them. It is then not an essence, in the sense of an invariant nucleus of traits. It is also not an order or a system or a law instantiated in them, but of itself universal. What then? Merleau-Ponty formulated the concept of a 'sensuous essence', a way each element leads to, involves, implicates, reflects, is in its own register equivalent to, the next. Thus when we see an apple, this identity is not something conceived at once like a concept, it is not an invariant found in all its various aspects, it is not a law or principle like triangularity found in all triangles. We see it, by looking, by looking at the way this shiny red and dense white involves, somehow makes visible, a certain sense of pulpiness, a certain juiciness, even a certain clear and homogenous taste. One sees it does not have that tomato look, that pear granularness, that peach feel. We can say that the identity is given in the way our perception moves from color to tactile value, to savor, the way our perception *is moved* from color to pulp to savor. Each particular element is what it is only by involving, leading to, reflecting in its own way the others. Each occupies its own spot and moment with something like its own scheme, its own way of filling, condensing or rarefying its space and its moment – and there is a relationship between this kind of whiteness and this kind of pulpiness; each reflects something of the scheme of the other. There is something like an apple-sense in that red and that white, and in that pulpiness felt or chewed, and in that taste. But again, that 'sense' is not something like an identity, an invariant or a principle instantiated in different registers of sensoriality. It would rather have to be conceived as a 'style', that is, as a general scheme which can be recognized in each of its variants, but which is not a universal, an identity the same with an addition of some differences. A style in the sense that personality is a style, a sensibly perceived scheme which makes all the conversations of a person recognizably his own, even though one can isolate in them neither identical elements nor identical arrangements of elements that recur.

The Transcendence of Things

This scrutiny of the things that we perceive already makes it impossible for us to suppose that there is in them something given – the 'sense-data', simples, and something we add to make things out of the data – the organization, the relations between them. For, on the one hand, without their cohesion, without their involvement in one another, the isolated sensuous aspects can no longer be said to be anything. And on the other hand, their cohesion and coherence is not a kind of unit, unity of meaning or universal, which we grasp at once, immediately or intuitively; it is sketched out, open-ended, caught on to progressively, as we go further. Perhaps we see enough to attach a name to it from the start, but what a winesap apple or the calvados distilled from apples really is and means is something that one understands in touching, smelling, chewing, savoring, without ever ending at something like the definitive key to it, in the sense that, one day, we possessed all there is to understand about a triangle.

But then the sensible elements themselves are not really particulars, are they? They should not be defined as items of being that are what they are, when and where they are. Not one of them is just a here-and-now particular, contingent and unfounded such that it can only be recorded or not recorded. Each of them goes beyond simple location; there is not one that is instantaneous, that does not prolong itself in duration. And there is not one that is simply here; a point of red reduced to itself is not visible and is not red; it needs to be reinforced, prolonged by other spots, to be red, and it is not simply red within its own borders, since it can be the red it is only if the background is the color or colors it is. And, we can say, the red of this apple could not be the red it is without repeating something of its inner diagram on the register of the tangible; this red is a tangible red, looks tangible, and is not this red without this tangible prolongation.

What then is this red? It is a moment of a scheme, a variant on a sensible scheme, that we encounter here and now, and on the register of the visible, but which we see prolonging itself beyond and elsewhere, and in depth. Existential philosophy had defined certain new concepts – the concept of ecstasy, or of transcendence – to fix a kind of being that is by throwing itself out of its own given place and time, without dissipating, because at each moment it projects itself – or more exactly, a variant of itself – into another place and time. That is different from being everywhere and at all moments from the start. Ex-istence, understood etymologically would be that, not so much a stance as a movement which is by conceiving a divergence from itself or a potentiality of itself and projecting itself into that divergence with all that it is. This bizarre concept was formulated precisely to define the whole constitution of subjectivity, and thus to clearly, fundamentally, totally distinguish it from the way objective reality, the facts, are – which have to be located where and when they are, because for them existence is being at a point p and a time t.

What is now very extraordinary and very strange indeed is that this very concept, upon which the whole twentieth-century existential philosophy of subjectivity was built, is now found to be exactly the concept one needs in order to describe the sense data!

The more and more lucid sense of this explains the new descriptions of the sensible field we find in Merleau-Ponty's later writings. The sensible field is a realm of being where all points become pivots, all lines become levels, all surfaces become planes, all colors become atmospheres, all tones become keys, like in dodecaphonic music. There are not particulars, and universals; what there is are particulars generalizing themselves, a whole landscape concretizing itself momentarily in this red, a whole love given in condensation in a vase of flowers, a whole adventure or fatality sounded in five little notes. Each one given is the spot or moment in which a schema of being is being elaborated. The painters have a precise knowledge of this; their knowledge consists in knowing what a color does – to a field, to another color, to a zone of space; in knowing what a line does – to the zone it molds, the space it bunches up, bulges out, or flattens, to the color, to the field of tensions; in knowing what shapes move, creep, crawl, set up movement in a whole field – and this knowledge is not conceptual, is not a possession of laws or principles. But thus it is that they know how, with a few lines, a few strokes of color, how to paint *things*.

It is the essence, the schema, the style that is given from the start; our perception does not first see the black color of the ball-point pen, but goes straight to the substance, something like a somber power condensing there, occupying a region there, of which the black color, the dense matter, the hard solidity are variants. The thing itself, then, is this matrix, this pregnancy!

The Hold on Things

What now about the sensing of things? Classical epistemology, distinguishing between the de facto multiplicity of sense data and their relationships, whether additive or synthetic, in the thing perceived, distinguished also between a passive and an active side involved in the perception. There would be a passive receptivity for the sense data, and an active collating or synthesizing of them. The sensing properly so-called would be a passive being-impressed by sense impressions. In Husserl's phenomenology, intentionality then intervenes, to take these sense impressions to mean something, and thus to identify them, synthetically taking them as signs of one and the same signification.

The sensing Merleau-Ponty takes to be active from the start; he conceives the receptivity for the sensuous element to be a prehension, a '*prise*', a 'hold'. The idea is Heideggerian; several times Merleau-Ponty says that in the handling that explores the tangible the very operation of perceiving is visible – and that looking – palpating with the eye – is a variant of it (VI 175). The tactile datum is not given to a passive surface; the smooth and the rough, the sleek and the sticky, the hard and the vaporous, are given to a movement of the hand that applies itself to them with a certain pressure, pace, across a certain scope, and they are patterned ways in which this movement is modulated. 'The hard and the soft, the grainy and the sleek, moonlight and sunlight in memory give themselves not as sensorial contents, but as a certain type of symbiosis, a certain way the outside has of invading us, a certain way we have to welcome it' (PP 317).

The striking experiments of Goldstein and Rosenthal enable us to extend this insight to visual data: the emergence of blue induces a sliding up-and-down movement across the body schema, the emergence of orange an increased tension and extension of the body. But for Merleau-Ponty this should not be described as evidence of a motor reaction in the whole body-schema once the color has been sensed; rather it is in and by the modulation of the motility of the look, and of the whole body, that the blue or the yellow is sensed, taken up, communicated with.

Thus the moist, the oily, the sleek, the restful green and the aggressive orange are palpated by the hand or the look, which takes up, in its own motility, in its own stance and pace, something which in it is a modulation of its own motility, and which, in the thing, is the sensuous essence, the essence of oiliness or green, an essence which has to be conceived verbally, as the way of occupying its space and time actively, a way of condensing or rarefying its space and moment, a way of bulging it out or hollowing it out, a way of polarizing, molding, spreading its tension across a certain field. But that inner sense of the green is also realized in its own way in the register of the tangible, the pulp of the watermelon, and in the register of flavor and odor; it is the inner sense of the watermelon, and it is already the whole watermelon that is captured by the sweep of the eye.

The sizes and shapes of things is also captured actively in this kind of prehension; it is in dilating the scope of my look or my grip, eventually filling out the whole field, that is, approaching the limit of what my look or my hearing can hold together before it, that the bigness of a visual object, or the vibrancy of a sound, is felt, becomes manifest, comes to be. It is in experiencing the articulation of the wall receding, become less for me, that I feel that end of it receding from the hold I have on it, and thus oriented away from me, receding into distance. It is my hold on it, the degree to which its form and grain are clear and distinct to me, the degree to which I feel myself centered on it, that determines the normal, true, or right appearance of things from the variants, from mere appearances, or the abnormal appearances. It is in the equilibrium of my gaze, traveling about the rim, that the circular is sensed, and comes to be for me.

This already brings us to a second idea involved in perception as a prehension, a 'prise'. On the one hand, it means that the sense datum is in reality not a point of opacity, a particular occupying a here and now, but is a kind of essence, in the verbal sense, a transcendence or an existence, which occupies a domain and a trajectory of duration actively, in a certain way, with a certain movement or schema or effect. And that is what is picked up by the palpation of the hand or eye, by the motility of the sensitive body.

On the other hand, this prehension tends to a maximum. The normal or normative appearance is one given with as much clarity and distinctness as possible. From the first the sensitive body captures not only a visual modulation, but something that is more than that, that reverberates across all the registers of sensoriality; from the first it is the whole sensibility of the body that is turned to something, both eyes converge on it, all the body surfaces center on it. The relationship of the sensitive body with its surroundings tends to a state of maximum, when the body, in all its powers, is geared into the setting, centered on something, when there is an inner sense of equilibrium, maximum adjustment, centering, responsiveness, interrelationship. It is then that the presence and apparition of something appears normal, right and true, that the spatial axes, the sense of what is up and what is down, what is close and what is far, what is left and what is right, stabilize – as can be vividly seen in the successive days of Stratton's reversed retinal image experiment. Here 'prise' means something like a hold on a world. An appropriation. There is something like an intrinsic body norm or finality, when it tends not to the sensing of fleeting and fragmentary sensory data, but to the presence of fully and clearly articulated intersensorial things, things that are such as to be compossible with other such things in the cohesion and continuity of a world. At such moments the body itself is equilibrated, integrated, wholly activated, and centered.

This state is basically practical. It is the state at which the body can operate in its field, deal with these things in the most centered, integrated, and thus forceful or efficacious ways. Stratton reverses the retinal images by special eyeglasses, and thus disconnects the visual field from the tangible. The sense of the world, its layout, becomes normal and integral again, right and right-side-up when the subject comes to be able to function again, to reach for and find things, to move and to act. Merleau-Ponty's term is 'inhabit'. Normal and true perception is a being-in-the-world, in the strong sense of inhabiting the world, that is, having a world, holding on to a field of operations, having it within reach or in one's grip, possessing it, being efficaciously adjusted to it. Here the 'prise', the prehension involved in perception is a possession or appropriation, a com-prehension. That is, not an intellection, but a coordinated and coordinating hold.

Here we see clearly that despite the Husserlian theme of the primacy of perception, which Heidegger begins *Being and Time* by repudiating, Merleau-Ponty's analysis is much more Heideggerian than Husserlian. There is a primacy of perception – at least with regard to the second-level fields of conceptual representation, and perhaps with regard to the emotional and evaluative presentifications. But what is perceived does not appear, for Merleau-Ponty, as it does for Husserl, to be a stratum of bare things, factual data which are or are not, are given or are not given, and whose givenness and factuality consists especially in the immediacy, presence, plenitude of sense data, that 'flesh and bone' of things. To be sure, Merleau-Ponty does not believe that our life opens from the first upon a complex of *ta pragmata* as Heidegger describes them, implements, nodes of instrumental or dynamic relatednesses, vectors of transmission of force, gear and obstacles. But the colors, sounds, lights, shapes, and shadows are not out there as concretions of immediacy, opaque qualia, plenary moments of presence confronting an intuition. The colors are condensing or rarefying, contrasting and veering into depth; the points are pivoting, the lines doing something, damming up space, vibrating it, the tones are echoing across the silent regions of chromaticity, tacticity, luminosity, and shadow, and reverberating into reality whole things. And the sensitive and motile body is exposing itself to these vibrations, is capturing them with its own movements, is centering itself and integrating its forces upon them, is giving itself a figure, an intersensorial thing it can deal with, is giving itself a field to its own measure, to the measure of its own dealings and preoccupations, a field that is basically a field of operations, a practical field, a habitat of its own.

Here the example of the gesture is a key for us. The hand that rises to hail a face in the crowd is not preceded and made possible by a representation of the one recognized, a representation by which he would be recognized. It is not preceded by a process that lays out representations across distances and measures those distances against one another or against some scale. It is the hand itself that recognizes the friend, who is not there as a form represented, but as a movement and a cordiality that solicits, and what it solicits is not a cognitive and representational operation, but a greeting, an interaction, this very movement of my stance in this field of social interactions. And it is the hand itself, in its reach, in the range of its wave that signals my presence and my welcome, that measures the distance between us. It is with this kind of model that we should conceive of the recognition of the brash and garish colors of the Snopes suburbs, the bluegreen waters of the coral seas, the lines of the giant sequoias.

The Comprehension

The thing is a unity of a diversity of aspects. Its diverse sensuous aspects are themselves received, taken up, by the perceiving subject on its diverse sensitive surfaces and organs. They must themselves be unified, for the subject, perhaps at the level of the central nervous system, where all the sensations of the body are assembled. But the unity of a thing is not simply that of a unity by spatio-temporal juxtaposition of elements: a sensible thing is a unit in that it has one sense, one identity. It is a unity by coherence and not only by cohesion. Its sensuous aspects belong together even if they are separated spatially and temporally. Thus the subject of perception must also involve an agency which synthetically unifies the sensuous aspects of a thing for itself, and which would have to first intuit or produce the one sense, one identity or one meaning that could function as the unifying factor. This agency would be the comprehending mind as such, the understanding involved in combining with sensation to produce a perception. This mind is defined as the seat of concepts, of the forms of unity.

This classical explanation has been transformed by Merleau-Ponty in certain fundamental ways. The comprehending or synthesizing agency has been identified with the body itself.

The key point is just how the unity involved in a thing is to be conceived. To be sure, the diverse sensuous aspects are not simply juxtaposed, additively. There is a coherence; they belong together intrinsically; there is an inner logic, or system, or relationship between them, the diverse sensuous aspects manifest a common essence or sense. But what exactly does this mean? Husserl conceives of their relationship as a relationship of sign with signification; each of the sense data are significant; the mind takes them to mean the presence of something, some one and the same thing. Perception consists in taking the color data in the sphere of vision, the tactile data in the sphere of touch, the taste data and smell data all to indicate, to manifest, to express, to mean the presence of something, of the apple, which is the transcendent identity-pole signified by all these senses. Thus they all belong together, because each is a parallel reference to one and the same identity-pole.

But Merleau-Ponty's analysis has given us a different conception of the unity involved. What one perceives, when one perceives the apple, is not that there is an identity-pole intuited or conceived to which both this color and this pulpiness refer; it is rather that one sees that this red looks pulpy, and juicy, and tart, and the sense of the apple is just the peculiar way this red involves and makes visible a certain pulpiness and juiciness, and makes visible too a certain tart sense. The sense of the apple, and the sense of the pear, is just this complex, this coming-together of a certain multiple reverberation across all the dimensions of sensoriality. One does not really have an idea of an apple and a pear, in the sense that one has an idea of a triangle or a circle. The sense of the apple there is just this way a certain zone of color bulges out before you, tangible already, touchable, graspable, and sending across your sensibility a foretaste of a certain substantial and sleek, homogenous and full mouthful.

This presupposes and requires in us not a power to produce an ideal identity-pole, but rather a multiple and diverse capacity to take hold, to prehend that apple-way of filling out a spot of space and duration, diverse organs of motile prehension, which intercommunicate, that is, where what takes form on one register is reverberated across other registers, each time in its own way. That is the sensibility, the *sensus communis* of classical epistemology, which classical thinking was mainly wrong in locating in the central nervous system, since it was working with a physiology which supposes that each sense organ was a specialized and autonomous apparatus specialized for certain kinds of stimuli and thresholds, and that the diverse senses were only assembled at a central sphere. But in fact modern physiology has come to conceive of the nervous circuitry as anatomically decomposable but physiologically one, and that the operation of the whole is at the level of the parts, not working by additively combining the separate functionings of the parts, but rather working by determining the functionings of each of the parts, its focus and its threshold, in function of the functioning of all the other parts. The sensibility is in this sense a whole, a Gestalt. It is not only a total system where whatever is received, prehended, taken up in one part is reverberated across all the other parts and sensitive surfaces, but, conversely, the energization and capacity of any part is determined at each moment by the centering, focus, threshold level, of all the parts. The sense of the apple, taken up by the look, is immediately communicated to all the rest of the body sensibility, and thus what is prehended is not a visual scheme only, but something intersensorial from the start. But the level of excitability of the whole sensibility, its fatigue or its distraction or disintegration, affects the functioning of the sight; the apple becomes more and more visible to the degree that the whole sensibility of the body centers on it, and one sees its form in the measure that it becomes for the awakened hand more and more palpable.

But this communication within the body, within the sensibility, should not be conceived as something automatic, as though the nervous circuitry were simply a system where any agitation that affects it is reverberated throughout. There is an internal action, by which the sensibility determines its own receptivity, its own thresholds, and by which it determines its own focus. At every moment the body is not absolutely excitable, but determines its own level of excitability, which can be determined by determining the sensory thresholds of the moment. And at any moment the body is centered, to a greater or lesser extent; as Goldstein wrote, the body always does but one thing at a time – and perceives but one thing at a time, one figure against the ground of the rest. The sensibility is positioned, is postured, is focused in on an objective.

These thoughts lead us to connect the sensibility, in its Gestaltist unity, as the sphere where the diverse sensorial receptivities communicate, with the posture of the body. The motility of the body, the way its forces and tensions are coordinated, forms a postural schema. The posture has to be conceived as a Gestalt, a way all the positions and movements of the body are internally adjusted to one another; it is not simply the sum of the positions of the parts each determined by the force of gravity and the outside pressures. It is the axis of the whole that positions each of the parts. But the postural schema is not simply a diagram of the way all the parts are equilibrated; the body does not tend to a state of rest, but tends to maintain a state of tension centered in a particular direction. This direction or focus is practical: the body positions itself over its objective or its task. Thus the perception of an exterior objective, as something soliciting the coordinated hold of the body, determines the postural schema.

But, conversely, it is the posture, that is, the motile way the body centers and converges all its receptor surfaces upon an objective, that centers the sensibility. It is the finality of that posture that determines the level of excitability, the sensory thresholds. It is the finality of picking up the apple and eating it, that determines the visual threshold of the moment.

Thus the movement in Merleau-Ponty is to the sensibility, conceived as a Gestalt, and extended throughout the body, as the comprehending, synthesizing agency which yields the perception of a unified intersensorial thing. And the active spontaneity at work within the sensibility, determining its direction and operation at the moment, is not the spontaneity of a spiritual factor, but is rather identified with the corporeal motility. What spontaneously coordinates and centers the focus of the whole sensibility is the body's posture. This posture has to be seen as a whole, an integrating axis, which is spontaneous, self-determining. And practical. It focuses itself upon tasks, objectives.

At this point we have reached a kind of ultimate in the explanation. What there is, in the body, is a movement spontaneously assembling its parts, positioning the members according to one coordinated and equilibrated axis, that stands by itself, or moves by itself. This movement arises in the body finalized by an exterior pole: the body positions itself before some task, makes something an objective for itself by this positioning. The ultimate is this movement which can be decisively described as objectifying and integrating. A movement integrating the parts and phases of the body into one axis, or one arc. And making something into the objective of that axis, that move. Nothing is an objective except in terms of that move, for that move. And there is no such positioning, posturing movement within the body except in function of an objective.

It is then this movement that should be called, in the most basic and ultimate sense, intentionality, or ex-istence. It integrates and focuses the sensibility, producing the emergence of an integral and intersensorial, motor objective. And it assembles, integrates the body and its sensitive surfaces, not by the force of some selfsame law, but by a laternal, transitional, continuous movement of intercommunication.

Thus what we have to correlate is the thing, in its essence, in its intersensorial unity, and the postural schema of the body. What comprehends the sense, the essence, the intersensorial unity of the thing is the common sensibility of the body, integrated and positioned by the postural schema – the motor intentionality, or ex-istential arc as a whole. There is in the body something like an intrinsic knowledge of how to center, how to position itself, how to take hold of things, such that they are given and manifest in their intersensorial essence. There is something like a knowledge of the essence of an apple in the body – a practical knowledge, a praktognosis, a knowledge of how to deal with such a thing, how to station oneself before it, how to apply oneself to it, such that its sense, its way of being makes itself felt. This does not mean that the body possesses in itself something like the formula of the apple, the formula of how to put the sense data together, the principle or the law that makes sense data into an apple. Its knowledge is practical and is indistinguishable from its sense of itself: it is a knowledge of how to deal with an apple, how to position oneself before it, how to focus on it in such a way that its sense gets taken up by the diverse sensitive surfaces of the body, and how these diverse ways of taking hold of it get coordinated and integrated, laterally.

And this also explains why the essence of the apple is something transcendent and exterior. It is in the red of the apple, but also leads beyond the red, in the pulp and in the savor, and the progression toward it takes the form of a progressive mobilization of the body faculties along lines and in a direction that essence lays out. Within reach, held by the body, it functions nonetheless as a line of exploration and behavior ever sketched out in advance, still beyond what the body has appropriated at any stage. The essence of the apple is like a theme or style of being comprehended already in its first movement, but existing only in the diversity of its variations, grasped only as the family resemblance of the variations, and whose variations are never yet exhausted as long as the apple is there.

The Universal

The essence, according to Husserl's and the most elementary possible definition, is the universal. The sense of the apple is in all its visual profiles, and in all its sensory aspects. It is in all apples. It is not only in all the apples of my sphere of experience, but also in all the apples of the sensible fields of experience of all the others; it is what we share out of the particularities of our sensory experiences. These items were what led classical epistemology to conceive of the essence as an ideality, something selfsame that transcends, or recurs the same, in any moment and in all places. There would have to be something the same in all of us, an impersonal or interpersonal transcendental ego, to account for the possibility of its being the same for me as for anyone. How is this universal nature of the essence accounted for in Merleau-Ponty's phenomenology?

On the one hand, the essence recurs in all its particular manifestations – in all the visual aspects of the apple, and in all its diverse sensuous aspects – not in the way that a selfsame and identical ingredient recurs in different compounds, nor in the way that a law or principle recurs in each of its instantiations. But in the way that a musical theme is one in all its variations, or in the way that one style is found in all the novels of an author who speaks with his own voice, or in the way that one gait is visible through the various steps over uneven ground. Here there is a kind of universal, or general schema which cannot be grasped separately, which can only be grasped in the differential of the instances in which it is realized, by a kind of oblique sense that senses how the particular might be varied without disintegrating its identity.

But the sensuous element in the apple is a transcendence. It is a *Wesen* in the verbal sense, something like a way of occupying space and time, which, since it is what holds this space and time together, holds itself together, maintains itself, promotes itself across a certain domain and a certain duration. A world-ray, Merleau-Ponty will say, in the notes of *The Visible and the Invisible.* And this red is not only at work here, in this place and moment, on these lips, or in the petals of this rose; it is a node in the field of the visible, a punctuation in the field of color; it has its effect elsewhere, where there are colors it is reinforcing or contrasting with, and all the other reds are having their effect on it, enforcing or thickening it. It is not just that, de facto, there are to be seen elsewhere something that resembles it. It is that the visual field is one fabric, and each of its concretions precipitate the tensions of a certain surroundings, and send their tensions across a certain region. What got started here, now, in this rose or in these lips, is going to have its prolongations and reverberations elsewhere, in other hours of the world.

If it is going to be that way for others too, besides me, others who dwell in different zones of the sensible with different bodies, that must be, to be sure, that the rose or the lips I see are also what they see, that this rose sends its essence onto their eyes as it does on mine. And that it is somehow with one subjectivity that we all comprehend the universal essence of the rose. That is true. But this universal subject is not a transcendental subjectivity beneath the body, or beyond the body, because it would have to be everywhere one and selfsame, as bodies cannot be.

The universal subject, the 'one' that perceives in me as in anyone, is an intercorporeality. Transcendental criticism had reasoned that if the triangle is to be one and the same for all rational cognitive agents, then the agency of rational cognition is itself someone one and undivided, that reason is one and the same in everyone. There is certainly also this kind of argument in Merleau-Ponty. Except that, first, the universal is not really the order of ideal and conceptual rational essences, over and beyond the sensible realm; it is the order of sensuous essences. The universal, the common, is the world itself, the sensible, brute or wild or sensuous being. And the universal subjectivity is not the rational faculty, but the sensitivity, the flesh, which for classical philosophy is exactly the particular and particularizing faculty, the faculty that always grasps but the particulars. But our flesh is not one in its matter, but rather in its stances, its schemas of movement, which organize its sensibility. Thus the universal subject is the flesh as the element in which schemes and diagrams of motility communicate, laterally, varying one another. A scheme of movement is something my body catches on from another body, a posture or stance is something my body picks up from another body is something which from the first is not something I see, look at, or understand, but rather which I feel, in my own postural schema, by my own postural schema, as one of its own possibilities. And it is in this continual contagion of schemas of posture and movement, this sphere where every particular position schematizes itself, maintains itself as the theme of a series of possible variations, that corporeality becomes one, common, that each of us is for himself and for the others a variant on corporeality in general.

Representation

The two fundamental innovations in Merleau-Ponty's analysis of perception – its existential or ecstatic concept of the sensuous, and the idea of a prehension, or motor intentionality, involved in sensing – also seem to tend to make this account one that reduces perception to behavior, to practical adjustment and interaction, and makes that behavior governed from the outside, from the vibratory or radiant moments of sensuous material which elicit that behavior. Merleau-Ponty's phenomenology brings out the motor basis for perception, makes perception but an abstraction from behavior, from praktognosis, makes the essential in sensing the behavioral or motor response. And puts the initiative in the terms outside; the prehension that is elicited is always held by the sensuous element and its movements. It is true that the relationship of the outside and the body is no longer conceived mechanically, or according to a linear causality; it is rather in the essences of the things, their verbal, active, vibratory or radiant ways of affecting, occupying a domain of space and time, that Merleau-Ponty sees their action on us.

But there is still something lacking in all this. In what sense is this an account of perception – that is consciousness and self-consciousness? In what sense is this an account of the representation of the world – the presentation of the world to someone?

Perception, as consciousness of a world, as the original appearing of a world, the world forming an apparition – is not explained by explaining how the world produces a representation of itself, a picture of itself, within us, and by explaining how there is in us a sphere of consciousness in which such a representation could be formed. What has fundamentally to be understood is the occurrence of a presentation, a presence, the event whereby distant and separate beings are nonetheless present to us, affect us where we are by their own natures and characteristics.

The notes to *The Visible and the Invisible* were working more and more with the concept of dimensionality. Points become pivots, lines veer into axes, patterns become schemas, planes veer into depth. What there is is not particulars and frameworks in which they are positioned, but rays – world-rays. Diagrams and patterns of being that prolong themselves in depth, across space and time, forming a differential sequence of variants. Then, when one touches upon such a ray somewhere, one slips into a whole schema, a whole world. Such is the original format of the sensible. All the liquidity, freedom and transparent coolness of the water is present in the ripple with which the wind and the sun make it visible in the pool, but one cannot see these ripples without seeing also the wind and the sun and the tiles at the bottom of the pool, and the setting of green cypresses which situate the pool in this park. Each moment, each relief of such a sensuous being, such a ray of the world, presents a whole world. Not as a portrait represents the original, nor as a mental image might depict the original outside, but as the whole Gestalt is present in the position and functioning of each of its parts, as the whole character of someone is present in the few lines the caricaturist draws on paper, as the whole essence of a love is present in an embrace. This is the fundamental fact, this dimensionality of sensible being, this differentiation which is its veritable way of being, which is the Being of these beings.

This differential, this ordered succession of figures of presence in depth, does not require a mind that would see the different figures of the water or the red, and then synthetically unite them so as to be able to recognize them, and compare them, and see that one is a representation, or a new presentation, of the other. Rather one makes contact with one configuration, and *through* it one is already in touch with its variants and its axis of variation – in the way if one's hand is in the glove, one does not need a new experience, and an outside point of view, to get into the presence of the outside of the glove; it is already given, as the concave is given in and through the convex.

It is then not a subjective power of forming representations that explains how it is that the rays of the world can be present, though distant. They themselves prolong themselves across space and time; to be rays and dimensions of being is their very essence. Being – sensible being – comes in dimensions; for it to be is to differentiate itself, to dimensionalize itself. The subject, our flesh, is but a certain field, a certain visible, tangible, auditory, palpable field in which whatever is visible, tangible, auditory can prolong itself, can make its presence felt, can send something of its schema, its schematic essence.

These schemes and diagrams of visible, tangible, auditory being are actively taken up, taken hold of, prehended, by the motility of our flesh. Our flesh then is something like an element, a sphere of generality, a sensible field, which can capture all the schemes and styles of the visible, palpable, resounding world, because it is itself visible, palpable, sonorous, and because it is motile by itself. Its motility is not just the reaction the presentation of something distant provokes in our body; it is the very way that presentation is taken up, received, realized. The body can be the register or field in which all the schemes and styles of sensible being can be presented because it is itself a sensible being that continually schematizes itself, makes a gait of its movement, a gesture of its displacement, makes of each of its here-now particular configurations or positions into a posture or attitude maintaining itself by varying itself continuously.

But perception is the presentation of something to someone, the apparation of a field of being laid out across the distances to someone; it involves this emergence of a someone, an ipseity, a selfsameness. Where, how, is this pole, this center, to which the distant things are present, formed? One does not perceive something without perceiving oneself – what is the nature of this perception? Merleau-Ponty refused to conceive of the self as an ideality, as an identity pole, maintained the same, given, intuited or posited. There is not an inner circuit where consciousness is immediately and adequately present to itself, in the core of all consciousness of the world.

Rather it is in the act of *moving oneself* that he felt the secret was to be found. In its motility the body moves itself. It is in this moving-oneself that the first ipseity, the first reference to self germinates. The self that is moved is not perceived as something positive: to move oneself is not to first perceive oneself, and then move oneself. Indeed every perceiving of oneself is already a moving of oneself: the first example Merleau-Ponty reflected on was the old Aristotelian case of the body that touches itself, and, in the touching of something tangible identifies itself, identifies this tangible something with the very movement that is touching it. The identification, the synthesis of inside and outside, the closure of the circle, the setting into motion of the circle of referentiality, is realized in that: in a body which by moving itself, that is, by displacing itself, gathers itself together, inscribes the presence of each of its parts in the whole, takes up a posture, is one and someone for itself.

It is strange, Merleau-Ponty wrote, when I try to clear up just what I mean by 'the seer', all I find in the visible – the body, the body the others see, and which I do not see only because for me to perceive it is still to move it, to be the self forming in that motility. It is then with one and the same motility that my flesh captures the movements and diagrams of the remote things, and moves itself, and forms the circle of referentiality which is the self. It is by displacing itself, by differentiating itself, that our flesh captures the differentiations, the world-rays, of the sensible field, and sketches out its own unity and selfness, its own identity. The first unity, the first identity, that by which a self, an identity-pole, is first constituted, is realized in the bending back upon itself of the body that touches itself, sees itself, hears itself. In this folding back or this overlapping, it also touches, sees, hears, the presence of all visible, tangible, resounding things.

Levinas on Memory and the Trace

EDWARD CASEY
State University of New York at Stony Brook

> What is this original trace, this primordial desolation?
>
> Levinas, *En découvrant l'existence avec Husserl et Heidegger*, p. 208

I

Let me start with the following paradox, one that arises from the very idea of trace: what seems at first exceedingly limited in scope and secondary in status is capable of drawing together the most divergent realms of human experience and theories about that experience. On the one hand, the ordinary notion of trace is that of a mere mark left by an entity or an event of which it is but the finite and fragile reflection. Its nature seems to consist in a self-surpassing operation whereby its meaning or value lies *elsewhere* – namely, in that *of which* it is the trace, that which the trace signifies by a self-suspension of its own being or happening. On the other hand, despite this apparent disposability, the concept of trace has proved indispensable in several quite disparate domains: the neurophysiology of memory, the graphematics of writing, and the overcoming of metaphysics. (Indeed, just because the activity of tracing is so critical to all three arenas, we can no longer afford to regard them as so disparate, and we begin to suspect the possibility of a deep alliance between them.) This is not to mention the rather uncanny way in which a concern with the unsuspected importance of traces brings together Heidegger, Derrida, and Levinas with such unlikely bedfellows as Plotinus, Descartes, and Peirce – all six of whom regard traces as strictly unexpungeable and even as having a certain primacy.

Traces primary? How could this be if they are *ex hypothesi* the mere residua of entities or experiences held to be more fundamental or more pure? For example, *sensation* (though it is more than one example among others, being exemplary of them all). Sensing has often been assumed, after Aristotle, to be the unique ontogenetic source of experiential contents, whether these be sensible forms, intuitive givens such as space, time, and Firstness, or richly laden *Gestalten*. Just because sensation has been viewed as so openly receptive of these contents – *and* because its manifestations are so constantly changing (constantly changing precisely because so rich: intolerable if held steadily the

J.C. Sallis, G. Moneta and J. Taminiaux (eds.), The Collegium Phaenomenologicum, 241–255.
© *Kluwer Academic Publishers.*

same) – some form of fixation and preservation is called for. This demand is clearest in the case of *memory*, whose very function is normally considered to be one of recording or registration – that is to say, fixation in memory traces that can be stored and retrieved with maximum ease. In the words of Descartes:

> How we find in the memory the things which we desire to remember. Thus when the soil desires to recollect something, this desire causes the gland, by inclining successively to different sides, to thrust the spirits towards different parts of the brain until they come across that part where the traces left there by the object which we wish to recollect are found; for these traces are none other than the fact that the pores of the brain, by which the spirits have formerly followed their course because of the presence of this object, have by that means acquired a greater facility than the others in being once more opened by the animal spirits which come towards them in the same way. Thus these spirits, in coming in contact with these pores, enter into them more easily than into the others, by which means they excite a special movement in the gland which represents the same object to the soul, and causes it to know that it is this which it desired to remember.[1]

In his celebrated article 'In Search of the Engram,' Karl Lashley remarked on how very modern this Cartesian conception is. The idea of facilitation via traces survives not only in Freud's 'Project for a Scientific Psychology' (1895) but also in contemporary pursuits of the elusive engram, an entity never entirely abandoned even if decried as difficult to specify in detail: is the engram a neurone, a group of neurones, a reticular network, a hemispheric epiphenomenon, a hologram? However conceived, it keeps on making a ceremonious reappearance in neurophysiological treatments of memory.[2]

The mention of 'en-gram' already points to another area where trace has figured so powerfully and in an exactly analogous way: namely, *writing*. Just as effervescent sensations and errant memories require tethering to traces, so slippery speech demands *grammata* or written letters to tie down its wayward course. Like the statutes of Daedulus, spoken words in particular call for the quasi-permanence of written language. As Plato would put it, the 'sparks' of living discourse need the supplement of writing. Even if writing is berated in the *Phaedrus* as *hypomnemic* in status – a crutch or *aide-mémoire* – it is notable that Plato's own dialogues were *written out* (and this not for esorteric purposes alone). From here it is but a short step to Derrida's effort in the *Grammatology* and elsewhere to show that the supplementary is in fact a *sine qua non*: precisely parallel to Freud's point that it is the memory of the trauma, and not the trauma itself, that is pathogenic. In both instances, the traces exceed their own origins, whether in living speech (*parole*) or lived experience (*Erlebnis*).

If these were not merely introductory remarks, it could also be shown how the concept of trace in Heidegger's notion of metaphysical epochs begins by being indispensable (each epoch must have and leave its mark) and ends by assuming a certain primacy – as is seen most strikingly in Heidegger's retrieval of the pre-Socratics, whose work consists wholly in fragmentary written traces. What might seem a mere physical requirement – to produce visible/readable adumbrations of a thought that has its own independence and integrity – exhibits its own fundamentality. (I say 'a *certain* primacy' and '*its own* fundamentality' in order to avoid falling back into the very metaphysics of origin which Heidegger and Derrida have deconstructed so effectively.) More than stubborn persistence – itself striking enough – we witness here, as in the equally salient cases of Plato and Freud, a reversal of priorities. Traces as fixation-points in/of memory, language, and history (and not just the history of metaphysics but doubtless other forms of history as well) are more than depository and repository in function, or defensive in strategy, or conservative in value. They must, therefore, be more, or other, than the clues or reminders to which they are so often reduced by other thinkers, most notably Descartes. They have a status, function, and value of their own that exceeds their materiality just as it surpasses their facilitating effect. In what can this unsuspected strength consist?

II

It is just here that Emmanuel Levinas comes straightforwardly to our aid – or as straightforwardly as this perpetually enigmatical philosopher ever will! Traces, ultimately understood, will prove as enigmatic as Levinas' own writing; they will not be assimilable to any discrete 'phenomenon,' where this last word implies manifestation, disclosure, clarity – not to mention context, horizon, and perspective. Indeed, it is in an essay entitled 'Enigma and Phenomenon' (first published in 1965) that Levinas underscores the elusive the importance of traces. About enigma itself Levinas says that it is

> this way for the Other (*Autre*) to call for my recognition while preserving its *incognito* ... this way of manifesting itself without manifesting itself [as phenomenon] ... The enigma is not a simple equivocation wherein two meanings [significations] have equal opportunities and the same light. In the enigma, the exorbitant meaning [*sens*] has already effaced itself in its apparition.[3]

With this statement we are on the trail of the trace as non-phenomenal: that is, as non-present (i.e., as *not* the empirical sign of an absence) yet not as fading presence either (i.e., as an evanescent sign) or even as sheer absence. We have to do, rather, with a form of absence that has inscribed itself in material presence in such a subtle manner as already to have eluded its own presentation. And this is just the enigma in question:

> the disturbance [effected by traces] is a movement that proposes no stable order in conflict with a given order, but a movement that already carries away the meaning [*signification*] which it brings with it: the disturbance disturbs the [phenomenal] order without troubling it deeply. It enters into it in a fashion so subtle that it has already withdrawn from it . . . It insinuates itself – retires from it before entering it (ED, 208).

Here, I may remark in passing, we begin to see the trace of Levinas on Derrida – a trace that, true to form, has also been withdrawn in advance (I refer, of course, to Derrida's essay 'Violence and Metaphysics,' the text in which this very enigma is enacted.) But in the above citation we can also begin to glimpse how the trace can possibly enjoy a certain priority over that of which it is a trace. It does so by escaping the phenomenal presence to which its own origin remains bound. Or, more exactly, the trace escapes the binary metaphysical choice between being either sheer presence or an equally sheer absence – while not being their compromised compound either.[4] Yet this is possible only if we also do not take the trace as pointing to an absence or presence outside itself:

> The opening of the empty [that is effected by the trace] is not only the sign of an absence. The figure traced on sand is not the element of a path but the very emptiness of the past. And that which has withdrawn is not evoked, does not return to presence – not even to an indicated presence (ED, 208).

I have cited at some length from 'Enigme et phénomène' because it is indissociable from the still more important essay of 1963, 'La trace de l'autre.' And it does so precisely by calling into question 'indication' and 'presence' – and above all the *phenomenon* of 'indicated presence' – as an adequate model for understanding the trace in its enigmatic, non-phenomenal form.

III

I shall not, however, follow 'On the Trail of the Other' in any consecutive fashion – nor confine myself to it alone. Instead, I shall bear down on the respective roles of memory and trace: 'respective' because the two terms are never brought together expressly by Levinas, despite their considerable affinity for each other via the bridging notion of 'indicated [past] presence.' In fact, the two terms suffer very disparate fates – memory being subject to critique and severe limitation, trace to critique followed by an equally extreme expansion.

Let us begin with memory. For Levinas the positivity of memory resides in its very negativity. As is made abundantly clear in *Totality and Infinity*, memory is critical for 'psychism' and thus for 'separation.' Memory is the very pro-duction of interiority by the hollowing out of the past – an interiority which, in the form of 'recollection,' is basic to dwelling and possession, economy and labor:

> Memory recaptures and reverses and suspends what is already accomplished in birth – in nature. By memory I ground myself [qua separated psychism] after the event, retroactively ... Memory realizes impossibility: memory, after the event, assumes the passivity of the past and masters it. Memory as an inversion of historical time is the essence of interiority.[5]

The ambivalence in this passage cannot be gainsaid: to 'realize impossibility' by mastering 'the passivity of the past,' to 'invert' historical time, to 'suspend' what is 'already accomplished': these sound like Pyrrhic victories, however essential they may be in the creation and fortification of what Sartre might call 'the circuit of selfness' and what Levinas calls simply 'egoism' or the Same. If it is true (as is stated at the beginning of 'The Trace of the Other') that 'I am myself, not because of such and such a trait of character ... [but] because I am *already* the same – me myself, a selfness,'[6] this being always-already-the-same-self is the dubious work of memory, which achieves self-enclosed egoism as 'the tautology of selfness' (TO, 34).

The memorial work is dubious on three counts, each of which serves to delimit and to indict the voracious narcissism of psychism itself:

a) Memory is mainly a matter of *control* in the interest of constructing a well-protected refuge where thought can be free to reverse the course of time:

> The world which confronts thought cannot do anything against [a] free thought capable of interior refusal, of remaining free in the face of truth and of existing first of all as the origin of what it receives, of *controlling with memory what preceded it* (TO, 41. My italics).

Here memory is reduced to a defensive strategy of defiant control, even at the price of contravening historical truth (i.e., confabulating where it suits it).

b) Memory thus manipulates the past not so as to respect or explore it more deeply but primarily for the sake of a *future* in which the world will be more coherently the province of the psychism:

> memory replaces the past itself into this future, where the search and the historic interpretation will be risked. The traces of the irreversible past are taken for signs which assure the discovery and unity of a world (TO, 35).

Here memory and traces are allied – though still not as memory traces! – in a common project of future-oriented knowledge of the world, with all that this implies of the thematized and the phenomenal.

c) Most seriously, memory brings with it a *nostalgia* that locks it into a circuit of return to the same. Levinas opposes the fatherlandless Abraham to Ulysses returning to Ithaca ('*Nostoi*' was the name for the larger epical cycle of which the Odyssey formed a leading part). Moreover, any such nostalgia is a matter of need; or more exactly, all need is essentially nostalgic:

> [need] coincides with the consciousness of what has been lost; it is essentially a nostalgia, a longing for return. (TI, 33: desire, in contrast, 'does not long to return, for it is a desire for a land not of our birth' (TI, 33–41)

The nostalgic needful nature of memory helps to explain its deep penchant for recapture and reproduction – for re-presentation of the past. It might seem to undercut the controlling and future-oriented aspects of memory; but in fact it contributes to the same end as they: the maintaining and strengthening of the psychism as the domain of the Same.

What is most problematic is Levinas' seemingly willful restriction of memory to 'recollection' understood in the threefold sense just discussed. A lacuna is left which only the notion of trace will come to fill like a scar gowing uneasily over an open wound. The lacuna to which I refer concerns the 'absolute past' (TI, 130) that is introduced by the Other. In contrast with the thematized, phenomenal past – 'the historical, the *fact*, the *already [having] happened*' (TI, 65; my italics), which is forever disappearing behind its own manifestations – the 'passé absolument révolu' (TO, 43; 'over and done with') cannot be recaptured in any representational format. *This* past, the past 'given' in and by the Other who is present in his or her manifestations, is not even subject to the action of the *après coup*. The after-the event efficacy of recollection which Freud termed *Nachträglichkeit*. The 'posteriority of the anterior,' whereby 'the *After* or the *Effect* conditions the *Before* or the *Cause*' (TI, 54; cf. also 170), still remains within the self-generating sovereignity of interiority. This means that, like the anticipated future, the retro-dicted past can be condensed in an image – unlike the absolute past or the future of an 'absolutely patient action' (TO, 38). Neither the absolute past nor the liturgical future can be represented in an image; in this regard they rejoin retentions and protentions, which cannot be imaged either. (And for the same reason: *proximity* so great or so subtle as to resist representation of any kind, even though the proximity of the Other is by no means the propinquity of primary memory or anticipation.)

The difficulty to which I am pointing is found in the fact that Levinas disallows any memory whatsoever, whether primary or secondary, retentional or recollective, imagistic or non-imagistic, of the absolute past. This might seem to follow logically enough from the very epithets by which he attempts to circumscribe such a past: 'a past that was never a present,'[7] 'a past that was before the past' (TI, 170), 'the deep past, never past enough' (Valéry's phrase cited at TI, 170; TO, 43), and especially 'immemorial past' (TO, 43). Don't all of these imply precisely that there can be no memory at all, *of any kind*, of such a past, which becomes thereby unrecuperable by *any* memorial power? It is tempting indeed to become persuaded of this; but consider only three dissenting instances that come to mind:

Plato: he allows anamnesis (or better *mnēmē*) of forms experienced by the soul before its present personal life;

Eliade: he conceives myths and rites to be a commemoration (hence a form of memory) of origins in *illo tempore*, another prepersonal past (neither Plato nor Eliade would require explicit representations of any such past);

Freud: he came increasingly to see that 'screen memories' screened a past that *never was*, yet one that still, even as fiction, exerts itself in the pathological present; Freud also remarks that we can forget that of which we were never conscious, not because it was fictitious, but because it gave rise to an unconscious memory trace.

Consider further that we must be able in principle to remember those experiences in which the absolute past of 'exteriority' presented itself in the Other. This memory cannot be recollective in any usual sense since the face that is the vehicle of such a past is said to be 'stripped of its own image' (TO, 40); the face is not a thematized content that could be re-presented in any memory image. But surely there has to be at least the possibility of remembering faces as themselves purveyors of an absolute past. What kind of memory is this? Why is there no name for it in Levinas' writings?

IV

Once again it is a question of a supplement: the place of the unnamed and unspecified memory is *taken by the trace* – the trace of the Other. Indeed, even this place is a non-place: place as site or clearing (*le site éclairé*) is supplanted and replaced by *'le Non-Lieu de la trace'*[8] wherein a non-measurable proximity, an epiphany of the face, is realized. What kind of a trace, realized in such a non-place, is this?

As so often in coming to understand Levinas, we must here undertake a *via negativa* in interpreting him. The trace in question, the trace that stands in for the missing *memoria*, is *not* a material imprint discovered in the world. For any such imprint is a mere *effect* of a causal process itself belonging to the phenomenal realm. Much as Kant identifies causality with objective succession in the Second Analogy, so Levinas remarks:

> Cause and effect, even reported by time [i.e., as required by objective succession], pertain to the same world. Everything in things is exposed, including what in them is unknown: the traces which mark them are all part of this fullness of the present; their history is without a past (TO, 46).

More precisely, effects in the phenomenal world can be *taken* as traces; but if they are, they do not necessarily designate a particular past. For this latter to happen the effects qua traces must be further construed as signs – that is, as signifiers in relation to the past as signified. The relation is really one of cor-relation, of 'rectitude' (*droiture*) in which the two terms, signifier and signified, are regarded as somehow compresent in the sign, as modes of manifestation within the semiotic horizon of disclosure.

Such a sign relation Levinas sometimes terms 'symbolic' (TO, 42); but usually he calls it 'indicative' (TO, 43; ED, 207–8, 234). All he says about it is that it is the point of 'insertion of space into time' – 'the point where the world inclines toward a past and a time' (TO, 45). We could equally well characterize it in Husserlian terms as a situation where one actually known reality (*Bestand*) motivates us to believe in the presumptive existence of an indicated reality – in this case, the past as historical fact. Husserl's own examples of indicative signs include 'signs to aid memory, such as the much-used knot in a handkerchief, memorials, etc.'[9] To this we can add, as in a continuing series, Levinas' own instances of the detective utilizing clues, the hunters talking game, and the historian investigating ancient civilizations. (Cf. TO, 44.) In every instance, 'all is arranged in an order [i.e., an order of actual or presumptive existence], in a world where each thing reveals the other or reveals itself in its own functioning' (*ibid.*). But therein lies the problem: for the order is strictly phenomenal – a particular modality of being in which everything figures as a 'this' or a 'that' concatenated into the contents of propositions: 'states of affairs' as Husserl would say. Here all is a matter of manifestation or dissimulation in 'a plastic and mute form' (TO, 40). Even signifier and signified are plastic and mute in the case of indicative signs: 'the sign and its relation to the signified are already thematized' (EW, 234).

If I have emphasized the indicative status of empirical traces – which can only signify a determinate past of closed fact – it is not only in order to grasp what the non-empirical trace of the Other is *not* like but also to help us understand better why Levinas is so severe in his treatment of recollective memory. Such memory is intimately allied with indicative sign-consciousness, for both attempt to recapture, to make things come back; each is a paradigm of re-presentation; and each therefore fails to attain the absolute past. As Levinas puts it in 'Enigma and Phenomenon':

> [Indicative signs] re-establish between indicating and indicated terms a conjunction, a simultaneity, and [thereby] abolish depth. A relation that would not create simultaneity between its terms, but would hollow out depth on the basis of which expression [could] approach, must make reference to an irreversible past, immemorial and irrepresentable. But how are we to refer to an irreversible past, that is, to a past which this reference itself would not make come back – in contrast with memory, which brings back

the past, and with the sign, which recaptures [*ratrappe*] the signified? (ED, 207).

V

How indeed? How are we to make reference to the absolute past without the referring vehicle being any kind of sign or symbol, much less an effect, of the referent? If such a vehicle cannot be representational in an indicative manner, then it cannot be a form of communication or manifestation either – given Husserl's reduction of communication to indication. Nor can it be iconic in Peirce's sense of an isomorphic representation of the same by the similar; by extension, it cannot be a matter of repetition: thus the mimetic thread that binds together *mnēmē* and *hypomnēsis* in Derrida's reading of the *Phaedrus* is not pertinent here.[10] Nor can it be any combination of the iconic with the indicative (e.g., as in footprints or fingerprints, which represent in both ways at once); or in the triple combination of index, icon, and symbol that we find in petroglyphs, ideograms, or hieroglyphs. The very idea of a referring *vehicle* is in question if 'vehicle' means a material bearer in the manner of Scheler's *Träger* of values.

We know the nominal answer: the reference is made by the trace. Not by the empirical trace that we have just discussed and dismissed but by what Levinas calls the 'authentic' or 'original' trace.[11] What then is this strange entity or non-entity that escapes all ordinary causal and representational formats – and yet that is an essential supplement of the memory of the absolute past?

To make matters worse, Levinas himself regards this pure trace as itself an 'enigma' in his strict sense of what cannot be made intelligible: 'such is the trace by its emptiness and its desolation.'[12] The enigmatic emptiness of this trace of traces – this 'super-imprinting' (TO, 44) – is propounded in at least two paradoxes:

the tracing of the traces is accompanied by its simultaneous effacing – its own retreat;[13]

this trace 'disturbs the order of things in an irreparable fashion' (TO, 37), yet this *dérangement* of the world order is not even noticed by us: 'l'insolite se comprehend'.[14]

Now both of these paradoxes exemplify the very nature of enigma: 'to manifest over all without manifesting oneself.'[15] How can this be? Can we understand the 'action' of the *archi-trace* – Derrida's locution is here practically irresistible – without making use of Levinas' own earlier explanatory terms such as 'expression' or 'revelation' (these were doubtless the names for the proto-trace in *Totality and Infinity*)? We might start with Kant's Third Analogy, that which treats community or reciprocity. Recall the celebrated lead ball placed on a pillow, and ask yourself if this situation is one of authentic tracing. Here there is neither causality of succession nor indication: instead, there is an immediacy of tracing since we cannot meaningfully distinguish between the moment at which the ball is placed on the pillow and the moment at which its imprint (i.e., the indentation) is made. Similarly in the notion of 'the trace of the Other,' the trace does not exist at a different time from the Other: the subjective genitive 'of' in 'the trace of the Other' precludes this.

Nevertheless, we cannot say that this trace exists *at the same time* as the Other. The simultaneity entailed by Kantian reciprocity is possible only in a phenomenal order in which two items co-exist in the same illuminated temporal field. It is the very exclusion of such synchrony that leads Levinas to the notion of diachrony. The trace of the Other is neither compresent with it nor posterior to it in an objective succession. It is a matter of what Levinas calls in *Otherwise than Being* 'the strange temporal itch, a modification without change [which as alteration requires succession]'[16] – in short, a diastasis, a *déphasage* or getting out of phase with itself. This diachronous dispersion begins with the now of the present – no longer conceivable as pure 'primal impression' – and extends to the past of retention or recollection: a past no longer recuperable. But if so, haven't we rejoined, as if tunneling from another side of the mountain of Otherness, something like an absolute past that was never a (pure) present? If the trace of the Other is related to this past diachronously, then it is always out of phase with regard to it, a phasing out so complete that there was never an unphased now-point. (Notice how we also rejoin, across another otherness, Derrida's deconstruction of pure punctuality in *Speech and Phenomena*.)[17]

But I say '*something like* an absolute past' because this past presumably never had (or was) a present of any kind, not even an impure phased-out one. The latter belongs to subjectivity, whereas the trace is precisely the trace *of the Other*. Its originality answers to the originarity of the *Urimpression* – an originarity which is not removed by its (auto-)deconstruction. Precisely as such, it too remains other: other *of* the Other. And it is such an other just because of its refusal to become present, to become complicitous with *a* present. This is what Levinas means by its power to disrupt temporal order – or more exactly, to inter-rupt it: to insert itself *between* present moments without itself ever becoming such a moment itself:

> What is this original trace, this primordial desolation? The nudity of the face facing us, expressing itself: it interrupts order. But if this interruption is not taken up (*reprise*) by the interrupted context so as to receive a meaning (*sens*) from it, this is because from now on and already, it has been ab-solute: the immersion [*la partie*] was abandoned before commencing, the dis-engagement took place before the engagement ... (*ED*, 208).

In other words, the engagement (with the Other) cannot become a present – not because it has not inserted itself *long enough* to become one (for that would imply that it is itself a synchronous slate of time) but because it has entered into the time of the same in a 'strange' way that does not make present – cannot become present. And in this presentlessness it can be only a past, a past that is ab-solute precisely by its refusal to dissolve into any present: such is its emptiness and desolation, deprived of the plentitude (even as dephased) that only presence in the present can give.

This does *not* mean, however, that the trace of the Other is the trace of an absence;[18] it is the trace of an Other who is perfectly present – present in an irreversible past. This Other is the *Il*, the He: 'the trace is the presence of whomever, strictly speaking, has never been there; of someone who is always past' (TO, 45). The face itself is 'the trace of He-ness (*illéité*)' (*ibid.*, 46), and *it* is certainly a form of presence. More critically, the trace itself is presence, but a presence that is neither material, nor semiotic, nor synchronic. Its presence is that of passage, *la passe*.

VI

We must now come to terms at last with the structure and significance of the original trace in four concluding remarks and two remaining questions.

1. As we have just seen, the working of such a trace is that of *passage*: 'it is the passage itself toward a past which is farther removed than any past and from any future, a passage which is still taking place in my time. It is the passage toward the past of the Other . . .' (TO, 46). This may sound like explaining the obscure by the still more obscure, but it is, in fact, a quite specific movement that it is in question. '*La passe*,' in contrast with any mere mark or sign, is the very tracing of the trace, the massive non-phenomenal fact of such tracing (Heidegger might call it '*das Dass*,' the sheer that-it-is of the tracing). It finds its most exemplary case, paradoxically, in the effort to cover up one's traces in accomplishing the 'perfect crime': it is a matter of the 'sur-impression,' the 'imprint' (*empreinte*) one leaves in the very attempt to efface one's empirical traces (Cf. TO, 44). Here one has 'passed by absolutely' (*ibid.*), leaving as trace only the sheer passing itself. So, too, in the case of writing: the sheer writtenness of a text signifies that its author has passed by its perceived surface, which is in no way to be reduced to an indication of the author's intentions or his subliminal significations. In this respect, every written sign is an original trace, though not every such trace need occur as this kind of sign.

2. One may suppose that the sheer passage of the Trace[19] answers to the

empty desolation that characterizes it as non-empirical: each is the obverse of the other. We can understand this two-sidedness of the Trace in two ways:

a) *temporally*: the diachrony of pure passage – its active dehiscence – takes the place of the inactive synchrony of Tracing. For *la passe* can be said to be the very emblem of diachronous movement, the sur-impression which any such movement leaves in its wake. We could also speculate that this sur-impression is the supplement for the problematized *Ur-impression* of Husserl.

b) *spatially*: the Trace is 'the insertion of space into time' (TO, 45) not in the Bergsonian sense of a degraded *durée* but as a 'profile' (*ibid.*, 46) that belongs to no-place. Having no site of its own (which would be the equivalent of a synchronous present), it is located in a Non-Site (*Non-Lieu*) that is as diastatic as is diachrony itself.

3. Construed as pure passing by, the Trace cannot be considered as any kind of 'simple presence' indicating or signifying an equally simple absence (i.e., non-entity). In simple presence phenomena are co-present in a world. (Cf. TO, 46.) But does this mean that the terms 'presence' and 'absence' have no application here? Certainly not. This becomes clear in passages from 'The Trace of the Other':

> 'the supreme presence of the face is inseparable from supreme and irreversible absence' (44) 'the absolute of the presence of the Other' (46)

We are reminded of how for Heidegger *Anwesenden*, simple presences, are inconceivable apart from *Anwesen*, Presence – and how the 'early trace' (*die frühe Spur*) of their very difference is what has been forgotten.[20] Derrida, commenting on Heidegger, points to the essentially self-effacing character of any such trace. But from this he draws a very different conclusion than does Levinas:

> The trace is not a presence but is rather the simulacrum of a presence that dislocates, displaces, and refers beyond itself.

But where self-effacement means the direct deconstruction of presence for Derrida, for Levinas it has the more subtle sense of diachronous retreat or withdrawal – which can leave presence, indeed even being, intact. For the Trace is said to be the 'weight,' the 'indelibility' of being itself (TO, 45). Moreover, the Trace that at once differentiates and conjoins presence, absence, and being is not utterly extinguished or forgotten – as could occur with a trace situated in the *history* of being. It is itself powerfully present in *la passe*, whether the passage occurs in the expression of a face or in the style of one's writing.

4. If Presence must be retained to sustain the force of pure passage, Absence has to be kept to account for the absolute past that was never a present: 'in the

trace there has passed a past which is absolutely complete (*révolu*). Within the trace the irreversible revolution is sealed' (TO, 45). The fact that this past is *révolu* – fulfilled, finished – shows that we do not have to do with simple absence, lack of fulfillment on the model of an empty intention or unfulfilled promise. It is a matter of what we could call 'hard absence,' the absense of a sheer pastness that answers to the soft presence of sheer passage ('soft' because diachronously distending).

We are left with two residual difficulties:

a) Despite the difference between presence and absence that has just been affirmed – and despite the fact that Levinas needs to keep the Trace less than entirely effaced – he *also* continues to exalt 'the marvel of the infinite *in* the finite' (TO, 42). The marvel occurs not on the model of immanence – i.e., recapture in the interiority of memory or signs – but so as to preserve transcendence itself: 'transcendence is maintained as transcendence always completed in the transcendent' (TO, 43). The Trace brings Presence and Absence together in a third way as well: neither as illumination nor as dissimulation but as Presence-of-Absence-in-Passage. Presence and Absence *come to pass*, and they do so as always already having done so. But how does such coming to pass rejoin these metaphysical ultimates in a way that is genuinely beyond Being, while retaining Being's gravity – as well as its indelibility?

b) Closely related is the problematic position of the '*Il*' in all this. I say 'position,' for He-ness *is* 'position in the trace' (TO, 46). Position, a spatial term, is another way of saying non-immanence; it means taking up a stand in the trace. The 'in' is critical – as is suggested by the fact that the phrase 'in the trace' is used no less than five times on the last page of 'The Trace of the Other.' What is going on here? Perhaps the following. Where the face can be said to be the trace *of* the Other, that is, the more or less direct emblem or expression of the Other, the face is in turn *in* the trace of the He:

> The face is by itself visitation and transcendence. But the face, completely open, can at the same time be in itself because it is in the trace of He-ness (*illéité*). (TO, 46)

Could it be that while any human activity (from holding stones to writing) is always a trace of the Other, of transcendence, by virtue of bearing the imprint of pure passage – signifying that 'someone has already passed' (*ibid.*) – the face is a privileged place (i.e., non-place) of passage because it is itself not only a trace of the Other but is *in* the trace of the He? In other words, its tracing as pure passing finds itself already positioned in another tracing. This tracing traces the passing not of just any other but of the He: tracing and passing each being raised to the second power. (In fact, tracing is raised to the third power if we include empirical tracing!) Also, this would mean that others are themselves caught up in this ultimate Trace, which is also the trace of 'God.'

Such seems to be the purport of the enigmatic last paragraph of 'The Trace of the Other':

> The God who has passed is not the model of which the countenance will be the image. Being in the image of God does not signify being the icon of God, but to find oneself in His trace . . . He does not show Himself except in His trace, as in the thirty-third chapter of *Exodus*. To go toward Him is not to follow the trace which is not a sign. To go toward Him is to go toward the Others who are in the trace (TO, 46).

Let me only remark in closing that this paragraph's placement at the end of the essay is itself tracelike in the very sense now being wondered over. Itself a trace of Levinas' passage as a writer with a face, it is in the position of being, precisely as such as passage, a trace of the He who is in the final position. Or we could say, equivalently, that the absolute past adumbrated by the trace of the Other itself gestures toward an eternity that not only 'gathers together all times' (TO, 46) but ab-solves them all, too, thereby bringing to term the place of traces in the Other – in Him of whom we have no memory but from whom we retain a trace . . . *nothing but* a Trace.

Notes

1. René Descartes, *Passions of the Soul*, Article XLII.
2. See, for example, *The Pathology of Memory*, ed. G.A. Talland and N.C. Waugh (New York: Academic Press, 1969), *passim*; and Paul Rozin, 'The Psychobiological Approach to Human Memory' in *Neural Mechanisms of Learning and Memory,* ed. M.R. Rosenzweig and E.L. Bennett (Cambridge: MIT Press, 1976), pp. 3–46.
3. Emmanuel Levinas, *En découvrant l'existence avec Husserl et Heidegger* (Paris: Vrin, 1949), p. 209. (Hereafter 'ED.')
4. Originally, however, Levinas comes dangerously close to such a compromise: 'une absence qui est la présence même de l'infini' (ED, 231).
5. Levinas, *Totality and Infinity*, trans. A. Lingis (Pittsburgh: Duquesne University Press, 1969), p. 56. Cf. also pp. 53–4, 56, 127, 170 (Hereafter 'TI.')
6. Levinas, 'La trace de l'autre,' *Tijdschrift voor Filosofie* vol. 25 (1963), p. 605. (Hereafter 'TO.' I shall follow the pagination and, for the most part, the translation by D.J. Hoy: 'On the Trail of the Other,' *Philosophy Today,* vol. 10 [1966], pp. 34–47. The above citation is from p. 34 of this translation.)
7. Levinas, *Otherwise than Being or Beyond Essence*, trans. A. Lingis (The Hague: Nijhoff, 1981), p. 24.
8. ED, 231.
9. Edmund Husserl, *Logical Investigations*, Inv. I, section 2, trans. by J.N. Findlay (Atlantic Highlands: Humanities Press, 1970), I: 270.
10. See Jacques Derrida, 'Plato's Pharmacy' in *Dissemination,* trans. B. Johnson (Chicago: University of Chicago Press, 1981), pp. 111–12.
11. 'Authentic trace' is mentioned at TO, 44; 'original trace' at ED, 207.
12. ED, 207. The designation of the trace as an enigma occurs at *ibid.,* p. 211.
13. 'It withdraws as easily as it inserts itself' (*ibid.*, 208).
14. *Ibid.,* p. 206.

15. *Ibid.*, p. 209.
16. *Otherwise than Being or Beyond Essence*, p. 35. Cf. the entire discussion at *ibid.*, pp. 31–4.
17. See Derrida, *Speech and Phenomena,* trans. D. Allison (Evanston: Northwestern University Press, 1973), pp. 60–70.
18. Nevertheless, Levinas does say that 'the face is in the trace of the Absent' (TO, 43) and that 'the Other proceeds from the absolutely Absent' (*ibid.*).
19. Hereafter I will capitalize 'trace' when I refer to Levinas' notion of 'original trace.'
20. See Derrida, 'Différance,' in *Speech and Phenomena*, pp. 156ff.
21. Ibid., p. 156. Derrida does say, however, that 'the trace has, properly speaking, *no place*, for effacement belongs to the very structure of the trace' (*ibid.*; my italics).

The Silent Anarchic World of the Evil Genius

ROBERT BERNASCONI
Memphis State University

I

Husserl and Heidegger are, more than any others, the thinkers with whom Levinas is in constant dialogue. From the late 1920's when he attended their lectures in Freiburg, through the 1930's when he more than anyone else was responsible for introducing their thinking into France, until the present day when it seems as if it is still virtually impossible for him to write a philosophical essay without referring to one or other of them, Husserl and Heidegger provide Levinas with his starting-point. But it is a starting-point with which he never remains content so that it is invoked only as a basis for saying more. The relation with the Other is presented always as 'beyond intentionality' or 'otherwise than being.' When it comes to the task of giving a more positive account, Levinas' favourite recourse is to turn to Descartes. It was above all Descartes who gave Levinas his own voice with which to show what Husserl and Heidegger and indeed, if we are believe to him, the whole tradition of Western ontology from Parmenides on failed to recognise and preserve.[1] This is already clear from the very title of *Totality and Infinity*. Rosenzweig may have provided the critique of totality, a critique to which Husserl and Heidegger were assimilated, but it was from Descartes that Levinas borrowed the word by which he sought to think and say transcendence and thus rupture this totality.

The role which Descartes plays in Levinas' thinking is all the more striking when one bears in mind the place Descartes occupied in the thinking of Husserl and Heidegger. Descartes had inspired and also guided Husserl in his quest for a rigorous science of philosophy, and one suspects that it is partly as a consequence of Descartes' importance for Husserl that Heidegger is so severe on Descartes. This is not only the case in *Being and Time* where Descartes is castigated for evading ontological questions, but it is striking that even later Descartes is asked to play a more prominent part in the transformations of truth which is the *story* of the growing oblivion of Being than in the saying of

J.C. Sallis, G. Moneta and J. Taminiaux (eds.), The Collegium Phaenomenologicum, 257–272.
© *Kluwer Academic Publishers.*

the *destiny* of Being. Thus Levinas finds himself in marked disagreement with both Husserl and Heidegger on the question of the interpretation and assessment of Descartes' *Meditationes de Prima Philosophia in qua Dei existentia et Animae immortalitas demonstratur*. But how could such a text which plays such a central role in the history of Western ontology be thought to offer the resources with which that history might be disrupted?

The force of this question might lead a reader of *Totality and Infinity* to regard Levinas' reference of the word *infinite* to Descartes as of only incidental interest. Is it not the case that it is only possible to sustain the interpretation of Descartes which lies behind this reference so long as many details of Descartes' text are ignored? Do we not do better under these circumstances to disregard Descartes and concentrate on whatever it is that Levinas is attempting to say with this word? Is it not, as it were, a question only of 'influence' which is of little or no philosophical interest? The word *infinite* is surely in this context to be thought of as Levinas' word so that the issue of its source is at most of only marginal concern. Or is there something essential about the fact that it is with Descartes' word that Levinas finds his voice?

For Levinas the task of 'thinking transcendence' represents a contradiction or rather an impossibility for thought. The importance of Descartes from this perspective is that he engages this issue. Descartes' proof of the existence of God in the Third Meditation takes as its basis the fact that I as a finite being cannot think the infinite. And yet I have the idea of the infinite, an idea which Descartes will say is more certain than that of the *cogito* and so therefore, we must assume clearer and more distinct. It is because the idea of the infinite is one that I as a finite being cannot have produced of my own accord, that I cannot entertain on my own account, one that Descartes is led to conclude that it must have been put in me by an infinite being. It is because it is an idea I cannot think that it must be thought in me by a God who must therefore exist.

Levinas is not concerned with this line of thought as a proof for the existence of God, so he immediately disregards Descartes' explicit intentions. To ask for a proof of God's existence is, so far as Levinas is concerned, irreligious to the point of blasphemy in much the same way as to set about justifying or providing a foundation for ethics is already to have subordinated ethics to ontology to the point of immorality (AQ 150/117). What does engage him is the attempt to stay with the infinite as an excess or surplus, a thought which is not a thought, a thought which I cannot think but which is rather thought in me, so accomplishing a reversal or overturning of intentionality. The idea of the infinite is unthinkable to the point where it has to be said of this thought that 'it is not a thought' (TI 186/211).

Levinas, in offering his account of Descartes' Third Meditation, remains silent about such terms as 'objective reality' and 'formal reality' as if he was attempting to divorce the 'infinite' from the ontological presuppositions which govern its appearance in Descartes' text.[2] And yet it is readily apparent that any attempt to paraphrase Descartes' proof without recourse to them is lame, depriving the original at once of its rigour. Furthermore, that Descartes conceives of God onto-theo-logically is not something which can readily be subtracted from Descartes' text. The *similitudo* between man and God which Descartes explicitly evokes in his text is translated into a continuum of increasing degrees of reality which connects man and God (AT VII 51/HR i 170). To this extent, the Cartesian God is not transcendent in the sense of being radically Other. Precisely the rupture with being that Levinas finds announced in Plato's phrase 'the good beyond being' seems to be lacking in Descartes' Third Meditation which is essentially conceived in terms of Being. Levinas therefore breaks not only with Descartes' intention to prove the existence of God, but also with the whole conceptual apparatus in which that attempt is couched. Levinas transforms the meaning of the Cartesian text when he conceives the height and superiority of God not ontologically but ethically. Levinas is no Cartesian and does not share Descartes' assumptions. But this simply renders more pressing the question of whether Levinas' appeal to Descartes' word 'infinite' is anything but an extrinsic misuse of Descartes' text.

Levinas' reading of Descartes is, for the most part, not concerned with textual details. And yet there is one specific paragraph of the Third Meditation that Levinas constantly quotes and directs his readers to. That is the closing paragraph of the Third Meditation which does not take the form of an ontological affirmation. Here at least, if not in the preceding discussion, Descartes is led to a relation with the infinite which 'overflows thought and becomes a personal relation' (TI 187/211).

> . . . it seems to me right to pause for a while in order to contemplate God Himself, to ponder at leisure His marvellous attributes, to consider, and admire, and adore, the beauty of this light so resplendent, at least as far as the strength of my mind, which is in some measure dazzled by the sight, will allow me to do so. For just as faith teaches us that the supreme felicity of the other life consists only in this contemplation of the Divine Majesty, so we experience that a similar meditation, though incomparably less perfect, causes us to enjoy the greatest satisfaction of which we are capable in this life (AT VII 52/HR i 171).

If this closing paragraph is not to be dismissed as hypocritical, a concession to an audience Descartes was eager to impress perhaps, then Descartes is not simply thinking the God of onto-theo-logy, but also the God before whom one kneels. It is here that Levinas finds the initial justification for his transformation of Descartes. 'To us this paragraph appears to be not a stylistic ornament or a prudent homage to religion, but the expression of this transformation of the idea of infinity conveyed by knowledge into Majesty approached by a face' (TI 187/212).

And yet, whether we grant this or not, how could Levinas' appeal to the notion of the infinite be understood as anything but an alternative candidate for the role of ground or fundamental principle, in spite of every protest that he might make to the contrary? Does not his constant use of the language of origins, foundations and conditions place him firmly within the ontological discourse he seeks to challenge? Cannot Levinas' attempt to dispute the fundamental place accorded to ontology by means of insisting on the primacy of the ethical be quite legitimately objected to on the basis that he seems to dispute the primacy of ontology only by asserting another alternative ontological thesis? Similarly, the role he accords to the Other as Infinite may be thought to replace the *cogito* as the commencement and principle of experience, but does not the explicit appeal to Descartes show how unready he is to challenge the fundamental framework of Western thought? All attempts to paraphrase Levinas' thinking are particularly prone to formulations which are vulnerable to these objections. But is it any different with Levinas' own texts? How could his claim to have put in question the fundamental status traditionally accorded to ontology be taken seriously, so long as he retains the characteristic methods and discourse of Western ontology?

II

In order to clarify the questions raised by Levinas' adoption of Descartes' word, it may prove helpful to recall certain aspects of Derrida's discussion of Levinas in 'Violence and Metaphysics.' There Derrida adopted the argument – already familiar from Hegel – that opposition always implicates itself in what it opposes and applied it to Levinas' claim to have broken with the tradition of Western philosophy. On the basis of this argument any attempt to transcend the tradition would remain bound to the tradition by its very intention to surpass it. This does not mean that we are simply locked within the tradition, for any reading of a text which sets out with these considerations in mind also finds that to be *inside* is to be implicated in the *outside*. The susceptibility of Western philosophy to this argument is a consequence of the fact that it has been governed by the logic of opposition although, as Hegel already found, these oppositions are not secure. They 'will not stay in place, will not stay still' (Eliot). Derrida, as is well known, renounces the dialectical procedure which gives rise to the *Aufhebung* of the opposition. Instead he adopts the procedure or strategy of so-called double writing by which the very susceptibility of the tradition to what I have called this Hegelian argument draws these oppositions irremissibly to *undecidability*. In this way Derrida formulates the double bind of so-called 'double reading.' Insofar as an author attempts to transcend the tradition, he or she must be found to be already inside, but in so far as an author stands inside, he or she must be found to be already outside. This gives the appearance that Derrida is forever *opposing* the text he is reading and attempting to situate it elsewhere. But this is only an appearance, the result of a completely one-sided perspective where an attempt has been made to separate Derrida's contribution from whatever text he has been reading. It is therefore something to which anyone who sets out to be *for* or *against* Derrida is always prone.

This double strategy already governs 'Violence and Metaphysics' where the explicit focus is the language with which the thinker performs his or her task.[3] In this essay Derrida reflects on how Levinas' efforts to 'renounce philosophical discourse' (ED 163/110) were governed by 'the necessity of lodging oneself within traditional conceptuality in order to destroy it' (ED 165/111), which means 'to dress oneself in tradition's shreds and the devil's patches'' (ED 165–166/112). Not that one has any alternative but to depend on this traditional conceptuality which one can nevertheless no longer speak with confidence or in the manner of assertion. The whole question is rather how one addresses or responds to this 'necessity,' this question of a conceptuality which destroys itself. And for Derrida that means drawing it explicitly into this curious 'logic' of inside-outside that I have just described and which Derrida makes his focus because he believes that these terms govern the traditional logos (ED 132/88). So in a passage Derrida added when the essay was republished in *Writing and Difference* in 1967 we read, 'And if you will, the attempt to achieve an opening toward the beyond of philosophical discourse, by means of philosophical discourse, which can never be shaken off completely, cannot possibly succeed *within language* – and Levinas recognizes that there is no thought before language and outside of it – except by *formally* and *thematically* posing *the question of the relations between belonging and the opening*, the *question of closure*' (ED 163/110). It is a formula whose complexity suggests that it is no more easier to pose even the question of the opening 'formally and thematically' than it is to say the infinite.

But when Derrida comes to examine Levinas' appeal to the word *infinite*, he does not focus on how Levinas has lodged himself in traditional conceptuality or seek to make his practice more explicit according to the rules of a game he, Derrida, more than anyone else has drawn up. (Not that he was by any means the first to play the game, except insofar as one believes that there is no game unless the rules are formally established.) To be sure, Derrida acknowledges the necessity of having recourse to philosophical discourse in the attempt to renounce it specifically with reference to the notion of infinity: 'it is necessary to state infinity's *excess* over totality *in* the language of totality' (ED 165/112). But having raised the question of how Levinas attempts to say *the infinite* within philosophical discourse, Derrida does not pursue it. Instead he asks whether the negative prefix of the word *in-finite* does not betray a sense of opposition or negation. And if the infinite exteriority of the other cannot be designated otherwise than negatively, 'is this not to acknowledge that the infinite (also designated negatively in its current positivity) cannot be stated' (ED 167/113)?

> As soon as one attempts to think Infinity as a positive plenitude (one pole of Levinas' nonnegative transcendence), the other becomes unthinkable, impossible, unutterable. Perhaps Levinas calls us toward this unthinkable-impossible-unutterable beyond (tradition's) Being and Logos. But it must not be possible either to think or state this call. In any event, that the positive plenitude of classical infinity is translated into language only by betraying itself in a negative word (in-finite), perhaps situates, in the most profound way, the point where thought breaks with language. A break which afterward will but resonate throughout all language (ED 168/114).

It would be unwise to conclude without hesitation that Derrida has reversed his own procedure and imposed on the word *infinite* not the 'logic' which disturbs opposition, but the logic of opposition itself. And indeed Derrida subsequently returns to this question of the rupture between thought and language. This occurs during a meditation on the notion of the infinitely other, a meditation which Derrida introduces as indicative of the difficulties Parmenides might have had with Levinas' discussion of the Other, but which he himself also wants to underwrite. So '*Other than* must be *other than* myself. Henceforth, it is no longer absolved of a relation to an ego. Therefore it is no longer infinitely, absolutely other' (ED 185/126). Derrida refuses to dismiss such considerations which

> would mean that the expression 'infinitely other' or 'absolutely other' cannot be stated and thought simultaneously; that the other cannot be absolutely exterior to the same without ceasing to be other; and that, consequently, the same is not a totality closed in upon itself, an identity playing with itself, having only the appearance of alterity, in what Levinas calls economy, labour and history. How could there be a 'play of the Same' if alterity itself was not already *in* the Same, with a meaning of inclusion doubtless betrayed by the word *in* (*dans*)? (ED 186/126–127)

Derrida seems here to be continuing his play with the word 'infinite' so that it is now to be understood not simply as bearing the sense of negation, but that of inclusion as well. And if that is how we are to understand this passage, then it could be associated with Derrida's discussion of Hegel's use of the word *aufheben*, for Derrida makes it clear that he admires the way Hegel draws on the duplicity and difference inherent in the word *aufheben*, even if he does not follow the practice the word describes (ED 167–168/113/114). This could also be said to be the point at which *logic* passes' toward the beyond of philosophical discourse' into 'a kind of unheard-of graphics' (ED 163/111). Derrida with this phrase, which was another addition to the 1967 version of the essay, has in mind such graphics as the crossing out of Being in Heidegger or his own word *différance*. But it would seem that Derrida has also recognised a duplicity and difference in the graphical play of the prefix of the word *in-finite*.

In 'God and Philosophy,' an essay which can in large measure be understood as a reply to Derrida's 'Violence and Metaphysics' although Derrida is never mentioned there by name, Levinas acknowledges that we must read the 'in-' of *infinite*, not only as a negation of the finite, but also as meaning that the 'infinite' is found within the finite, 'as though – without wanting to play on words – the *in* of Infinity were to signify both the *non* and the *within*' (DVI 106/GP 133).[4] This makes more explicit what Derrida has said by referring to an 'inclusion' of alterity in the same. And yet was it not already said by Levinas in *Totality and Infinity* itself? Indeed was this not Levinas' own guidance in the Preface as to how the book was structured?

> This 'beyond' the totality and objective experience is, however, not to be described in a purely negative fashion. It is reflected *within* the totality and history, *within* experience. (TI xi/23)

The terms of Levinas' title *Totality and Infinity* do not stand in simple opposition to each other. Levinas' language of transcendence and his insistence on the 'beyond Being' do not mean that we should suppose the infinite to stand outside the totality, as if to find the way to the infinite it was necessary to leave the totality behind. Hence *in-finite* says inclusion as well as negation. And hence, to take up Derrida's comments on economy, labour and history, Levinas explicitly says that his account of labour is an attempt to show how it already implies the relation with the transcendent (TI 81/109). Was Derrida, as it sometimes appears, really unaware when he wrote 'Violence and Metaphysics' of this whole strain or tendency in Levinas' discussion of the infinite? Just as one might find oneself persuaded to ask whether Derrida was aware when he called Levinas' account the other becomes 'unthinkable-impossible-unutterable' that for Levinas the whole issue of transcendence arose because of its character specifically as unthinkable, so one might also ask if he can have really thought that Levinas had entirely neglected the discussion of inclusion? Or does Derrida lead his reader to make these protests because he is following as faithfully as possible Levinas' own line of thought which constantly issues in the most extraordinary tensions, not least that between the infinite as 'exterior' to (TI 171/197) and yet within the finite? And yet does not Derrida show that the tension between the infinite as both non-finite and within-the-finite must take another form than that between a 'positive' and a 'negative' infinite, precisely because the only route to the positive is by means of the negative which as negative yet denies access to the positive? So, for example, 'If I cannot designate the (infinite) irreducible alterity of the Other except through the negation of (finite) spatial exteriority, perhaps the meaning of this alterity is finite, is not positively infinite' (ED 168/114). And does not Derrida also recognize that Levinas would not want to maintain that the infinitely Other is a positive infinitude precisely because of its ethical meaning as someone for whom I can never do enough? Is this not also the meaning of such concepts as 'trace' and 'desire' in Levinas? Hence Derrida writes that 'within philosophy and within language, within *philosophical discourse* (supposing there are any others), one cannot simultaneously save the themes of positive infinity and of the face' (ED 169–170/115). Hence the necessity of destroying or rather deconstructing philosophical language, a task which can only be undertaken by lodging oneself within that language. Hence the necessity of the turn to Descartes.

III

Levinas' preoccupation with Descartes' Third Meditation is focused initially on the surplus of this thought which is not a thought, which is unthinkable because it transcends thought, which exceeds the order of being, even if in being said it is also returned to the order of being. If in the first instance he concentrates on separating this thought from the language of being and thus from the traditional conceptuality in which it is immersed in Descartes' text, this is neither in disregard of the necessity of lodging oneself within traditional conceptuality nor of the broader context in which it is to be found. Levinas did not isolate the word *infinite* from Descartes' text. There are a number of other discussions of Descartes in *Totality and Infinity*, as also elsewhere, which show that it was not a single 'concept' that Levinas sought to evoke with this word, but a 'structure' of thinking (DEHH 171). The 'formal design' of this structure is ultimately that of 'separation,' for it is not the case that the infinite is to be conceived in terms of our absorption or participation in it as source. Rather, 'the production of infinity calls for separation, the production of the absolute arbitrariness of the I or of the origin' (TI 268/292). It is separation which accomplishes the rupture with participation and thus allows for transcendence.

But what does it mean to speak of the 'absolute arbitrariness of the I or of the origin'? How can the I be an origin in respect of infinity without denying the very meaning of the word in Descartes' discussion? And in what sense is the I arbitrary? In a section of *Totality and Infinity* called 'Truth and Justice' Levinas approaches these questions in a way which greatly contributes to an understanding both of his own procedures and of his reading of Descartes. He begins by drawing attention to a tradition in Western thinking that attaches unique importance to the free spontaneity of the I. But he then observes how philosophy as critique (in the sense of a 'tracing back' (*remonter*) to preconditions) puts itself – and the freedom of the I – in question by going back 'beyond its own origin' (TI 54/82) and 'penetrating beneath its own condition' (TI 57/85).

> To philosophize is to trace freedom back to what lies before it, to disclose the investiture that liberates freedom from the arbitrary. Knowledge as a critique, as a tracing back to what precedes freedom, can arise only in a being that has an origin prior to its origin – that is created. (TI 57/84–85)

To construe the task of seeking foundations as an attempt to attain an objective knowledge of knowledge is to begin by assuming the freedom of the I and to forget its very arbitrarines (TI 57–58/85). But to attend to this the arbitrary nature of freedom is already to entertain morality. For 'morality begins when freedom, instead of being justified by itself, feels itself to be arbitrary and violent' (TI 56/84). The suggestion seems to be that the ambitions of epistemology are only fulfilled when it recognises itself as morality; that is to say, when critical philosophy recognises that its source lies in this same welcome accorded to the Other that also puts in question my freedom as arbitrary (TI 58/85). Claims of this kind are not prominent in Levinas' thinking, but they do play an important role and serve to justify, for example, Levinas' attribution of an underlying ethical structure to Descartes' thinking. Philosophy as ontology is a thinking of the totality, a totalitarian thinking, but philosophy as metaphysics, in the unique sense Levinas gives to that word, may be defined in terms of a rupture of participation in the totality.[5] 'Metaphysics' is not to be understood as bearing the meaning it has in Heidegger or Derrida. What Levinas calls 'metaphysics' in *Totality and Infinity* corresponds to what in *Otherwise than being or beyond essence* is characterised as 'interruption,' an *interruption* of ontology. Indeed he asks there with reference to the issue of the closure (*fermeture*) of philosophical discourse whether 'its interruption is its only possible end' (AQ 24/20). The passage from ontology to metaphysics may thus be understood as, in Derrida's phrase, the passage to 'an opening toward the beyond of philosophical discourse.'

Levinas finds in Descartes' sensitivity to the question of the order of the *cogito* and the proof of God's existence a passage of this kind. Many readers of Descartes have felt a certain unease about the relative ordering of the *cogito* and the proof of God's existence in the Third Meditation, an unease which – along with certain other assumptions about the text – has given rise amongst some commentators to the notion of a Cartesian Circle. Levinas does not construe this question as a problem requiring immediate solution if the 'argument' of the text is not to fall into disrepute. Rather it constitutes Descartes' greatest discovery, so that it is ultimately this structure, rather than simply the concept of infinity alone, that is for Levinas inscribed in Descartes' word 'infinite.' It is the relation of the same and the other, the relation which the *cogito* maintains with the Infinite, which is called 'idea of infinity' (TI 19/48).

Levinas does not believe Descartes to have instituted a philosophy which takes its basis in the *cogito*, nor does he regard the *cogito* as simply provisional and so subsumed in the infinite. Instead Descartes is understood to have opted not for a single but for what one might call, to borrow a phrase Derrida used in another context, 'a double origin' (ED 435/299). Its applicability to Levinas' discussion is suggested by the following quotation.

> The ambiguity of Descartes' first evidence, revealing the I and God in turn without merging them, revealing them as two distinct moments of evidence mutually founding one another, characterized the very meaning of separation. The separation of the I is thus affirmed to be non-contingent, non-provisional. The distance between me and God, radical and necessary, is produced in being itself. (TI 19/48. Cf. also DEHH 174)

Levinas refuses to compromise this 'non-contingent, non-provisional' separation of the I. Hence he holds fast to what he calls this Cartesian order (TI 155/180), where the chronological order remains distinct from the 'logical' order and neither is subordinated to the other (TI 25/54). He thus refers to what is otherwise named the order of discovery or of reason and the order of being. The order by which the cogito is placed before God allows for a progression from one to the other which maintains separation. When we read the Second Meditation, what is 'older than the cogito' is still to come.

Just as Levinas was found earlier to say that it is the welcome accorded to the Other which puts in question my freedom, Descartes is clear that the commencement of the *cogito* remains antecedent to it and that what underlies the quest for certainty is a doubt which has its source in the idea of the Perfect, that is to say in the Other as infinite. 'Certitude itself is sought because of the presence of infinity in this finite thought which without this presence would be ignorant of its own finitude' (TI 186/210). Levinas is referring here to this famous passage in the Third Meditation.

> I see that there is manifestly more reality in infinite substance than in finite, and therefore than in some way I have in me the notion of the infinite earlier than the finite – to wit, the notion of God before that of myself. For how would it be possible that I should know that I doubt and desire, that is to say, that something is lacking to me, and that I am not quite perfect, unless I had within me some idea of a Being more perfect than myself, in comparison with which I should recognise the deficiencies of my nature? (AT VII 45–46/HR i 166)

It is only in relation to the infinite that the subject discovers itself as finite and so is able to take the path of doubt which leads to the *cogito* (TI 186/210). In other words, 'The *cogito* in Descartes rests on the other who is God' (TI 58/86). Just as in Descartes the infinite allows the finite as doubt, so in Levinas the welcome of the Other is 'the shame that freedom feels for itself' (TI 58–59/86). Furthermore, Levinas understands Descartes to have said that 'certitude itself is sought because of the presence of infinity in this finite thought' (TI 186/210), so finding the process of deduction in Descartes whereby the infinite is – impossibly and yet necessarily – in the finite.

The 'ambiguity' of the order of Descartes' text is also addressed by Levinas when he refers to the I as both 'atheist and created' (TI 60/88). It is 'atheist' in its separation as a free individual prior to the infinite and yet 'created' in the sense that this freedom is capable of being put into question by an origin that is prior to its origin in a sense that points 'beyond atheism' (TI 61/89). This ambiguity is clearly reflected, or rather is *traced*, in the ontological language of Descartes' text. And indeed Heidegger documented this very ambiguity when he wrote that 'the *res cogitans*, as *fundamentum absolutum et inconcussum* the eminent *subjectum*, is at the same time a *substantia finita*, that is *creata*, in the sense of traditional metaphysics.'[6] It is an ambiguity which belongs only to that unique moment in the history of metaphysics, which is why Levinas could say none of this in his own voice, but only by clothing his own thought in the 'tradition's shreds and the devil's patches.'

IV

That the *cogito* discovers its support in the infinite *après coup* – after the fact – is the 'posteriority of the anterior' (TI 25/45). But it does not await Descartes' recognition that his doubt as an acknowledgement of his finitude was dependent on the idea of the infinite which he already held in advance. This 'posteriority of the anterior' is already inscribed in Descartes' text as the evil genius.

Levinas' consideration of the evil genius may be found at the beginning of the section 'Truth presupposes justice.' The evil genius, it may be recalled, was introduced by Descartes in the first instance to extend the range of issues which might be put in doubt following the discussion of dreams and madness. But this doubt is not only more extensive but more potent than any doubt that we can engender by reflecting on the fallibility of our senses. From where does it get this potency? What is its force? Levinas finds in Descartes' appeal to the hypothesis of an evil genius more than a rhetorical device. What would the world be like were it governed by an evil genius? A world of pure spectacle, 'an-archic, without principle, without a beginning' (TI 63/90). This an-archic world which is not a world is introduced by Levinas to explore the possibility of a 'world' without language which presented itself simply as a spectacle to a solitary I. Levinas joins the text of the *Meditations* with his own account of the *il y a*, the 'there is,' that he had himself offered in *De l'existence à l'existant* (TI 66/93). 'It is immediately there. There is no discourse. Nothing responds to us, but this silence; the voice of this silence is understood and frightens like the silence of those infinite spaces Pascal speaks of' (EE 95/58). In the 'there is' we are confronted only with appearances – shadows which may or may not be of something more substantial. There is no certain passage from the appearance to the thing itself. The 'there is' is characterised by 'the silence and horror of the shades' (Racine), the vigilance of insomnia, the horror of the night (EE 98–113/60–7).

Appearance is not simply nothing; still less does it present itself as straightforward illusion so that it itself would bear the signs which would enable me to dismiss it and save me from being misled by it. Appearance is threatening precisely because it only *might* deceive me; it is equivocal. We find the fiction of the evil genius so powerful because it expresses the sense in which we feel ourselves mocked by this equivocation (TI 64/91). It is the very uncertainty of phenomena – as the silence of the 'there is' – which convinces us of the possibility of an Other, the evil genius, behind the appearances. I am most solitary in my solitude when I am confronted by the sense of an other confronting me with malign intent. Levinas recognises this other in Descartes' account of the evil genius.

Even though Levinas began by referring to a world without language, a world which was absolutely silent, he nevertheless comes to refer to the 'lie of the evil genius' (TI 64/91). It is not a lie in any ordinary sense. 'The evil genius' lie is beyond every lie; in the ordinary lie the speaker dissimulates himself, to be sure, but in the dissimulating word does not evade speech, and hence can be refuted.' By the same token the silence of this silent world cannot be understood as silence in the ordinary sense of the word, silence as the absence of speech.

It is tempting to read this passage as a kind of 'deconstruction' of the opposition between silence and language. The 'original' silence of this silent world would then be language just as much – and as little – as it is silence. For it would be outside or rather undecidable between the opposition of language and silence as the silence of language. Just as this an-archic word would seem to occupy the place (or rather 'non-place') Derrida accords to Rousseau's state of nature in *De la grammatologie*, so this 'an-archic silence' would correspond formally or structurally to Derrida's 'arche-writing' which is neither writing nor speech. It would be a silence before silence, an ante-silence, and thus equally an ante-language. But Levinas does not use the world *ante-language*; he writes of an *anti-language*. Anti-language is the language of mockery, laughter held back, a language which is so little language that there is no appropriate response to it and 'to respond would be to cover oneself with ridicule' (TI 64/92). The appearances offered by the evil genius are signs which decline every interpretation. They are the inverse of language, 'like a laughter that seeks to destroy language, a laughter infinitely reverberated where mystification interlocks in mystification without ever resting on a real speech, without ever commencing' (TI 64/91). The silence of the so-called silent world is not the silence of the absence of speech, but 'the silence that terrifies' (TI 64/91). And the terror is terror of the evil genius.

The *arche-* or *ante-language* of a deconstruction turns into the *anti-language* of Levinas. The difference between the words, a difference which appears in writing but not to the ear (at least in standard English) suggests the graphics of arche-writing itself. But the difference is not contained by arche-writing which it does not leave untouched. Levinas introduced his discussion of the evil genius with the notion of 'a world absolutely silent that would not come to us from the word, be it mendacious.' On these terms, silence would be as little absence of speech as speech. But Levinas found himself unable to maintain such a restriction and he subsequently reintroduced language by referring to the lie of the evil genius. The special character of the lie lay in its silence, but it was 'as though the silence were but the modality of an utterance' (TI 64/91). The attempted destruction of language ('it seeks to destroy language') fails. For even though it was silence in respect of language, it was nevertheless the silence of an Other. This is even more explicit when Levinas writes of the silent world that 'as an-archic, at the limit of non-sense, its presence to consciousness lies in its expectation for a word that does not come' (TI 66/93). A solitary silent world of spectacle is not solitary, silent, a world nor a spectacle. 'A world absolutely silent, indifferent to the word uttered, silent in a silence that does not permit the divining, behind the appearances, of anyone that signals this world and signals himself by signaling this world – be it to lie through the appearances, as an evil genius – a world so silent could not even present itself as a spectacle' (TI 66/94). The silence which is undecidable between language and silence, is a silence which is already governed by a reference to the Other.

But does this not mean that in this notion of the expectation of a word we have been brought back to a conception of silence as the absence of speech? Not at all. The values of presence and absence remain under erasure with reference to this original 'silence' which is nevertheless a lie.[7] The Other is indestructible, non-deconstructable, already undecidable, an-archic, always an interruption of the language of being. Not that the notion of anarchy itself can be allowed to remain without further interrogation. Such an interrogation is most explicit in *Otherwise than being*. 'Anarchy is not disorder as opposed to order . . . Disorder is but another order, and what is diffuse is thematizable. Anarchy troubles being over and beyond these alternatives' (AQ 128/101). But already in *Totality and Infinity* it is clear that the an-archic world is not an-archic in contrast with a world which is ordered with reference to the Other or for which the Other is 'the principle of phenomena' (TI 65/92). Rather, its an-archic character is a consequence of its having at its heart a relation with the Other as evil genius (TI 66/93).

And yet can one silence the thought that the Other in the form of the evil genius merely serves as the *principle* of this anarchy? It would be prudent to hesitate before such a question and not to attempt to answer it too quickly. To acknowledge a 'principle' within anarchy, however dangerous a formulation, might be less prone to misunderstanding than to allow anarchy itself to be set up as a principle (AQ 128n3/194n3). But it should already be apparent how far Levinas must have led us for that already to be a question. That the *cogito* is not only a principle that 'interrupts itself by way of the idea of the Infinite' (DVI 106/GP 133), but is also the work of infinite negation, a movement of descent towards the 'there is,' indicates the ambiguity to which the thinking of *principles* has been brought. If the ontological language of origins, foundations and conditions seems to predominate *Totality and Infinity* on one's first reading of it, Levinas' own reading of Descartes subsequently emerges as Levinas' own way of transforming that language. *Totality and Infinity* is itself a fractured discourse. To show this it would be necessary to point beyond Levinas' intentions to the way that book cannot be contained by formal logic, as the logic of non-contradiction, a logic governed by opposition. I have only been able to hint here at how that is done, but insofar as it is possible, it is possible because the tradition interrupts itself in order to say what cannot be said in terms of being.[8]

Abbreviations

AQ *Autrement qu'être ou au-delà de l'essence* The Hague, Martinus Nijhoff, 1974; trans. A. Lingis *Otherwise than being or beyond essence* The Hague, Martinus Nijhoff, 1981.

AT *Oeuvres de Descartes* eds. C. Adam and P. Tannery, Paris, Vrin, 1897–1913.

DEHH *En Découvrant l'existence avec Husserl et Heidegger* Paris, Vrin, 1974.

DVI *De Dieu qui vient à l'idée* Paris, Vrin, 1982.

ED *L'Écriture et la différance* Paris, Seuil, 1967; trans. A. Bass *Writing and Difference* University of Chicago, 1978.

GP 'God and Philosophy' trans. R. Cohen *Philosophy Today* 22, 1978 pp. 127–147.

HR *The Philosophical Works of Descartes* trans. E.S. Haldane and G.R.T. Ross Cambridge, Cambridge University Press, 1968.

TI *Totalité et Infini* The Hague, Martinus Nijhoff, 1961; trans. A. Lingis *Totality and Infinity* Pittsburgh, Duquesne University, 1969.

Notes

1. Already in the 1949 essay 'De la description a l'existence' the last paragraph of Descartes' Third Meditation was evoked (DEHH 97) and a discussion of infinity may be found (DEHH 101–2). In 'L'ontologie est-elle fondamentale?' the word 'infinity' may be found used in relation to the face, *Revue de Métaphysique et de Morale* 56 (1951), p. 95. But as a corrective to over-emphasising the importance of Descartes, it should be noted that even before these essays and without reference to Descartes Levinas may be found in *De l'existence à l'existant* emphasising the importance of separation in the form of the substantiality of the subject with a view of the 'good beyond being' (EE 168/97).
2. The disproportion of 'objective reality' in respect of 'formal reality' is observed in *Éthique et Infini* (Paris: Libraire Arthème Fayard et Radio France, 1982), p. 97; trans. R. Cohen, *Ethics and Infinity* (Pittsburgh: Duquesne University Press, 1985), p. 91). And in 'God and Philoso-

phy' we read that 'the cogitatum's 'objective reality' bursts open the 'formal reality' of the cogitation' (DVI 105/GP 133). In the same place Levinas writes 'In interpreting the immeasurability of God as a superlative case of existing, Descartes maintains a substantialist language. But for us that is not what is unsurpassable in his meditation' (DVI 104/GP 132). Levinas' most forthright statements about the way Descartes' idea of a perfect Being as an idea of the Infinite surpasses the idea of being may be found in the reply he made to a letter written by José Etcheveria after the delivery of 'Transcendance et Hauteur,' *Bulletin de la Société française de Philosophie* LIV (1962), pp. 112–3.

3. I have attempted to sketch the way in which this strategy already governs 'Violence and Metaphysics' in 'The Trace of Levinas in Derrida' *Derrida and Differance*, ed. D. Wood and R. Bernasconi (Warwick University, Coventry: Parousia Press, 1985).
4. 'Le *non* et le *dans*.' Similar discussions are found elsewhere. See particularly 'Beyond Intentionality' trans. K. McLaughlin *Philosophy in France Today* ed. A. Montefiore (Cambridge: Cambridge University Press, 1983), p. 113. This essay corresponds to no single published French text, but the passage in question is a shortened version of one to be be found in 'Amour et révélation' *La charité aujourd'hui* Paris, Ed. S.O.S. (1981), p. 145. See also DVI where the *dans* is identified with 'l'affection du Fini.' These discussions post-dating *Totality and Infinity* deserve separate examination, but reference to them is sufficient to show that Levinas does not refer to this discussion of infinity when in 'Signature' he says that 'the ontological language which *Totality and Infinity* maintains . . . is hereafter avoided.' *Difficile Liberté* second edition (Paris: Albin Michel, 1976), p. 379; trans. Mary Ellen Petrisko, ed. A Peperzak, *Research in Phenomenology* 8 (1978), p. 189. It is more likely that Levinas refers to the transcendental language of conditions which permeates *Totality and Infinity*, although it is not entirely absent later on. The way this apparently transcendental language might be read as having an-other-than transcendental meaning is indicated at the end of this paper and was given a more thorough treatment in my presentation to the Collegium Phaenomenologicum in 1985.
5. 'Martin Buber et la théorie de la connaissance,' *Nom Propres* (Montpellier: Fata Morgana, 1976), p. 49; trans. 'Martin Buber and the Theory of Knowledge,' *The Philosophy of Martin Buber*, ed. P.A. Schilpp and M. Friedman (La Salle, Illinois: Open Court, 1967), p. 149.
6. *Nietszche II* (Pfullingen: Neske, 1961), p. 433; trans. J. Stambaugh *The End of Philosophy* (New York: Harper & Row, 1973), p. 30. On the question of the trace of 'metaphysics' in the language of ontology, see AQ 216/170: 'Does not the discourse that suppresses the interruptions of discourse by relating them maintain the discontinuity under the knots with which the thread is tied again? The interruptions of the discourse found again and recounted in the immanence of the said are conserved like knots in a thread tied again, the trace of a diachrony that does not enter into the present, that refuses simultaneity.'
7. Levinas' notion of *expression* which is elucidated in terms of presence and specifically the superiority of speech over writing may seem to contradict this and serve as an open invitation to a Derridian reflex. I say 'Derridian' to avoid introducing the name of Derrida himself, who is noticably restrained in his comments on this topic, even though he shows himself very well capable already in 1964 of outlining the general direction which will be taken by 'Plato's Pharmacy' (ED 150–153/101–103). It should any way be noted that Levinas does not use the term *expression* in anything like the sense given to it by Husserl. The idea of a universal thought which dispenses with communication is dismissed (TI 44/72). Levinas makes much of the attendance of the speaker at his own manifestation and he thereby comes to lend his support to the Platonic condemnation of writing in favour of the mastery of speech (TI 41/69). Nevertheless a more careful reading shows that the issue is praise for an always renewed deciphering (TI 157/182) and not the ideal of a total presence where all our questions will be answered, although there are phrases which suggest this. One only needs to reflect on the theme of the failure of communication as it recurs throughout Levinas' thinking. But there is also no doubt

that on this, as on a number of other related questions (the place accorded to experience, for example), Levinas has learned from Derrida's essay and reformulated his thinking in consequence.

8. This essay is based on a presentation given to the Collegium Phaenomenologicum in July 1983.

Jewgreek or Greekjew

JOHN LLEWELYN
University of Edinburgh

Das Sein selber das Strittige ist.
Martin Heidegger

On the one hand and on the other hand. This is a pattern one finds in and among the writings of Derrida. It is a pattern one used to find in leading articles of *The Times* of London. In *The Times* the outcome was either a neutral, middle of the road compromise or a dissolution of an apparent conflict through the exposure of an equivocation in the terms in which the views of the parties to the dispute were expressed. This essay will come round to considering whether it is a meeting of extremes of this latter sort that we find in the essay by Derrida which is entitled 'Violence and Metaphysics' and which ends with the citation of the words 'Extremes meet' from 'perhaps the most Hegelian of modern novelists' (WD 153; 228).[1] We can assert at the start that if Derrida subscribes to the idea that extremes meet, he certainly does not subscribe to the idea that they meet in some neutral middle ground, for example a higher or deeper synthesis such as is posited by the aforementioned Hegelianism.

It is not only in Hegelian phenomenology and ontology that Derrida encounters difficulties. He encounters them in Husserlian phenomenology and Heideggerian ontology also, as, to mention only three of his publications, *Speech and Phenomena, 'Ousia* and *Grammē'* and 'The Ends of Man' demonstrate. Now Hegel, Husserl and Heidegger are arraigned too by Levinas, and declared guilty of advocating philosophies of neutrality. How then is it possible for Derrida in 'Violence and Metaphysics' to question the coherence of what Levinas writes in *Totality and Infinity* and before?

In seeking an answer to this question via Derrida's comments on Levinas' comments on Hegel, Husserl and Heidegger, we shall not be able to avoid 'the prosaic disembodiment into conceptual frameworks that is the first violence of all commentary' (WD 312; 124). This violence will be all the starker in our treatment of Hegel because, although he is, as Derrida says, the philosopher most on trial in *Totality and Infinity,* the bearing of the comments on him will be for the most part only implicit in those made on Husserl and Heidegger. In Levinas' own writings explicit references to Husserl and Heidegger are more

J.C. Sallis, G. Moneta and J. Taminiaux (eds.), The Collegium Phaenomenologicum, 273–287.
© Kluwer Academic Publishers.

numerous than they are to Hegel, so it is not surprising that this should hold for 'Violence and Metaphysics' and in turn for our exposition.

From the explicit references that are made to Hegel in 'Violence and Metaphysics' we soon learn that Derrida is perhaps by no means the least Hegelian of modern philosophers.[2] The extent to which Levinas qualifies as a candidate for that description may be gauged from his reaction to the doctrine of self-consciousness put forward in *The Phenomenology of Spirit.* There Hegel writes:

> I distinguish myself from myself, and in so doing I am directly aware that what is distinguished from myself is not different. I, the selfsame being, repel myself from myself; but what is posited as distinct from me, or as unlike me, is immediately, in being so distinguished from me, not a distinction for me.[3]

Levinas has two things to say about this. First, the identity of the I (*moi*) and the self (*soi*), my selfsameness, is not a provisional condition destined to be revealed as merely provisional in the light of a dialectical transition to its truth. Second, this unrendable (*indéchirable*) identity of the I and the self is not the 'I am I' that Kant had already classified as a purely formal tautology. It is the concrete identity of an I at home in its world, *chez soi*. The world is over against me, hence other, but it is a world in which I am more or less free to exercise my power to make things, to take things into my possession . . . and to give them to others.

> The identification of the same is not the void of a tautology nor a dialectical opposition to the other, but the concreteness of egoism. This is important for the possibility of metaphysics. If the same would establish its identity by simple *opposition to the other*, it would already be a part of a totality encompassing the same and the other (TI 38; 8).

By metaphysics Levinas means Desire for what is beyond *phusis*, beyond nature and need: my relationship, which is not a surveyable relation, to the ab-solutely other, the Other (*Autrui*) who commands me, the Stranger who disrupts from over there the being at home with myself in a world where what I lack is nevertheless something that might satisfy a need. The Other is incapable of satisfying Desire. He commands me, and the more I respond to him the greater becomes my responsibility, the more I am called upon to sacrifice. The metaphysical is ethical Desire that supervenes upon happy atheism as the unhappiness of a religion that is supererogatory as regards enjoyment and need, 'un besoin luxueux,' a 'need' surplus to need.

The Other is not the subject matter of theology or theory. He surpasses all understanding. I cannot represent him. I cannot represent him even as another I. 'He and I do not form a number. The collectivity in which I say "you" ["*tu*"] or "we" is not a plural of the "I". I, you – these are not individuals of a common concept' (TI 39; 9). For Levinas subjectivity is my being subject to the

Other, my being his servant, which is not to say his slave. Hence, while I cannot represent him, neither can he stand in for me. No one can be my substitute. Only in the universe of need is that possible, in the system in which I am the centre. In the asymmetrical system of metaphysical ethics I am accused, subjective as absolutely accusative.

The Littré states that *Autrui* never occurs in the subject place of a sentence, but is always governed by a preposition. But the Littré and older grammar books are not reliable guides to the metaphysics of the Levinasian *Autrui*. *Autrui* is governed by nothing. *Autrui* is the Governor. He is the Master and Teacher. As is Emmanuel Levinas presumably vis-à-vis his reader. And the reader of *Totalité et Infini* will not read far before he discovers '*Autrui*' in sentences of which it occupies the subject or the object place. Grévisse notices that this practice is not so rare as some grammarians maintain, and he quotes examples from half a dozen modern authors who include Proust. One French grammarian permits himself the philosophical observation 'In fact, the world is made up of *soi* and *autrui*.' Levinas would beg to differ on the grounds that this leaves out of account the goods on which we live, but he would agree with the implication, assuming that the *autrui* with a lower case *a* here is intended to be equivalent to *les autres*, that *Autrui* is *not* of this world. *Autrui* is exorbitant. He is absolutely unenglobable (EDE 199). He is no more among that of which the world is 'made up' than is the Cartesian Maker of the world. Descartes' Creator is a safer guide to the unique status of the *Autrui* whose denomination with an upper case Alpha is not the name of a case and not a proper name. *Autrui* is absolutely other as is according to Descartes the Infinity of God which overflows our idea of it, and that idea is not one we can generate by negation of the idea of our own finiteness.

Yet the singularity of the Other demands the plural pronoun *Vous*. Perhaps Levinas exaggerates the distance between Buber and himself, as Derrida and Buber maintain (WD 314; 156).[4] But Levinas' preference for the respectful *Vous* makes it plain that the Other is not inferior to me and I am not equal with him, implications that could be carried by speaking of the relationship as that of a *je* and a *tu*, and were evidently carried by Buber's *Ich* and *Du*. Despite the clarifications of the Postscript which Buber added to *I and Thou*, its final paragraph still adheres to the idea of mutuality between God and man. There is no mutuality between the I and the Other. That is the force of Levinas' assertion that the Other is Highness. I have to look up to him in his Humility that commands.

To him. As well as being Majuscule and Majesty, the Other is masculin, like Bossuet's *Autrui* (see Littré again). But this masculinity is for Levinas metaphysical, not biological. It is metaphysically, ethically, speaking that the Other is Father. Not biologically or theologically.

Levinas' perception of his departure from Buber can be put in Heideggerian language by saying that I and the Other are not participants in *Mitdasein*. To say that the Other is Dasein is already to say that he is indeterminately *da*, here or there. According to Levinas, the Other is always only over there and up there. He is *Illic*.

And he is Illeity. This illeity is not the itness or the thatness of an object in my world which Buber and Marcel, followed by Levinas, distinguish from the Thou. Nor is it the Thou of familiarity. The illeity of the face of the Other is not of my world. It is absolved from it. It is the extra-mundane origin of the Other's absolute alterity (EDE 197-202).

Levinas would have us understand that this absolute alterity is other than the alterity of Hegelian dialectic. It does not admit of totalization. Not my recognition of the Other, but my recognition of his irrecuperability is the condition of my showing him respect. I fail to show him respect if I regard him as another I.

Derrida asks whether this is so. Is not my treating another as another I a condition of my treating him with respect? Are not Hegel and Husserl and Kant closer to the truth of this matter than Levinas? Unless I treat another as another I, how can one make the distinction Levinas wants to make no less than these other philosophers between persons and things like stones, the distinction he contends Buber blurs in admitting that it is not only with persons that I can have an I-Thou rapport? Has Levinas been led perhaps to question the Kantian, Hegelian and Husserlian standpoints here, Derrida wonders, because he has given insufficient attention to the distinction between the transcendental and the empirical? Cannot a *Phenomenology of Spirit* and a *Logic* permit a *conceptual* assimilation of the other and the I in a social whole that transcends them without this destroying the *factual* alterity of the other? And is not this factual alterity of the other compatible with his being another I *factically* within the *epoché* of transcendental phenomenology that suspends questions of empirical and metaphysical fact? Levinas may be forgetting Husserl's warning against confusing creation and constitution, a warning Levinas himself repeats in *The Theory of Intuition in the Phenomenology of Husserl* where he emphasizes the distinction between Husserl's transcendental idealism of noematic meanings and the metaphysical sensualism of Berkeley, the distinction that § 89 of *Ideas* captures in the dictum that meanings do not burn. The constitution of the other with which the fifth of the *Cartesian Meditations* is preoccupied does not make the other a part of my world, even if phenomenological constitution is an operation of the meditating philosopher's own consciousness. Within the *epoché* that abstracts all but the ego's sphere of ownness, Husserl writes in § 44 of the *Cartesian Meditations,* 'I, the reduced "human Ego" ("psychophysical" Ego) am constituted, accordingly, as a member of the "world" with a multiplicity of "objects outside me." But I myself constitute all this in my "psyche" and bear it intentionally within me.' However, nothing in this 'world,' any more than the phenomenological consciousness of the ego whose noetic 'psyche' – or 'psychism,' as Levinas would say – has this world as its noematic object, 'is worldly in the natural sense (hence all the quotation-marks).'

Is there not room for Levinas to say about the ethical something parallel to what Husserl says about the psychological: that it is parallel to the phenomenological? Derrida does not have recourse to this notion of parallelism in framing his questions for Levinas in 'Violence and Metaphysics.' If we think that he might have cast his questions in this form, we shall be committed to acknowledging that to read the paragraphs in 'Violence and Metaphysics' on Husserl as a defence of Husserl would be short-sighted. It would be to neglect the 'difficulties' he raises for and from Husserl in the paragraphs Derrida devotes to this parallelist doctrine elsewhere. On the one hand and on the other hand. Derrida writes with both hands. But the hands do not write parallel texts. He is ambidextrous alright. He is also ambisinistrous. Sometimes the right hand plays the left-hand part while the right-hand is played by the left. In 'Violence and Metaphysics' this double crossing of hands is practiced in the opening paragraphs that tentatively pose the question of the question, and in the pages at the end that recapitulate some of the historical and structural or, rather, historico-structural reasons why this question remains open. Still, if we leave out of account these outer movements and the wider context of the essay that Derrida's other compositions supply, we could be forgiven for believing that Derrida's chief aim is to demonstrate that Levinas does violence to the dialectical phenomenology of Hegel, the transcendental phenomenology of Husserl and to the fundamental ontology and essential thinking of Heidegger.

Not only does Levinas appear to misread Husserl on constitution; he compounds this error by paying too little heed to Husserl's insistence that there is no constitution of horizons, only horizons of constitution (WD 120; 177). This insistence is a mark of phenomenology's respect for the physical object and the other self. This respect is the spirit of Husserl's teaching that there can be apodicticity without adequacy. That is to say, for example, that the physical object has profiles with which neither I nor even God can be confronted. And the horizon that lies beyond that which confronts me in my living present is an analogue of the other's experience, an experience that I can never enjoy. 'If', observes Derrida, 'a consciousness of infinite inadequation to the infinite (and even to the finite) distinguishes a body of thought careful to respect exteriority, it is difficult to see how Levinas can depart from Husserl, on this point at least. Is not intentionality respect itself?' (WD 121; 177-8).

And, Derrida asks, turning to Levinas' polemic with Heidegger, what about *Fürsorge, Seinlassen* and *Sein*? Do not these Heideggerian notions accomodate the respect for the Other that Levinas believes Heidegger's thinking fails to show? Care (*Sorge*) on Levinas' interpretation of Heidegger, is Dasein's envelopment of its world in an initially practical project. It regards the Other as a co-inhabitant of the world that I comprehend. To do this, Levinas says, is to do violence to the Other by ignoring the ethical alterity that resists the embrace of a neutral being-with as much as it resists the power of the 'I can' of transcendental phenomenology and the categories of Hegelian dialectic.

However, what Heidegger means by care is not, as Levinas usually assumes, a structure of practice as opposed to theory. Since it is an existential-ontological structure, it is prior to the distinction between the theoretical and the practical, therefore prior to the ethical (SZ 193, 300). Further, the manifestation of *Sorge* that Heidegger calls *Fürsorge,* solicitude, does not have to be a taking over of the Other. Authentic being-with 'helps the Other to become transparent to himself *in* his care and to become *free for* it.' It 'frees the Other in his freedom for himself' (SZ 122). How can this be a violation? Does not this letting be of the Other which is neither interference nor indifference leave room for everything that Kant means by moral respect? There's the rub. For Kant moral respect is the essence of freedom. For Levinas freedom is anchored in the satisfaction of the ego's need. For him egoity is autonomy and heteronomy is ethical Desire for the Other. The Kantian order is inverted. And with it the Heideggerian. In *Kant and the Problem of Metaphysics* Heidegger ties in his thinking of *Seinlassen* with Kant's analysis of the notion of respect.[5]

There are other aspects of Kant's metaphysics of morals that Levinas cannot endorse, despite the indebtedness he avows. Thus, although Levinas' Other who commands me to command has something in common with Kant's categorical imperative, it is difficult to see how Levinas could accept Kant's idea that what commands my respect in another person is the rationality that that person embodies. For that rationality is embodied also in me as a citizen with equal rights and duties in the kingdom of ends. In that kingdom God too is a citizen subject to the same moral law as we are. In Levinas' face to face the Other and I are not equals. If this is a reservation Levinas would make regarding Kant, it is one that would carry over to Heidegger. Levinas could agree with Derrida that Kant, Hegel, Husserl and Heidegger provide for respect for persons. He could continue to object that they do not provide for sufficient respect or for respect of the right kind rightly directed. But we should continue to require assurance that this objection does not stem from a failure to perceive that a transcendental or ontological symmetry is compatible with a factual or ontic asymmetry.

Is Derrida's suspicion that Levinas does fail to perceive this compatible with Derrida's assertion that Levinas is not claiming to outline *a* morality? If we take Kant's metaphysics of morals as a specimen of what is not *a* morality, but a purely formal structure that would yield *a* morality only when applied in concrete historical circumstances, there is nothing to prevent his citing specific injunctions – Do not break promises, Do not commit suicide, and so on – as examples of maxims that the moral law would require or allow in certain or indeed in all historical circumstances. Levinas says, however, that 'Thou shalt not commit murder' is the first word (*le premier mot*) that I read in the Other's eyes (TI 199; 173). This sounds like the basis of *a* morality, even if to describe the basis as a principle or maxim would be to risk lapsing into the tradition questioned by Levinas which substitutes 'ideas for persons, the theme for the interlocutor and the interiority of the logical relation for the exteriority of interpellation' (TI 88, 60). We can agree at least that 'Thou shalt not commit murder' would be only the beginning of a moral code. And so conspicuously absent from *Totality and Infinity* is any serious attempt to draw up a table of commandments (though a second one might be 'Give to the other the bread from thy mouth') that maybe we should understand Derrida's denial that Levinas is purporting to give us *a* morality as a denial that 'Thou shalt not commit murder' is even a rudimentary morality. Maybe we should after all read this commandment as the Levinasian version of Kant's formulation of the categorical imperative calling upon us to 'Act in such a way that you always use humanity, whether in your own person or in the person of another, never simply as a means, but always at the same time as an end.' That is to say, 'Thou shalt not commit murder' would be the command to abstain from doing violence to the other by treating him as though he were subsumable within a causal nexus, conceptual system or a referential totality (*Verweisungsganzheit*) of the sort Heidegger describes in §§ 15–17 of *Being and Time*. Levinas' 'Thou shalt not commit murder' would be a 'version' only because it is doubtful whether he would be in favour of our *using (brauchen)* humanity as an end, and because, as noted above, Kant's scheme is symmetrical, whereas his is initially hierarchical. Initially and ultimately. For it is by way of the face of the second person (you), of the Master, of the Other (*Autrui*) that I have access to the third person, Others (*les Autres*), to humanity, to justice, and to language or discourse (*le langage*). Alphonso Lingis often gives 'conversation' where Levinas has *langage.* With good reason, even if it can sometimes seem that there is little *con*versation in the face to face, but instead the Master addressing me and me as in my turn Master responding by addressing third parties. This impression is not dispelled by the following passage which shows Levinas outlining an account of humanity that he hopes will preserve precedence for plurality over totality while escaping both the neutrality of Anyone (*das Man*) on which Heidegger's analysis of Dasein is based and the kind of subjectivity on which Husserl grounds his analysis of society.

> The third party looks at me in the eyes of the Other – language is justice. It is not that there first would be the face, and then the being it manifests or expresses would concern himself with justice; the epiphany of the face qua

> face opens humanity. The face in its nakedness as a face presents to me the destitution of the poor one and the stranger; but this poverty and exile which appeal to my powers, address me, do not deliver themselves over to these powers as givens, remain the expression of the face. The poor one, the stranger, presents himself as an equal. His equality within this essential poverty consists in referring to the *third party,* thus present at the encounter, whom in the midst of his destitution the Other already serves. He comes to *join* me. But he joins me to himself for service; he commands me as a Master. This command can concern me only inasmuch as I am master myself; consequently this command commands me to command. The *thou* is posited in front of a *we*. To be *we* is not to 'jostle' one another or get together around a common task. The presence of the face, the infinity of the other, is a destituteness, a presence of the third party (that is, of the whole of humanity which looks at us), and a command that commands commanding (TI 213; 188).

*Con*versation as intimate exchange between an I and a thou who love and forgive each other takes place against a background of a we of justice and service in which I am joined not only by the You who is the Other, *Autrui*, but also with Others, *les Autres*, who are his equals, but not mine, for the third party that looks at me in the eyes of the Other is also my Master, another Other, and I have a greater responsibility than anyone else. 'We are all guilty of everything and before each other, but I more than anyone,' as Dostoevsky writes in *The Brothers Karamazov*. And, as Levinas writes in *Totality and Infinity,* brotherhood presupposes fatherhood, a fatherhood that is a key to an ethical monotheism presupposed by the ontological atheism of the free self cultivating its own garden.

In '*Le mot je, le mot tu, le mot Dieu,*' an article published by *Le Monde* in 1978, continuing the dialogue with Buber and Marcel, Levinas writes:

> that above the neighbour's gravity in being or nothingness, without ontology, fraternity should be capable of being invested with an excessive importance, through which meaning is taken on immediately by the God who '*opens my lips*' (Psalm 51, 15), therein lies the great originality of a mode of thinking in which the word God ceases to orientate life in stating the unconditioned ground of the world and cosmology, to reveal, in the face of the other man, the secret of its semantics.[6]

Transcending atheistic egoity, fraternity depends on monotheistic but atheological paternity.

> Human fraternity has then two aspects: it involves individualities whose logical status is not reducible to the status of ultimate differences in a genus, for their singularity consists in each referring to itself. (An individual having a common genus with another individual would not be removed enough from it.) On the other hand, it involves the commonness of father, as though

> the commonness of race would not bring together enough. Society must be a fraternal community to be commensurate with the straightforwardness, the primary proximity, in which the face presents itself to my welcome. Monotheism signifies this human kinship, this idea of a human race that refers back to the approach of the Other in the face, in a dimension of height, in responsibility for oneself and for the Other (TL 214; 189–90).

The God here appealed to is not a first cause, but Infinite Goodness that interpellates me from beyond Being, *epekeina tes ousias,* and therefore beyond the possibility of mystical union; conscience that cannot be incorporated by my freedom or encompassed by the conceptualizing of my consciousness: 'in conscience I have an experience that is not commensurate with any a priori framework – a conceptless experience' (TI 101; 74).

'Conceptless experience'? That would not be a bad translation of the *Erfahrung* which for Heidegger is the experience of the sense (*Sinn*) of Being, the experience which is certainly not Dasein's consciousness of an object, but Dasein's experience that is a *Seinlassen* and therefore at the same time the *Fahren,* the passage – in Levinasian language, *la passe* (EDE 201) – that is Being's history and history's Being. History that is a differing, as Derrida observes when he says that Levinas appears not to have taken to heart Heidegger's statement in the 'Letter on Humanism,' 'Identity and Difference' and elsewhere that Being is not a concept or category and that the Same is not the concept of identity or equality. 'The Same shuns all haste to resolve differences in the Equal' (WD 317 n. 67 and n. 68, 318 n. 80; 206, 214). Levinas equates or at least assimilates Heidegger's Being to his own *il y a*, the neutral presence of the absence of every determinate thing, 'essential anonymity' (EE 58; 95). A more fitting assimilation would be to the word of the *Sophist* that 'teaches us to think that Being – which is other than the other and other than the same, is the same as itself, and is implied by all genres to the extent that they are – far from closing difference, on the contrary liberates it, and itself is what it is only by this liberation' (WD 317 n. 66; 205–6). As Derrida also says, Being is foreign to the finite totality without being an infinite totality or a higher existent. If it is neither a concept or essence nor an existent, but what makes the distinction between essence and existence possible, how can Levinas attribute to it an oppressive domination in contrast to the non-totalitarian domination by the Other? The thinking of Being is no more onto-theology than is ethical Desire. And since the thinking of Being which is Being's thinking is the truth which is the unconcealing, *a-letheia*, of Being that is inseparable from concealment and primordial erring, 'how can one accuse this thinking of interminable wandering of being a new paganism of the Site, a complacent cult of the Sedentary?' (WD 145; 213). This thinking is always under way from one ontic epoch to another, being diverted from the light of Being by each of its ontic determinations. 'The unconcealment of beings, the brightness granted them, obscures the light of Being.' 'As it reveals itself in beings, Being withdraws.' That withdrawal is itself Being's *epoché* (EGT 26; 310). Being is always historically disclosed-undisclosed in existents. So there is no cause for complaint that Heidegger makes beings factually secondary to Being. Could it even make sense to state the entailment of this thesis, to state that Being is factually, ontically, prior to beings?

However, although Derrida adduces ample evidence that Levinas is not attentive enough to the *Unzuhause* in Heidegger's thinking that invalidates the interpretation of it as a thinking of pure *chez soi,* there remains the difference that whereas it is Being that conceals itself according to Heidegger, what does not appear according to Levinas is the face of an existent. The face of the Other is a nonphenomenal trace not because it is a noumenal thing in itself, but because it is ethical command – the rumour of the Kantian Critiques that there remains the ghost of a chance that, unknown to us, the ethical has an ontological foundation, that rumour Levinas believes he has scotched (TI 178-9, 181; 153, 156-7). Also, once we have recognized the *unzuhause* aspect of Heidegger's thinking, must we not recognize also that it betrays a nostalgia for the *Behausung* of Dasein? And is it not Heidegger who tells us that language is the house of Being? Derrida reminds us in 'The Ends of Man' that Heidegger's man seeks the overcoming of homelessness, *die Überwindung der Heimatlosigkeit* (M 128; 154). But he reminds us as well that the *Heimat* here in question is not a nation or three acres and a cow. Nor is it a community of nations. If there is nostalgia here it is for what is Greek, where by what is Greek is not meant, say, the Ithaca of Ulysses. But is there nostalgia here? Or is there rather nomadism?[7] Both and neither. 'When we are historical we are neither a great nor a small distance from what is Greek. Rather, we are in errancy toward it' (EGT 26; 311). 'The Site, therefore, is not an empirical Here but always an *Illic*: for Heidegger, as for the Jew and the Poet,' the poet Hölderlin in connection with whose poem *Heimkunft* Heidegger comments that the word 'country' is 'thought in an essential sense, not at all a patriotic sense, not a nationalist sense, but rather, from the point of view of the History of Being' (WD 319 n. 80; 214).[8] What is near may also be far off, a notion that is as nonsensical (*Thörig* is Hölderlin's word) as that of a wandering Greek or a wandering Jew who senses that the proximity of home is inseparable from the separation of exile, that 'if man is to find his way once again into the nearness of Being, he must first learn to exist in the nameless.'[9]

Given that 'In our manner of speaking, "Greek" does not designate a particular people or nation, not a cultural or anthropological group,' and that 'What is Greek is the dawn of that destiny in which Being illuminates itself in beings and so propounds a certain essence of man' (EGT 25; 310) we must return to the question: How can the Jew be true to his Jewishness? But what is the essence of Jewishness to which the Jew is to be true? The very question is

Greek. For even if the answer we make is that it is of the essence of Jewishness to give priority to experiencing the existent over the thinking of essence, this is a Greek distinction that has as its condition the nonconceptual Being and Same that is the wonder with which Greek thinking, philosophy, begins: the very opening of the question and the openness of the naked face of the Other who commands and accuses me.

> Here it is a question of knowing whether the trace permits us to think presence in its system, or whether the reverse order is the true one. It is doubtless the *true order*. But it is indeed the *order of truth* which is in question. Levinas' thought is maintained between these two postulations (WD 108; 160).

It is as philosopher that Levinas maintains that justice is presupposed by truth and that prophecy and proffering are above and beyond philosophy. There is no inconsistency in this, it might seem. But there is at least a 'difficulty' if philosophy comes on the scene with the verb to be. If that is so, how could we escape the totalitarian violence which Levinas associates with predication? Only Derrida suggests, by postulating a language without verbs; for predication implies the verb, in particular the unparticular verb to be. The language without which there could be no justice and no ethical command would have to be a language of pure invocation. 'The Greeks, who have taught us what *Logos* means, would never have accepted this' (WD 147; 219). If we cannot accept this, must we accept silence? But pre-logical silence would surely be a greater violence than the 'secondary war' against the silence of pre-historical night waged to win secondary peace by polemical Being articulating itself historically in the brightness of the concept.

In the polemic between the Jewgreek and the Greekjew, Derrida poses this dilemma:

> Like pure violence, pure nonviolence is a contradictory concept. Contradictory beyond what Levinas calls 'formal logic.' Pure violence, a relationship between beings without face, is not yet violence, is pure nonviolence. And inversely: pure nonviolence, the nonrelation of the same to the other (in the sense understood by Levinas) is pure violence. Only a face can arrest violence, but can do so, in the first place, only because a face can provoke it. Levinas says it well: ' Violence can only aim at the face' ('La violence ne peut viser qu'un visage' TI). Further, without the thought of Being which opens the face, there would be only pure violence or pure nonviolence. Therefore, the thought of Being, in its unveiling, is never foreign to a certain violence (WD 146-7; 218).

Is this dilemma resolved as soon as Levinas acknowledges the distinction between the conceptual sense of Being and Heidegger's nonconceptual sense? We seem to be on the way to a resolution if we can agree with Derrida that 'Levinas doubtless would not deny that every historical language carries within it an irreducible conceptual moment, and therefore a certain violence' (WD 148; 219). For the difference between Levinas and Heidegger to vanish altogether, would it be enough if Levinas admitted that he has been speaking of Being in only one of the senses Heidegger distinguishes? To put a finer point on the question, could Levinas say that *non*conceptual Being is compatible with the respect that he holds is due to the Signifier, where the Signifier is not the acoustic image or the mark that along with the signified concept makes up the sign of Saussurean semiology, but is the Other who addresses me and to whom I say 'Speak, Lord, for thy servant heareth'? Is the Signifier above nonconceptual Being? If we emphasize that nonconceptual Being determines itself historically in concepts, in order that the Signifier shall not be submerged we shall have to emphasize no less what for Heidegger is in excess of the concept. We must then ask whether the Signifier is excluded or shown disrespect by the way Heidegger thinks that excess. What answer are we to give to this question?

One answer, an answer we have found Derrida giving to this question, is that if my ethical relationship to the Signifier is a relationship within the ontic field, no disrespect to the Signifier is shown, because Heidegger's thinking of Being is thinking that thinks what in *Being and Time* he still calls the ontological, the thinking of nonconceptual Being as distinguished from beings. Since Heidegger distinguishes in the ontic field beings that are Dasein and beings that are not, beings whose being is comprehended through existentials and beings of which the being is comprehended through categories, has Heidegger not allowed for everything that Levinas demands? Levinas cannot complain that to talk of comprehension here is already to fall short, since he is himself attempting to enable us to comprehend the relationship of the Other to me, to grasp that that relationship is a nonrelation or a 'relation of relations' and cannot be comprehended from the point of view of the so-called impartial spectator, the *uninteressierte Zuschauer,* as what is required is neither interest nor disinterest, but *dés-inter-esse-ment.*

In presenting his account, in revealing, for example, that the Signifier does not reveal himself, Levinas does not deny that he is giving an account of the essence of being. Exteriority, he says, is 'the essence of being' (TI 292; 268). This does not mean that the being the essence of whose being is being described cannot be a being that surpasses being: it is precisely in the relation to exteriority that being, Levinas tells us, 'produces' and surpasses itself (TI 302, 304; 278, 281): superlates. But this surpassing of being must show itself in the extension of the meaning of words, in the manifold senses of *on* and *logos*, of 'being' and 'description' or 'account,' in order to permit that what can be given one sort of description cannot be given a description of another sort; in order to permit that something may be coherently described as indescribable, metadescribed as resistent to, for example, phenomenal description. The point may seem trivial, 'merely semantic,' as the saying goes. It begins to look less trivial as soon as we see that it leads to the question whether 'something' (as it occurs, for instance, in the sentence two before this one) is descriptive, to the question whether 'being' is a predicate, and to the problem of the analogy of being. The philosophers who have debated these questions for two thousand years have been fighting battles in what Derrida calls secondary war. And Levinas is waging this war when he says that it is of the essence of being to transcend being, to transcend essence, or, as the tidy-minded wish he would say, to transcend 'essence' to essence, or essence to 'essence.' Where it is a question of transcending essence, being, knowledge, intentionality, phenomenology, etc. to their namesakes, Levinas employs inverted commas no more than Heidegger does when, on his account, phenomenology comes to include as its topic not only what appears but also the disappearing of being. Indeed, what in Heidegger and Levinas may appear to be a mere strategy of rhetorical style is itself a passage in the history of being, understood in the sense which most preoccupies Heidegger, the sense he says we so readily forget, the sense which Levinas forgets, thereby demonstrating a sameness once more in his difference with Heidegger. What Levinas forgets, Derrida says, is the *as such* of metaphor. He couples the human face and the hidden face of God, but in offering us this metaphor he forgets the metaphorization that is going on here, thus betraying his 'etymological empiricism, the hidden root of all empiricism' (WD 139; 204). 'As Hegel says somewhere, empiricism always forgets, at very least, that it employs the words to be.'

So is that the conclusion Derrida reaches in 'Violence and Metaphysics' that Levinas is appropriated by the Greeks, by Heidegger if not also by Hegel? No such conclusion is reached. No conclusion is reached. The question and the question of the opening of the question is left open. The essay ends by asking:

> Are we Greek? Are we Jews? But who, we? Are we (not a chronological, but a pre-logical question) *first* Jews or *first* Greeks? And does the strange dialogue between the Jew and the Greek, peace itself, have the form of the absolute, speculative logic of Hegel, the living logic which *reconciles* formal tautology and empirical heterology after having *thought* prophetic discourse in the preface to the *Phenomenology of Spirit*? Or, on the contrary, does this peace have the form of infinite separation and of the unthinkable, unsayable transcendence of the other? To what horizon of peace does the language which asks this question belong? Whence does it draw the energy of its question? Can it account for the historical *coupling* of Judaism and Hellenism? And what is the legitimacy, what is the meaning of the *copula* in this proposition from perhaps the most Hegelian of modern novelists: 'Jewgreek is Greekjew. Extremes meet'?

Do the extremes meet? If they do, it is the strange meeting Derrida describes as a 'reciprocal surpassing,' the kind of meeting Levinas describes at the end of the essay on Derrida 'Tout autrement':

> The ridiculous ambition to 'improve' a true philosopher is certainly not part of our plan. To cross his path is already quite something and probably just what is to be expected of a philosophical encounter. In underlining the primordial importance of the questions Derrida poses we have wanted to express the pleasure of making contact at the heart of a chiasmus.[10]

For although it may have begun to seem from what we have said in this essay on Derrida on Levinas that a philosophical encounter of a closer kind between Levinas on the one hand and on the other hand Heidegger could be expected if only Levinas accepted that nonconceptual ontology or thinking of Being is prior to the ontic, and that morality eventuates as an aspect of the ontic after first philosophy divides itself into morality, logic, theory of knowledge, and so on, Levinas is explicit that 'Morality is not a branch of philosophy, but first philosophy' (TI 304; 281) and shows no sign of revising that thesis in the works he has written since having the opportunity to think about Heidegger again in the light of 'Violence and Metaphysics.' As he puts this thesis in *Totality and Infinity, logos* as vocation and invocation precedes *logos* as thesis. As he puts it in *Otherwise than Being or Beyond Essence, logos* as Saying, *Dire,* is prior to *logos* as the Said, *Dit.* But if, on pain of begging the question, priority must be prior to *logos* in both of these senses, prior to the Jew and prior to the Greek, how are we to understand, let alone answer, Derrida's question whether we are first Jews or first Greeks?

Notes

1. Abbreviated references in the text are as follows: pages in the original are given after a semi-colon when an English translation is cited:

EDE: Emmanuel Levinas, *En découvrant l'existence avec Husserl et Heidegger* (Paris: Vrin, 1982).

EE: Levinas, *Existence and Existents,* trans. Alphonso Lingis (The Hague: Nijhoff, 1978); *De l'existence à l'existant* (Paris: Vrin, 1981).

EGT: Martin Heidegger, 'The Anaximander Fragment,' in *Early Greek Thinking,* trans. David Farrell Krell and Frank A. Capuzzi (New York: Harper and Row, 1975); *Holzwege* (Frankfurt am Main: Klostermann, 1972).

M: Jacques Derrida, 'The Ends of Man,' in *Margins of Philosophy,* trans. Alan Bass (Chicago: University of Chicago Press, 1982; Brighton: Harvester Press, 1982); *Marges de la philosophie* (Paris: Minuit, 1972).

SZ: Heidegger, *Sein und Zeit* (Tübingen: Niemeyer, 1972).

TI: Levinas, *Totality and Infinity,* trans. Alphonso Lingis (Pittsburgh: Duquesne University Press, 1969; The Hague: Nijhoff, 1969); *Totalité et Infini* (The Hague: Nijhoff, 1980 [1961]).

WD: Derrida, *Writing and Difference,* trans. Alan Bass (Chicago: University of Chicago Press, 1978; London: Routledge and Kegan Paul, 1978); *L'écriture et la différence* (Paris: Seuil, 1967).

2. See John Llewelyn, 'A Point of Almost Absolute Proximity to Hegel,' forthcoming in the proceedings of the conference on Deconstruction and Philosophy: The Texts of Jacques Derrida, sponsored by the Philosophy Department of Loyola University of Chicago, March 1985. The present essay could perhaps be said to suggest that the relationship of Derrida to Levinas is one of what the latter would call ab-solute proximity.
3. G.W.F. Hegel, *The Phenomenology of Spirit,* trans. A.V. Miller (Oxford: Clarendon Press, 1977), p. 102.
4. See P.A. Schilpp and M. Friedman, eds., *The Philosophy of Martin Buber* (La Salle, Illinois: Open Court, 1967; London: Cambridge University Press, 1967), p. 723.
5. See John Llewelyn, 'Heidegger's Kant and the Middle Voice', in David Wood and Robert Bernasconi, eds., *Time and Metaphysics* (Warwick: Parousia Press, University of Warwick, 1982).
6. Levinas, 'Le mot je, le mot tu, le mot Dieu', *Le Monde,* March 19–20, 1978, p. 2. I am grateful to Gustave Calamand for sending me a cutting of this.
7. I am grateful to Adriaan Peperzak for a shrewd comment on this question.
8. Heidegger, 'Letter on Humanism,' in David Farrell Krell, ed., *Martin Heidegger Basic Writings* (New York: Harper and Row, 1977; London: Routledge and Kegan Paul, 1978), p. 217; *Wegmarken* (Frankfurt am Main: Klostermann, 1976), p. 338.
9. Ibid., p. 199; p. 319. Derrida, *Margins*, pp. 128-9; p. 154.
10. Levinas, 'Tout autrement,' in *Noms propres* (Montpellier: Fata Morgana, 1976), p. 89.

The Economy of the Body in a Post-Nietzschean Era

JEFFNER ALLEN
SUNY Binghamton

Since Nietzsche's aphorism 'The Madman,' the question of embodiment has stood, albeit uneasily, on the philosophical horizon. If God is dead, what is the status of his murderer, the human subject? If God, the totality of codes that constitute Western metaphysics, no longer exists, must not the human subject, that complex of mind, body and desire, have died at the same time? To be sure, for Nietzsche, it is we who made the God that became the ideal of truth, goodness, and life-denying beauty. Yet it would be a hasty philosophical sleight of hand if we failed to note that we, the murderers of that ideal, are implicated in the subsequent, fundamental shift of all structures of meaning.

The death of the human subject as 'soul,' 'ego,' or 'pure consciousness' is considered definitive by most recent continental philosophers. The 'subject' is a fiction that can no longer be thought as standing behind the field of experience or behind the text. The body as subject, however, has received an uncertain dismissal. Foucault has indicted any retrieval of the body as the product of ahistorical reflection that ignores the modern dislocation of those conceptual systems in which the body once had meaning. The phenomenological recovery of the body as 'flesh' and the post structuralist 'writing the body' have, nevertheless, claimed to trace a movement of the body out of metaphysics.

The point of departure for all of these interpretations of the body is to be found, I propose, in their distinct economic evaluations of the body. The post-Nietzschean era is marked by a shift from what I will term a *metaphysical economy* to a *philosophical economy*. Each economy, each circulation of meaning, value, and the basics of daily life, institutes a split between that which it will admit and that which it will exclude. The metaphysical economy of identity and presence assumes a hierarchy of origins. Its dominant modes of exchange are substitution and reversal: with the death of God the human subject stands in for the divine subject and takes its place as all that the divine subject once represented. When the body subject is substituted for the human subject, explicitly reversing the hierarchy of mind and body, the metaphysical

J.C. Sallis, G. Moneta and J. Taminiaux (eds.), The Collegium Phaenomenologicum, 289–307.
© *Kluwer Academic Publishers.*

economy continues as a closed circle of equivalences. A philosophical economy, in contrast, retrieves that which has been suppressed by metaphysics: difference and absence. Such an economy is termed 'philosophical' because it is in the space of difference and absence that thinking can take place.[1] There is no closed system of exchange in the philosophical economy, but an open relationality of barter in which there is never the Same. In the absence of a common denominator, the only truth is incomplete, meaning is deferred: the body can be spoken of only by speaking of quite other things.[2] When thought from the perspective of a philosophical economy, the body posited by the metaphysical economy is a lingering remnant of a theological world view; the body, *if* it can be posited within a philosophical economy, is one moment of a new beginning. Whereas Foucault maintains that only the first alternative is viable, the later Merleau-Ponty and Barthes claim that the second alternative not only is possible, but already is underway.

Through analysis of the economies of the body that are developed by Foucault, phenomenology, and post structuralism, I will argue that the death of God need not be accompanied by the demise of the human subject *as* embodied individual. The retrieval of the body need not be an attempt to reinstate the Same. Evaluation of the body in terms of the Same is itself metaphysical, for it assumes that the body is a counterfeit that copies, or reproduces, a point of origin. In the circulation of a metaphysics that made, forgot, and then believed to be eternally true all of its creations, *the body, like all else, is a mere fiction. This body defrauds metaphysics by artifice which, unlike metaphysics, it recognizes as precisely that.* Counter to those who place the body exclusively in the domain of the metaphysical economy, and as a challenge to the current scope of a philosophical economy, I will show that interpretation of the human subject as embodied individual constitutes both a way out of metaphysics and a critical step in the formulation of non-metaphysical social philosophy. The body, embedded in the post-Nietzschean shift of economies, itself places in question the significance of that shift.

Writing with One's Feet

The primary obstacle to a revaluation of the body within a philosophical economy has been the issue of anthropocentrism. As long as language and truth are reduced to the body subject, Heidegger's critique of the body in *Being and Time,* and Foucault's assessment in *The Order of Things,* are more than justified.[3] The *homo farber* of the metaphysical economy is the self-declared maker of all value and meaning, outstanding evidence of the failure to admit that 'man' too is a function of that making.

The prevalent and unconditional extension of the charge of anthropocentrism to any possible valuation of the body is, however, difficult to substantiate. Such a claim equates all conceptions of the body with the natural body of philosophical anthropology, and all versions of philosophical anthropology with the metaphysical economy. Even Heidegger, who in *Being and Time* describes the 'body subject' as mired in metaphysics, an 'I-Thing encumbered with a body,' offers in his later work a clue to a philosophical interpretation of the body: 'Bodily being does not mean that the soul is burdened by a hulk we call the body .... We do not "have" a body; rather we "are" bodily.'[4] These passages may indicate that for Heidegger 'bodily being,' unlike the 'body subject,' stands apart from the metaphysical limits of philosophical anthropology.

One need not rely on filling in a lacuna in Heidegger's writing to suggest that the body can be conceived as in-the-making and the body is not necessarily man-made. The unconditional charge of anthropologism is more totalizing than the evidence supports. To the body subject of metaphysical philosophical anthropology there may be juxtaposed the circulation of the body in a philosophical economy: the body *as* event. The body subject of metaphysics has a fixed 'nature' that serves as a monolithic measure of value and meaning; bodily being is heterogeneous, shaped by the artifice of language and truth. The question is whether an initial philosophical conception of the body can be sustained without falling back into metaphysics.

This dilemma, faced by recent continental analysis of the body, is prefigured, albeit without a definitive resolution, in Nietzsche's work. *Zarathustra* reclaims the body: 'body am I entirely and nothing else.'[5] Nietzsche retrieves the body not as another subject, but as an event: ' "I," you say, and are proud of that word. But greater is that in which you do not wish to have faith – your body and its great reason: that does not say "I"; but does "I." '[6] Yet Nietzsche's delineation of the body as event remains incomplete. His poem 'Writing with One's Feet,' from *The Gay Science,* is paradigmatic of that moment in which interpretation of the body circles back to metaphysics:

Not with my hands alone I write:
My foot wants to participate.
Firm and free and bold, my feet
Run across the field – and sheet.[7]

In this poem, language has shifted from the mouth to the writing of hands and feet. Such writing remains, however, a writing 'with' the body: the instrument of an originary body that has discovered a new aspect of its nature (the feet). 'Writing with One's Feet' is still not a writing the body: a discovery of the body as event, the body as text. While transcending field and sheet the feet run and fall – into the circulation of metaphysics.

DISPLACEMENT, ILLUSION, AND FICTION

Whether all conceptions of the body are inherently metaphysical depends not on the critique of philosophical anthropology, which is justified only in part, but on the epistemological categorization of the body as 'illusion' or as 'fiction.' Foucault and others who understand the body solely as 'illusion' argue that the body is displaced by the end of metaphysics: affirmation of the body prolongs metaphysics. Barthes and those who define the body as 'fiction' maintain that the body is one element in the displacement of metaphysics: affirmation of the body limits metaphysical claims. The theories of truth that inform these epistemological designations, and not the consideration of 'man' *per se*, bring the former to consider the body contemporaneous with metaphysics and therefore anthropocentric, and the latter to view the body apart from metaphysics and freed from the critique of anthropocentrism.

Reference to a passage on truth and illusion, by Nietzsche, offers an orientation to these epistemological designations:

> If he does not wish to be satisfied with truth in the form of a tautology – that is, with empty shells – then he will forever buy illusions for truths.[8]

The claim that the body is displaced by the end of metaphysics and the claim that the body is one element in the displacement of metaphysics both pursue a critique of the guardians of metaphysics. Neither interpretation countenances the buying of illusions for truths. The former view, especially as developed by Foucault, vividly evokes a picture of how the body has been coined by the philosophical anthropology of Western metaphysics. While precluding the purchase of illusions, however, this interpretation continues to buy illusions and to accept these illusions as *un*truths.

Illusions are 'bought' whenever they are thought to be exchangeable in the metaphysical economy of signs, all of which are measured by their distance or proximity to truth. Illusions are accepted as untruths when, by a reversal of their relation to the measure of truth, or by a reversal of truth itself, they are thought to be exchangeable in an economy of untruth rather than in an economy of truth. Even the rejection of illusions as untruths entails an acceptance of the metaphysical economy in which there are illusions, for illusions must first be accepted in order to be rejected as such.

Foucault's reversal of the truth of the body and his subsequent rejection of its untruth function, thus, as instruments of metaphysical truth making. Belief is invested in metaphysics through the conviction that the metaphysical economy of truths and untruths has constructed *in toto* its subject matter and is, therefore, the final word on that which it claims to have made. The body as illusion is reduced to the system that is claimed to be its maker and is assumed to be consumed in that making. That the body need not circulate in the traffic of truth and untruth which is measured by metaphysics remains outside of consideration.

The option to buying illusions for truths, presented by Nietzsche in this passage, is that of being satisfied with truth in the form of a tautology: 'empty shells.' Yet, one may note, shells are empty not because they are tautological, centered at the selfsame point of identity, but because they have no center. Empty shells are the sign of absence.

Nietzsche's descriptions of fictions, like his description of empty shells, often are apt. His interpretations of these descriptions tend, however, to miss the possibility of absence. That '. . . all are fictions that are of no use,' or that 'mere fiction [is] constructed of fictitious entities,'[9] need not mean that fictions are to be rejected, but that fictions are of no use, have no hidden purpose, are comprised solely of other fictions: that fictions pertain to an economy *other* than the metaphysical. This interpretation of fiction informs Barthes' analysis of the body: the body as fiction cannot be reduced to illusion; the body is, accordingly, one element in the displacement of metaphysics.

The economy of the body in a post-Nietzschean era thus presents itself as an array of diverse economies divided according to their understanding of the body as 'illusion' or as 'fiction.' A critical analysis of these economies will be undertaken not to assimilate their distinctive authors – Foucault, Merleau-Ponty, Barthes – to one another, but to examine further the issue of displacement. The coining of the body in each of these economies reflects a concern with displacement in terms of the relation of the body to sameness and difference, nature and artifice, subjectivity and individuality.

Foucault and the Economy of the Body: Circulation Between the Threads of Power

The genesis of the body that is metaphysical is demonstrated convincingly by Foucault, but his critique of the body is limited by its investment in the totality of the Same. To the extent that Foucault's analysis of the economy of the body does not stand apart from the Same, it precludes that the body might be seen apart from metaphysics. His critique of the body comes to a premature closure, secured by the self referential circle of the metaphysical economy.

For Foucault, the void left by the death of God has created a space in which philosophy is again possible. Nietzsche's aphorism, 'The Madman,' is interpreted by Foucault to state unequivocally that the death of God marks the end of 'man.' Foucault sets forth an uncompromising critique of any attempt to hold on to the shadow of the human subject. Philosophy, in particular, is claimed to have fallen into an anthropological sleep, 'as if it were unaware that with the death of God "man" too is erased like a face drawn in sand at the edge of the sea.'[10]

The body is not natural, Foucault argues, but the product of the unacknowledged artifice of a metaphysical making that would establish the body as origin. Discourse that affirms the body, akin in this sense to Nietzsche's last man, prolongs the buying of illusions for truths that distinguishes the metaphysical economy and ignores the untruth of that illusion. The artifice of which the body is the effect is an elaborate political technology: 'a set of material elements and techniques that serve as weapons, relays, communication routes and supports for the power and knowledge relations that invest human bodies and subjugate them into objects of knowledge.'[11] Bodies are not the center of meaning giving activity, but are subjected, used, transformed and improved: docile.[12] An unusual reference by Foucault to bodies other than docile is his comment that 'subtle coercion' exercises 'an infinitesimal power over the active body.'[13]

Both subjectivity and individuality are considered by Foucault to be illusions that are untruths. Subjectivity is referenced as one of the last anthropological constraints, a preserve of Western discourse. Even the phenomenological historicizing of the subject must be disbanded, Foucault maintains, to account for the constitution of the subject within a historical framework.[14] The individual, too, is an effect of the mechanisms of power and an element of its articulation: 'Not only do individuals circulate between its threads [the threads of power]; they are always in the position of simultaneously undergoing and exercising its power.'[15]

An alternative to this economy is suggested, though not developed, in the conclusion to the first volume of Foucault's *History of Sexuality*: 'We need to consider the possibility that one day, perhaps in a different economy of bodies and pleasures, people will no longer quite understand how the ruses of sexuality, and the power that sustains its organization, were able to subject us.'[16] Yet the actuality of the body described in Foucault's works is one in which revolt at the level of the body is stayed by the mechanisms of power and its ever more subtle manifestations.[17] How Foucault's focus on the Same tends to preclude the active body and revolt, and to relegate 'a different economy of bodies and pleasures' to the status of mere possibility, may be clarified by analysis of his reflections on the emancipation of subjugated knowledges.

The emancipation of subjugated knowledges that is formulated by Foucault has for its aim the association of discourses that have been 'disqualified' from the hierarchy of knowledge and sciences, and of 'naive' knowledges located 'low' on that hierarchy, with the 'buried' knowledges of erudition.[18] In this association, Foucault maintains, there is located the force of critical discourse.[19] The emancipation is described by Foucault as one of 'unqualified' or 'directly disqualified' knowledges 'that are opposed primarily not to the contents, methods or concepts of a science but to the effects of the centralizing powers.'[20] The 'local' knowledges are reactivated in 'a kind of attempt to emancipate historical knowledges from that subjection, to render them, that is, capable of opposition and struggle against the coercion of a theoretical, unitary, and formal scientific discourse.'[21] Foucault's articulation of this emancipation is limited, however, in two senses. First, it articulates the freeing of subjugated knowledges not *from* the Same, but *in order to* challenge the Same. Secondly, it assumes that these knowledges, if emancipated, will share the same goals as those of his discourse.

Such an assumption institutes over 'local' and 'disqualified' knowledges a sovereignty of the Same, especially in that it abstracts these knowledges from their own contents, methods, styles, and indigenous concepts in order to place them in the service of a presumed common project. This difficulty, inherent in Foucault's emancipation of subjugated knowledges, bears directly on his analysis of the economy of the body. What if, contrary to the emancipation envisaged by Foucault, some local or ethnological knowledges exercise a positive discourse of the body that might not be reducible to the body of the metaphysical economy? What if some subjugated knowledges prioritize a claiming of the body over insurrection against centralizing power? Or if some subjugated knowledges find in the affirmation of the body a rupture with centralizing power? On the one hand, Foucault criticizes those who would begin first with ideological questions and who raise second, or not at all, the question of the body: 'to all those who still wish to talk about man, about his reign or his literature ... to all those who wish to take him as their starting-point in their attempts to reach the truth ... we can answer only with a philosophical laugh – which means, to a certain extent, a silent one.'[22] On the other hand, Foucault's development of the body question is itself imbued with ideological claims: the dismissal of difference by the establishment of a central focus, that of the opposition to, and struggle against, the Same. Foucault's emancipation of subjugated knowledges reimposes the Same by the erasure of difference, perhaps most significantly, by its erasure of the recognition of its own difference.

The paradox of a discourse against the Same which, because composed of the codes of that distribution of power, precludes a rupture with, and contributes to, its circulation, is characteristic of Foucault's interpretation of the body. Although not all nursery rhymes have a claim to philosophical wisdom, that of 'Humpty Dumpty' illustrates several implications of this paradox. One may remember that 'Humpty Dumpty,' like many nursery rhymes, enjoyed a lengthy circulation in the public world of power and politics before its original sense was reduced to a single meaning and made an instrument of disciplinary power in the creation of docile bodies in the nursery.

That Humpty Dumpty, that frail body which will be referred to as H.D., fell and could not be restored, is the most prevalent but by no means the only possible interpretation of the rhyme. That H.D., a subject of the King, fell on the King's side of the wall, which is why all the King's horses and all the King's men tried to put H.D. together again, even though they failed, also need not have been the actual situation. H.D. might have fallen on the other side of the wall, in which case the King's horses and King's men may have failed because they could not cross to the other side of the wall and still be the King's men; or they may have failed because they crossed to the other side and in the absence of those codes to which they were accustomed, they found 'nothing.' Perhaps H.D. never was a subject of the King. Or, more surprisingly, H.D. may have lived all along on what the King presumed was 'his' side of the wall, lived by codes that were not the King's, and never have been the King's subject. Difference is affirmed in all of these alternatives, for H.D. is interpreted as the tale of a tumble that takes the life out of the supposed correlation between the Same, bodies, and power – or, what was said at the time, a tumble that took the 'life' out of the British Parliament.[23]

The recoded versions of this tale not only improve the outcome for Humpty Dumpty, who in the customary modern interpretation dies on the day that he falls, but change the sense of the rhyme. No longer is the body an illusion which, because it is embedded in the Same, cannot secure itself and is moving slowly to its end. The body is active, a survivor that can be understood only from the direction of difference. 'Humpty Dumpty' need not be a report *of* the Same, fabricated by the King's men, but a report *about* the Same that is told from a perspective of difference. The whirling described in Nietzsche's aphorism, 'The Madman,' tells of the unchaining of the earth from its sun, the rupture of effect and cause, a plunging, a straying and feeling the breath of empty space.[24] The omnipresence of the Same in Foucault's account of the economy of the body hides the history of that turbulence.

Merleau-Ponty and the Economy of the Body: 'This Strange System of Exchanges'

In the turbulence brought forth by the death of God there is, Merleau-Ponty claims, an upsurge of negativity: there is the open space of non-coincidence.[25] Merleau-Ponty's development of his early assertion, 'I am my body,' gives full expression to Nietzsche's exhortation to break with the despisers of the body, to start from the body, methodologically, without coming to any decision about its ultimate significance.[26] His *Phenomenology of Perception,* which he later criticizes for its assumption of a Cartesian subjectivity, affirms the lived body as fluid, dynamic, a 'perpetual incarnation'[27] through whose intentionality space, time, speech, and the world are constituted. The lived body incarnates consciousness which, both reminiscent of Nietzsche's claims in *Zarathustra* and portending Heidegger's discussion of bodily being in his later writings, is not a matter of 'I think,' but of 'I can.'[28] In Merleau-Ponty's working notes for *The Visible and the Invisible,* which along with 'Eye and Mind' is the major text where he develops an ontology of the body, the flesh of the world assumes the primacy he once gave to the lived body. The flesh is 'not matter, is not mind, is not substance. To designate it, we should need the old term, "element."'[29] The flesh of the body is thought by Merleau-Ponty as non-coincidence: a wave, 'this circle which I do not form, which forms me'; a reversibility, 'our body is a being of two leaves' in which there is a double reference between the body sensed and the body sentient, each calling for the other; and an intertwining, 'visibility sometimes wandering and sometimes reassembled.'[30] The radicality of the turn out of metaphysics that is effected by the shift in Merleau-Ponty's positive discourse on the body is aptly indicated by his surprising observation, 'for the first time I appear to myself completely turned inside out under my own eyes.'[31]

Discussion of Merleau-Ponty along with Foucault and Barthes may seem startling, so often is phenomenology opposed to post structuralism as the continuation of metaphysics is to the end of metaphysics. Such an opposition, at least with regard to the body, relies unduly on an identity politic of philosophical interpretation in which each philosophical movement maintains its individuality by neglecting to recognize and pursue overlapping and pluralist claims. The approach to the issue of displacement that is traced by Merleau-Ponty's sustained, positive discourse on the body is highly suggestive of how the body might be an element in the displacement of metaphysics. That suggestion is perhaps more important than any definitive resolution that his work may, or may not, have achieved.

The body, for Merleau-Ponty, is imbued with nothingness. Negativity inhabits touch, and for this reason the body is an ontological dimension and not an empirical fact.[32] The body is in perpetual non-coincidence with itself, forever escapes itself; it does not reach itself, does not appropriate to itself what it touches and sees. The body is not an actor caught in the web of its instrumentality, but an openness upon the world.[33]

Merleau-Ponty's interpretation of nothingness as 'the difference between identicals'[34] enables him to supplant the assumption that the body must be either natural or the product of artifice by an ontological conception of body reflexivity. Silence, understood not as the contrary of language but as the 'absence of the word due,' displaces the natural body that is present in Merleau-Ponty's early writings in the form of the tacit cogito, a substratum of body identity.[35] The body as the product of artifice is dismissed by appeal to an interiority of the flesh that neither precedes nor results from our actions.[36] The effects of our articulations are, Merleau-Ponty concedes, contingencies without which humanity would not exist, but they do not bring it about that there is a single person. 'Humanity,' if understood as the self identical sum of effects, is a Cartesian ideal that neglects depth and attempts to explain the human in terms of the mechanics of things. The body reflexivity that Merleau-Ponty proposes instead traces an ontological approach to the body as event. 'There is' a human body only once there is a blending *between* touching and touched, which never coincide.[37] The economy of the body is, thus, a metamorphosis of touching and touched that is called by Merleau-Ponty, 'this strange system of exchanges.'[38]

The nothingness of the body dislodges the 'I' as a fixed point of reference: 'My "central" nothingness is like the point of the stroboscopic spiral, which is who knows where, which is "nobody."'[39] By inversion of the traditional metaphysical conception of the 'I,' the nothingness of the 'I' is given primacy over its thingliness. 'Negativity – ungraspable in person . . . since it is nothing' is called the 'primary I'; the 'named I' is the objectification of that negativity. The 'I' is defined, but not displaced, by two distinct circulations: the economy of absence that characterizes the primary 'I,' 'the unknown to whom all is given,' and the economy of presence that makes of the 'named I,' 'an object.' Merleau-Ponty refers once to the 'primary I' as that 'before which there is something,' suggesting that both economies of the 'I' might be distinguished from still a third and more fundamental ontological circulation.[40]

Merleau-Ponty's economy of the body might appear to stand apart from the conflict between metaphysical and philosophical economies. The body of his phenomenological ontology seems to be neither illusion nor fiction. 'There is' the body: the body is not an epistemological construct, but an ontological given. The perceptual logic of the movement that touches and movement that is touched, which is uniquely suggestive of a non-metaphysical economy of the body, is brought to a metaphysical stand, nevertheless, by Merleau-Ponty's idealist presuppositions. His multiple attempts to secure an ideal ground for 'this strange system of exchanges' pull the body back into the metaphysical economy of truth and illusion.

In Merleau-Ponty's analysis of the 'I,' the 'primary I' might be thought originary because it is that of which the 'named I' is the representation, but not the origin, for it is 'the one *to whom* all this occurs' (italics my emphasis). The function of the 'primary I' is, however, undeniably foundational. It serves as an ideal ground of identity and truth. In this sense, Merleau-Ponty's interpretation of the 'I' merely transfers the natural body and its metaphysical assumptions to an ontological level.

An idealism is also present in Merleau-Ponty's discussion of body reflexivity. His position is not simply that where the negative would be 'there is' body reflexivity: the fold.[41] He maintains, rather, that 'there is' a '"pure" ideality' of the double reference of the body which derives from 'the fundamental mystery of those notions "without equivalent".'[42] This ideality 'is' the flesh, but the converse does not hold, the flesh is not the ideality. A metaphysical hierarchy is thereby established, for the '"pure" ideality' has a greater proximity to origin and truth than does that in which the ideality is incarnate.

The open space of non-coincidence likewise is imperiled by Merleau-Ponty's imposition of the ideal of the Same. The return of the Same renders determinate the indeterminacy of the open space of non-coincidence. The indeterminacy of the open space is, on the one hand, a recognition of nothingness. Merleau-Ponty aptly remarks that he approaches the abyss by an '"indirect" method': '"negative philosophy" like "negative theology."'[43] This indeterminacy functions, however, as an affirmation of the non-recognition of difference. The open space of non-coincidence is at once every possibility and no possibility, a continuation of the ever more subtle presence of the Same. The difficulties faced by Foucault's economy of the body have not vanished, but as a consequence of Merleau-Ponty's repatterning of the Same in the indeterminate, have not been broached. Merleau-Ponty states, '. . . these *facts* have no *explicative power*. They express differently an ontological relief.'[44] Yet, even *if* Merleau-Ponty's ontological 'facts' were devoid of explicative power, they would not be exempt from interpretation. The neutrality of his statement fails to recognize and affirm difference, and thereby sets forth a metaphysics of the Same which is so much taken for granted it scarcely is noticed.

The tumble into metaphysics, present in each of Merleau-Ponty's attempts to secure an ideal grounding for his ontology, assumes its most critical dimension in the perceptual logic by which his economy of the body is defined. The perceptual logic of touching and touched, although reversible at will, has a unidirectional structure. The unidirectionality appears in the *Phenomenology of Perception*:

> When one of my hands touches the other, the hand that moves functions as subject and the other as object.[45]

The unidirectional structure continues in *The Visible and the Invisible*:

> My left hand is always on the verge of touching my right hand touching the things, but I never reach coincidence; the coincidence eclipses at the moment of realization, and one of two things always occurs: either my right hand really passes over to the rank of the touched, but then its hold on the world is interrupted; or it retains its hold on the world, but then I do not really touch it.[46]

The system of exchanges moves in one direction: touching to touched. The exchange of the hands, from the active to the passive, in the *Phenomenology of Perception*, opens to an ontological grounding in *The Visible and the Invisible*. No longer are the hands in the exchange caught in the web of their own actions. There is an anchor, a 'hold,' albeit only one, which identifies the hand that is 'touching.' The 'hold' is transferred from hand to hand, but is not displaced.

In this logic, 'the difference between identicals' is marked not by nothingness, but by the Same. The rule of the Same, expressed in the oblique identity of the hand that is 'holding' with that which it 'holds,' regulates the possibilities of the perceptual logic. The rule of the Same confers on the hand that is touching, by virtue of that hand's proximity to the ground, a primacy that is maintained until its 'hold' is magically interrupted. Each moment in the system of exchanges is a step away from the truth of the Same and into illusion: the 'world' . . . the hand with its 'hold' on the world . . . the hand which reaches for that hand and its 'hold.' The body which 'there is' only in relation to its 'hold' on the Same is not without illusion.

Barthes and the Body: A Catastrophic Collapse of Economies

The repeated fall of the body into a metaphysical circulation is brought to a halt, at least in principle, by Barthes' body of bliss. Barthes' interpretation of the body as fiction is concomitant with the collapse of that economy in which there can be illusion.

An affirmation of plurality and a positive discourse of the body are, for Barthes, integral to activity that follows the death of God. Writing the body is both 'anti-theological,' it refuses to fix meaning, it refuses God, reason, science, and law, and apart from 'the theological,' for it releases 'a multi-dimensional space in which a variety of writings, none of them original, blend and clash.'[47] Plurality is affirmed exuberantly by Barthes, who speaks of a 'triumphant plural' of which '. . . the networks are many and interact, without any one of them being able to surpass the next.'[48] Contrary to those who would give primacy to the deconstruction of language and who frequently consider discussion of the body superfluous, Barthes argues that the reformulation of language is contingent on the deconstruction of normative ideas of the body. The 'plural body' is introduced by Barthes and is referenced indirectly under the phrase 'to write the body,' where next to an anatomical sketch Barthes notes, 'Neither the skin, nor the muscles, nor the bones, nor the nerves, but the rest: an awkward, fibrous, shaggy, raveled thing, a clown's coat.'[49]

'I speak from my own body,' a phrase ascribed to Barthes, marks the transition from phenomenology to deconstruction with regard to the body. The subjectivity of the lived body disappears as the subject unmakes itself, dissolving into the tissue, the text.[50] 'Language' does not speak, in contrast to Heidegger's phenomenological ontology, nor does 'man' speak, counter to the tradition of metaphysical philosophical anthropology. Body speaks unto body; 'language lined with flesh' writes aloud.[51] In the spirit of Nietzsche's wisdom of the body, Barthes institutes 'scription': 'when my body pursues its own ideas.'[52] 'Writing with One's Feet,' writing which is but the instrument of an originary body, is displaced by 'scription,' writing which is 'the hand and thus the body . . . not the *soul* but the subject.'[53] Scription also brings to an end the naturalization of language and truth, for the stereotype, a repetition of the word as though it were natural, and the morality of truth, a solidification of old metaphors, occur, Barthes claims, when the body is missing.[54]

The 'materialist subject,' and the subject, 'not as illusion, but as fiction,' are prominent themes in Barthes' work. The fictive subject is individual and irreducible. My fictive identity as individual is, for Barthes, 'a final, rarest fiction.'[55] When I imagine myself as individual I uphold not a metaphysical personhood, but a staging of self in 'the theater of society,' not an illusion of unity, but an affirmation of the plural, not a transcendent entity that would precede or exceed writing, but that which is born simultaneously with the text.[56] An individuality is, moreover, 'the given which makes my body separate from other bodies,' that which 'can be divided no further.'[57] The fatality of my individuality is that 'my body will never be yours.'[58] The reduction of an individuality, that final rarest fiction, to amorphous being, or to a blank slate, is itself a metaphysical imposition. No discourse can reduce one body to another.[59] The erasure of my individuality is an illusion of metaphysics and, as is evident once one stands apart from that economy, is impossible.

Does Barthes' positive discourse of the body accomplish all that he claims for it? Or, is it necessary that some natural body be posited in order to sustain any positive discourse on the body, such that the displacement of metaphysics by reclaiming the body is vitiated from the start? Barthes, like Merleau-Ponty, often seems to render a positive discourse of the body only by retaining a natural aspect of the body. At the limits of scription we find a certain essentialism, an assumption of the 'natural' wisdom of the body, the imprint of an anthropologism that Barthes renounced but did not entirely avoid. Yet the essentialism that might be attributed to Barthes' writing the body by a first, metaphysical glance dissolves upon examination. His anti-essentialist statement that writing is that space 'where our subject slips away, the *negative* where all identity is lost,'[60] may seem to conflict with his affirmation of the material subject and its fictive identity. The conflict is resolved, however, if a distinction is made between metaphysical and non-metaphysical contexts, in this instance, between the subject and the principle of identity of the metaphysical economy and the subject and identity as fiction. Barthes' reference to the body of the writer as 'the most real and intimate part of him'[61] claims, when approached from a non-metaphysical direction, no more than the constellation of fictive identities without which the writer here and now would not be. When considered from a perspective that is not enclosed in the metaphysical, Barthes' embodied individual appears not as an ontic 'fact' that enters into the valuations of a metaphysical philosophical anthropology, but as an irreducible difference, a plurality that defies erasure.

Desensualization, the hostility of philosophers toward the senses that was so disparaged by Nietzsche, is brought to a close by Barthes' body of bliss.[62] My historical subject, according to Barthes, balances the contradictory interplay of the senses in the form of cultural pleasure and of non-cultural bliss. The metaphysical economy of the dividing line, represented quite literally as '/,' constitutes the economic system of cultural pleasure. The economy of the dividing line upholds all epistemologies of the law, for it sustains the power of legal substitution, which is the basis of meaning.[63] The ingredients of illusion – just equivalences and contrasting opposites, circulatory codes, rules of exchange, and lines of propriety – all are sustained by the line that divides.

Cultural pleasure ignores non-cultural bliss; bliss does not correspond to or satisfy, but surprises and exceeds the desire of cultural pleasure. The body of bliss produces not the absence of the lawful, but its nullity.[64] At present out of place, adrift, the body of bliss nullifies epistemologies of the law; it takes the life out of Parliament.

Does not the enthusiastic reach of the body of bliss, exceed its formidable embrace? Bliss, Barthes writes, 'can erupt, across the centuries, out of certain texts that were nonetheless written to the glory of the dreariest, of the most sinister philosophy.'[65] Similarly, bliss erupts out of the body that has, for centuries, been claimed by the metaphysical circulation. Bliss exercises a force of suspension, 'a veritable *epoché*, a stoppage which congeals all recognized values.'[66] That which is placed in suspension is the legislator of values and meaning: the dividing line. Whereas Foucault's analysis of the body focuses on the power of the Same, Barthes' interpretation of the body emphasizes the power of the dividing line that gives rise to the Same and the different, the present and the absent, to the endless duplicity of inversions and substitutions that sustain metaphysics. Once the dividing line is suspended there is, Barthes claims, 'a generalized collapse of economies . . . the economy of language . . ., the economy of genders . . ., the economy of the body (its parts cannot be interchanged . . .), the economy of money.'[67] This collapse, the end of all economies of truth and meaning is, in Barthes' words, 'catastrophic.'

Yet, what actually collapses? It is on this point that Barthes' approach to the body is ambiguous. Barthes seems committed to the drifting, atopic, body of bliss, whose eruption stops the economies of law and meaning and brings about their collapse. The sudden shift brought about by the 'revolutionary and asocial' body of bliss marks the end of economics.[68] Barthes is also committed, however, to a dual economy that is to be balanced by the historical subject. Here cultural pleasure and non-cultural bliss are affirmed as the double surface of reality and utopia, the alternation of two values by which the writer bestows meaning.[69] While Barthes often dismisses the dual economy as reactive and tactical, he also invokes that economy as necessary to the writerly art that precedes from meaning and governs it.[70]

This ambiguity reflects Barthes' metaphysical position on the transcendence of the body of bliss, and its resolution requires that that metaphysical stance be overcome. The body, Barthes writes, 'exceeds the exchange in which it is caught up: no commerce in the world, no political virtue can exhaust the body.'[71] The excess of the body of bliss situates that body apart from culture and, at the same time, places it in need of culture. The body of bliss, which is posited as non-cultural, 'erupts' only in the midst of culture. Its atopic force, like a lightning bolt from out of the blue, requires that the body of cultural pleasure be there to receive its impact. In this sense, the body of bliss reinstates the economy of the dividing line, but at a new level: the division between elements of the metaphysical economy shifts to a division between the metaphysical economy and a non-metaphysical economy. Is not a culture constituted, however, by the body of bliss? And need the identity of that culture depend on that body's exercise of transcendence?

Barthes' body of bliss presupposes a metaphysical univocity. Although the body is plural, its non-metaphysical 'drifting' is parasitic on the Same, on that body whose circulation is enclosed in metaphysics. If, however, the implications of Barthes' triumphant pluralism were followed consistently, economies, like bodies, would be plural. Amidst a plurality of non-metaphysical economies, each with an individual culture, an irreducible circulation, the body of bliss might be one possibility among many.

Counterfeit Bodies

In the circulation of metaphysics that made, forgot, and then believed to be eternally true all of its creations, the body, like all else, is a fiction. The fraudulence of the body is not that it is fabricated in imitation of an original fact which it is not. The body defrauds all economies of fact by artifice, which it recognizes precisely as that.

Metaphysics mistakes fiction for illusion when it believes that the body is its counterfeit. Most recently, this belief has been given new credence by the assertion that the body is a last shadow of metaphysics, that the body, no matter how conceived, is but the counterfeit of the Same. It is not coincidental that such a claim, which reaffirms the scope of metaphysics and thereby contributes to its restoration, emerges with Nietzsche's heralding of the death of God. Plurality is banished as metaphysics attempts once more to consume what it believes – uneasily – to be its own creation.

The demise of metaphysics is effected, however, not by the incursion of what is foreign to it, but by metaphysics itself. Umberto Eco shows, in *The Name of the Rose*, that the Western metaphysical tradition is destroyed not by the burning of the library at Alexandria by 'infidels,' but by its own attempt to silence what it perceives to be foreign. In this instance, what is thought most dangerously foreign is Aristotle's treatise on laughter, which is isolated and walled in at the heart of all metaphysical circulation.

Eco's account of the risibility of the 'foreign' bears directly on the body, though he does not explore its significance. Laughter is exiled in *The Name of the Rose* not by chance, but because of its extraordinary effect on the body: laughter makes the human body appear to be no longer human. Or, in other terms, laughter so radically changes the relations between the 'parts' of the body that the metaphysical economy can no longer recognize what it once believed to be its own. Specifically, laughter is held to turn the face of 'man' into the face of a 'monkey': to annul the dividing line between 'human' and 'animal,' and by implication, the line between what Western metaphysics perceives to be European and what it perceives to be African.[72] The endeavor to insure that the body of 'man' not circulate in any economy other than metaphysics turns, however, against itself. The keeper of the secrets of the body, in a futile final attempt to legislate meaning, consumes that which metaphysics would keep secret and ignites the edifice of 'knowledge.'

While the Same consumes itself, the body drifts. The body, counterfeit, is outside the law: the annulation of the law. This body challenges the metaphysical economy, and also the current scope of philosophy. The counterfeit body brings with it an insistence on the plurality of ideas and values which are transacted in local currencies, and which often have no exchange value elsewhere. The counterfeit body enables a recognition of the plurality of economies which are sometimes in conflict, sometimes harmonious, and often oblivious of one another.

The formulation of a non-metaphysical social philosophy that undertakes the difficult task of situating itself *within* the most common of experiences *and* beyond metaphysics is a crucial step in the exploration of local economies. Such a social philosophy gathers experimentally that which is outside what has most frequently been considered philosophical – the everyday, the ordinary, the commonplace, at least to some – and that which lies apart from what is considered the correct, because accepted, scope of philosophical articulation. An insistence on the plurality of non-metaphysical economies is consistent, as well, with Barthes' reflections on ethnology and fiction:

> The ethnological book . . . noting and classifying all of reality, even the most trivial, the most sensual aspects; this encyclopedia does not adulterate the Other by reducing it to the Same; appropriation diminishes, the Self's certitude grows lighter. Finally, of all learned discourses, the ethnological seems to come closest to a Fiction.[73]

An ethnological approach to the body need not be the loss of philosophy, but the articulation of plural economies of the body that might jolt, and thereby displace, the persistence of metaphysical illusion.

Notes

1. Michel Foucault, *The Order of Things: An Archeology of the Human Sciences* (New York: Random House, 1970), p. 3 42; Martin Heidegger, *The End of Philosophy,* trans. Joan Stambaugh (New York: Harper and Row, 1973), pp. 14, 15.
2. Rodolphe Gasché, '*Ecce Homo* or the Written Body,' *Oxford Literary Review* 7 (1985), pp. 3–24.
3. Heidegger, *Being and Time*, trans. Macquarrie and Robinson (New York: Harper and Row, 1962), p. 142; 'Letter on Humanism,' *Heidegger: Basic Writings,* trans. David Krell (New York: Harper and Row, 1977), pp. 189–242; Foucault, *The Order of Things*, pp. 385–7.
4. Heidegger, *Being and Time,* p. 142, *Nietzsche,* vol. 1, *The Will to Power as Art,* trans. David Krell (San Francisco: Harper and Row, 1979), pp. 98, 99; *Heracleitus Seminar 1966/67,* trans. Charles Seibert (University: University of Alabama, 1979), p. 146. It is interesting to note that Edmund Husserl, too, altered his initial, seemingly inexorable critique of philosophical anthropology in his later writings. See my 'Husserl's Philosophical Anthropology,' *Philosophy Today*, 21 (1977), pp. 347–55, which was presented at the founding conference of the Collegium Phaenomenologicum, June, 1976.
5. Friedrich Nietzsche, *Thus Spoke Zarathustra*, trans. Walter Kaufmann (New York: Viking Press, 1966), p. 34.
6. Ibid.
7. Nietzsche, *The Gay Science,* trans. Walter Kaufmann (New York: Vintage, 1974), p. 63.
8. Nietzsche, 'On Truth and Lie in an Extra-Moral Sense,' *The Portable Nietzsche,* trans. Walter Kaufmann (New York: Viking Press, 1968), p. 45.
9. Nietzsche, *The Will to Power,* trans. Walter Kaufmann and R.J. Hollingdale (New York: Vintage, 1968), pp. 266, 306.
10. Foucault, *The Order of Things,* pp. 342, 385, 386.
11. Foucault, *Discipline and Punish: The Birth of the Prison,* trans. Alan Sheridan (New York: Vintage, 1979), p. 28.
12. Ibid., p. 136.
13. Ibid., p. 137.
14. Foucault, *The Archaeology of Knowledge,* trans. Alan Sheridan Smith (New York: Harper and Row, 1972), pp. 12, 15; *Power/Knowledge: Selected Interviews and Other Writings 1972–1977,* ed. Colin Gordon (New York: Pantheon, 1980), p. 117.
15. Foucault, *Power/Knowledge,* p. 98.
16. Foucault, *The History of Sexuality,* vol. 1, *An Introduction,* trans. Robert Hurley (New York: Vintage, 1980), p. 159.
17. Foucault, *Discipline and Punish,* pp. 306, 307.
18. Foucault, *Power/Knowledge,* pp. 81, 82; *Discipline and Punish*, pp. 61, 67, 73.
19. Foucault, *Power/Knowledge,* pp. 81, 82.
20. Ibid., p. 84.
21. Ibid., p. 85.
22. Foucault, *The Order of Things*, p. 342. See also *Power/Knowledge,* p. 58.
23. *Oxford English Dictionary: The Compact Edition,* vol. 1 (Oxford: Oxford University Press, 1971), p. 1348.
24. Nietzsche, *The Gay Science,* p. 181.
25. Maurice Merleau-Ponty, *The Visible and the Invisible,* trans. Alphonso Lingis (Evanston: Northwestern University Press, 1968), p. 250.
26. Merleau-Ponty, *The Phenomenology of Perception,* trans. Colin Smith (London: Routledge, Kegan and Paul, 1962), p. 150; Nietzsche, *The Will to Power*, p. 283.
27. Merleau-Ponty, *The Phenomenology of Perception,* p. 166.

28. Ibid., p. 137.
29. Merleau-Ponty, *The Visible and the Invisible,* pp. 139, 250.
30. Ibid., pp. 140, 137, 138.
31. Ibid., p. 143.
32. Ibid., p. 255.
33. Ibid.
34. Ibid., p. 263.
35. Ibid.
36. Merleau-Ponty, 'Eye and Mind,' tr. Carleton Dallery, *Primacy of Perception* (Evanston: Northwestern University Press, 1964), pp. 163, 170.
37. Merleau-Ponty, *The Visible and the Invisible,* pp. 263, 264.
38. Merleau-Ponty, 'Eye and Mind,' *Primacy of Perception,* p. 164.
39. Merleau-Ponty, *The Visible and the Invisible*, p. 264.
40. Ibid., pp. 246, 264.
41. Ibid., p. 264.
42. Ibid., p. 152.
43. Ibid., p. 179.
44. Ibid., p. 256. For another development of this theme see 'Through the Wild Region: An Essay of Phenomenological Feminism,' *Review of Existential Psychology and Psychiatry,* special issue on Merleau-Ponty, 18 (1986), forthcoming, which was first presented at the Collegium Phaenomenologicum, July, 1979.
45. Merleau-Ponty, *Phenomenology of Perception,* p. 315.
46. Merleau-Ponty, *The Visible and the Invisible,* pp. 147, 148.
47. Roland Barthes, *Image-Music-Text*, trans. Stephen Heath (New York: Hill and Wang, 1977), p. 146.
48. Barthes, *The Grain of the Voice: Interviews 1962–1980,* trans. Linda Coverdale (New York: Hill and Wang, 1985), p. 242; *Roland Barthes by Roland Barthes,* trans. Richard Howard (New York: Hill and Wang, 1977), p. 60.
49. Barthes, *Roland Barthes by Roland Barthes,* p. 180.
50. Michel-Antoine Burnier and Patrick Rambaud, *Le Roland Barthes sans peine* (Paris: Ballard, 1978), p. 41. Barthes, *The Pleasure of the Text,* trans. Richard Miller (New York: Hill and Wang, 1975), p. 64; *Le Grain de la voix* (Paris: Seuil, 1981), p. 184.
51. Barthes, *The Pleasure of the Text,* pp. 66, 72.
52. Ibid., p. 17.
53. Ibid., pp. 17, 57.
54. Barthes, *Roland Barthes by Roland Barthes,* p. 90.
55. Barthes, *The Pleasure of the Text,* pp. 61, 62.
56. Ibid., *Image-Music-Text,* p. 145.
57. Barthes, *The Pleasure of the Text,* p. 62; *The Responsibility of Forms,* trans. Richard Howard (New York: Hill and Wang, 1985), p. 170.
58. Barthes, *The Responsibility of Forms,* p. 170.
59. Ibid.
60. Barthes, *Image-Music-Text,* p. 142.
61. Barthes, *The Pleasure of the Text,* p. 72.
62. Nietzsche, *The Will to Power,* pp. 253, 434; Barthes, *The Pleasure of the Text,* p. 16.
63. Barthes, *S/Z: An Essay,* trans. Richard Miller (New York: Hill and Wang, 1974), pp. 88, 215, 216.
64. Barthes, *Roland Barthes by Roland Barthes,* p. 112; *The Pleasure of the Text,* pp. 57, 62.
65. Barthes, *The Pleasure of the Text,* p. 39.
66. Ibid., p. 65.

67. Barthes, *S/Z*, p. 215.
68. Barthes, *Roland Barthes by Roland Barthes,* p. 49; *The Pleasure of the Text,* p. 23.
69. Barthes, *Roland Barthes by Roland Barthes,* p. 76.
70. Ibid., p. 49.
71. Barthes, *The Responsibility of Forms,* p. 171.
72. Umberto Eco, *The Name of the Rose,* trans. William Weaver (New York: Warner, 1983), pp. 149–53, 573–85.
73. Barthes, *Roland Barthes by Roland Barthes,* p. 84.

The inevitable and slips of the tongue

J.M. HEATON

Introduction

Some years ago I saw a young man who consulted me as he wanted psychotherapy. After recounting the history of his childhood and adolescence during which he was orphaned he said 'Oh well, I suppose it was all *inviteable.'* I looked at him with an expression of puzzlement. He repeated 'Yes, it was all inviteable.' I repeated to him what he had said to me. He began to look embarrassed. And after several minutes of confusion he managed to say: 'I meant it was all *inevitable.'* I pointed out to him, and over the years I proved right, that his slip of the tongue depicted a central problem in that he did not clearly understand the nature of destiny and wanted to 'invite' and so control, important events in his life rather than see that what happened to him and what he was were inextricably bound together. By wanting to invite events he was denying himself. So no wonder he was in confusion and unhappy.

His stance towards his life reminded me of a remark made by Kierkegaard in his Journal in 1848.[1] 'I am overwhelmed by gratitude for all that providence has done for me. How is it possible for things to go so well? Poetically speaking I can only say that there is nothing that has happened in my life of which I cannot say, that is the very thing which suits my nature and disposition; I lack nothing. I was unhappy in my love; but I simply cannot imagine myself happy unless I were to become a different person altogether. But in my unhappiness I was happy. Humanly speaking, I am saved by one already dead, my father; but I simply cannot imagine myself having been saved by someone living. And so I became an author in exactly the way which suited the latent possibilities of my nature; and then I was persecuted – oh, had that been wanting my life would not have been mine. There is melancholy in everything in my life, but then again an indescribable happiness.'

The Best of all possible worlds

Now Kierkegaard's understanding of the nature of destiny is often associated

J.C. Sallis, G. Moneta and J. Taminiaux (eds.), The Collegium Phaenomenologicum, 309–318.
© *Kluwer Academic Publishers.*

with the notion that our world is the best of all possible worlds and leads to the problem of justifying the ways of God to men. If God is good why does he allow evil in the world? Surely a good God would create the best of all possible worlds?

The most celebrated formulation of the problem is attributed to Epicurus.[2]

> God either wishes to take away evils and cannot, or he can and does not wish to, or he neither wishes to nor is able, or he both wishes to and is able. If he wishes to and is not able, he is weak, which does not fall in with the notion of God. If he is able to and does not wish to, he is envious, which is equally foreign to God. If he neither wishes to nor is able, he is both envious and weak, and therefore not God. If he both wishes to and is able, which alone is fitting to God, whence, therefore, are these evils, and why does he not remove them?

The problem was taken up and discussed with great vehemence in Islam following al-Ghazali's statement.[3] 'There is not in possibility anything more wonderful than what is.' This statement engendered controversy, at times including physical violence, from the twelfth to the nineteenth century. It seemed to its critics to lead to a restriction of divine omnipotence. For if nothing in possibility is 'more wonderful' or more perfect than what exists here and now then God seems very weak. We just need to contemplate Milton's catalogue[4] of some mens' ills to see the point of this:

> Immediately a place
> Before his eyes appeared, sad, noysom, dark,
> A Lazar-house it seemed, wherein were laid
> Numbers of all diseas'd, all maladies
> Of ghastly Spasm, or racking torture, qualmes
> Of heart-sick Agonie, all feavorous kinds,
> Convulsions, Epilepsies, fierce Catarrhs,
> Intestin Stone and Ulcer, Colic pangs
> Demoniac Phrenzie, moaping Melancholie
> And Moon struck madness, pining Atrophie,
> Marasmus, and wide wasting Pestilence,
> Dropsies, and Asthma's, and Joint-racking Rheums.

Surely modern medicine can improve on that? If God is omnipotent why does He not create more and more excellent worlds ad infinitum?

The critics of al-Ghazali laid emphasis on the 'necessary' coming-to-be of the world. The act of creation itself for them was totally ruled by necessity. But if this were so then there was no real act of creation. They had the ideal of the purity of the logical 'must' before their eyes and so assumed that everything was logically determined. But creation is not an event occuring in the world and implies freedom and freedom is not some sort of abstract object that is ruled by logic.

This argument in Islam is mirrored in European thought in Leibniz's disagreement with Spinoza. Spinoza stated[5] 'All things must have followed of necessity from a given nature of God, and they were determined for existence or action in a certain way by the necessity of divine nature.'

Leibniz[6] protested that God acts sub ratione boni and not sub ratione perfecti. Creation is an act of will and power and is not to be understood in terms of His nature which is subject to logical necessity. Leibniz's idea that our world is organised to be the best of all possible worlds is of profound importance for it led to his insight that of all possible processes, the only ones that actually occur are those that involve minimum expenditure of action (the principle of least action). This was basic to the development of theoretical physics and led to the development of the calculus of variations and minimal surfaces which has applications in pretty well every branch of science.

The world as it is may be perfect but it only comes to be after a prior act of divine creation. The very fact that in this world there are perfect and imperfect beings is decisive proof of God's perfection in creating the world. The following analogy from the Islamic tradition illustrates this.[7]

If there were a king who had many storehouses – a storehouse of jewels, a storehouse of gold, a storehouse of silver and a storehouse of coins – and he then gave alms from all his storehouses, he would be absolutely generous. But if he gives from one storehouse and not from the others he can be deemed miserly in relation to what he has not given.

But there is no doubt the God, in this world which He produced, gives from all His storehouses.

In this story the king represents God and the precious metals various degrees of wisdom and the coins evil people. Without the coins we would not be able to recognise the value and the distinction of the precious materials.

The point of al-Ghazali's statement 'There is not in possibility anything more wonderful than what is' was to invite men to have complete trust in God so they did not despair over evil or over a good that eluded them. Men are arrogant and presumptuous so they must learn to be before God 'like an infant who knows no refuge other than his mother's breast.'[8] This position does not mean that we must be merely resigned before the decrees of fate, it is not a stoic position. It should lead to a changed perception of the world; being in touch with the Being of the world rather than being hypnotised by events and their causes and effects. So whatever happens to the person is perceived not in terms of his selfish desires but in terms of the divine will. God is seen as the only real agent, every action of man is the expression of His will.

> Not even the casual glance of a spectator nor the stray thought in the mind comes to be outside the sphere of His will. He is the originator; He causes recurrence; He is the effecter of what He wills.[9]

> Were men, jinn, angels, and devils to join together in order to act in motion a single atom in this world, or to bring it to rest, without God's will and volition, they would be incapable of that.[9]

This is the point where it is appropriate to turn to consider slips of the tongue apparently trivial stray thoughts which Freud's genius raised to importance.

Determinism and Slips of the Tongue

Freud ended 'The Psycho-pathology of Everyday Life' with a chapter on determinism. He thought that he had shown that 'certain seemingly unintentional performances prove, if psychoanalytic methods of investigation are applied to them, to have valid motives and to be *determined* by motives unknown to consciousness.'[10]

He gave an entirely psychological explanation of slips of the tongue. He compared them to dreams, jokes, and symptoms of neurosis and claimed that they were compromise – formations resulting from antagonism between the subjects' conscious intentions and thoughts that he has repressed. They are disorders of psychical functioning due to incompletely suppressed psychical material which, although pushed away by consciousness, has nevertheless not been robbed of all its power to express itself.

So in the example I gave of the young man saying 'inviteable' instead of 'inevitable' Freud's explanation would be that the young man secretly wished to control his life so that what happened would be only what he invited because of the pain of what had happened to him in his childhood. In the initial interview this wish broke through and so he said 'inviteable' instead of 'inevitable.'

In giving this sort of explanation Freud thought that he was demonstrating the strict determinism of all our psychic acts. An apparently arbitrary psychical act can be shown to be determined by unconscious psychical processes. The unconscious thought is understood as being some sort of object which is present though hidden in the unconscious where it can act causally on consciousness and so cause the slip of the tongue. This hidden object can be discovered by the technique of free association which Freud thought he had discovered.

Freud considered he was giving the cause of slips of the tongue and other parapraxes. He thought motives were causes and that by finding an unconscious motive he was finding a cause of a psychical process and so restoring complete determinism to mental life and making it amenable to scientific investigation.

Cause and reason

We must now consider the difference between reasons and causes. In Freud's understanding of cause, the one usual in science, a cause and its effect are distinct existences so that the existence of the cause does not logically imply the existence of the effect, or vice versa. Furthermore, if a sequence is a causal one then there is some description of the situation that falls under a law. Science seeks to explain sequences of events by putting forward hypotheses as to what law the causal sequence obeys and then by experiment and observation it seeks to prove what universal propositions are true of the sequence, i.e., what law the sequence obeys.

Freud explains slips of the tongue in this way. Subjection to the pleasure principle is the general law that mental events obey and he tries to show how slips of the tongue obey this law.

Now is a motive a cause? Consider this case. A and B are playing chess and both are experienced players. To the surprise of the spectator B makes an odd, apparently senseless move. When the game is finished B is asked 'What caused you to make that move?.' B answers 'I wanted to disconcert my opponent.' This answer gives B's reason or motive for making the move. Now when B gives this answer he is not offering an hypothesis for his move, there are no experiments we can do to prove or disprove what he says. We simply trust the speaker if he appears fairly sane and if his explanation seems to fit what we know of the circumstances, as they do in this case.

If, however, B had been in a panic or felt a momentary dizziness when he made the odd move he then might have said that the panic caused him to make the move and we the onlookers might also say that panic caused him to do something odd. So here there is a causal relation: an event, panic, might cause another event, an odd move in chess. Our general knowledge of human behavior confirms that this is so.

Now let us turn to slips of the tongue and other parapraxes. An odd move in chess could be a parapraxis for we might not know why we did it. But does Freud actually treat it as a causal matter? No, the person at first cannot give a reason for the move so he will tend to explain it in a causal manner: 'something made me do it' is a common phrase. But Freud does not accept this. He asked the person to say whatever comes to mind; to stop speaking and trying to find an explanation and ponder awhile. In the famous 'Aliquis' case[11] he tells his friend 'I must only ask you to tell me, candidly and uncritically, whatever comes into your mind if you direct your attention to the forgotten word without any definite aim.' Freud then made comments, well aimed questions and shrewd observations from his knowledge of human nature and customs to the person free associating. And when he found a reasonable explanation which he and the person who had made the slip agreed upon then he stopped his enquiries and declared he had found the answer.

His method then is not like that of a scientist investigating a cause by hypothesis and experiment but that of a man who gives a person time and encouragement to find a reason and to speak a truth.

Freud went on to develop a theory which purported to give the causes of slips of the tongue because he wanted to show that determinism rules our mental life. But an examination of his actual practice shows that he did not find causes but uncovered reasons with patience and subtlety.

Determinism and reason

So we must ask what is the relation between determinism and reasons. If we uncover reasons for slips of the tongue, dreams and neurotic symptoms does that mean our mental life is ruled by determinism? Or are reasons arbitrary so we can never discover any order in human life and everything occurs purely by chance? What is the place of causality in our mental life? Is causality our only refuge from chance?

We have seen that Leibniz criticised Spinoza's necessitarianism which assumes that blind necessity rules the world. God acts, Leibniz said, sub ratione boni and not sub ratione perfecti.

So what is reason? Leibniz formulated the commonplace, nihil est sine ratione, 'Nothing is without reason' or to put it positively 'Everything has its reason [or ground].'

Ratio [reason] is connected with *reor* [Latin] 'to hold the belief or opinion, think, imagine, suppose, deem' (Oxford Latin Dictionary). *Ratio* is the act or process or manner with regard to which we 'reor.' So the principle of reason emerges as saying that nothing (nihil) – be it what is thought, believed, imagined or supposed – nothing is as this being without its reason (ratio). So reasons pertains to being.[12] That is, there is an intrinsic relation between reason and being. The laws of reason are not determined from some place outside of being, imposed on it as from above, but are somehow connected with being so that we understand being from within.

Furthermore this implies that freedom is related to reason and being. For it is not possible to understand being – to think, believe, suppose or imagine something – unless there is freedom. For only something that exists as a free being could be subject to the lawfulness of reason. We do not say that automata are reasonable; they do not obey the laws of reason any more than an unconscious person does, they have no choice but to perform as they perform. A free being on the other hand always has the ability to disobey the laws of reason, he can put on a performance.

When we make a slip of the tongue it appears to have no reason. Ordinarily, people have said it happened by chance, or if they have wanted to be technical they have said slips are due to some mechanism such as cortical ataxia or inattention. These explanations give a reason – some causal mechanism or the 'action' of chance – but do not appeal to or recognise the reason of the person who makes the slip.

But Freud does appeal to the person's reason for he appeals to norms recognised by the person making the slip. Thus the slip must not exceed certain dimensions fixed by our judgment which we characterise by the expression 'within the limits of the normal.' And the same function must have been correctly performed before or we must believe ourselves capable of carrying it out correctly.[13] Thus if the young man simply did not know of the word 'inevitable' and its meaning it would not have been a slip of the tongue. He must be able to recognise the slip and recognise the reasons that are uncovered for it as being true.

So what is the evidence that the reasons uncovered for the slip are true? Now there are different modes of evidence according to what is being asserted. Observation is, of course, usually appealed to over empirical matters. But evidence for reasons is not an empirical matter. What is the evidence that 8 + 8 = 16? This depends on skills like counting and adding which have to be taught and which are unquestioned in the community. But what sort of evidence do we seek when we question whether we love someone or not or they love us? What evidence have I that my own hand is holding my pen? We are not taught these matters and they are not a matter simply of observation. For what observations can I make on myself that make me sure that I love or am loved? They are all defeasible. Similarly, if I doubt that this is my hand then it is no good looking at it and saying look I am moving it for in cases of such basic doubting how can I be sure that my memory still works or that I know the meaning of the words I use? But nevertheless I use my hand to hold the pen with perfect assurance and doubt simply does not enter here; similarly we can love and feel loved with assurance.

So we can say that somewhere we must begin with not doubting and that is not, so to speak, hasty but excusable: it is a part of judging. We do not explicitly learn the propositions that stand fast for us such as 'This is my hand that is holding the pen.' We can *discover* them subsequently like the axis around which a body rotates. This axis is not fixed in the sense that anything holds it fast, but the movement around it determines its immobility. No one ever taught me that my hand does not disappear when I hold my pen and don't pay attention to it but yet this is a fundamental presupposition of much of what I say in certain circumstances.[14]

So we can say that we have to be already in the world before we can observe things and make true statements about them. Our readiness to make causal statements about things is because we are perpetually engaged in producing one thing from another, in the know-how related to producing in our technically orientated world. So it is understandable that when we observe people making slips of the tongue we should ask how they are produced. What part of the neural mechanisms or the mental mechanisms produces the slip? Freud tried to put it this way when he explained them, in his case, or course, using mental mechanism to explain them. Thus concluding that our mental life is completely determined and that motives are causes.

Heidegger on Slips of the Tongue

Heidegger discussed slips of the tongue in 'The Nature of Language.'[15] He noted that in a slip of the tongue 'we leave unspoken what we have in mind and, without rightly giving it thought, undergo moments in which language itself has distantly and fleetingly touched us with its essential being.'

Language withholds the appropriate word and may put a false word in its place but if we attend to the slip then we may undergo an experience with language which may enable us to glimpse its essence.

What is it to undergo an experience with language? To undergo an experience with something is to be struck by it; it may even overwhelm and transform us. The experience is not of our own making, we suffer and submit to it. This is not the same as masochism in which we bring on the experience ourselves. Nor is it the same as fatalism in which we passively accept the blows of fate. So to undergo an experience with language is to let ourselves be claimed by it in its own time and way.

To experience language is not to gather information about it for the collector of information has some other end in view than allowing language itself to strike him. Also it is not the same as using language to describe, order, calculate, express feelings and all the other everyday uses to which it is put. For in these cases we are not submitting to language but using it to deal with each other and things in the world. Language then has, so to speak, got to hold itself back in order that we may use it. But when we submit to an experience with language, language itself bares its essence to us.

So what does Heidegger mean by the essence of language? To understand this we must let language speak for itself. It is not a tool which we can use or a system which we can explore. In a slip of the tongue we are taken unaware, we have no time to explore or use language. We have to submit, we often stop speaking and in Freud's language we may free associate or perhaps it is better to say we muse for a while; we allow words to float before our minds, we allow language to play with us and then we may remember, and a word that reveals comes to mind. The appropriate and competent word names something that we have forgotten. And in this naming that which we have forgotten comes to mind, it shows itself to us. So the essence of language is saying as showing.

When our young man said 'inviteable' for 'inevitable' by stopping him in his tracks we allowed language to show him both the distortion 'inviteable' which was so subtly and revealingly distorted and the normal word 'inevitable' which instead of just being slipped over as in idle talk revealed itself to him.

The saying of these words did not merely connect a word on one side and a concept on the other but the word itself was the relation which bodied forth the concept so that we could see it with some of its force and profundity. In speaking which is a saying we listen to the language speak and so for a moment speak thoughtfully.

So we can say that the concept only is itself fully there when the appropriate word names it. And this naming relates us to things and in so doing lets us see them as inseparably bound to us, it draws our attention to the way in which our being is always a being-together-with.

This allowing language to speak when we attend to a slip of the tongue cannot be subsumed under a method as did Freud when he claimed his method of free-association was the only really scientific instrument suitable for investigating the mind. By thinking his investigation was a method he subordinated himself to method and so method held coercive power over the development of his knowledge. It led him to see the mind in terms of mental mechanisms and to develop his psychology as a sort of physics of the mind. So psychoanalysis rapidly became assimilated to modern technology.

Ironically, Freud never attended fully to his own words and practice. Thus in the 'Aliquis' case at the beginning of his Psychopathology of Everyday Life he told his friend 'I must only ask you to tell me, candidly and uncritically, whatever comes into your mind if you direct your attention to the forgotten word without any definite aim.' But to be 'candid and uncritical' is not a method, all methods have an aim and he tells his companion to have no aim. To be candid is surely to allow a truth to show itself, to allow it to glisten (cf. candid from Latin 'candeo' to shine, be illuminated, to be white, to gleam, to become hot).

So by attending to slips of the tongue we may learn that language is that which holds and sustains things in their being. It opens up for us the inevitability of our being-together-with things; so we realise that we cannot pick and choose this being-together-with. The world is our destiny. It is not before us so that we can invite what we want from it. 'Welt is nie, sondern weltet' (World never 'is'; it 'worlds').[16]

When I would pray and think, I think and pray
To several subjects: Heaven hath my empty words;
While my invention, hearing not my tongue,
Anchors on Isobel: Heaven in my mouth,
As if I did but only chew his name;
And in my heart the strong and swelling evil

Of my conception. ——————————————————
—————————————————— O place! O form!
How often dost thou with thy case, thy habit,
Wrench awe from fools, and tie the wiser souls
To thy false seeming!

Measure for Measure, Act II,
Scene IV: 1–15

Notes

1. *The Journals of Sören Kierkegaard,* sel. and trans. A. Dru (London: Oxford University Press, 1938) [1848, § 771].
2. 'Epicurus,' quoted in E.L. Ormsby, *Theodicy in Islamic Thought* (Princeton: Princeton University Press, 1984), p. 63.
3. E.L. Ormsby, *Theodicy in Islamic Thought* (Princeton: Princeton University Press, 1984), p. 32.
4. J. Milton, *Paradise Lost,* Book 11, 477ff.
5. B. de Spinoza, *Ethics,* part 1, proposition 33 proof 1.
6. G.W. Leibniz, *Theodicy,* 'Essays On The Goodness of God, The Freedom of Man and The Origin of Evil,' trans. E.M. Huggard (New Haven: Yale University Press, 1952).
7. E.L. Ormsby, *Theodicy in Islamic Thought* (Princeton: Princeton University Press, 1984), p. 79.
8. Ibid., p. 43.
9. Ibid., p. 54.
10. S. Freud, *The Psychopathology of Everyday Life* (1901) Pelican Edition (1975), p. 300.
11. Ibid., p. 46.
12. M. Heidegger, *The Metaphysical Foundation of Logic,* trans. M. Heim (Bloomington: Indiana University Press, 1984), p. 109–17.
13. S. Freud, *Psychopathology,* p. 300.
14. L. Wittgenstein, *On Certainty,* ed. G.E.M. Anscombe and G.H. von Wright (Oxford: B. Blackwell, 1969), §§ 150–174.
15. M. Heidegger, 'The Nature of Language' in *On the Way to Language,* trans. P.D. Hertz (New York: Harper and Row, 1971), p. 59.
16. M. Heidegger, *The Essence of Reasons,* trans. T. Malick (Evanston: Northwestern University Press, 1969), p. 103.

Appendices

Programs of the Collegium Phaenomenologicum 1976–1985

1976 Organizational Meeting

Informal Talks
Emmanuel Levinas
Werner Marx

Seminars

Jeffner Allen	Husserl's Philosophical Anthropology
Samuel IJsseling	Heidegger's *Die Grundprobleme der Phänomenologie*
Bernd Jaeger	Towards a Phenomenology of the Passions
Giuseppina Moneta	The Teleology of Cognitive Experience
J.H. Nota	Max Scheler on His Phenomenological Method
Reiner Schürmann	The Ontological Difference and Political Philosophy
Thomas Sheehan	Heidegger and *die Sache selbst*
Carlo Sini	Phenomenology and the Foundation of Human Sciences
Jacques Taminiaux	Being in Husserl and Heidegger
Michael Zimmerman	Heidegger, Nietzsche and Authentic Temporality

1977

Topic: Husserl
Director: José Huertas-Jourda

Guest Lectures

Edward Ballard	The Relation between Lived Time and Objective Time

J.C. Sallis, G. Moneta and J. Taminiaux (eds.), The Collegium Phaenomenologicum, 321–329.
© Kluwer Academic Publishers.

Rudolf Berlinger	Die philosophische Rehabilitation der Krankheit
Emmanuel Levinas	Phénoménologie et Eveil
Thomas Sheehan	Heidegger, Aristotle, and Phenomenology
Stephan Strasser	The Ideal of God in the Later Philosophy of Husserl
Courses	
Jeffner Allen	Workshop in Husserl
Rudolf Bernet	Husserl's Theory of Knowledge
Richard Holmes	Husserl's *Cartesian Meditations*
Robert Jordan	Transcendental Philosophy as the Ideal of Phenomenology
Eduard Marbach	The Method of Transcendental Phenomenology
John Mayer	Transcendental Philosophy as the Ideal of Phenomenology
William McKenna	Practice in Phenomenology
Dallas Willard	Husserl's Early Philosophy
Specially Arranged Lectures	
William McKenna	Phenomenological ἐποχή and the Neutrality Modification
Carlo Sini	Phenomenology in Italy Today
Jacques Taminiaux	Immanence and Transcendence in *The Idea of Phenomenology*
Informal Presentations	
Samuel IJsseling	Current Work at the *Husserl Archiv Leuven*
Alexandre Métraux	Gurwitsch's Social Theory
Seminars	
Thomas Clifton	The Notion of Temporal 'Intercut'
José Huertas-Jourda	On the Two 'Foundations' According to Husserl – the Epistemological or Legitimizing, and Occasional or Actualizing
Samuel IJsseling	Heidegger and Phenomenology
Robert Jordan	The Transcendental Ego as 'Being-in-the-World'
J.N. Kaufman	Phenomenology of Personal Identity
	Phenomenology of Pre-linguistic Experience
Alexandre Métraux	On the Early Husserl's Theory of the Sciences
Giuseppina Moneta	The Phenomenological Way to Cognitive Certainty

J.H. Nota	The Unity of Life, Method and Doctrine in M. Scheler's Phenomenology
John O'Neil	The Mutuality of Accounts: On the Relationship between Common Sense and Scientific Knowledge of Society
Tom Rockmore	Fichte, Husserl and Philosophical Science
Thomas Seebohm	The Problem of Human Studies in Husserl's Late Philosophy
Herbert Spiegelberg	The Significance of the Brentano-Husserl Correspondence
Dallas Willard	Husserl's Critique of Extentional Logic

1978

Topic: Heidegger
Director: Thomas Sheehan

Lecture Courses

David Krell	Logic, Language, Logos
Reiner Schürmann	Heidegger and the Destruction of the History of Ontology
Jacques Taminiaux	The Origin of the Work of Art
Ernst Vollrath	Time in the Tradition and Temporality in *Being and Time*

Guest Lectures

Jeffner Allen	Madness and the Poet
André de Konig	Suspicion and Delusion
Hans-Georg Gadamer	On Phenomenology
Samuel IJsseling	Heidegger and the Question of Time
Bernd Jaeger	Dionysus and the World of Passion
J. Kohn	Heidegger, Hannah Arendt and the Will
David Kolb	Hegel and Heidegger as Critics
David Krell	The *Lichtung* in Transition
Werner Marx	Heidegger and the Task of Thought
William Richardson, S.J.	The Mirror Inside: The Problem of the Self (Heidegger and Lacan)
G. Rota	The Problem of Inductive Logic
Reiner Schürmann	Anti-Humanism: Marx, Nietzsche, Heidegger
Hugh Silverman	The Limits of Logocentrism (On the Way to Grammatology)

Special Seminars

David Krell	Heraclitus, Logos Fragment
Giuseppina Moneta	Heidegger's 'The Thing'
Gianmaria Polidoro	Language and the Body
Thomas Sheehan	*Being and Time,* section 7

Italian Colloquium

Alberto Caracciolo	Heidegger e il nichilismo (Heidegger and Nihilism)
Hans-Georg Gadamer	Heidegger e la fenomenologia (Heidegger and Phenomenology)
Carlo Sini	Heidegger e il problema del Segno (Heidegger and the Problem of Sign)
Gianni Vattimo	Il pensare e il fondamento (Thought and Ground)
V. Vitiello	Il problema del tempo in Heidegger e Hegel (The Problem of Time in Heidegger and Hegel)

1979

Topic: Merleau-Ponty
Director: Jacques Taminiaux

Lecture Courses

Thomas Busch	The Cogito in Merleau-Ponty's Philosophy
Amedeo Giorgi	The Psychology of Merleau-Ponty
David Krell	Language and 'Le chiasm'
Alphonso Lingis	Sensation in Merleau-Ponty

Seminars

O. Davis	Merleau-Ponty and Metaphysics
John Heaton	Merleau-Ponty and Psychotherapy
Samuel IJsseling	Phenomenology and Structuralism
Tom Rockmore	Merleau-Ponty, Marx, and Marxism
John Sallis	The Thing and the Natural World
Hugh Silverman	The Interrogation of Language
Robert Solomon	Merleau-Ponty and the Relationship between Phenomenology and Anthropology
Stephan Strasser	The Otherness of the Other interpreted by Merleau-Ponty and Levinas
Bernhard Waldenfels	The Silent Cogito and the Speaking Subject

Guest Lectures

Jeffner Allen	Through the Wild Region: An Essay in Phenomenological Feminism
Bernard Dauenhauer	Silence and Merleau-Ponty
John Heaton	The Phenomenology of Eyestrain
Stephan Strasser	Temporality in Levinas and Merleau-Ponty
Bernhard Waldenfels	Phenomenon and Structure in Merleau-Ponty
Stephen Watson	Pretexts: Language, Perception and the Cogito

Gurwitsch Day Lectures

Lester Embree (read by Alexandre Métraux)	How the Paths of Gurwitsch and Merleau-Ponty Intersected
Richard Grathoff and Wolters, P.	Gurwitsch's Notion of Milieu
William McKenna	Objects, Appearance, and Privileged Perception in Gurwitsch, Husserl, and Merleau-Ponty

1980

Topic: Studies in Hermeneutics and Interpretation
Director: Jeffner Allen

Seminars

Anna Cazzullo	Ricoeur and Hermeneutics
André de Konig	On Interpretation in Psychotherapy
Thomas Flynn	Sartre
Hans-Georg Gadamer	Sprache, Schrift, Lesen
	Truth and Method
Michel Haar	The Heideggerian Critique of Husserlian Phenomenology
John Heaton	Freud's and Heidegger's Interpretation of Slips of the Tongue
K. Heiges	Understanding, Reciprocity, and Certainty in the Philosophy of W. Dilthey
S. Kvale	The Relevance of Hermeneutics for the Interpretation of Qualitative Research Interviews in Psychology
Giuseppina Moneta	The Object and the Thing: from Phenomenology to Thought
J.H. Nota	Max Scheler's Solidarism or Prophetic Socialism

Clyde Pax	Ricoeur's Philosophy of the Will: A Textual Exegesis
James Risser	Truth in Art: Gadamer's Criticism of Kant's Aesthetics
Karl Schuhmann	R. Boehm's *Kritik der Grundlagen des gegenwärtigen Zeitalters*
Reiner Schürmann	Phenomenology and Ethics
Thomas Seebohm	Issues in Hermeneutics
Christopher Smith	Gadamer's Hermeneutics and Moral Theory
Kathleen Wright	*Ein Gespräch sind wir . . .:* on Conversations

1981

Topic: Phenomenology and Aesthetics
Director: John Sallis

Courses

David Krell	Aesthetics Male and Female: Derrida on Heidegger on Nietzsche on Kant on the Beautiful
Hugh Silverman	Merleau-Ponty, *Eye and Mind*
Joan Stambaugh	Nietzsche, *The Birth of Tragedy*
Jacques Taminiaux	Heidegger, *The Origin of the Work of Art*

Seminars

Anne Ashbaugh	Merleau-Ponty, Metaphysics and the Novel
Walter Brogan	Heidegger's Interpretation of Plato in *Nietzsche*
Martin Dillon	Merleau-Ponty, Indirect Language and the Voices of Silence
Veronique Fóti	Merleau-Ponty, The Visible and the Invisible
Michel Haar	Nietzsche, The Will to Power as Art
Samuel IJsseling	Philosophy as Work: A Reading of *The Origin of the Work of Art*
Theodore Kisiel	Heidegger's Overcoming of Aesthetics
Guiseppina Moneta	Intuition, Expression, Language in Croce's Aesthetics
William Richardson, S.J.	Heidegger, *On the Essence of Truth*
André Schuwer	Merleau-Ponty, Cezanne's Doubt
Charles Scott	Heidegger, Poetically Man Dwells
Thomas Sheehan	Heidegger, On the Being and Concept of *Physis*
Joan Stambaugh	Nietzsche, *Thus Spoke Zarathustra*

David Wood	Derrida, The Retrait of Metaphor
William Wurzer	Kant, *Critique of Judgment*

1982

Topic: Phenomenology and the End of Metaphysics
Director: John Sallis

Courses

Robert Bernasconi	The Ends of Metaphysics and Another Beginning
John Sallis	Phenomenology at the End of Metaphysics
Jacques Taminiaux	Heidegger and Hegel
David Wood	Writing at the Edge of Metaphysics

Seminars

Anne Ashbaugh	Heidegger, *Plato's Doctrine of Truth*
Bernard Dauenhauer	Heidegger, The Thing
Parvis Emad	Hegel in Heidegger's *Being and Time*
Veronique Fóti	Heidegger, Recollection in Metaphysics
Samuel IJsseling	Heidegger and the Destruction of Ontology
David Kolb	Heidegger, *Letter on Humanism*
David Krell	Heidegger, The End of Metaphysics
Rudolf Makkreel	Temporality and History in Dilthey and Heidegger: Some Comments on Heidegger's *Being and Time*
Giuseppina Moneta	The End of Ratio
Adriaan Peperzak	Heidegger, Hegel and the Greeks
André Schuwer	Derrida and Hegel

1983

Topic: Phenomenology and Language
Director: Robert Bernasconi

Courses

David Allison	Derrida's *Speech and Phenomena*
Rudolf Bernet	Husserl's first *Logical Investigation*
John Llewelyn	Derrida's 'Violence and Metaphysics'
Adriaan Peperzak	Levinas' *Otherwise than Being or Beyond Essence*

Seminars

Robert Bernasconi	Levinas and the Silent World of the Evil Genius
Edward Casey	Levinas 'On the Trail of the Other'
Pietro D'Oriano	Representational Difference
Parvis Emad	Heidegger on Husserl on Signs: *Being and Time,* section 17
Veronique Fóti	Derrida's 'Plato's Pharmacy'
Michel Haar	Language and Silence in Heidegger
Samuel IJsseling	On Reading and Writing
Giuseppina Moneta	Heidegger's Dialogue on Language
André Schuwer	Derrida's 'Differance'
Charles Scott	Heidegger's *Letter on Humanism*

1984

Topic: Phenomenology and the Crisis of Reason
Director: Parvis Emad

Courses

Robert Bernasconi	Heidegger, Technology, the Danger and the Turning
David Krell	The Crisis of Reason in 19th Century Thought
Charles Scott	Foucault: Reason in Question
Hugh Silverman	Textuality and the Crisis of Reason

Seminars

Rudolf Bernet	On Husserl's *Origin of Geometry*
Steven Davis	Art and Reason in Foucault
Parvis Emad	Nietzsche on Truth and Lie
Joseph Fell	Heidegger's Dispute with Ernst Jünger
Rodolphe Gasché	'Mise en Abyme': The Concept of Infinity in Derrida and Hegel
Samuel IJsseling	Questions Concerning a Phenomenology of Reading
Giuseppina Moneta	The Limits of Reason in Husserl's *Crisis*
Thomas Nenon	Philosophy as a Rigorous Science
John Sallis	Reason and Ek-sistence
Thomas Sheehan	Heidegger's Reading of LOGOS in Aristotle's *Peri Hermeneias*
Jacques Taminiaux	The Genesis of the Theoretical Attitude in the Early Heidegger; The Issue of Perception

1985

Topic: Thinking after Heidegger
Director: Charles Scott

Courses

Robert Bernasconi	Levinas: Dwelling and the Face
William Richardson, S.J.	Thought and Desire
John Sallis	The End of Philosophy and the Beginning of Thought
David Wood	Following Derrida

Seminars

John D. Caputo	Releasement and the End of Metaphysics
Edward Casey	The Place of the Work of Art
Franco Ferrarotti	Orientional Crisis in the Social Sciences
Eugene Gendlin	Non-logical Moves
David Krell	Vorstellendes Denken: A Representation
Kenneth Maly	Parmenides: Circle of Disclosure, Circle of Possibility
Mary Rawlinson	Reading Derrida, Reading Metaphysics
André Schuwer	Derrida's Reading of Freud
Charles Scott	Destruction and the Middle Voice in *Being and Time*
	The Self-overcoming of Nietzsche's Thought
Hugh Silverman	Derrida and the Theory of Textuality
Jacques Taminiaux	Heidegger and the Greeks in the Early Period
Mark Taylor	Blanchot: Philosophy-Art/Time-Space

Participants in the Collegium Phaenomenologicum 1976–1985

Allen, Jeffner	Husserl's Philosophical Anthropology (Seminar, 1976) Workshop in Husserl (Course, 1977) Madness and the Poet (Guest Lecture, 1978) Through the Wild Region: An Essay in Phenomenological Feminism (Guest Lecture, 1979)
Allison, David	Derrida's *Speech and Phenomena* (Course, 1983)
Ashbaugh, Anne	Merleau-Ponty, Metaphysics and the Novel (Seminar, 1981) Heidegger, *Plato's Doctrine of Truth* (Seminar, 1982)
Ballard, Edward	The Relation between Lived Time and Objective Time (Guest Lecture, 1977)
Berlinger, Rudolf	Die philosophische Rehabilitation der Krankheit (Guest Lecture, 1977)
Bernasconi, Robert	The Ends of Metaphysics and Another Beginning (Course, 1982) Levinas and the Silent World of the Evil Genius (Seminar, 1983) Heidegger, Technology, the Danger and the Turning (Course, 1984) Levinas: Dwelling and the Face (Course, 1985)
Bernet, Rudolf	Husserl's Theory of Knowledge (Course, 1977) Husserl's first *Logical Investigation* (Course, 1983) On Husserl's *Origin of Geometry* (Seminar, 1984)
Brogan, Walter	Heidegger's Interpretation of Plato in *Nietzsche* (Seminar, 1981)

J.C. Sallis, G. Moneta and J. Taminiaux (eds.), The Collegium Phaenomenologicum, 331–339.
© Kluwer Academic Publishers.

Busch, Thomas	The Cogito in Merleau-Ponty's Philosophy (Lecture Course, 1979)
Caputo, John D.	Releasement and the End of Metaphysics (Seminar, 1985)
Caracciolo, Alberto	Heidegger e il nichilismo (Heidegger and Nihilism) (Italian Colloquium, 1978)
Casey, Edward	Levinas 'On the Trail of the Other' (Seminar, 1983)
	The Place of the Work of Art (Seminar, 1985)
Cazzullo, Anna	Ricoeur and Hermeneutics (Seminar, 1980)
Clifton, Thomas	The Notion of Temporal 'Intercut' (Seminar, 1977)
Dauenhauer, Bernard	Silence and Merleau-Ponty (Guest Lecture, 1979)
	Heidegger, The Thing (Seminar, 1982)
Davis, O.	Merleau-Ponty and Metaphysics (Seminar, 1979)
Davis, Steven	Art and Reason in Foucault (Seminar, 1984)
de Konig, André	Suspicion and Delusion (Guest Lecture, 1978)
	On Interpretation in Psychotherapy (Seminar, 1980)
Dillon, Martin	Merleau-Ponty, Indirect Language and the Voices of Silence (Seminar, 1981)
D'Oriano, Pietro	Representational Difference (Seminar, 1983)
Emad, Parvis	Hegel in Heidegger's *Being and Time* (Seminar, 1982)
	Heidegger on Husserl on Signs: *Being and Time,* section 17 (Seminar, 1983)
	Nietzsche on Truth and Lie (Seminar, 1984)
Embree, Lester (read by Alexandre Métraux)	How the Paths of Gurwitsch and Merleau-Ponty Intersected (Gurwitsch Day Lecture, 1979)
Fell, Joseph	Heidegger's Dispute with Ernst Jünger (Seminar, 1984)
Ferrarotti, Franco	Orientional Crisis in the Social Sciences (Seminar, 1985)
Flynn, Thomas	Sartre (Seminar, 1980)
Fóti, Veronique	Merleau-Ponty, *The Visible and the Invisible* (Seminar, 1981)
	Heidegger, Recollection in Metaphysics (Seminar, 1982)
	Derrida's 'Plato's Pharmacy' (Seminar, 1983)
Gadamer, Hans-Georg	On Phenomenology (Guest Lecture, 1978)
	Heidegger e la fenomenologia (Heidegger and Phenomenology) (Italian Colloquium, 1978)

	Sprache, Schrift, Lesen (Seminar, 1980)
	Truth and Method (Seminar, 1980)
Gasché, Rodolphe	'Mise en Abyme': The Concept of Infinity in Derrida and Hegel (Seminar, 1984)
Gendlin, Eugene	Non-logical Moves (Seminar, 1985)
Giorgi, Amedeo	The Psychology of Merleau-Ponty (Lecture Course, 1979)
Grathoff, Richard and Wolters, P.	Gurwitsch's Notion of Milieu (Gurwitsch Day Seminar, 1979)
Haar, Michel	The Heideggerian Critique of Husserlian Phenomenology (Seminar, 1980)
	Nietzsche, The Will to Power as Art (Seminar, 1981)
	Language and Silence in Heidegger (Seminar, 1983)
Heaton, John	Merleau-Ponty and Psychotherapy (Seminar, 1979)
	The Phenomenology of Eyestrain (Guest Lecture, 1979)
	Freud's and Heidegger's Interpretation of Slips of the Tongue (Seminar, 1980)
Heiges, Kenneth	Understanding, Reciprocity, and Certainty in the Philosophy of W. Dilthey (Seminar, 1980)
Holmes, Richard	Husserl's *Cartesian Meditations* (Course, 1977)
Huertas-Jourda, José	On the Two 'Foundations' According to Husserl – The Epistemological or Legitimizing, and Occasional or Actualizing (Seminar, 1977)
IJsseling, Samuel	Heidegger's *Die Grundprobleme der Phänomenologie* (Seminar, 1976)
	Current Work at the *Husserl Archief Leuven* (Informal Presentation, 1977)
	Heidegger and Phenomenology (Seminar, 1977)
	Heidegger and the Question of Time (Guest Lecture, 1978)
	Phenomenology and Structuralism (Seminar, 1979)
	Philosophy as Work: A Reading of *The Origin of the Work of Art* (Seminar, 1981)
	Heidegger and the Destruction of Ontology (Seminar, 1982)
	On Reading and Writing (Seminar, 1983)

IJsseling, Samuel	Questions Concerning a Phenomenology of Reading (Seminar, 1984)
Jaeger, Bernd	Towards a Phenomenology of the Passions (Seminar, 1976)
	Dionysus and the World of Passion (Guest Lecture, 1978)
Jordan, Robert W.	Transcendental Philosophy as the Ideal of Phenomenology (Course, 1977)
	The Transcendental Ego as 'Being-in-the-World' (Seminar, 1977)
Kaufman, J.N.	Phenomenology of Personal Identity (Seminar, 1977)
	Phenomenology of Pre-linguistic Experience (Seminar, 1977)
Kisiel, Theodore	Heidegger's Overcoming of Aesthetics (Seminar, 1981)
Kohn, J.	Heidegger, Hannah Arendt and the Will (Guest Lecture, 1978)
Kolb, David	Hegel and Heidegger as Critics (Guest Lecture, 1978)
	Heidegger, *Letter on Humanism* (Seminar, 1982)
Krell, David	Logic, Language, Logos (Lecture Course, 1978)
	The *Lichtung* in Transition (Guest Lecture, 1978)
	Heraclitus, Logos Fragment (Special Seminar, 1978)
	Language and 'Le chiasm' (Lecture Course, 1979)
	Aesthetics Male and Female: Derrida on Heidegger on Nietzsche on Kant on the Beautiful (Course, 1981)
	Heidegger, The End of Metaphysics (Seminar, 1982)
	The Crisis of Reason in 19th Century Thought (Course, 1984)
	Vorstellendes Denken: A Representation (Seminar, 1985)
Kvale, S.	The Relevance of Hermeneutics for the Interpretation of Qualitative Research Interviews in Psychology (Seminar, 1980)
Levinas, Emmanuel	Phénoménologie et Eveil (Guest Lecture, 1977)
Lingis, Alphonso	Sensation in Merleau-Ponty (Lecture Course, 1979)

Llewelyn, John	Derrida's 'Violence and Metaphysics' (Course, 1983)
Makkreel, Rudolph	Temporality and History in Dilthey and Heidegger: Some Comments on Heidegger's *Being and Time* (Seminar, 1982)
Maly, Kenneth	Parmenides: Circle of Disclosure, Circle of Possibility (Seminar, 1985)
Marbach, Eduard	The Method of Transcendental Phenomenology (Course, 1977)
Marx, Werner	Heidegger and the Task of Thought (Lecture, 1978)
Mayer, John	Transcendental Philosophy as the Ideal of Phenomenology (Course, 1977)
McKenna, William	Practice in Phenomenology (Course, 1977)
	Phenomenological ἐποχή and the Neutrality Modification (Specially Arranged Lecture, 1977)
	Objects, Appearance, and Privileged Perception in Gurwitsch, Husserl and Merleau-Ponty (Gurwitsch Day Lecture, 1979)
Métraux, Alexandre	Gurwitsch's Social Theory (Informal Presentation, 1977)
	On the Early Husserl's Theory of the Sciences (Seminar, 1977)
Moneta, Giuseppina	The Teleology of Cognitive Experience (Seminar, 1976)
	The Phenomenological Way to Cognitive Certainty (Seminar, 1977)
	Heidegger's 'The Thing' (Special Seminar, 1978)
	The Object and the Thing: from Phenomenology to Thought (Seminar, 1980)
	Intuition, Expression, Language in Croce's Aesthetics (Seminar, 1981)
	The End of Ratio (Seminar, 1982)
	Heidegger's Dialogue on Language (Seminar, 1983)
	The Limits of Reason in Husserl's *Crisis* (Seminar, 1984)
Nenon, Thomas	Philosophy as a Rigorous Science (Seminar, 1984)
Nota, J.H.	Max Scheler on His Phenomenological Method (Seminar, 1976)

	The Unity of Life, Method and Doctrine in M. Scheler's Phenomenology (Seminar, 1977)
	Max Scheler's Solidarism or Prophetic Socialism (Seminar, 1980)
O'Neil, John	The Mutuality of Accounts: On the Relationship between Common Sense and Scientific Knowledge of Society (Seminar, 1977)
Pax, Clyde	Ricoeur's Philosophy of the Will: A Textual Exegesis (Seminar, 1980)
Peperzak, Adriaan	Heidegger, Hegel and the Greeks (Seminar, 1982)
	Levinas' *Otherwise than Being or Beyond Essence* (Course, 1983)
Polidoro, Gianmaria	Language and the Body (Special Seminar, 1978)
Rawlinson, Mary	Reading Derrida, Reading Metaphysics (Seminar, 1985)
Richardson, William, S.J.	The Mirror Inside: The Problem of the Self (Heidegger and Lacan) (Guest Lecture, 1978)
	Heidegger, *On the Essence of Truth* (Seminar, 1981)
	Thought and Desire (Course, 1985)
Risser, James	Truth in Art: Gadamer's Criticism of Kant's Aesthetics (Seminar, 1980)
Rockmore, Tom	Fichte, Husserl and Philosophical Science (Seminar, 1977)
	Merleau-Ponty, Marx, and Marxism (Seminar, 1979)
Rota, G.	The Problem of Inductive Logic (Guest Lecture, 1978)
Sallis, John	The Thing and the Natural World (Seminar, 1979)
	Phenomenology at the End of Metaphysics (Course, 1982)
	Reason and Ek-sistence (Seminar, 1984)
	The End of Philosophy and the Beginning of Thought (Course, 1985)
Schühmann, Karl	R. Boehm's *Kritik der Grundlagen des gegenwärtigen Zeitalters* (Seminar, 1980)
Schürmann, Reiner	The Ontological Difference and Political Philosophy (Seminar, 1976)
	Heidegger and the Destruction of the History of Ontology (Lecture Course, 1978)

	Anti-Humanism: Marx, Nietzsche, Heidegger, (Guest Lecture, 1978)
	Phenomenology and Ethics (Seminar, 1980)
Schuwer, André	Merleau-Ponty, Cezanne's Doubt (Seminar, 1981)
	Derrida and Hegel (Seminar, 1982)
	Derrida's 'Differance' (Seminar, 1983)
	Derrida's Reading of Freud (Seminar, 1985)
Scott, Charles	Heidegger, Poetically Man Dwells (Seminar, 1981)
	Heidegger's *Letter on Humanism* (Seminar, 1983)
	Foucault: Reason in Question (Course, 1984)
	Destruction and the Middle Voice in *Being and Time* (Seminar, 1985)
	The Self-overcoming of Nietzsche's Thought (Seminar, 1985)
Seebohm, Thomas	The Problem of Human Studies in Husserl's Late Philosophy (Seminar, 1977)
	Issues in Hermeneutics (Seminar, 1980)
Sheehan, Thomas	Heidegger and *die Sache selbst* (Seminar, 1976)
	Heidegger, Aristotle, and Phenomenology (Guest Lecture, 1977)
	Being and Time, section 7 (Special Seminar, 1978)
	Heidegger, On the Being and Concept of *Physis* (Seminar, 1981)
	Heidegger's Reading of LOGOS in Aristotle's *Peri Hermeneias* (Seminar, 1984)
Silverman, Hugh	The Limits of Logocentrism (On the Way to Grammatology) (Guest Lecture, 1978)
	The Interrogation of Language (Seminar, 1979)
	Merleau-Ponty, *Eye and Mind* (Course, 1981)
	Textuality and the Crisis of Reason (Course, 1984)
	Derrida and the Theory of Textuality (Seminar, 1985)
Sini, Carlo	Phenomenology and the Foundation of Human Sciences (Seminar, 1976)
	Phenomenology in Italy Today (Specially Arranged Lecture, 1977)

Sini, Carlo	Heidegger e il problema del Segno (Heidegger and the Problem of Sign) (Italian Colloquium, 1978)
Smith, Christopher	Gadamer's Hermeneutics and Moral Theory (Seminar, 1980)
Solomon, Robert	Merleau-Ponty and the Relationship between Phenomenology and Anthropology (Seminar, 1979)
Spiegelberg, Herbert	The Significance of the Brentano-Husserl Correspondence (Seminar, 1977)
Stambaugh, Joan	Nietzsche, *The Birth of Tragedy* (Course, 1981)
	Nietzsche, *Thus Spoke Zarathustra* (Seminar, 1981)
Strasser, Stephan	The Ideal of God in the Later Philosophy of Husserl (Guest Lecture, 1977)
	The Otherness of the Other interpreted by Merleau-Ponty and Levinas (Seminar, 1979)
	Temporality in Levinas and Merleau-Ponty (Guest Lecture, 1979)
Taminiaux, Jacques	Being in Husserl and Heidegger (Seminar, 1976)
	Immanence and Transcendence in *The Idea of Phenomenology* (Specially Arranged Lecture, 1977)
	The Origin of the Work of Art (Lecture Course, 1978)
	Heidegger, *The Origin of the Work of Art* (Course, 1981)
	Heidegger and Hegel (Course, 1982)
	The Genesis of the Theoretical Attitude in the Early Heidegger; The Issue of Perception (Seminar, 1984)
	Heidegger and the Greeks in the Early Period (Seminar, 1985)
Taylor, Mark	Blanchot: Philosophy-Art/Time-Space (Seminar, 1985)
Vattimo, Gianni	Il pensare e il fondamento (Thought and Ground) (Italian Colloquium, 1978)
Vitiello, V.	Il problema del tempo in Heidegger e Hegel (The Problem of Time in Heidegger and Hegel) (Italian Colloquium, 1978)
Vollrath, Ernst	Time in the Tradition and Temporality in *Being and Time* (Lecture Course, 1978)

Waldenfels, Bernhard	The Silent Cogito and the Speaking Subject (Seminar, 1979)
	Phenomenon and Structure in Merleau-Ponty (Guest Lecture, 1979)
Watson, Stephen	Pretexts: Language, Perception and the Cogito (Guest Lecture, 1979)
Willard, Dallas	Husserl's Early Philosophy (Course, 1977)
	Husserl's Critique of Extensional Logic (Seminar, 1977)
Wolters, P. and Grathoff, Richard	Gurwitsch's Notion of Milieu (Gurwitsch Day Lecture, 1979)
Wood, David	Derrida, The Retrait of Metaphor (Seminar, 1981)
	Writing at the Edge of Metaphysics (Course, 1982)
	Following Derrida (Course, 1985)
Wright, Kathleen	*Ein Gespräch sind wir . . .*: on Conversations (Seminar, 1980)
Wurzer, William	Kant, *Critique of Judgment* (Seminar, 1981)
Zimmerman, Michael	Heidegger, Nietzsche and Authentic Temporality (Seminar, 1976)